THE ~~BACKSTAGE~~ GUIDE
TO WORKING IN
REGIONAL
THEATER

THE ~~BACKSTAGE~~ GUIDE TO WORKING IN

REGIONAL THEATER

JOBS FOR ACTORS AND OTHER THEATER PROFESSIONALS

JIM VOLZ

BACK STAGE BOOKS
NEW YORK

_8-3-2009_

To: Erin Gilbreath
one of the world's
best people!

love—
jim

SENIOR EDITOR: Mark Glubke
PROJECT EDITOR: Gary Sunshine
ART DIRECTOR: Julie Duquet
DESIGNER: Areta Buk/Thumb Print
PRODUCTION MANAGER: Katherine Happ

Back cover photo by Evelyn Carol Case

First published in 2007 by Back Stage Books,
an imprint of Watson-Guptill Publications,
a division of VNU Business Media, Inc.
770 Broadway, New York, NY 10003
www.watsonguptill.com

Library of Congress Control Number: 2006927720

ISBN-13: 978-0-8230-7880-6
ISBN: 0-8230-7880-9

Manufactured in the United States of America

First printing 2007

1 2 3 4 5 6 7 8 9 / 15 14 13 12 11 10 09 08 07

This book is dedicated to my ever-supportive family,
Evelyn Carol Case, Nicholas Volz, and Caitlin Volz,
whose passion, independence, humor, and sense of adventure
always manage to inspire and amaze me.

CONTENTS

ACKNOWLEDGEMENTS

Grateful thanks to my marvelous editor, Mark Glubke, senior editor of Back Stage Books, who helped shepherd *How to Run a Theater* and *The Back Stage Guide to Working in Regional Theater* onto international bookshelves, to project editor Gary Sunshine, who added significantly to this book's substance, and to Back Stage Books publicist Lee Wiggins, and to copy editor Michele LaRue for all their advice, work, and support.

Heartfelt thanks to Cindy Melby Phaneuf and Abe J. Bassett, who reviewed this manuscript and offered important editorial, artistic, and historical guidance. Also, many thanks to Ben Cameron, Dana Gioia, Gilbert Cates, Paul Baker, Arthur Bartow, Robert Schenkkan, Gerald Freedman, Vera Mowry Roberts, Scott L. Steele, Sanford Robbins, Sid Berger, Kate Pogue, Roche Schulfer, John Jakes, Paul Nicholson, Dan McCleary, Richard Garner, Lesley Schisgall Currier, Fred C. Adams, R. Scott Phillips, Stephen Rothman, Richard Rose, James O'Connor, Kate Ingram, Tad Ingram, Andrew Barnicle, Rick Stein, Dick Devin, Steven Woolf, Ed Stern, Alan Rust, Gil Lazier, David W. Weiss, Scott J. Parker, Tom Markus, Ted Herstand, Kent Thompson, Emma Walton, Kevin Maifeld, Cindy Gold, Sidonie Garrett, Michael Detroit, Peter Brosius, Risa Brainin, Emily Petkewich, David Heath, Mark Hofflund, Michelle Kozlak, Ben Donenberg, Iris Dorbian, Jan and Griff Duncan, Julia and Geoff Elliott, Richard G. Fallon, Joel G. Fink, Bernard Havard, Susie Medak, Howard J. Millman, Charles Morey, Jonathan Moscone, Robert Moss, Jim O'Quinn, John Quinlivan, Murray Ross, Craig Belknap, Ralph Cohen, Kathleen F. Conlin, Lynn Landis, Timothy Near, and Victoria Nolan, who shared their wisdom and thoughts for the text.

Sincere thanks to Mark R. Sumner, Sallie Mitchell, Edwin Duerr, and Allen Zeltzer, for their theater history collections that provided vital background for the "Brief History of Regional Theater" and for their library contributions that have opened up the worlds of Eva Le Gallienne, Margo Jones, Nina Vance, and countless other American theater pioneers to new generations of theater students who appreciate theater history.

Special thanks to those who helped with regional theater and city information, including Chicago's Valerie Black-Mallon, Seattle's Stephanie Shine,

San Francisco's Toby Leavitt, and LORT's Adam Knight. Thanks to Bruce Goodrich, Gordon Goodrich, Dan Evers, Nikki Allen, Samantha Smith, Heather Biehl, Mary Waldron, and Jenny Spear for their Orange County assistance.

Collegial thanks to California State University President Milton Gordon, Dean Jerry Samuelson, and Chair Susan Hallman.

Finally, **loving thanks** to Betty Volz, Connie and Bob Mahle, Becky Phillips Volz, Chris and George Kuntz, John and Becky Volz, and my dear friends and the best actors I know-Robert Frederick Bailey, Michael J. Markus, and Mary Buehrle Squicciarino.

PREFACE

"Small opportunities are often the beginning of great
enterprises."

Demosthenes

Over the past year, I've received an outpouring of sage advice, pithy sayings, and fascinating words of wisdom from theater leaders throughout the United States. Artistic directors, producers, managing directors, casting directors, playwrights, freelance directors, and others have been amazingly generous in sharing their vision of theater and offering "tips of the trade" to help you.

There's great joy in assisting the next generation of American theater artists. This book offers you an overview of the field and many of the career planning resources you need to create, build, and nurture a life in the theater. From past experience, it's clear that the information contained in this book has the power to:

1 Assist you in identifying and defining your options for working in America's theaters;

2 Help you clarify your job-search, career-planning, and life-planning expertise;

3 Educate entry-level employees in the rich history, astounding artistry, risk-taking legacy, and self-sacrificing contributions of so many regional theater leaders and institutions;

4 Contribute to your future earning power through savvy career strategies;

5 Change your life with ethical, straightforward outreach, and networking that helps put you in control of your destiny and allows you to anticipate and plan for your future in the theater.

This guide to working in regional theater offers immediate strategies for breaking into the business, coupled with advice on how you can develop long-range career planning skills that may serve you in every area of your life. It also offers an overview of many of the largest and most successful professional theaters in America and contact information regarding many of the most successful service organizations, useful nonprofit theater support groups, and dedicated unions and collective bargaining organizations.

As a longtime producer, theater professor, and consultant to many of the nation's theaters, arts centers, cultural parks, and universities, I've been privileged to coach, lead, direct, or assist actors, directors, designers, choreographers, dancers, singers, craftspeople, board members, artistic directors, producers, and presidents of nonprofit operations while teaching in BA, BFA, MA, and MFA programs in a number of America's universities.

This book has been in the making for decades and began with a series of "Business of Acting," "Assertive Personal Marketing," and "Working in Regional Theater" seminars and workshops I used to conduct for regional and national theater organizations, undergraduate theater classes, graduate acting classes, and professional conservatory training programs.

There are already dozens of timely books on the market dealing with the evolving basics of the job search: résumés, interviews, cover letters, auditions, photographs, etc. This book identifies many of these resources for you, fills in the blanks, and details resources that have never been captured before in one book on regional theater.

My sincere thanks to the many theater leaders who contributed to this book and my absolute apology to all the brilliant artists and theater leaders whose names aren't included in this attempt to meld a bit of history with the realities of the job search.

Here's hoping this book ends up being worth at least 100 times what you paid for it. If you haven't already, consider adding to your library a copy of *How to Run a Theater* (New York: Back Stage Books, 2005). Together, these two volumes offer a unique insight into the sometimes harsh, oftentimes fabulous, oh-too-often surreal realities of the theater. Do write me (jvolz@fullerton.edu) and let me know what you'd like included in the next edition or a future book on the theater.

EVERYTHING YOU NEED TO KNOW ABOUT WORKING IN REGIONAL THEATER ... FROM THE PROFESSIONALS!

LIFE LESSONS FROM AMERICA'S ARTISTS AND EXECUTIVES

Whether you are wailing on stage or welding in the scene shop, there's the potential for a great life in the theater. Career choices in regional theater range from acting, directing, playwriting, and designing to costuming, set building, marketing, stage managing, fund-raising, and a whole host of other challenging, potentially career-satisfying positions that offer employees the opportunity to create theater.

The Fool Wonders, The Wise Man Asks (*Benjamin Disraeli*)

Fortunately, for those just heading into a high school, college, or theater training program, I've asked many of the nation's theater professionals to help guide you in your decision-making. Happily, they don't all think alike—many have found their own creative avenues to successful careers—and all have been stunningly candid, unpredictably blunt, graciously helpful, or all of the above! The great news is, *it is your life* and you can read through all this grand advice, listen to the debates of theater professionals who also had to make key life choices, and *decide for yourself what's best for you!*

Nobody's Sweetheart Is Ugly

Good news! If you are already in college or preparing for a career in the theater in other training programs, or already working in professional, community, university, or myriad other theaters, there are still plenty of extraordinary tips for managing your career and strategically planning for *your* life in the theater. An old Dutch proverb declares that "nobody's sweetheart is ugly," and regional theater is the "sweetheart" and artistic home of many quoted in this text. Keep this in mind as you weigh the advice. No doubt, many Broadway producers would regale you with the joys of life in New York and the thrills of Times Square. My contributors strive mightily to strike a balance in their advice about working in regional theater—but it's up to *you* to make your own choices!

As you might suspect, when you are fresh out of school, it sometimes seems impossible to break into the larger, more financially stable theaters or work your way past the volunteer or low-paying intern stages of any theater. For most of my over thirty-year career in the theater, it has driven me crazy when not-very-well-informed Broadway agents or film or television casting directors advise students and young actors, directors, designers, and crafts-people to go "cut your teeth and get experience in the regional theaters and come back when you've grown up." Ha! Generally, this is ridiculous advice as it's often harder to get a job in a League of Resident Theatres (LORT) venue than in any other theater in America. Perhaps community theaters, membership companies (where you pay to support the company), or smaller, generally volunteer-based companies allow you to "cut your teeth" with less-than-brilliant skills, but be ready for a highly competitive regional theater marketplace where polished skills and soaring potential are expected to mesh with unrelenting dedication, fervent loyalty, and long hours.

So where do you start and what do the leaders of American theaters have to say about working in their venues? It's great to have a career mentor and ongoing advisor, and I hope you will seek out many along the way. In the meantime, how wonderful to have so many theater professionals share their lifelong lessons and career advice with you in this book. I am so indebted and grateful to the many industry leaders and artists who "answered the call" to share their "best practices" with you.

This Is the Moment!

Before you plunge in, let me remind you that there are so many ways you can prepare NOW for your life in the theater. Seek counsel from your high school teachers, from your university professors, and from professionals with theater experience in your home community. Nurture relationships and gather written recommendations that will help you in the future. Research the Web sites of schools and/or training programs that interest you and sit in on classes, workshops, and seminars to determine if the work is right for you. Attend performances, read theater reviews, peruse trade papers, go to the library or bookstore and devour Theatre Communications Group's *American Theatre* magazine, Todd London's *The Artistic Home*, Robert Cohen's *Acting Professionally*, Tom Markus's *An Actor Behaves*, Sherry Eaker's *The Back Stage Handbook for Performing Artists*, William Ball's *A Sense of Direction*, and the myriad other books on the market.

Conduct an informational interview with someone who has the life and career you think you want and ask how he or she achieved success. Most people enjoy sharing their life stories—especially if they think they may be of help to you. An informational interview is a fact-finding session that you create by calling someone who has been successful at your dream job or a related job in the profession. You call them up, make it clear that you aren't applying for a job—that you would just appreciate 15 minutes of their time. Ask them to share their thoughts about how to break into their business, how they have enjoyed their career climb, and what advice they might have for you in regard to the profession.

Mentors and Mottos

Ben Cameron, longtime executive director of the national organization for the American theater, Theatre Communications Group (TCG), is one of the most articulate, engaging, embracing, and respected professionals in the field. He worked on the American theater's front lines for a number of years, was lured into the philanthropic and service communities, then returned to head TCG and devote time to "strengthen, nurture, and promote the professional not-for-profit theater." He discusses the mentoring process and offers advice about training and a life in the theater:

> I was blessed by being mentored by a number of people, of whom two rise to the top: the late Tom Haas, who was perhaps the most important figure for me, steering me toward graduate school, nurturing me as a director, teaching me how to read text in an uncluttered but heartfelt way; and the late Peter Zeisler, who during my NEA days taught me to see a field, not a string of separate theaters, while teaching me to value the concepts of service and leadership.
>
> Conservatory training is, for many in our field, indispensable: it provides a basic framework for thinking and instills a basic vocabulary and approach for work—a vocabulary that (like Picasso breaking out of the realistic tradition in which he had been trained but which was pivotal to his development) we will be increasingly shattering as we solve the problems and challenges that lie ahead for us, artistic and managerial alike. That said, mentor relationships are critical. I heard Lloyd Richards once say, when asked whether someone should enroll in a grad program, that the more important thing was to find the person with whom you needed to study and attach

yourself to them—a counsel that embraced, but did not mandate, formal grad programs.

My motto: Life is too short to be serious and too serious to be frivolous.

Paul Nicholson, executive director of the Oregon Shakespeare Festival, offers these seven thoughtful bits of advice:

1 Remember that we work for a theater that does not exist.
2 Before anything can be accomplished, some poor fool has to put something down on paper.
3 If you keep doing what you're doing, you'll keep getting what you're getting.
4 Winston Churchill's definition of planning: Ponder deeply, then act.
5 You cannot afford not to make the time for strategic planning.
6 There is nothing like the threat of being hanged in a fortnight to concentrate your mind.
7 The goal of every theater artistic director, managing director or general manager should be to enable the people they work with to make a life in the theater; just making a living is not enough.

Advice to the Players: Get Out of That Suitcase!

National Endowment for the Arts chair Dana Gioia has inspired and revitalized America's arts community. A working artist himself, Mr. Gioia directs those interested in regional theater "to keep working—no matter what the obstacles. I have only impractical advice, but for artists impractical idealism is ironically the most pragmatic: To read as much as possible, to act as much as possible, and to put your art at the center of your life."

Stage Directions magazine editor-in-chief Iris Dorbian encourages aspiring theater professionals to "be curious and open-minded. Learn something else besides theater—read newspapers, cultivate your brain, and get out there! Do some investigation of the theaters where you'd like to work and then find out if they offer internships in your desired area."

Jan and Griff Duncan, producer and artistic director of one of America's premier musical theaters, California's Fullerton Civic Light Opera, explain the upside and downside of a career in the theater:

Theater requires endless devotion/perseverance and a personal constitution that can accept rejection and a willingness to try again after failure. As a performer, it is "life out of a suitcase" and the constant judging of your ability (auditions). Theater is fickle and there will be failures. Each new production offers hope of success and it is enormously rewarding when that happens.

Sweep the Floors and Stay Out of Debt!

Near the breathtaking Zion National Park is Cedar City, Utah—home to a glorious complex of professional theaters and the Tony Award–winning Utah Shakespearean Festival. Fred C. Adams, one of America's wisest, most active, and most experienced theater producers, offers sound advice for all theater job seekers:

> I beg young promising theatrical entrepreneurs to refrain from debt. Borrowing money has proven to be the kiss of death to young and promising theater groups. Build first an audience, and that is done with credible high-quality work, then when the demand is great talk about building a theater.
>
> Sweep floors, usher, volunteer in the box office, learn everything you can from the ground up. My university courses were wonderful ways of learning what makes a script great, how you market, how to measure the taste of your audience—these were all great topics. But, no class can teach you how to approach a foundation for funding, what to look for in potential actors, how to maintain the theaters' restrooms. So learn what you can in school, then go out and immerse yourself in the actual day-to-day operation of a regional theater.
>
> I would tell any young dreamer to remember the advice my father gave me: "Hell is going to work eight hours a day at a job you do not love." Stay the course, pay your dues, and remember that the American theater is a very small family, so make no enemies, do not spread tales, and be honorable to your peers and even more to the people you hire.

Pseudolus, Pericles, or the Cover of *People* Magazine?

Perhaps the most well-placed LORT theater in America is California's Laguna Playhouse, a brisk walk from the Pacific Ocean and surrounded by glorious cliffs, leaping dolphins, and international intrigue. Laguna Playhouse artistic director Andrew Barnicle offers sane, sound, practical advice:

Recognize what the ultimate goal is and be honest with yourself. If you dream of being on the cover of *TV Guide*, by all means move to L.A. without regret. If visions of accepting a Tony put you to sleep at night, by all means move to New York. If playing Hamlet—even if you're too young—maybe in a storefront in South Dakota, gets you hot, then by all means move to South Dakota; just don't expect many people to notice. For nonactors (development directors, managers, designers), recognize that you will be overworked and not remunerated at the level of the regular commercial sector. You must love making a contribution to an art form you truly believe in, or that one-bedroom apartment and the ten-year-old Hyundai will get boring very quickly.

New York University's Tisch School of the Arts is one of the premier training grounds for theater students in many disciplines. Arthur Bartow, artistic director of the undergraduate Department of Drama, offers this canny advice:

See the work of as many regional theaters as you can and study their histories. Look at their current repertoires. Determine those artists who you admire and how you can fit into the structure of their theaters. Develop the skills necessary to do the work of those theaters. Once you are ready, start a communication with their casting directors and their artistic directors. Keep at them, continue to grow, and you will succeed.

The pathways for actors, directors, and designers are unique in their own ways. But knowledge is power no matter what your discipline. Gather as much skill as you can and be a person that others like to work with. Life is short and we would prefer to work with people whose company we enjoy rather than those who may be brilliant but take out all the air in the room. Remember, you are there to solve the problem, not be the problem.

Theater, film, and television director Craig Belknap is one of the rare directors who has managed to create a career in regional theater, Hollywood, and academia (California Institute of the Arts). Over the years, I've had the privilege of sitting on the hard benches of Washington, D.C.'s Folger Theatre, the plush seats of Alabama Shakespeare Festival's Stage, and the dark screening rooms of Hollywood's private studio theaters to watch his productions. A gentle, yet determined, assertive, and seasoned professional, Mr. Belknap shares his secrets for success:

> Work in all venues whenever and wherever you can, make contacts
> and *stay in touch*. For directors, until you run a theater, always
> remember that you are a "guest." If you want to be asked back, do
> your homework, stay on schedule, provide a positive atmosphere, and
> collaborate! Research the production. Stay *under* budget! Egos and
> indecision must *never, never* enter on-stage or off!

Located in America's heartland, the Dallas Theater Center helped define
the dramatic future of regional theater. In a recent letter from Paul Baker,
one of the pioneers of regional theater (and a co-founder of the Dallas
Theater Center), one begins to understand the demands of regional theater.
"Are you willing to donate eighteen hours a day for years to learn your
trade?" he asks. "Are you willing to sacrifice your energy and all you value?"

Do It Yourself!

Chicago has long been hailed as one of the most vibrant of America's theater
cities, and Joel G. Fink, professional director, casting director, and associate
dean of the Chicago College of Performing Arts helps explain why:

> If you are interested in regional theater, take the time to discover what
> a particular theater is doing now and if that is the work that you want
> to be doing. Of course, having lived in Chicago for the past decade,
> I have become used to groups of people with like artistic visions
> banding together to start their own theater companies. Companies
> like Steppenwolf, Lookingglass Theatre, Chicago Shakespeare Theater
> are all products of the Chicago mentality of "do it yourself!"

Howard J. Millman's favorite saying is, "Don't let the bastards get you
down." As producing artistic director of Florida's Asolo Theatre Company,
he urges "those interested in regional theater to believe in regional theater
for what it is, not a stepping stone for anything more. Let's all try to go back
to the original concept of acting companies created specifically for our communities doing work designed for our audiences."

Take Responsibility (and Stop That Whispering)!

Dan McCleary, associate artistic director of the much-revered Shakespeare
& Company in Massachusetts, offers a strong dose of reality and some historical perspective:

What's needed now is a strong sense of personal responsibility . . . the art of theater, and its inherent creative risk, increasingly is giving way to the industry of theater, and its inherent safety and fiscal assurance. As regional theater creativity becomes industrial, artists and managers become increasingly specialized and enclosed, driving to achieve financial or employment objectives in their area of specialization without knowing how their creativity cooperates with others. The result is that there are few Renaissance women or men, fewer artist-managers (like Shakespeare and Burbage, for instance), fewer resident companies of artists, and, sadly, even fewer regional theaters that we can call our artistic homes. An artistic home might be described as a safe, inspired place to do and say dangerous, inspired things.

As artistic director Tina Packer says, the function of theater is to speak that which can't be spoken. It's usually hard, ugly, messy, and there's no getting it right. It's live art with live people, and it demands caretaking and responsibility: responsibility for fellow artists, for knowing budgets, for fundraising, for marketing, for cleaning, for the playwright, for the audience, for the community.

My most recent experience at a large regional theater in the South exemplified the direct opposite of all of the above. It was a dangerous place to speak freely and a dangerous place to act anything other than safely. The halls were filled with fear and notes in boxes and whispers. The stages were filled with shows that looked like each other, and a palpable malaise hung over the facility and filled the artists. It was a living example of the death of regional theater. Thankfully, we know this is not the case in every theater. And in those theaters are usually people of responsibility; artist-managers who see the whole engine working, who care about their audience, who fill the office space and the stage with their humanity, and who take it upon themselves to be responsible for examining, questioning, and celebrating the human condition. Personal responsibility.

Is a University Education or a Graduate Degree in Theater Really Necessary?

"Only two things are infinite, the universe and human stupidity, and I'm not sure about the former," teased the wildly educated Albert Einstein.

A university education isn't for everyone and many directors, actors, playwrights, and craftspeople have succeeded in the theater without a college degree. However, many would argue that a fine liberal arts background as an undergraduate student, combined with specific graduate training in your chosen field, will help you make friends and colleagues who develop into future professional collaborators and networking buddies.

If you decide to pursue the university route, consider the advice offered below by many of America's leading professionals and do your research before going to an undergraduate school with a graduate program where all the best roles (on stage and off stage) go to the graduate students. Be savvy about researching graduate schools, applying for scholarships, and committing to training programs with connections to professional theaters that have made a financial investment and a training commitment to *you* (versus simply accepting your tuition payments and *processing* you through a series of prerequisite classes).

As the Emmy Award–winning producer for ABC's annual *Academy Awards* and producing director of Hollywood's The Geffen Playhouse, Gilbert Cates understands the theater. He cites Joe Papp, (founder of New York's Public Theater) as a key figure in American theater because "he dared to do what he thought was important. His reward was an audience of interested, earnest, and informed people." Cates offers this advice:

> Craft is Freedom . . . study, work hard, and don't accept defeat. I find university training an excellent background for theater. Many graduate programs offer first-rate educations in the theater. As past dean and continuing faculty member of the University of California at Los Angeles, UCLA School of Theater Film and Television, I am a big proponent and advocate of university training. My own training included a BA and masters at Syracuse University (1955 and 1965), and studies at the Neighborhood Playhouse.

Joel Fink, also the director of the Chicago College of Performing Arts Theatre Conservatory, explains the value of professional training:

> American actors today are faced with the greatest challenge of any actors in history. They are expected to have the craft and technique to handle works from all eras, all countries and all mediums. To make a living in the theater today, actors are expected to have both a breadth and depth of skills and abilities. Actors today can't rely on inspiration or opportunities to learn their craft "on the job." Whether through professional training, internships, or other means, actors need the training to enter the profession with the ability to meet a wide range of artistic demands.

This is one reason why MFA training programs have proliferated in America. Where else will a young actor get to work on Shakespeare, Chekhov, Ibsen, the Greeks, Comedy of Manners, musicals . . . as well as gain experience in film and television technique? Fortunately, summer companies such as the Illinois Shakespeare Festival, the Colorado Shakespeare Festival, the Utah Shakespearean Festival, and other festivals in almost every state offer students opportunities to work with seasoned professionals on Shakespeare and other classic texts, while pursuing degrees.

The University of Delaware is well known and respected for its Professional Theatre Training Program. The director of the program is professional director and educator Sandy Robbins, who encourages aspiring regional theater artists to:

Know the field. Travel and see everything you possibly can. Be aware of who is doing what where. Train at a conservatory that will equip you with the skills you will need and also provide entrée to the profession and introduce you in a meaningful way to those who hire.

Do not wait for opportunities; create them by making theater wherever you are with whatever means you have. I think it is impossible to contribute to the kind of theater I care about without knowing the literature and history of the theater.

I think it crucial to develop the skills of acting and/or directing for the stage. The most efficient way to do this is to train at a conservatory.

Finally, if it's the money that has you concerned, remember that scholarships are often available for financially needy and talented students and note that there are a lot of terrific theater professors at reasonably priced universities around America. Consider the words of Derek Bok (president of the not-so-reasonably priced Harvard University from 1971 to 1991): "If you think education is expensive, try ignorance."

Which University Is the Right University?

Making great contacts and networking through alumni, faculty, and staff connections is oftentimes one of the key reasons that parents, career counselors and theater professionals advocate attending more "high-profile" universities. Pulitzer Prize–winning playwright Robert Schenkkan addresses this issue:

I'm sure some training programs (professional or academic) are better than others and offer their graduates better connections and credits but I couldn't tell you who they are. And besides, they change drastically from year to year as people move from one program to the next. But certainly all regional theaters value talent and practical experience.

Not surprisingly, as executive director of the University/Resident Theatre Association (U/RTA), Scott L. Steele has strong views on preparing for a career in regional theater:

Those contemplating a career of any kind in regional theater, whether in acting, directing, design or management, should pursue training on a professional, graduate level. People should take time off after college, and then invest in attending a great MFA training program. This may seem an obvious recommendation coming from an executive direc-tor of U/RTA, but the fact remains that graduate training provides the fundamental skills, helps develop the natural talent and intellect, and offers the specialized education, that are all necessary, along with luck, for a career in theater. Of equal importance is that graduate training effectively provides the network of contemporary colleagues, as well as of accomplished professionals encountered during that training, which will, more than anything else, help a young professional to first gain work. Whether it is classmates starting a small theater company somewhere, or a new administrator seeking an entry-level job with an established theater, it is the relationships that are created over the three years of graduate training that make work happen. Perhaps 50 percent of the value in graduate training is the rich resource it provides for building this network. It is true in most other professions, and is no less true in the field of theater.

Education and Training: Liberal Arts, Conservatory, or Both?

Kent Thompson, artistic director at the Denver Center Theatre Company, reviews the balance of broad academic training, life experience, and conser-vatory training:

I always recommend a bachelor of arts degree from a liberal arts college rather than a BFA—I think the knowledge of the world that such a degree demands is very helpful in keeping the theater professional connected to the world. Peter Zeisler always derided his staff at TCG if they didn't read the newspaper—there's a grain of truth in his criticism—theater has to examine what it means to be human in the world today. You can't do that if you're disconnected or worse, uninformed.

For most theater professionals, an advanced degree from a major training program or conservatory (preferably attached to a professional theater) is the fastest way into the field. Such an experience will combine the classroom and independent study with practical work in the field. And provide you with lots of professional contacts in building your own network. Building and nurturing that network is the key to a successful career in professional theater. Otherwise, find the theater and the community you want to work in, apply for a job and work your way up.

The liberal arts are also high on Cincinnati Playhouse in the Park producing artistic director Ed Stern's list:

I am a firm believer in liberal arts training at the undergraduate level as I love for actors and directors and designers to have as wide a range of knowledge as possible. Graduate school is a time to focus on acting, directing, or designing as a designated field of study. And get good training. Develop good discipline. The difficulty of entering a field teeming with actors, directors, and designers underscores the need for the finest training and discipline possible.

A re-creation of Shakespeare's historic indoor theater, The Blackfriars Playhouse, may be found in the delightful hamlet of Staunton, Virginia, home to Shenandoah Shakespeare and the American Shakespeare Center. Embracing a "we do it with the lights on" philosophy, executive director Ralph Alan Cohen believes that audiences "should be in the show, not at the show." He also hails the value of a more general university education: "I still believe that a director has to have something to say and that something comes from a broad, liberal arts education."

A liberal arts education is at the top of Charles Morey's list as well. As artistic director of Utah's prestigious Pioneer Theatre Company, Mr. Morey offers advice to students and parents:

The best educated individuals make the best artists, artisans, and managers—not to mention colleagues. Go to a good college or university with a strong emphasis in the liberal arts. Do not go to an undergraduate conservatory program! (Parents, if you are reading this, do not allow your child to go to an undergraduate conservatory program! Refuse to pay for it.) Once you are enrolled in that good liberal arts program, major in theater if you must, but take tons of literature, dramatic and otherwise. Study history, art, music, philosophy, psychology, maybe even the sciences. Then when you have given yourself a well-rounded liberal education and when you have convinced yourself that absolutely nothing else but a life in the theater will make your existence bearable; then, work like hell to get into a *good* MFA program and when you're in it, work even harder.

In California, Marin Shakespeare Company managing director Lesley Schisgall Currier agrees:

If all you've ever studied is acting, you will be far less interesting on stage. Travel, explore the world, have adventures . . . then you'll have something to create theater about.

One of the few remaining classical repertory theaters in America is located in the historic Masonic Temple Building in Glendale, California. It has deservedly been hailed as Los Angeles' premier classical theater, and the theater's co-artistic directors, Julia Rodriguez and Geoff Elliott, offer this perspective on preparing for a career in theater:

The intensive conservatory atmosphere that we were happily a part of at ACT (in San Francisco) in the 1980s can't help but influence our answer . . . we feel it is essential for actors who are interested in pursuing serious stage work to attempt to enroll in one of the several great conservatories in the country, *organizations with working professionals on staff.* We have watched countless actors over the years who, without the benefit of solid technique, find themselves at sea when faced with difficulties arising out of the creation of character and pursuit of passion-filled objective.

Florida's oldest nonprofit professional theater, the Asolo Theatre Company, has a long established Conservatory for Actor Training, affiliated with Florida State University (FSU). Richard G. Fallon, dean emeritus at FSU, was one of the Asolo's co-founders in 1960 and he too recommends that students "prepare in university programs which have a relationship to a professional theater company." Dean Fallon also cajoles students to have a "love—of yourself, those who work with you, the audience, the theater, and your mission. You must have courage and dedication to see you through."

Rehearsing Hamlet or Reselling Houses?

Professional director Theodore Herstand offers the following pointers:

> Be prepared to struggle in your first years "out there" after you've been graduated. Some don't have to struggle, but most do. If you can't take it, get yourself a good life selling houses. That way, you can afford to go to the theater often and, perhaps, become a philanthropist who helps not-for-profit arts institutions.

Shakespeare's Friends author Kate Pogue sums it all up:

> Regional theater requires versatility, sensitivity to historical styles, and a commitment to a simple, hard-working, low-profile career as opposed to hope for fame and fortune. Actors need the most comprehensive vocal and physical training, and the broadest range of experience (personal and theatrical) they can find. They don't, however, have to go to the best and the biggest schools. At the undergraduate level they may be much better off at a small university, or local community college, where they can get decent training in all the theater skills, and lots of onstage experience, saving their specialized training for the graduate level.

Discover Me and Save Me from Academia!

We've all heard the Hollywood stories of stars "being discovered" at the local drugstore, on the beach, in the park, and through sheer serendipity. Is formal training, academic or otherwise, even necessary? "Life is my college," writes Louisa May Alcott. "May I graduate well, and earn some honours!"

Although he holds an MFA from the University of California, Davis, Richard Rose, artistic director of Virginia's Barter Theatre, writes:

> I am not an overall fan of the academic path, although it is the path we are currently following. I think education takes as much out of us as it gives us. Again, many of the artists of early regional theater found their education and career paths in doing, not in studying.

I think the most important aspect of training is learning every day and always striving to be better each and every moment. We have a saying here at Barter Theatre that "Art equals learning." If you want to call yourself an artist, you must learn always; first and foremost. We have found that those who succeed are not necessarily the most "talented," or the ones with the most "potential." Those who succeed in the long run in regional are the ones who strive to improve, never settle, never coast, and who have a real desire to learn. This has been a constant in my life. So, I don't care if you've gone to one of the elite universities, have a PhD, or if you are right off the street. Those who learn, succeed.

So the necessary training or preparation is "Learn from everyone you meet, everyone you study, and every situation. Especially learn from your mistakes. They are your greatest teachers."

One of the problems with academic learning is that even those programs that give their students permission to fail do not necessarily teach their students success through failure. Largely because there are no consequences.

Bernard Havard, producing artistic director of Philadelphia's Walnut Street Theatre, steers actors "to develop yourself into a triple threat (acting, singing, dancing) in order to make the most of your options," and advocates apprenticeships or internships as "the most crucial element for those contemplating careers—it's a wonderful way to sort things out and gain the first rung on the ladder to success."

Certainly, universities aren't for everyone and not every university does a great job of preparing students for careers in theater. If you are going to invest the time, money, strength, and energy in a university program, make sure it's right for you and that you find a good match. One of Mario Puzo's characters in *The Godfather* offers this challenging question: "*You go to college to get stupid?*"

And the Beaches Are Great, Too!

The graduate training process works for many. Stephen Rothman, chair of Theatre Arts at California State University, Los Angeles, offers this personal testimonial:

I had the unique experience of spending the last year of my MFA from Florida State at the Asolo Theatre full-time. This was the crucial experience for me. After years of classroom training I was thrust for an entire year into a position/internship at a LORT theater. Without that year my career would never have fast-tracked the way it did. This was a segue for me from training to doing it and it was what *truly* gave me a career.

Decorum: On Stage and Off Stage

Winston Churchill defined a gentleman as "a man who is only rude when he intends to be." Gil Lazier, longtime dean of Florida State University and the Asolo Theatre Conservatory, expresses similar sentiments:

> It's really about attitude if you have the requisite talent and skill. You must be easy to work with—positive, optimistic and friendly. Otherwise, your first job could be your last. You need to make employers want to rehire you for the next gig. This work not only requires efficiency, creativity and skill, but also a high level of diplomacy, no matter what area is involved. You've got to get the job done with ease and good will in an intense environment. Be positive and honest. If you can't be positive and honest at the same time, be honest in the most positive way you can!

Lynn Landis, managing director of Philadelphia's The Wilma Theater, puts it more succinctly: "Keep the drama on stage."

Still, some people just like to shake things up! Berkeley Repertory Theatre managing director Susan Medak feels that her job is to "challenge orthodoxy." She explains that "To keep us from getting stale, my job is to make sure we aren't falling back on easy answers. At Berkeley Rep, our staff jokes that 'Flexibility is a four letter word!' But in fact, when we 'embrace flexibility,' we make it possible for a broad range of artists to do their best work."

"Never think the work isn't valued," cautions Steven Woolf, artistic director of The Repertory Theatre of St. Louis. "The chance to make art and investigate texts and themes is a privilege and a responsibility. Our work in our communities is part of the social fabric of our cities and vital to the society in our towns."

As esteemed acting guru Stella Adler notes: "Life beats down and crushes the soul, but art reminds you that you have one."

The Big Picture: What Many Universities Fail to Tell You

Certainly, there's no one way to train for a life in the theater and there isn't a standard theater curriculum that is taught in America's training institutions.

Consider this book "Everything You Need to Know About Working in the Theater that You Didn't Learn in Class" and you will find some ingenious, effective tools that will help you throughout your career. "The great difficulty in education," writes George Santayana, "is to get experience out of ideas."

GET EXCITED OR EXCITE YOURSELF!

"Visit the theaters you admire or are curious about," insists longtime Alabama Shakespeare Festival artistic director, past TCG president, and current Denver Center Theatre Company artistic director Kent Thompson. He adds:

> See their work, meet their artists and administrators. Find out what kind of theater you want to work in. At the same time find a community that you can invest in personally and professionally, for these theaters work only with deep local roots and many on-going connections to the larger professional field. Find out what artists—playwrights, directors, actors—most excite you when you go to the theater; then work with them or work at the theaters they frequent.
>
> Or start your own theater.
>
> Always remain curious and always remain critical (that is, define your own aesthetic, your own vision of what theater can become in 21st-century America).

BE AGGRESSIVE, SAY YES, DO YOUR HOMEWORK, KEEP THE FAITH!

Playwright Robert Schenkkan explains that aspiring regional theater workers must "pursue it aggressively" and remember that "it's the people who run the theater that matter; relationships are important."

There's a wonderful regional theater in Upstate New York known as Syracuse Stage where artistic director Robert Moss offers reliable advice, plain and simple:

> Say "YES" as often as possible. See every play as if it's never been done before. Avoid the word "just" as in—"it's just a living room." Go to your heart more often than your brain for answers. When going to work at a regional theater, try to understand it as an ongoing entity of which you will be a part. Go to its Web site before you arrive. Do some research. Be smart. Introduce yourself to the whole staff.

"Be familiar with the players," asserts professional director and educator Jim O'Connor. He explains:

One would hardly be prepared to be a physicist without the knowledge of past and present contributors to this discipline. The same should be expected of those who aspire for careers in the regional theater. It is essential that one always be prepared with a number of interesting projects that might fit at particular theaters and be prepared to actively present these proposals and have a good idea of personnel to implement them. Most important and certainly most difficult of all is to position oneself so that the work can be seen by artistic directors from the regional theaters.

"Keep the faith," notes Barter Theatre artistic director Richard Rose. "It is important work that regional theaters are doing . . . regional theaters are now the heart, soul, and still, training ground for American theater. My second piece of advice: Don't give in. Success can lead to conservatism. Keep your ideals and boldly go where no one else is going. If you don't who will?"

Noted theater historian Vera Mowry Roberts offers three simple tips: "First, be proficient in your art. Second, love people. Third, expect hard, long work hours."

AND MOM SAID NEVER TO TALK ABOUT POLITICS OR RELIGION

"Like any other career in the arts, it is important to know what's happening in the wider world (in the arts as well as politics and economics). All of this has impact on our work," asserts Repertory Theatre of St. Louis artistic director Steven Woolf. He explains:

Whether it's interpretive in a new way in looking at a text or
if you are an administrator trying to run and maintain a company,
the more knowledge you have, the more well equipped you are.
If you are thinking about running a company, then knowing as much
as you can about all the elements of the theater is crucial—from
design to construction to balance sheets to being able to stock
the rest rooms with supplies. The more you know, the better
everything works—on the artistic side, the technical side and the
administrative side.

OKAY, SUPERMAN, *SMALLTOWN* IS NOT *SMALLVILLE*!

"My advice, of course, is to work anywhere and everywhere," counsels Ed Stern. "Do not presume a theater in Smalltown, USA, can only do small work. Certainly the day and age of simply waiting in New York to be 'discovered in New York' is gone. The range of opportunities in regional theater far outweighs the option of hoping for the occasional straight play just to be 'seen' in New York City."

"Be well educated. Be well trained. Work hard." Obvious but often ignored advice from professional director and Pioneer Theater Company artistic director Charles Morey, who adds: "Be the type of person with whom I would like to spend eight hours a day in a windowless rehearsal room. Be intensely disciplined in your work habits and work ethic. Your competition will have all those attributes listed above. And you probably have to locate yourself in one of those half dozen cities in the country whence many if not most of the regional theaters hire."

IF I WERE A RICH MAN!

For those interested in regional theater work, "Marry great wealth!" jokes Tom Markus, author of one of the best, most practical, and funniest books on the theater, *An Actor Behaves: From Audition to Performance.* "Otherwise," he commands, "find the strength in yourself to know that your rewards come from the work you do. The yuppie mantra says that the one with the most toys wins. If your toys cost money, regional theater is not for you. But if your toys are your experiences, your memories, the gifts of your labors that you give to your audiences, then you will die richer than Bill Gates."

A professional director and longtime artistic director, Mr. Markus admonishes aspiring theater professionals to "travel the world, as far and as often as you can. See how other people live, learn what they value, wonder at the myriad ways they make theater. Travel in your mind—read, read, read. Go to museums. Go to concerts. Think. Think harder. Read. I have two mantras I always have posted above my desk. The first is my own (so far as I know): Take the work very seriously, but laugh at yourself. The second is Beckett's: 'No matter. Try again. Fail again. Fail better.'"

TAKE RISKS!

Jonathan Moscone, artistic director of the California Shakespeare Theater, echoes the sentiment: "Take risks. Read. Go to museums, travel, experience as much of life as possible. Intern anywhere you can. It's the best first step into a career."

The phenomenal producers and performers of Cirque du Soleil take risks onstage and offstage and, although they are definitely a for-profit corporation, they do tour and perform regionally throughout America. Their production and performing team now includes nearly 2,400 employees—and it all started with creative risk taking and a dream.

FORGET THE RISKS, JUST LEARN YOUR CRAFT. (AND DON'T EXPECT ME TO SAY THANKS!)

"Craft, Craft, Craft, learn it, practice it, own it!" insists Alan Rust, director of Connecticut's Professional Actor Training Program at The Hartt School. "You need a solid education to be able to embrace the broad scope of material that is explored in regional theaters," adds Mr. Rust.

Marin Shakespeare managing director Lesley Schisgall Currier offers this bit of advice about working in the field:

> Never expect gratitude. (We work so hard and very often end up feeling that our work is not recognized, rewarded or respected. Learning to find self-gratification in the work is a great gift you can give yourself. After all, despite how hard we work, we are extraordinarily fortunate to do what we do.)
>
> Treat your fellow theater artists with respect. Returning phone calls, responding to (even unsolicited) scripts or résumés, caring about the often transitory artists without whom we cannot create collaborations, sharing knowledge, volunteering time to support the organizations that support our theaters—all these things are essential. The successful future of this young thing we call America's regional theaters depends not only on the longterm health and vitality of individual organizations, but also on continuing to learn to collaborate as a field to create viable career opportunities for artists, communicate our value, and become an essential part of the fabric of American life across the nation.

IF I LIVE IN DENVER, WHY DO I HAVE TO GO TO NEW YORK TO GET CAST IN DENVER? WHAT, NOT ANYMORE?

Emma Walton, co-founder of Sag Harbor's Bay Street Theatre in New York, offers extremely valuable advice on connecting with directors and the ongoing reality of many regional theaters when it comes to casting: New York still rules! According to Walton:

> Depending on whether their interests are creative or administrative, my advice to those interested in regional theater work would change. At Bay Street, we cast almost exclusively out of New York City, so actors interested in working here need to have relationships with agents, casting directors, and directors in order to be submitted. Housing is a big issue for us, being located as we are in one of the most expensive resort communities in America—so if an actor or

designer has local housing it's a big plus. Finally, though, we find that a lot of the actors, designers, stage managers, etc. that we employ have prior relationships with directors and are brought in by their request. So it's important to cultivate relationships with directors.

For administrative roles, it's another thing. In addition to experience in their specific field, it's critical for our staff members to be willing to multi-task, and to be team players. Any one of us is as likely to be found serving concessions one night, or painting a bathroom or replacing a lightbulb as we are doing our more job-specific tasks . . . and anyone who isn't willing to get their hands dirty once in a while doesn't last long. It's not a line of work that offers a great deal of salary. It takes a small staff of very dedicated people who are interested in a different reward—a creative, collaborative "thinking outside the box" kind of life, with a spirit of fun about it—to make a small regional theater like Bay Street survive and thrive.

I think anyone interested in making a life in regional theater has to have a good deal of healthy perspective, and a willingness to place the good of the whole organization before any individual agendas or ambitions. Beyond that, I think to have had some practical theater experience is critical—it's hard to be a good producer, or write a great, compelling press release about a show, or be a collaborative tech director etc. if you don't have a very clear understanding of what the creative process of making theater entails. And the more experience the better—I worry about the kids coming out of college programs now who are so specialized they can't cross over from one department to another. Better to have been onstage, backstage, at the light board and sound board, in the box office—as much experience and understanding of all the components as possible. That's the only real way to develop the spirit of collaboration and the mutual respect that working in the theater demands.

As you will discover when you review the theater listings in this book, many theaters now cast in their own hometowns and invite potential employees to visit with them right there in their own regional cities (including Chicago, San Francisco, Minneapolis, Phoenix, Seattle, Omaha, and Los Angeles).

Beware the Potential Pitfalls

Regional theater in America is a growing, changing, evolving beast of a profession and many of the "innovations," cost-cutting measures, and practices wreak havoc for employees, visiting artists, managers, and audiences. Financial realities and poor executive planning are sometimes the case, but, oftentimes, the concerns center on employees who don't meet the basic expectations of their employers. "The one sign I still have up says, 'It ain't all bright lights and glamour,'" explains artistic director Steven Woolf.

DON'T BE PITIFUL!

Designer, educator, and consultant David Weiss doesn't mince words:

> As for training, don't get me started. It is pitiful how little some of our so-called "young artists" know these days. Play analysis? Who needs it? I have watched designers go through a full course of MFA training without ever understanding that ours is an art of collaboration and that it starts with the play. But what is worse, far worse, is that they cannot bring any true knowledge or experience to the table. They are almost unaware of the fine arts beyond the most conspicuous examples—the *Mona Lisa*? Sure, I've seen pictures of that. But do aspiring lighting designers, just as one example, have any understanding or appreciation of the magnificence of their art as expressed by Rembrandt, Rubens or Carravaggio, just to name a very few? Too often they do not. And it goes on from there into literature, history, geography, and the basic sciences—in other words, the liberal arts. Well, you know the rant as well as I do. Unfortunately, the problem starts all the way back in primary school these days.

JOINT PRODUCTIONS USUALLY MEAN FEWER PEOPLE WORKING

A growing trend during tough economic times is for theaters to share the cast/director/designers, etc. and move original productions between theaters as "joint productions." Jim O'Connor warns that "there are fewer and fewer acting, directing, and design positions available as the composite number of individual productions on a national scale decreases due to the multiple stops of individual productions."

SEARCHING FOR IBSEN, CHEKHOV, STRINDBERG, AND SHAW

It may be harder to find truly brilliant classical work on stage. Professional director and educator Sandy Robbins offers a bit of history:

> It is my view that today we lack models of the kind of theater that inspired me—we have few resident companies in this country and few, if any, truly distinguished companies performing the classics in

rotating repertory. I was blessed to see many, many extraordinary performances and I believe that it is more necessary today than it was in the past to see a wide variety of theater in this country and abroad so as to see performances that inspire.

WOULD YOU LIKE FRIES WITH YOUR FEYDEAU?

Kent Thompson talks about the challenges of a career in the theater and offers advice on artistic and personal survival:

The hardest thing about the first decade of your career in this profession is keeping yourself engaged and growing as a person and as an artist. This requires an investment in your own personal development as a person. And it requires an investment in the larger cultural, political and social life of the community that you're in. You may have to work as a waiter or temp or whatever, but go to theater, work out in a gym, read, participate in sports, visit museums, travel the country, campaign for a political or social cause, write ... do whatever will keep you alive as a person. And stay disciplined about developing your artistic discipline. Our artistic endeavors (whether we're a manager or an actor) always reveal how curious we have been as human beings, how much we have sought what life offers us, and how disciplined we have been in preparing ourselves for the rigors and practice of the art form.

THE CHECK IS IN THE MAIL (NOT THAT IT'S ABOUT MONEY)

Laguna Playhouse artistic director Andrew Barnicle lists more than one of the potential pitfalls in the business:

Advice: You can only be sure that you've got the part when you are standing on stage on opening night. Mantra: It's never about money, but it's always about money. Pithy quote—from Bernard Sahlins, founder of Chicago's Second City to his company before a New York opening: "Just remember guys, in New York City, if you're one in a million, there's thirteen o' yas." Others: Theater, and especially casting, is not a democracy. Thank goodness. And the strongest personality in the room *will* direct the play.

A FINAL NOTE

According to a recent Theatre Communications Group (TCG) report, non-profit theaters contributed more than $1.46 billion to the US economy and a significant portion of most theaters' budgets is for payroll. There may very well be a job or a career for you in regional theater. But how much of that payroll will trickle down to you? In Chicago, The Goodman Theatre's executive director Roche Schulfer explains:

> We have to find a way to improve the dismal economic situation for the American stage actor. Every producer in the country should make this issue a priority. At the same time, if we don't solve the problem of chronic undercapitalization in our industry, we can't do much for actors or other theater professionals. We must do more to advocate with funding sources for multi-year support and other creative ways to provide for an infusion of capital to theaters that want to expand their artistic capacity.

In conclusion, do your research, hone your skills, network with potential employers, and see if this field is right for you.

PART II

A BRIEF HISTORY OF REGIONAL THEATER IN AMERICA

CARRYING THE ARTISTIC TORCH

"At a time when theatres were dark across America, plays began to be given from the Atlantic to the Pacific, not only in city theatres, but in parks and hospitals, in Catholic convents and Baptist churches, in public schools and armories, in circus tents and universities, in prisons and reformatories, and in those distant and unfrequented camps where 350,000 of America's youth are learning all they know about life and art."

Hallie Flanagan, *Federal Theatre Project/WPA brief before the House of Representatives*, 1938, page 3.

An Introduction to America's Nonprofit Theater Movement

Why is it so important for current theater practitioners to have a feel for the history of America's "regional theater movement" and why is theater history a requirement (and often dreaded component) in virtually every college and university theater program in America? Perhaps popular novelist Michael Crichton says it best in his medieval romp, *Timeline*, when he notes that "history is the most powerful intellectual tool society possesses."

Or, to quote Mark Hofflund, esteemed managing director of the Idaho Shakespeare Festival:

> Typically, I find that our awareness (among theater leaders) rarely goes back beyond our lifetimes and we only know about the things we invented. Yet, tying those inventions to our predecessors is richly rewarding and interesting. Invariably, it also ties us to existing movements whose relevance we may have discounted.

At the 2005 Tony Awards celebrating the best of Broadway at Radio City Music Hall, Tony Award–winner Norbert Leo Butz implored the audience to "support regional theater around the country" and paid tribute to San Diego's Old Globe Theater, "who gave us a home to create this play [*Dirty Rotten Scoundrels*]."

It is truly remarkable how quickly the tables have turned. Historically, of course, Broadway sparked the creative process and provided the playwrights, actors, dancers, singers, musicians, directors, designers, plays, and musicals through production in New York, through cast albums that made their ways into homes throughout America, and through touring productions to major cities, state-to-state throughout the United States. Today, the process is often reversed as regional theaters provide the artistic home and incubation period for many Broadway shows, including Pulitzer-, Tony-, and Drama Desk Award–winning plays and musicals.

Pulitzer Prize–winning playwright Robert Schenkkan (*The Kentucky Cycle*) offers these insights:

> I owe my career to regional theater. With one exception, all my plays
> have first been produced in regional theater before going to NYC.
> The regional theater movement has kept theater alive in this country.
> With Broadway and now even Off-Broadway too expensive to
> develop new work, as often as not it is in the regional theater that
> new plays are being commissioned, written, developed, and produced.

Even accomplished poet and NEA Chair Dana Gioia notes that "the growth of regional theaters has been the most important development in American theater in the past forty years."

Emma Walton, co-founder of New York's Bay Street Theatre, explains that regional theaters have "more or less replaced the old 'out-of-town tryout' period for a Broadway show—these days most Broadway shows were developed in the regions, at places like the Old Globe, Steppenwolf, Denver Center Theatre, etc. These theaters afford the creative teams the opportunity to develop their material in a safer environment, using what they learn from audiences and local critics but protecting the show from the kind of national press that can kill a production before it makes a transfer.'"

The regional theater movement has evolved in surprising ways. Laguna Playhouse executive director Richard Stein offers an abbreviated history and advice for those who wish to work in the field:

> The regional theater in America has evolved from being a passionate
> alternative to commercial New York theater, to a foundation-driven,
> cookie-cutter institutional formula heavily dependent upon govern-
> ment funding, to an entrepreneurial quasi-commercial nonprofit
> hybrid struggling to survive and attract audiences in an electronic age.
> To some, the heyday of the regional theater is long past, but I think

> what is emerging has the potential to be a more democratic and plu-
> ralistic institution that more closely mirrors our national character. It
> will be a sort of return to regional theater's roots and a rejection of
> its rigid, insular, and elitist adolescence ... anyone who contemplates a
> career in regional theater must be passionate about the art and be
> able to communicate that passion to others.

So, if indeed regional theater is returning to its artistic roots, an added bonus to reviewing the history of the movement is that it may very well provide insight into the future.

The Vision of a Nonprofit Regional Theater

"Vision: the art of seeing things invisible."

Jonathan Swift

Long before the beginning of what we now call the nonprofit theater move-ment, theater companies spanned and grew with the country. From the early 1800s until the 1870s, once-itinerant actors found work, and a home, in for-profit resident repertory theater companies. In the decades that followed, economic and technological changes altered the theater industry, creating a need and setting the stage for a new, *nonprofit* movement.

In the 1920s, this new wave of theaters began springing up across the country. Its leaders were visionaries-artists, educators, community organizers. Their new theaters generally focused on the compelling nature of the plays and the dynamic and exciting process of theater. Hundreds of nonprofit theaters suddenly surfaced in makeshift neighborhood theaters in small towns, midsize cities, and bustling metropolitan areas. Stephen Langley deftly chronicled the changes in these new nonprofit theaters that, instead of being led by profit-driven producers, were being governed by boards of trustees and artistic directors with "their sights fixed on artistic rather than commer-cial goals." (Langley, *Theatre Management and Production in America*, p. 169)

The 1934 guidebook, *B'way Inc! The Theatre as a Business* is one of the earliest published books on theater management in America. Author Morton Eustis offers a look at producing in America prior to the emergence of the nonprofit theater movement:

> Anyone who has money—or the ability to beg, or borrow it—can
> become a theatrical producer. Talent, background, theater training,
> common or garden business sense, he need not have ... to see his

name in electric lights glimmering above that of the star and the play, he has only to take an option on a script, any script will do; engage a cast, director and technical staff; post a bond with Actors' Equity; sign a few standard contracts; rent a theater, and order the curtain to be raised on another glamorous Broadway first night . . . producing a play can be a delightfully remunerative pastime.

Eustis, B'way Inc! Theatre as a Business, p. 18.

That same year, *Theatre Arts* editor Edith J. R. Isaacs writes:

Any living theater must have five essential qualities:

It must have an entity, an organism that can be recognized, as you recognize a human being, by certain traits of character and of physical presence that are marks of a personal life.

It must have permanence in some one or more of its fundamentals. It may be a permanence of place or of leadership, as in the Moscow Art Theatre, or the Vieux Colombier or the Neighborhood Playhouse; of repertory, of course, of company, or of idea, as in Meiningen or the Théatre Libre or the Provincetown, or of any two or three of these combined; but they must have something that stands firm and rooted, something not too transitory, in that transitory world of the theater where performances die as they live, each day, as a production is set up, played through and struck.

It must have the power of growth, of progress, both in its permanent and its impermanent factors, because times change and it must change with them . . .

It must bear within itself, the power of generation, the element of renewal, a force that, having flowed out of its own inner strength and integrity, can bring back fresh strength from a newer, younger world.

And finally it must have a goal that is essentially a theater goal. There is no reason under the sun why the leader of a fine theater should not hope to gain money, or power, or preferment from the enterprise. But these are by-products of theatrical success, not essential theater goals, which must always be in some way related to the performance of good plays by actors of talent, and the consequent development of the theater's innate power of entertainment, edification, exaltation, escape, and social persuasion.

There has probably never been an organized theater of importance that did not have, to some extent, these five qualities.

Isaacs, Broadway, Inc!, p. 191.

Predating the regional theater movement by almost three decades, these views of the American theater are both wonderfully visionary and, in today's world, absolutely laughable. Producing a play as a "delightfully remunerative pastime" is a concept that would elicit a chuckle from most Broadway producers while nonprofit theater producers might be rolling in the aisles. Although Broadway has arguably been the longtime center of America's commercial theatrical universe, many would note that, today, America's true national theater lies in the artistically, aesthetically, culturally, ethnically, socially, and politically diverse nonprofit resident theaters that are spread from coast-to-coast. This would no doubt please the many pioneers of the nonprofit theater who were dedicated to artistic excellence and the production of creative work that was often being overlooked in favor of more financially promising commercial shows on Broadway.

The Debates Begin

"It is not an exaggeration to say that regional theater saved American theater," explains Arthur Bartow, artistic director of the undergraduate Department of Drama, New York's Tisch School of the Arts. According to Mr. Bartow:

> The regional theater movement galvanized American theater at a time when commercial theater was at its nadir. It generated jobs for theater artists and inspired universities to create professional training programs to supply qualified actors, designers, and directors to feed the burgeoning theaters. It exposed thousands of theatergoers to classical dramatic literature that had been neglected by commercial theater. Later in the movement, the development of new and established playwrights was almost solely in the hands of regional theaters as commercial theater shrank from the risk of producing new plays. Regional theater created a national thirst for play going that fed not only nonprofit theaters but commercial theaters as well.

"Without the regional theater movement, we'd all be living in New York competing for the five jobs available on Broadway, or, if we chose to live elsewhere, we'd be working at Walmart doing community theater," contends Pioneer Theatre Company artistic director Charles Morey. The regional theater is 'Theater in America.'"

"The regional theater movement has, of course, transformed the landscape for theater in America," explains Ben Cameron, longtime executive director of the Theatre Communications Group (TCG). Mr. Cameron notes that "theaters of all shapes and sizes, springing from diverse aesthetic and cultural traditions, now constitute a true theater ecology in our country. Audience numbers from every source affirm the growing impact of this movement—audiences at an all-time high, and musical and nonmusical theater the top two performing arts forms for public participation today."

Scott L. Steele, executive director of the University/Resident Theatre Association (U/RTA) based in New York, weighs in with passion on the movement:

> The regional theater movement did not just impact theater in America. This movement created theater in America. Good theater outside the mainstream certainly existed prior to the development of regional or resident theaters, but it was a rather disparate group. The strength and growth that unity can provide came with the regional movement, as defined in the fifties and sixties. Of course, I'm totally biased, having grown up in Washington, D.C., with Arena Stage, The Washington Theatre Club (now extinct), and The Folger Theatre Group (now The Shakespeare Theatre).

Richard Rose, artistic director of Virginia's Barter Theatre, offers:

> In the beginning, regional theater served mostly to bring Broadway to the people, giving access to the shows created on Broadway and allow-ing audiences all over the nation to experience those shows. While places like the Barter and Cleveland and La Jolla did do a lot of new works and spawned many new authors, actors, designers, directors, etc. who went on to great careers, one could argue that regional theater was, in the beginning, merely an outgrowth of summer stock: a place for actors (and other theater artists) to work and hone their craft in anticipation of working on Broadway or in film. It was a training ground. Regional theater was the "farm team" to Broadway's "major league."

Gerald Freedman, professional director and dean of Drama at the North Carolina School of the Arts, explains that "the regional theater movement has evolved in a different manner than first conceived, as a kind of national theater with numerous dispersed satellites. Individual regions would find their unique voice and birth ensemble companies of professional caliber to bring a steady stream of quality theater, classics, current and new plays to enrich areas of the United States far from New York, Chicago, San Francisco. No longer would these outposts be dependent on touring companies with no regional roots." He asks crucial questions: "Without regional theater, where would we train our young actors, directors and designers? Where would our new playwrights find an outlet for their voice? Where would audiences experience the thrill of live performances in this time of mechanical reproductions?"

In no uncertain terms, noted author and professional director Tom Markus explains the potential influence and impact regional theater can have on a community:

> It has brought the life-nurturing experience of professional-quality live theater to millions of Americans, improving the quality of their daily rounds by providing them with an alternative to foolish movies and more foolish television. It has given hope and enlightenment to our young people and confirmation and vitality to our old. It has infused our society with the wisdom of the great writers of the past and the insights of the promising writers of the future. It has placed artists in each community, living side-by-side with postmen, dentists, electricians, and stockbrokers. Without regional theater, America would slide into ignorance and vulgarity.

Ted Herstand, professional director, historian, and Professor Emeritus at the University of Oklahoma, explains that "regional theater has provided a venue more conducive to new-play development than is found in the commercial theater. In a very real sense, the National Theater of America is the not-for-profit regional theater. The commercial professional theater is, more than ever before, dependent for whatever success it may have on the quality of regional theater that feeds it people, plays, and productions."

Longtime Florida State University/Asolo Theatre Conservatory dean, Gil Lazier, summarizes the overall impact of the regional theater movement by noting that "it's fostered more good American playwrights by providing them with more venues for artistic development than New York ever could. It's given American actors a chance to have normal lives by becoming members of resident companies and receiving steady incomes so that they can have homes and families. It's permitted professional productions of classic plays, seldom seen in New York except through imports, thus keeping alive a repertoire of great theater."

Laguna Playhouse artistic director Andrew Barnicle provides a bit of historical perspective:

> It is crucial to remember that the national theater of America has always been an organism in flux—in the 1830s every city had a

resident rep company that supported traveling stars in a common repertoire of slightly rehearsed plays. The expansion of the railroads during the Civil War created the possibility of entire productions touring, scenery et al., which rendered the resident companies obsolete. The actors all moved to New York so they could go on the road. The monopolies of the Syndicate and others desultorily formulized touring shows until there was an overwhelming need for an art theater movement, which eventually led to the small literary minded regional theaters in the early 20th century. This eventually resulted in the Off-Broadway and not-for-profit regional theater movement. Now, ironically, the commercial producers are partnering with the not-for-profits. Who would have guessed?

Jim O'Connor, professional director and head of the MFA Directing program at the University of South Carolina, notes the historic importance of college and university theaters in the development of the American theater:

> The regional theater movement along with its more widespread but less product-focused university theater has been the major force in maintaining the viability and visibility of the art of theater in the United States. While serving as the prime production archive of past cultures, the regional theater has simultaneously served to produce the major new writers for theater. Even a short review of the seasons of regional theaters will reveal that they are a combination of historically important scripts, new works written by resident or itinerant authors, and commercial works from Broadway with the first two categories most prominent. During the past several decades, the flow of material has reversed from what had been the import from Broadway to the regional theater to one from the regional theater to Broadway.

A Rose by Any Other Name

"I dislike the term 'regional theater,'" notes Geffen Playhouse and longtime Academy Awards producer Gilbert Cates. "I find it patronizing. The only regional theater in America is on Broadway. The rest is American theater." The Goodman Theatre's savvy executive director, Roche Schulfer, concurs: "I prefer the term 'resident' to 'regional' in referring to theaters that operate outside of the New York metropolitan area. I think that 'regional' implies that a theater serves a particular section of the country or that it is defined by its relationship to a specific geographic area, such as New York. 'Resident,' on the other hand, more accurately describes a theater with an ongoing history in a community and a strong connection to local artists, audiences, and supporters." Murray Ross of Colorado's Theatreworks also sees it this way: "To my mind, 'regional theater' sounds like a minor league franchise or branch . . . we don't think of ourselves as a regional theater—just as a theater . . . a good theater not in the Broadway or West End region." "Just for the record, one could argue that New York (Broadway) is just a large regional theater," adds the Barter's Richard Rose.

Robert Moss, artistic director of New York's Syracuse Stage, looks at the positive side: "There are so many major theater artists on Broadway who were brought up and nourished in the regions—it is a record we can be proud of."

Still, however one labels the burgeoning growth of regional, resident, local, community, or "home" theaters in America, it's clear that these theaters are changing the face of audiences and introducing many new faces as playwrights, actors, directors, and other theater professionals. As Marin Shakespeare Company managing director Lesley Schisgall Currier explains, "The regional theater movement has added a new chapter to the history of theater in America, providing myriad companies that serve the melting pot of communities and sub-communities throughout the 50 states. The most vital American theater today is gestating not on Broadway, but in communities all over the nation where artists are finding their own voices, reimagining the classics, providing creative opportunities for students of all ages, and making meaningful and entertaining theater that forges long-lasting relationships with other individuals and organizations."

Back to the Beginnings: Little Theater and Community Theaters

It is important to credit the many "little theaters" and "community theaters" that were a part of the American fabric long before the American regional theater movement began to fully blossom in the 1960s. To quote professional designer and University of Virginia Professor Emeritus David W. Weiss, "Keep in mind that long before anyone coined the phrase 'regional theater,' there was some serious activity out in the boonies. It was called stock, of course, and it wasn't just in the summer."

Writing about American drama during colonial times (and earlier), theater historian Walter J. Meserve offers this perspective:

If early attempts at dramatic literature were wild, one could surely describe the beginnings of an American theater as stormy. Performances of plays were opposed by local and colonial governments and by certain religious groups. Bankruptcy was a common hazard for theater managers. Playwrights were constantly subjected to abuse by theater managers, actors, and the public . . .

Just three hundred years ago, the first recorded play written in English in America, *Ye Bare and Ye Cubb* (written in 1665), was performed in Accomac, Virginia. During the intervening years, the advance of American drama to a position of world significance has been slow and painful.

Meserve, *An Outline of American Drama,* pp. 1 and 359.

"On Tuesday I speak at Andover on 'A Possible National Theater,' my old theme, slightly changed," writes Lady Gregory in a letter to Kenneth Macgowan, dated January 17, 1915.

In his 1916 study, Arthur Edwin Krows writes:

I welcome the various American experiments of little theaters, big theaters, open-air theaters, women's theaters, children's theaters, and the rest, for they signify a place for everything and everything in its place—with pleasure for all, varying scales of prices stabilized in each theater, for development of clientele, and, above all, support of plays for which it would be impossible at the time to secure general public approval . . . Shakespeare's plays, which were written for theaters in the open air in the daytime, have proven admirable when performed in the open air (in America).

Krows, *Play Production in America,* pp. 362-363.

"I am still full of the idea that one will be started in America—a tree with a root in every state." Kenneth Macgowan's *Footlights Across America: Towards a National Theater,* traces the "extent, nature and significance of the non-commercial theater of America." *Footlights* follows 14,000 miles of the author's travels helping to pinpoint the location of over 1,050 community and university theaters throughout the United States. He notes that George Pierce Baker of Yale University "has listed 1,800 names of producing organizations" and that *Theatre Arts Monthly* "has been in correspondence" with 1,000 groups (not counting the 6,000 high schools "that produce as part of their class work anywhere from one bill of short plays to twenty-five bills of long and short, and 6,000 more high schools with dramatic clubs that give at least one play a year").

He writes:

> The history of the little theater movement in America is a history of many things. It is a history of variegated efforts in acting, playwriting, direction, scene design, the organization of audiences, the financing and building of theaters. It is a history of amateur exhibitionism—the raw material of the stage—and of strongly talented artists who could make use of that material. . . . It is, in short, a history of aesthetic, social, and economic change."
>
> Macgowan, *Footlights Across America*, p. 41.

Boston's Toy Theatre (1912), Chicago's Little Theatre (1912), New York's Neighborhood Playhouse (1915), Massachusetts's Provincetown Players (1915), Ohio's Cleveland Play House (1915), New York's Washington Square Players (1918), California's Laguna Playhouse (1920), Chicago's Goodman Theatre (1925), and California's Pasadena Playhouse (1925) were just a few of the more than 2,000 theaters established throughout America by the mid-1920s, according to Drama League of America and Theatre Communications Group records.

Two of these groups emerged from a group of actors, writers, and artists who were mounting informal shows at the Liberal Club, labeled as the center of intellectual life in New York's Greenwich Village. Theater historian Jack Poggi tells the story:

> Out of these experiments two groups emerged, the Provincetown Players and the Washington Square Players. The two began to go in different directions. The Provincetown Players, more concerned with developing new writers, tried to preserve their freedom by remaining small and modest. The Washington Square Players, more concerned with improving production standards, expanded quickly and deliberately.
>
> Poggi, *Theatre in America*, p. 109.

"Perhaps the happiest development of the 1920s was the success of the Theatre Guild of New York City . . . the founding fathers of the Guild were veterans of the defunct Washington Square Players," writes Garff B. Wilson. Between 1920 and 1930, the Theatre Guild produced 67 plays including the works of Eugene O'Neill and Elmer Rice.

Writing about the growing professionalization of little theaters in the 1920s, Kenneth McGowan describes the "definite professionalizing of the actors," the cost of new productions, the salaries of directors, and "somewhere in the neighborhood of twenty-five plays a year" performed at The Cleveland Play House in Ohio. He describes The Goodman Theatre in Chicago's "handsome and finely equipped playhouse which the Goodmans built on the lake front" maintaining "an entirely professional company of sixteen actors . . . nine new plays and two or three revivals, and the average run of about four weeks. All this—the school and its losses included—is done on a budget of $120,000." In McGowan's travels to the Pasadena Community Playhouse in California, he discovered a company that "caters to both a winter and a summer audience," producing 28 plays and 322 performances a season, with a producing staff of 16, with 24 people "in the work of administration," and a budget over $145,000. (Macgowan, pp. 99–100.)

Universities Play a Significant Part in the Regional Theater Movement

Universities were expanding their dramatic activities as well in the late 1920s, and McGowan found that "not much less than 150 colleges have a course in the production of plays." He concludes that "universities have fed the new American theater, sending playwrights to Broadway, and actors, directors, audiences, and ideals to the local theaters." (Macgowan, p. 154.)

In a Northwestern University thesis survey of 383 universities conducted by Miss Lucile Calvert in 1928–29, she found the following as the "most active universities" who responded to her survey:

University	Number of Annual Productions	Number of Performances
Carnegie Tech	20	128
Cornell	20	40–50
Northwestern	14	68
Iowa	14	40–50
Yale	13	34
North Carolina	6	130

Macgowan, *Footlights Across America*, p. 110.

"If one goes back to Norris Houghton's book *Advance from Broadway*, we discover that when he wandered around the country in the 1930s trying to get a handle on theater in our country, he found mostly amateur theater along with a fairly lively road business," explains designer and longtime Institute of Outdoor Drama consultant David W. Weiss. "There was plenty of community and college theater that was of reasonably good quality but not much beyond that. After the war, however, and largely because of the financial help made available from the Ford Foundation, the regional theater as we know it now began to exist and thrive," adds Mr. Weiss.

Groundbreaking Theaters and Forceful Leaders Emerge

Eva Le Gallienne's Civic Repertory Theatre (1926) and the Group Theatre (1931) in New York were important artistic forces. Miss Le Gallienne, who presented an ambitious repertory of plays from 1926 to 1932, helped clarify the terminology we still use today:

> There was much confusion about just what repertory means . . . 'Repertory' derives from the Latin Reperio, 'to find again.' Its definition in the standard dictionary is 'a place where things are stored or gathered together' . . . A Repertory Theater, then, is a repository theater, a theater in which plays are gathered together and kept alive. Alternating performances of a wide range of plays is the only way to prolong their life. A permanent company is the only kind able to resume a play after months lapse from the current schedule without prohibitively arduous rehearsals. . . . In other words true repertory is the natural and normal form of the theater.
>
> Steinberg, *The History of the Fourteenth Street Theater*, pp. 86-87.

The mission of the Group Theatre, as reviewed by Harold Clurman in *The Fervent Years*, was "to lead full lives disciplined by a unified moral and intellectual code that would direct them toward smiling goals of spiritual and material well-being." The first directors included Mr. Clurman, Lee Strasberg, and Cheryl Crawford, and the actors included Elia Kazan, Stella Adler, Clifford Odets, Franchot Tone, J. Edward Bromberg, and Morris Carnovsky.

Important work was also being developed outside New York in Virginia's Barter Theatre (1933) and the Pittsburgh Playhouse (1933). The Barter Theatre's visionary Robert Porterfield attacked the Great Depression with the motto: "With vegetables you cannot sell, you can buy a good laugh" as his theater traded/bartered food and animals for theater tickets.

As a means of battling unemployment, Hallie Flanagan Davis headed up the Federal Theatre Project in 1935 and employed over 10,000 people in 40 states in hundreds of productions. She labored to create an initiative based on economic necessity that would be uniquely American, involve government subsidy, and present the best theater work of the day. In her landmark book, *ARENA, The Story of the Federal Theatre,* Ms. Flanagan Davis explains that the Federal Theatre worked on performing projects where "each region and eventually each state would have its unique, indigenous dramatic expression." (*ARENA,* page 371.) In a 1938 report to the House of Representatives, she offered a history lesson in international arts support:

> Government support of the theatre brings the United States into the best historic theatre tradition and into the best contemporary theatre practice. Four centuries before Christ, Athens believed that plays were worth paying for out of public money; today France, Germany, Norway, Sweden, Denmark, Russia, Italy and practically all other civilized countries appropriate money for the theatre.
>
> Flanagan Davis, *Federal Theatre Project/WPA brief before the House of Representatives, 1938* p. 1.

Unfortunately, the Federal Theatre's progressive contributions to the cultural life of the nation ended on June 30, 1939, when it was killed by an act of Congress.

While the political and censorship battles were raging in Congress—in part over Mark Blitzstein's controversial play, *The Cradle Will Rock,* the investigations of the Dies Committee on Un-American Activities, and charges that the Federal Theatre's activities were "communistic"—theater in the regions continued to flourish. In an April 5, 1940, address delivered by Frederick H. Koch at a "Southern Regional Theatre Festival" (commemorating the founding of The Carolina Playmakers in 1918–19), Professor Koch reviewed much of the rich history of American theater including "Folk Drama," "The Negro Drama," "The Tenant Farm Drama," "Drama in Extension (schools outreach)," "Plays of a Country Neighborhood (playwriting)," "Mexican Folk Plays," "Carolina and Canada," "A Chinese Playmaker," "The Professional and the People's Theatre," "Communal Drama of American History" and "Trouping (regional touring from the Carolinas to Boston, St. Louis, Dallas, Washington, D.C., and to myriad other cities through 45 plays and 36 tours).

The University of North Carolina's George R. Coffman welcomed the "Regional Theatre Festival" to the "Drama in the South" convention (that included speeches by playwrights Clifford Odets and Paul Green and author Zora Neal Hurston) and proclaimed that "critics and historians of American drama gave him (Professor Koch) first ranking as leader of a regional movement for native drama." Even Orson Welles, founder of the Mercury Theatre and well-known Broadway and Hollywood actor-director, sent greetings and wrote, "It is groups like yours which stimulate and keep the American Theater alive." Critics Brooks Atkinson and Stark Young sent greetings, along with philanthropist John D. Rockefeller, director Kenneth MacGowan, historian Allardyce Nicoll, and playwright Lynn Riggs.

In his address titled "A Playwright's Credo," playwright Clifford Odets tendered these words of advice to the assembled crowd:

> If America is to grow up in a creative sense the artist must realize how much he is like the life around him . . . America is a country of beginners, in the theater as in many other things. I believe that here it is certainly fact—that the parochial, not the cosmopolitan, is the beginning of truth.
>
> "A Playwright's Credo," *The Carolina Play-Book*, p. 105.

So, theater certainly existed in the "regions" long before what may eventually be known as the Golden Age of America's Regional Theater (when theaters were flourishing in the mid-20th century). However, it seems that for many current theater professionals with short memories (or an abbreviated view of America's theater history), the most important "regional theater movement" will always be tied to the founding of currently existing, generally thriving, and much-revered large institutions whose founders and ongoing leaders helped shape current production standards, theatrical architectural wonders, the collective bargaining of union contracts, and the artistic visions that currently spark 21st-century plays and productions.

The US Outdoor Drama Movement

Exciting, invigorating, often epic productions featuring historic, adventurous moments from America's past, passionate moments of religious drama, or even rambunctious Shakespearean productions provided theater in the regions long before the term "regional theater" was used to describe the nonprofit movement that was soon to follow. In Bulletin #42 in the University of North Carolina Institute of Outdoor Drama files, the "Preliminary Guidelines for Outdoor Epic Drama" clarifies the community partnership:

Regional outdoor drama production as it exists in America today, regardless of whether the production is of an original historical play or established as a festival of classics, has almost entirely been developed by non-profit historical and cultural organizations which stress cooperation between local groups, foundations, education, and government.

With the help of the Federal Theatre Project, the Civilian Conservation Corps, and President Roosevelt's New Deal, the citizens of Roanoke Island, North Carolina, first produced Pulitzer Prize-winning playwright Paul Green's famed outdoor historical drama, *The Lost Colony*, in 1937. According to Scott J. Parker, executive director of the Institute of Outdoor Drama (IOD) since 1990, *The Lost Colony* intended to run only one summer, was such a success that it continued each summer thereafter (except during World War II), and spawned the US Outdoor Drama movement, which currently numbers nearly 50 productions across America. Designed to preserve and celebrate the heritage of the country and to increase tourism, the historical plays are based on significant events and performed in amphitheaters on or near the sites where the events occurred.

Mark R. Sumner, Institute of Outdoor Drama executive director from 1964 to 1989, explains:

> Green followed the success of *The Lost Colony*, in 1937, with *The Common Glory* at Williamsburg, Virginia, in 1947, and Kermit Hunter, then a UNC graduate student, wrote his famed *Unto These Hills* in 1950 for the Cherokee Indian Reservation in the mountains.

David W. Weiss offers this view of America at the time:

> When Paul Green launched the first of his outdoor dramas, *The Lost Colony*, the world was a much simpler place. The simplicity of entertainment in those days, for children and adults, made going to an outdoor drama a highlight in vacation travel. It was alive! We went to an outdoor drama to see people who might have walked on the very spot we were looking at. And that was important because we also knew something about the historical events we were witnessing. There was truly a sense of pilgrimage, there was a reason we came to this place. We knew we would see history come to life. For decades the outdoor historical drama was an important part of summer travel. At a show one often heard people in the audience

talking about other outdoor dramas they had seen. Families often planned the route of their vacation travel so that two or three dramas might be enjoyed.

As an expert on outdoor drama, Mr. Sumner prophesied so much of the future of the theater (and the fears of theater producers) in a 1973 fiftieth anniversary program for the Carolina Dramatic Association:

> Unless the whole field of outdoor theatrical endeavor keeps its eyes on constantly improving production and acting standards, it is also quite possible that other and cheaper forms of entertainment through pay television, videocassette, and cable television will replace the outdoor drama in the minds of the audience. New electronic devices for presenting performances will bring more and more control to the hands of a few individuals at the top of corporate entertainment structures.
>
> Unless live theatrical forms can manage to hold huge segments of the American public in regional theaters showing regional original material, we may end up buying all our performing arts in electronic packages sold like sausages in plastic tubing . . . the opportunities for imaginative directors, paid positions for new performers, and the need for new writers and new managers are great, as are the opportunities for increasing service to the public . . . we have the opportunity to create a national drama as vital as the festival of the ancient Greeks, where the awe of nature is real and where live actors uphold the dignity of man.
>
> *The Carolina Handbook*, p. 41.

The Beginnings of the Regional Theater Movement

While the US Outdoor Drama movement was taking shape in small communities throughout America, legendary theater continued to surface and flourish in sometimes wonderful, sometimes bizarre, barely functional indoor spaces in New York and throughout the country. The Cleveland Play House (1915), Laguna Playhouse (1920), Arizona's Phoenix Theatre (1920), and Chicago's Goodman Theatre (1925) may have led the way, but the Oregon Shakespeare Festival (1935), San Diego's Old Globe Theatre (1937) and New York City's The Mercury Theatre (1937) weren't far behind.

"The 1930s were the great era for the proliferation of summer theaters of all kinds," explains Garff B. Wilson. "They spread from coast to coast, varying from earnest amateur groups performing in converted barns to professional companies presenting big-name players in well-equipped playhouses. As an instrument to assist and encourage the activities of the noncommercial theaters, the National Theatre Conference (NTC) was founded in 1930 . . . Not directly related to the noncommercial theater but of great importance to the American stage was the establishment in 1926 by the Dramatists' Guild of the now famous 'Minimum Basic Agreement,' which guaranteed to playwrights the permanent ownership of their plays and a fair share of the profits derived from them." Mr. Wilson provides additional history:

> In 1896 American performers had formed an association called the Actors Society to protect their welfare. It had proved ineffective. In 1913 a new organization called Actors' Equity Association had been founded; for six years it had tried futilely to obtain from managers and producers an agreement which would guarantee actors a fair wage, no more than eight performances a week and none on Sunday, a limitation on free rehearsal time, certain travel benefits, and other protections against unreasonable demands. Producers and managers had delayed, evaded, and refused. Finally, in 1919 Actors' Equity had called a strike. It had closed almost every playhouse on Broadway for four weeks and had ended in victory for Actors' Equity. Now in 1926, seven years after the actors' strike, the playwrights gained comparable protection under the Minimum Basic Agreement. Thus ended the long exploitation of the American dramatist, an ugly feature of the theatrical scene for almost two hundred years.
>
> Wilson, *Three Hundred Years of American Drama and Theatre*, pp. 375-376.

Theater support groups began to organize. Barnard Hewitt provides an overview of theater in America in the 1930s, 1940s, and 1950s:

> Some individuals and groups attempted to find remedies for the theater's ills. Everyone was alarmed by the scarcity of good new plays, and efforts were made to encourage the beginning playwright. The Bureau of New Plays, headed by Theresa Helburn, in the thirties, and the New Dramatists' Committee of the Dramatists' Guild, in the forties and fifties, provided advice, criticism, and a kind of introduction to the profession.
>
> In 1946 a group of producers, actors, playwrights, and critics, seeking a united front for an attack on the whole theater problem,

organized and set up offices as the American National Theatre and
Academy (ANTA) . . . it engaged in a great variety of activities, all
well-intended and most of them useful.

Hewitt, *Theater USA*, p. 486.

A brochure published by ANTA lists services ranging from job counseling and placement to information on international theater matters, to speakers for conferences and meetings, to a variety of publications to an annual national conference designed to bring together representatives of theaters to exchange ideas and information "related to the development of the American Theater."

Theaters were continuing to sprout up in unlikely spots. Mr. Hewitt notes, "Off-Broadway theater had always existed, but not since the Washington Square Players, the Provincetown Playhouse, and the Greenwich Village theaters in the teens and early twenties had it commanded such attention from the public and the critics. This phenomenon was virtually limited to New York. Dallas, Texas, Washington, D.C., and perhaps one or two other large cities could boast resident companies long enough established to be called permanent, but attempts to establish them in Philadelphia and Chicago, for instance, had failed." He concludes in a way that makes you wonder where he was hiding his crystal ball:

If professional theater Off-Broadway—and some of it deserved to be
called 'professional'—continued to flourish, not merely within metropolitan New York but in other cities across the length and breadth of
the land, the dream of ANTA and all other lovers of theater would
be realized—a genuine renaissance of living theater in America.

Hewitt, *Theater USA*, pp. 486-487.

In Hallie Flanagan's *Dynamo*, published in 1943, she discusses America's needs and the power of theater in a way that resonates eerily with the America of recent years:

America needs power, and because we are at war we think of
this power in terms of men, money, and machines. . . . We shall
need as never before the energy that can create life, and this is
the very pith and marrow of the theater. The creation of life is the
essence of all real theater; it is the raison d'être of the theater
in the college. Such a theater first finds and then releases youth's
burning energy, an energy not only intellectual but biological,

spiritual and emotional, not to be ignored by processes concerned
with the development of complete human beings.

Flanagan, Dynamo, pp. 3-4.

While many theater historians and critics were writing about the poten-
tial of America's theater future, others were working to fulfill it. Actors
Studio (1947), Dallas's Theatre '47 (founded by Margo Jones in 1947),
Houston's Alley Theatre (founded by Nina Vance in 1947), Washington,
D.C.'s Arena Stage (founded in 1950 by Edward Mangum, Zelda
Fichandler, and Thomas C. Fichandler), Circle in the Square (1951), Actors'
Workshop in San Francisco (1952), Stratford Shakespeare Festival in
Ontario, Canada (1953), New York Shakespeare Festival (1954), Milwaukee
Repertory Theater (1954), Williamstown Theatre Festival (1955), and the
American Shakespeare Festival in Stratford, Connecticut (1955) are just a
few of the theaters established to produce new work and the classics during
the early years.

Why were these theaters so important? As Louis Kronenberger
explained in the *Best Plays of 1954-55*, "Real achievement, genuine stature,
is indeed what Broadway fell short of most; what Broadway concerned itself
with was seldom at a very high level." Fortunately, there were regional theaters emerging to pick up the artistic slack. Regional theater pioneer Margo
Jones met Tennessee Williams in 1942, directed his plays at both the
Pasadena Playhouse and Cleveland Play House, garnered a Rockefeller fellowship in 1944, incorporated the Dallas Civic Theater in 1945 (with
Tennessee Williams and designer Jo Mielziner as board members), and
opened the theater under the name Theatre '47 in June 1947. She started
the company with eight to nine Equity actors at salaries of 75 dollars per
week and the theater sat 198 in the audience (*The Handbook of Texas Online*,
www.tsha.utexas.edu). Her words are prophetic: "We must create the
theater of tomorrow today. What our country needs . . . is a resident professional theater in every city with a population over one hundred thousand."
(Jones, *Theatre-in-the-Round*, 1951, pp. 3-5.) Dubbed "the Texas Tornado"
by Tennessee Williams, Margo Jones was a champion of many emerging
playwrights and shared her vision and fervor with both Nina Vance and a
very young Zelda Fichandler.

Nearby in Houston, Texas, the Alley Theatre's Nina Vance also started
her theater in 1947, with the $2.14 it cost to send 214 postcards to everyone
she thought might want to get her theater off the ground. Working in an
87-seat dance studio for the first two years, the Alley finally converted an
old fan factory in 1949.

A year later in Washington, D.C., Zelda Fichandler and co-founders rented an old movie house, raised $15,000, and started Arena Stage (originally as a commercial corporation and later reorganized as a nonprofit). In a January 2005 article for *American Theatre*, Zelda Fichandler reviewed her passion for the theater:

> I think the following is my "why" for sustaining a life in the theater for over a half a century. It's about the audience: my friends and neighbors; the visitors of different colors; the despairing who lead tight, circumscribed lives; the rich and comfortable who in the dark may experience guilt and the rich and comfortable whose hunger can never be assuaged; the wide-eyed children in their one good dress; the lonely one in a single seat; the Masons in their funny hats; the cognizant and the non-knowing; the old who can forget about dying for a few hours; the egoists; the damned; the teenagers who under their bravado and with rings in every part of their anatomy yearn to be useful. The Audience, the terminus of all our work. God bless them all.

Out west in the 1940s, San Francisco drama critic Luther Nichols noted:

> There were also strong indications that regional self-realization was being achieved in such semi-professional groups as the Workshop and Interplayers of San Francisco, and the Players' Ring, Stage Society, Hollywood Repertory Theater and Negro Ebony Showcase Theater in Southern California.
>
> Cory, The Dallas Theater Center, p. 3.

Other dates of great importance to the nonprofit theater movement would include the commitment of the Ford Foundation to provide millions of dollars of philanthropic support to the arts (1957). In 1959, the Ford Foundation even developed three-year grants to help resident theaters create permanent companies—Arena Stage received $127,000, the Alley Theatre received $156,000, and San Francisco's Actors' Workshop, with directors Herbert Blau and Jules Irving, received $156,000.

Back in Dallas, a Cleveland Play House veteran, Beatrice Handel, teamed up with Robert D. Stecker and Paul Baker to create the Dallas Theater Center in 1959. In Paul Baker's own words:

> "For me, at least, the theater is faith ... it is the faith that each one of us must find this individual creative force and make it grow and take

form. It is the faith that this individual creative force may be used to change and improve our lives and our perspective toward contemporary living. It is a faith developed out of experimentation and expenditure of every form of energy. It is the faith that must be expressed in action."

Cory, *The Dallas Theater Center*, p. 24.

Broadway Musicals Spur Regional Theater Development

The "golden age of musical comedy" on Broadway in the 1940s, 1950s, and 1960s (*Oklahoma!*, *Carousel*, *Annie Get Your Gun*, *Brigadoon*, and *Kiss Me Kate* in the 1940s through *Guys and Dolls*, *The King and I*, *Peter Pan*, *West Side Story*, *The Music Man*, *Gypsy*, and *My Fair Lady* in the 1950s through *Camelot*, *Oliver!*, *Hello Dolly!*, *Fiddler on the Roof*, *Man of La Mancha*, and *Cabaret* in the 1960s) seemed to coincide with a decline in the production of classic and new American plays on The Great White Way due to financial and marketability concerns. New York ticket prices were spiraling due to the high cost of producing on Broadway. At the same time, many cities around America were beginning to hunger for their own "arts teams."

Acclaimed author Helen Sheehy, who captured the wit, soul, and story of Margo Jones in her marvelous biography *Margo*, discusses Broadway's aversion to risk in regard to the production of new plays: "The fact is, Broadway as it existed in the 1940s and 1950s as a producing force . . . simply has not survived" (Sheehy, *Margo*, p. 270).

To the dismay of many American playwrights who were hoping for production on The Great White Way, more and more Broadway plays in the mid-to-late 20th century were finding their roots in British imports and the new-play development efforts of America's nonprofit theaters. To quote the late Peter Zeisler, longtime executive director of the Theatre Communications Group:

> A very interesting thing happened in the fifties and the beginning of the sixties, sociological, really. After the war, cities throughout the country were really tired of relying on the Northeast to provide them with culture, and they wanted their own. At the same time, remember that in 1950 there was no professional baseball team west of St. Louis. There was no football team west of, I don't know where. Suddenly, to be big league, all these cities had to have their own, and among the things they had to have was a professional theater. That was the mark of a big-league town. *Look* magazine had

a series of most little cities in America, which were the big-league
cities, and to be a big-league city you had to have a baseball team,
you had to have a professional theater. They all had symphonies, so
that didn't count. That really started the not-for-profit theater. Then, a
few years later when the NEA started, the government started to
recognize theaters, not really support them, but recognize them—
that really changed the landscape.

TCG Oral History Project, 2001.

Partly fueled by Broadway production concerns, the nonprofit theater
movement was experiencing unparalleled growth by the late 1950s and
1960s. Many of the theaters that would provide opportunities for new
playwrights, employment for actors, training programs for eager students,
and astute leadership to help shape the resident theater movement were
emerging. Florida's Asolo Theatre Company (1960), Ohio's Cincinnati
Playhouse in the Park (1960), Minnesota's The Children's Theatre
Company, and the Utah Shakespearean Festival (1961) were a few of the
early companies.

As the number of regional theater operations continued to grow, there
was a pressing need to communicate, collaborate, and share information
among the many theater leaders, especially those which set up shop far from
the bright lights of Broadway. There was also a need for coordination that
was articulated by corporations and foundations who were looking for ways
to evaluate funding requests to support these emerging arts organizations.
Fortunately, the Theatre Communications Group (TCG) was founded in
1961 and provided a national forum and communications network for the
rapidly expanding nonprofit professional theater field. W. McNeil Lowry,
vice president of the Ford Foundation, declared the arts one of the foundation's five major priorities and encouraged the creation of an organization
that would be championed by leaders in the theater profession. He offered
a three-year grant to create TCG and the Ford Foundation was the sole supporter of the service group for a decade.

The Guthrie Takes Shape

In the meantime, Minnesota's Guthrie Theater began to take shape and was
founded in 1963. The idea for the Guthrie Theater began when Sir Tyrone
Guthrie, Oliver Rea, and Peter Zeisler decided that there were indeed options
for staging theater with integrity far from the lights, costs, and commercialism
and critics of Broadway. To quote the theater's 25th anniversary program:

They wanted to create a theater with a resident acting company that would perform the classics in rotating repertory. Sir Tyrone Guthrie believed that a company of actors performing the classics in rotating repertory would form and nurture an artistic family; a family whose most important contribution would be the feeling of intimate companionship between audience and stage. In the end, it was this unique actor-audience relationship that has sustained the Guthrie as a prototype for an important new kind of theater.

In order to make this dream come true, Guthrie and his colleagues knew their theater had to be located far from the boom-or-bust psychology of Broadway. The Broadway atmosphere was conducive neither to producing the great worlds of literature, nor to cultivating the artists' talents, nor to nourishing an audience. The relationship the Guthrie wanted between audience and stage, artist and community, was in complete contrast to the commercial environment on Broadway.

This idea was introduced to the American public in a small paragraph on the drama page of the *New York Times* in 1959. "Was any city outside of New York interested in providing a home to a new theater?" asked Brooks Atkinson, theater critic.

Livingston, *The Guthrie Theater*, p. 1-2.

Again, Peter Zeisler added another perspective to the shifting sands of the development of theater in America:

The classic repertoire was really a great unknown to American actors. When we started the American Shakespeare Festival in Stratford, Connecticut, in '55, I interviewed over a thousand actors in New York for that first season. My first question was, "What was the last Shakespeare play you've done professionally?" None of them had ever done Shakespeare professionally. A few had worked at the Old Globe in San Diego, but otherwise they hadn't done any Shakespeare since college. You can't scratch an actor now who hasn't done Shakespeare any number of times. There's a total change.

Once the Guthrie and a few other theaters started to examine the classic repertoire, actor training changed radically in this country. Before that, actor training consisted of learning how to sit on a sofa and hold a martini glass. There was no voice work, no movement work. It was all realistic modern drama. Suddenly, enormous physical demands were being made on actors. Suddenly it became necessary to have voice work and movement work in the training programs that there'd never been before. The not-for-profit theater really started at Arena Stage in Washington, D.C., and the Alley Theatre in Houston. But the Guthrie was the first large company. We played in rotating rep, which nobody else did; we had forty-seven Equity actors, unheard of in this country; and we were doing work at a very high technical level. We had designs by Tanya Moiseiwitsch, one of the premier designers in the world. That, I think, demonstrated that you didn't have to be on 44th Street.

TCG Oral History Project, 2001.

An Explosion in Regional Theater

The continued growth of nonprofit theaters in America was nothing short of startling. The same year that the Guthrie was founded (1963), Seattle Rep was organizing on the West Coast; Center Stage was emerging in Baltimore, Maryland; Trinity Repertory Company surfaced in Providence, Rhode Island; and the Goodspeed Opera House created a home in East Haddam, Connecticut. In 1964, the Actors Theatre of Louisville began operations in Kentucky, Hartford Stage Company began in Connecticut, the Missouri Repertory Theatre took up residence in Kansas City, and both the PCPA Theaterfest and South Coast Repertory spearheaded operations in California.

Between 1964 and 1974 at least 90 new nonprofit companies surfaced nationwide and between 1975 and 1985 over 90 more companies jumped on the bandwagon. To quote Garff B. Wilson:

The American dream of many centers of dramatic inspiration and activity came close to being realized during the 1960s. The decade was outstanding for the spectacular development of regional profes- sional theaters and of university theaters. . . . The development of regional professional companies has been generously supported by the private philanthropic foundations of the nation. Even more signifi- cant, perhaps, was the establishment of the National Foundation on the Arts and Humanities in the mid-1960s. After almost two hundred years, the federal government recognized its obligation to aid and encourage cultural activities. . . . In 1965 the commitment was finally made and the foundation was established. It includes two groups, the National Endowment for the Arts (NEA) and the National Endowment for the Humanities (NEH).

Wilson, *Three Hundred Years of American Drama and Theatre*, p. 476.

Activism, Social Change, and Cultural Diversity

Not surprisingly, many theaters promoting activist causes and celebrating the cultural diversity of a changing America surfaced in the 1960s. In California, Tim Dang's East West Players (1965) emphasized the Asian-Pacific American experience and Luis Valdez's El Teatro Campesino (1965) explored the "curative, affirmative power of live performance," imagining a "worldwide cultural fusion of our times." Philadelphia's Freedom Repertory Theatre (1966) produced plays from the rich African American canon, New York's INTAR Hispanic American Arts Center (1966) aimed to "see Hispanic voices take their place in the forefront" of America's arts expression, and San Francisco's Magic Theatre embraced a "phenomenal diversity of cultures and means of artistic expression."

Two other dates of importance during this time period include the first League of Resident Theatres (LORT) and Actors' Equity Association contract (1966), and the creation of the now-defunct Foundation for the Extension and Development of the American Professional Theatre (FEDAPT) in 1967. FEDAPT assisted more than 700 performing arts companies over two decades and published comprehensive "Monographs" and "WorkPapers" detailing the creative fund-raising efforts, planning strategies, managerial relationships, season selection, board structuring, and overall "problems and difficulties" of the not-for-profit theater during a key growth period of the regional theater movement. Frederic B. Vogel and Nello McDaniel served successively as executive directors of FEDAPT. According to Actors' Equity Association and ANTA lists, 40 resident Equity theaters from 22 states were operating in 1966-67.

Other theaters of historic significance to the regional theater movement opened their doors in the 1960s, including Seattle's A Contemporary Theatre (1965), San Francisco's American Conservatory Theater (1965), New Haven's Long Wharf Theatre (1965), New York's Roundabout Theatre Company (1965), The Repertory Theatre of St. Louis (1966), Yale Repertory Theatre (1966), Arizona Theatre Company (1967), Los Angeles's Mark Taper Forum (1967), Georgia's Alliance Theatre Company (1968), California's Berkeley Repertory Theatre (1968), Wisconsin's Madison Repertory Theatre (1969), and Washington, D.C.'s The Shakespeare Theatre, founded in 1969 as the Folger Theatre.

"While the establishment of the theater in the Lincoln Center has interested many people, the work of the Tyrone Guthrie Theater in Minneapolis and the increased number of workshop theaters and summer stock companies in various American cities are equally impressive," wrote author Walter J. Meserve in 1965. "College and university theaters now attract professional actors and actresses, who work with students in creating productions of taste and excellence. If there is a contemporary theater movement at all, it is obviously designed to spread theater throughout America."

Children's Theater Takes One Giant Step Forward

Children's theater, long a staple in community theaters, schools, and parks and recreation programs, took a major leap forward when The Children's Theatre Company was founded in 1961 in Minneapolis, Minnesota. Other significant companies followed, including St. Louis's Metro Theater Company (1973), Seattle Children's Theatre (1975), Tempe, Arizona's Childsplay (1977), Dallas Children's Theater (1984), and Bethesda, Maryland's Imagination Stage (1992). Seattle Children's Theatre managing director Kevin Maifeld explains the children's theater phenomenon:

> Our belief is to produce "ageless" theater so that a grandparent, parent, and child can attend and have an equally rewarding experience. When this happens, we open the magical world of theater to a child and reinforce the importance of it to the parent and grandparent. We also believe in producing theater at the highest professional level so that children seek quality in the future.

ASSITEJ/USA is the United States Center for the International Association of Theatre for Children and Young People. Founded in 1965, the organization's primary objective is to help in the development of professional theater for young audiences and international exchange by sponsoring national and international festivals and forums, facilitating artist exchange, and providing publications to the theater community.

Today, youth theater is a major component of many nonprofit theaters. Many artistic directors who originally scoffed at the idea of "kiddie theater" and "community outreach programs" seemed suddenly to shift their thinking when funding dried up for the arts but remained for "educational programs." While there are indeed artistic leaders with an inherent appreciation for youth theater, the realities of funding and audience building inspired many others to address the broader cultural and educational needs of their home communities. Today, educational programs and children's theater are well developed in many regional theaters and a key part of the mission statement for many professional theaters. Peter Brosius, artistic director of the Tony Award–winning The Children's Theatre Company in Minneapolis, explains:

The field of theater for young people is one of the most dynamic areas of the professional theater. New theaters are being born every day. New multi-million dollar professional facilities to house professional theater for young people are being created across the country.

Will Regional Theater Last?

Many theaters faced financial and organizational challenges and the word was still out on the future of the American regional theater movement when Jack Poggi wrote *Theater in America, The Impact of Economic Forces, 1870–1967*:

> It's too early to tell whether the resident theaters will last. The fact that very few have closed since the movement began is encouraging. The fact that problems are accumulating faster than solutions can be found for them is discouraging. It is quite possible that the boom in resident theaters is a fad of a newly culture-conscious middle class . . . With all its weaknesses, the resident theater movement has accomplished more for the theater outside of New York in the last ten years than was accomplished in the preceding fifty.
>
> Poggi, *Theater in America*, pp. 240-241.

Although Mr. Poggi felt that the days of the "rugged individualist who sets out to build a theater on his own appear to be over," professional theaters continued to sprout up in unlikely spots throughout the 1970s, including Indianapolis's Indiana Repertory Theatre (1972), Montgomery's Alabama Shakespeare Festival (1972), Rochester, New York's GeVa Theatre (1972), Gainesville, Florida's The Hippodrome State Theatre (1973), Knoxville, Tennessee's Clarence Brown Theatre Company (1974), Minneapolis, Minnesota's Illusion Theater (1974), Pennsylvania's Pittsburgh Public Theater (1974), Kentucky's Roadside Theater (1974), and Little Rock's Arkansas Repertory Theatre (1976). Well-known "actor driven" non-profit theaters also materialized during this period, including New York's The Wooster Group (1975), Chicago's Steppenwolf Theatre Company (1976), and Massachusetts's Shakespeare & Company (1978).

In 1976, Benjamin Mordecai, then producing director of the Indiana Repertory Theatre, offered these remarks at a Foundation for the Extension and Development of the American Professional Theatre (FEDAPT) gathering:

> They [Cincinnati Playhouse artistic director Word Baker and Actors Theatre of Louisville artistic director Jon Jory] stated that anyone in

this day and age who has intentions of opening a large-scale professional resident theater has got to be out of his mind. The odds
against its succeeding are extraordinary.

Mordecai, *Indiana Repertory Theatre*, p.5.

In hopes of assisting other theater entrepreneurs, Mr. Mordecai provided
a brief list that captured Indiana Rep's formula for success. The list includes:

- An exceptional group of bright, talented people that were dedi-
  cated to accomplishment;
- A locale that was ready with an audience;
- Outstanding foundation and government support;
- A combination of an historic landmark and an inner-city location,
  which enhanced the appeal of the Theater;
- A good artistic product.

Mordecai, *Indiana Repertory Theatre*, pp. 20-21.

Perhaps noted historian Vera Mowry Roberts says it best: "In my early
days of traveling around the country as president of the American
Theatre Association, students asked how they could make it in NYC. By
the early 1980s, they were saying, 'I'm going to make theater where I am.'
Phenomenal.'"

Jumping on the Bandwagon

Despite the warnings of extraordinary odds against success, many larger
American cities jumped on the bandwagon in the 1980s in hopes of round-
ing out the cultural opportunities and quality of life for their surrounding
communities. Colorado's Denver Center Theatre Company, Oregon's
Portland Repertory Theater, California's San Jose Repertory Theatre, and
Washington, D.C.'s Woolly Mammoth Theatre Company all surfaced in
1980, while Boston's Huntington Theatre Company, California's Shakespeare
Santa Cruz, New York's Ubu Repertory Theater, and Los Angeles's West
Coast Ensemble all followed two years later, in 1982.

Local Heritage, Community Outreach, and HIV

By this time, many theaters were rejecting the idea that they needed to
recycle old Broadway hits or even attempt to mirror the commercial practices
of popular New York theaters and touring shows. Instead, many theaters

looked to their own communities and worked to tell the indigenous stories of their unique regions. Theater at Lime Kiln (1984) tackled the heritage, culture, and history of its Virginia home with a small resident company. Ohio's Cleveland Public Theater (1983) was created to serve serious emerging theater artists while confronting and examining "the political and social milieu which shapes our lives."

Societal issues certainly influenced the work and missions of promising nonprofit theaters. New York's Irondale Ensemble Project (1983) established extensive outreach programs in the New York City jails while the Irondale AIDS Improv Team worked with NYC students on matters of safe sex and the facts of HIV infection. On the West Coast, Seattle's Alice B. Theatre (1984) emphasized providing a "true clear voice" as a lesbian and gay theater for all people.

There's More than One "Quiet Crisis" in the Arts

FEDAPT's 1989-1990 Annual Report, titled *WorkPapers, The Quiet Crisis in the Arts*, by Nello McDaniel and George Thorn, discussed very loud and forceful attacks on the National Endowment for the Arts and "the quiet crisis" centering on the mounting debt, organizational dysfunction, shrinking human resource pool, high turnover, and low morale of many in the ranks of struggling regional theaters. Over a dozen theaters had closed the year prior to the report, which called for the development of "new paradigms to lead and effect change for these new realities."

New York's Nonprofits Offer Broadway Alternatives

Certainly, many New York theaters were founded over the years to fill the void of actual plays on Broadway. Broadway's 1980s focused on blockbuster musicals (think *42nd Street, Barnum, Joseph and the Amazing Technicolor Dreamcoat, Nine, Cats, La Cage aux Folles, Les Misérables, Starlight Express, Into the Woods*, and *The Phantom of the Opera* and you get the general idea). New York's Primary Stages (1985) emerged to develop and produce new plays by American playwrights and the Atlantic Theater Company (founded by David Mamet and W. H. Macy in 1985) worked to produce "affordable plays that speak to a new generation of theatergoers."

While myriad, smaller Off-Broadway and Off-Off Broadway theaters were surfacing in New York City, mega-institutions also offered Broadway alternatives. The Lincoln Center Theater (1985) gave a glorious home to new playwrights and audiences in search of American plays and the Public

Theater/New York Shakespeare Festival (founded by Joseph Papp three decades earlier) continued to "put the voices and the experiences of all Americans" on stage.

Finding a Home in Regional Theater

In 1985, the Theatre Communications Group leaders organized discussions with artistic directors of America's institutional theaters and discovered, according to author Todd London in *The Artistic Home*, that "the single most pressing concern . . . is to find ways of keeping the most talented artists in the theater . . . as work in television and film continues to offer extraordinary compensation and celebrity." Other areas for discussion included the creative and collaborative needs of artistic directors; desires for more institutional flexibility with subscriptions, scheduling, and rehearsal time; and the development of future audiences. Lloyd Richards, longtime dean of the Yale University School of Drama and artistic director of Yale Repertory Theatre, explained the groundbreaking discussions:

> In 1985, a group of theater trustees asked their own artistic directors a wonderfully explosive question: Beyond money and survival, what do you want—what is your vision, and what will it take to get you there?. . . This collection of statements does reveal that the tremendous surge of artistic energy and daring which forged, established and validated the nonprofit theater movement in this country more than twenty-five years ago still exists.
>
> London, *The Artistic Home*, p. ix.

As many of the larger "institutional theaters" were contemplating their future plans, more adventurous, homegrown companies took root throughout America. Santa Monica, California's Cornerstone Theater Company (1986) commissioned multilingual plays and produced "epic interactions between classic plays and a dozen rural towns." Dayton, Ohio's The Human Race Theatre Company (1986) featured contemporary scripts introducing "opposing ideas and concepts" within society, while Atlanta's Actor's Express (1988) produced plays "like a stick of dynamite that holds within it the possibility of exploding our preconceptions of ourselves and the world around us."

Arlington, Virginia's Signature Theatre (1990) balanced emotionally charged contemporary musicals and plays with school programs, The AIDS Project, a musical theater series, an Emerging Playwrights Series, and a

Cultural Exchange Night. In the Garage Theatre in Chelsea, Michigan, The Purple Rose Theatre Company (1991) declared its belief that "there are creative and revelatory voices in America's heartland worth exploring and listening to" and, back in Minneapolis, the Jungle Theater (1991) was formed as a playwrights' theater.

Although a number of regional theaters ceased operations in the 1990s due to fund-raising woes, the impact of various regional recessions, or leadership issues, over 100 new nonprofit professional theaters were established between 1992 and 2006, including New York's Tectonic Theatre Project (1992), Hailey, Idaho's Company of Fools (1992), Massachusetts's Barrington Stage Company (1994), Los Angeles's Geffen Playhouse (1994), New Mexico's Santa Fe Stages (1994), Austin, Texas's Rude Mechanicals (1995), Philadelphia's 1812 Productions (1997), Idaho's Boise Contemporary Theater (1997), Nevada Theatre Company (1997), Vermont's Northern Stage (1997), Boston Theatre Works (1998), Fort Myers's Florida Repertory Theatre (1998), Chicago's Congo Square Theatre (2000), Milwaukee Shakespeare (2000), Iowa's New Ground Theatre (2001), Atlanta's Out of Hand Theater (2001), and Hartford, Connecticut's HartBeat Ensemble (2002).

Into the New Millennium

Kent Thompson, recent Theatre Communications Group president and artistic director of the Denver Center Theatre Company, shares notes on how the development of regional theater has created a pathway for future theater artists to develop careers in the business and in related businesses:

> The regional theater movement has impacted theater in America in three significant ways:
>
> 1 Replacing Broadway and commercial theater as the birthing place of new plays and musicals. It's hard to think up a major new musical or play that did not start its life in a regional theater today. We are the research and development wing of theater in America.
>
> 2 Creating a national network of professional theater artists, managers, and craftspeople. Quite simply, the regional theater movement has created the means for people to earn livelihoods in professional theater across the United States. To live in and participate in the fuller life of the community; to buy a home or an apartment. To have a life in the theater as a full-time profession.

3   The regional theater movement remains the single most
    effective training ground for artists throughout the performing
    arts/entertainment worlds. Actors, playwrights, writers, techni-
    cians have all developed their careers in regional theater. The
    skills they've learned and the experience they have earned
    have made them valuable and viable candidates for work in
    commercial theater, television, film, theme parks and cruise
    ships, production companies, commercials, etc. This is a double-
    edged sword as it has led to a "brain drain" from the regional
    theater field.

Regional Theater Today

So where are we today? In 2007, nonprofit theaters in America continue to
emerge, struggle, flourish, and, hopefully, dig deep roots in their home communities. According to arts council and city arts service agencies, over 1,000
nonprofit theaters exist in just four American cities alone: New York (400),
San Francisco (300+), Los Angeles (210+), and Chicago (140+).

One not-so-scientific but very twenty-first-century way of assessing the
growth of American theater is to research the number of entries that appear
on the World Wide Web. If you follow America's favorite pastime and
Google "nonprofit theater in America," a mind-boggling 13,600,000 entries
appear (which seems miniscule compared to the overwhelming 79,200,000
entries for "Theatre in America"). The Internet provides fascinating background research on regional theater, but the best overview of the movement
still emanates from the hearts and mouths of its artists.

"Theater in America is a collective of bold, visionary artists and those
dedicated to creating and supporting the creation of art," maintains
Shakespeare Festival/LA's producing artistic director, Ben Donenberg.
"The regional theater movement is a collective of one set of artists and supporters that contribute an important and meaningful component of the
quiltwork."

Stage Directions magazine editor-in-chief Iris Dorbian adds that regional
theater "provides a wonderful, noncommercial option to the rampant, for-
mulaic commercialism of Broadway."

Professional theater, film, and television director and California Institute
of the Arts faculty member Craig Belknap puts it another way:
"Unfortunately, for the most part, Broadway has become Las Vegas East.
The regional theater movement is where it's at. *Angels in America* and *The
Kentucky Cycle* would never have gotten to New York without the regions."

Stephen Rothman, chair of Theater Arts at California State University, Los Angeles, explains how regional theater has opened up a whole new world of possibilities:

> For my generation of artists who graduated from universities in the early 1970s, regional theater has a tremendous impact as not only our segue from academia into having a first job but once there it became clear that there was now a place to spend your artistic life beyond Broadway and Hollywood. In other words, regional theater opened up a whole new career path that did not exist before. It once was if you wanted a life in the Theater, that meant New York or L.A.—now you could have that life and live in your own home area, be that Sarasota, Florida, Cleveland, Ohio, or Seattle, Washington.

"Regional theater is the lifeblood of theater in America," note Jan and Griff Duncan, producers of one of America's largest musical theater operations, the Fullerton Civic Light Opera. "It is the regional theater that invests in the outreach programs so important in cultivating present and future audiences. National touring companies reap the benefits of this and if regional theaters should disappear, audiences would disappear in a few years as there would be no development in place. Regional theater also involves the local public in the process and gives them a sense of satisfaction regarding the arts and the place they live."

"The regional theater movement has impacted all aspects of theater in America, from playwriting and dramaturgy, to acting and directing and design," adds longtime casting director and associate dean of the Chicago College of Performing Arts, Joel Fink. "As the price of doing theater in New York has skyrocketed, regional theaters have become the incubators for new theater work and new theater workers."

Susan Medak, managing director of Berkeley Repertory Theatre, explains that "the regional theater movement spawned a generation of people outside of New York City who attend theater with regularity, who see it as central to their lives, many of whom have chosen to make their own careers in the theater. And I think that while generations of theater-goers in cities outside New York were raised on Theatre Guild tours which brought great artists and great plays to large theaters in major cities, the regional theater movement spawned a sense of community pride in artists from their own communities and supported a repertoire that continues to be regionally specific. The entire sense of what 'theater' is has gone from the limited nature of national tours to a sense that local theater communities include everything from commercial tours to institutional companies to small storefront theaters."

Asolo Theatre producing artistic director Howard J. Millman agrees. "The regional theater movement has completely transformed theater in America," says Millman. "It has taken the highest quality of artistic work from Broadway to most of the country. The great work of the American theater now begins outside of New York. Regional theater has created more work for all theater artists around the country. The American public has become more sophisticated in its theatrical tastes and knowledge because of the regional theater movement. We have moved from a commercial venture to the center of the cultural fabric of many American communities. Theater is no longer 'Show Business.'"

So, what does this history and the regional theater movement have to do with today's actors, directors, craftspeople, and audiences? To quote *Shakespeare's Friends* author Kate Pogue, "It placed theater artistically on a par with symphony orchestras, art museums, ballet, and opera—a huge development in the attitude of the American public. It has offered stable career opportunities across the country to thousands of actors, directors, designers, technicians, managers, and front-of-house personnel. It has revived classic plays and created new plays, challenging the creativity of producers, writers, designers—and audiences."

For younger theater practitioners it may be hard to understand the challenges and responsibility that are inherent in pursuing a career in regional theater. John Quinlivan, managing director of the Geva Theatre Center, articulates the big picture: "A sense of community is formed around each regional theater. Each theater is, in a sense, 'owned' by that community. It is an awesome responsibility that we must all take very seriously."

Sandy Robbins, freelance director for many professional theaters and director of the University of Delaware's Professional Theatre Training Program, puts it another way:

> The regional theater movement has, for the majority of Americans, provided the only serious professional theater available to them in or near where they live. I am one of many theater professionals whose early theater experiences were provided entirely by regional theaters.
>
> My view is that, while the range of quality in regional theaters varies enormously, it is nonetheless true that theaters like the Guthrie, Trinity Repertory, ACT, Ashland, and others maintained a high standard for a long enough duration of time to set an example of acting and directing that still influences those who saw or worked

with them. This influence is then handed on to others who see the work of those under the influence of those early models.

Finally, the impact of these theaters has been and continues to be substantial on the development and production of new work that eventually gets to Broadway and Off-Broadway, and from there to the rest of humanity.

Bonding with home communities has emerged as a central theme for regional theaters eager to develop artistically and survive in a highly competitive American arts, entertainment, and tourism market. Edward Stern, Cincinnati Playhouse in the Park producing artistic director, believes that "the key element for me in regional theater is how it empowers the individual communities to create professional high-quality theater. Touring companies cannot focus as regional theaters can on extensive education outreach programming. Theater must do a better job of developing future audiences. Regional theater can and should have that capability and focus. Moreover, regional theaters can do so many of the plays that never would tour into those individual communities."

Repertory Theater of St. Louis artistic director Steven Woolf concurs:

> Theater in America has been forever changed because of the regional theater movement. Once audiences and communities began to understand and embrace their stake in professional theater in their own towns, it became clear that Broadway was no longer really going to define artistic output in this country. Now, truly, Broadway is a great marketing machine and nothing carries a kind of shimmer like something called "a Broadway show." But it has been clear over the past twenty years or so that almost every play to find its way to Broadway has started in the regional theaters in this country. Now, musicals are working much the same way. So the development line has changed and the not-for-profit regional theaters are producing the work the commercial field wants. This is a major shift in the landscape in a very short amount of time. Ultimately the discerning views and artistic sensibilities of audiences outside of New York are really determining what the New York audiences are seeing. This is something that no one ever envisioned at the beginning of this movement.

Fred C. Adams, founder and executive producer emeritus of the Utah Shakespearean Festival, adds that "a new vitality has found its way into the 'formula'-driven Broadway scene. A vitality born of upstart regional theaters that were not afraid to try something new, or in some instances something really old. Look at *Angels in America* with its birth at the Eureka Theatre of San Francisco, or *Big River* from La Jolla. The August Wilson canon saw the light of day at Yale, and the Humana Festival has spawned many major pieces like *Crimes of the Heart*. American theater, today, *is* its regional theaters, promoting new and exciting works or keeping the meaningful classics alive for our young promising actors to 'cut their teeth' on."

Today, over 400 nonprofit theaters are signed up as Theatre Communications Group members and more than 1,200 nonprofit theaters in America representing professional, community, youth, college, and university theaters. Many of the larger nonprofit theaters are featured in other areas of this book and each has contributed in significant ways to the development of theater in America.

It's outside the scope of this book to try to catalogue all of America's regional theaters or the many leaders, pivotal players, and supporters of the nonprofit arts movement in America. Still, marvelous historical quotes and words of wisdom from many of the nation's theater leaders (past and present) are included throughout and in the overviews of many of America's largest theater companies. This summary is intended simply to indicate the youth, ambitions, and needs of a resident theater movement that has long been ill defined and poorly compared to its mainstream, commercial counterpart, Broadway. In other areas of this book, you will find listings of nonprofit theater associations guilds, contracts, and profiles of the Theatre Communications Group (TCG), League of Resident Theatres (LORT), Shakespeare Theatre Association of America (STAA), Institute of Outdoor Drama (IOD), and many other key institutions that support America's theaters.

What Does the Future Hold?

"Regional theaters must continue to find ways to re-invent themselves so they can better serve the communities and audiences where they reside," contends Utah Shakespearean Festival managing director R. Scott Phillips. "A strong voice for new thoughts and ideas must prevail in America," notes Mr. Phillips. "I am convinced that regional theater companies must be the leaders in contributing to that strong new voice."

Regional theaters will have to be savvy, creative, flexible, entrepreneurial, and ferociously committed to a palpable artistic vision and strategic financial planning if the forward movement is to continue. The "original, older" regional theaters are morphing, adapting, and reinventing themselves to survive the ever-changing funding, audience, and entertainment trends of the 21st century and many start-up theater companies are plunging in with a whole new set of dreams, ideals, hopes, and production plans. Perhaps it's too obvious to note that regional theaters are changing because America is changing—America's people, American cities, America's sense of security, and America's desires and needs are shifting as the world's technology, governance, population, politics, and economic realities shape the nation.

Recent American census population statistics suggest that the "urban renaissance" that helped breathe new life into many cities at the end of the 20th century seems to have stalled somewhat in the 21st century. As real estate prices have skyrocketed in many major cities, many city planners are seeing a resurgence of interest in smaller communities. Looking to the future, it remains to be seen where the cultural growth and future homes of nonprofit theaters will develop. For example, virtually every Southern California community, regardless of size, has its own nonprofit theatre and many of the over 200 nonprofit Shakespeare festivals are located in the tiniest of towns, far from the bright lights of New York, Chicago, Los Angeles, or Seattle.

So, what does this mean for America's theaters? It means that the tremendous growth in many of America's smaller cities and suburbs may create opportunities for professional theaters eager to serve these new communities. It means that in a few of the larger cities where sky-high housing and theater rental costs once were formidable, creative spaces may now open up for emerging theater companies. No doubt, it also means that the larger cities that continue to grow (oftentimes as settling points for waves of immigrants as in Los Angeles, Phoenix, Fort Worth, Houston, etc.) will spawn new theaters that address the desires and needs of a culturally diverse community.

Scott L. Steele, executive director of the University/Resident Theatre Association (U/RTA), offers another prediction:

> The next "movement," or framework in which American theater will grow will be found on campuses across the nation. Operating relationships between schools, and particularly graduate training programs, and professional theaters of diverse sizes and kinds, will be the source of growth for current theater companies, and the seedbed of future companies. This is not new. There are existing examples of such marriages. Nevertheless, it is a process that is gaining interest among theater professionals, professional artists (who are also professional

teachers), and academicians and administrators. Such relationships come in different formats and are not always easy to maintain, but the potential for mutually beneficial results is a powerful reason for making the commitment. One result, when such relationships enrich theater production on campus, is that it might, just might, manage to harvest a part of the elusive "new audience" that theater is always seeking. And U/RTA, as the primary interface between professional theater and the world of professional, graduate training, is already serving as a resource for this movement. Like a good matchmaker, U/RTA is encouraging the dialogue that can lead to programming and operating relationships. Future professionals should look at theater-school relationships as invaluable resources. Such partnerships are going to be the focus of a lot of major activity, and will drive new and different theater production in many places.

Looking to the future, Utah Shakespearean Festival Associate artistic director and casting director Kathleen F. Conlin expects that regional theater will continue to "decentralize theater excellence, provide employment for numerous theater artists, and inspire students throughout the country by offering internships and career entry while providing artistic presence for non-commercial plays—which will move on to commercial success."

Cindy Melby Phaneuf, producing artistic director of the Nebraska Shakespeare Festival, predicts the growth trends will continue: "There are only positives to working in regional theater. There are more choices for directors and actors and designers. Playwrights and new plays can be nurtured with tender, loving care. Regional theater provides the freedom to risk, to test the limits."

The Goodman Theatre's longtime executive director, Roche Schulfer, offers a much briefer history and his own set of predictions:

> What does the future hold? Overall, I think we are entering a new phase in the evolution of the resident theater movement. Phase One was the founding mothers and fathers who came from the East and spread theater across the country like Johnny Appleseed. Phase Two was the heyday of the not-for-profit/commercial producer collaboration, which by the mid-nineties, turned Broadway into a showcase for the best in theater from around the country.
>
> The next phase will be about creating deeper roots in our respective communities. We are past the point of legendary founders and the obsession with Broadway megahits. We now have many theaters

that are led by people who come from the community they serve (or somewhere other than New York City). In this new phase, artists, trustees, and staff have to work together to identify and promote the value and importance of theater (and all the arts) in this precarious world. It has less to do with "who is in charge" of a theater and more to do with how we work together with mutual respect and trust to create quality art in our communities. This phase will be embodied by theatrical institutions with the highest standards of excellence and the deepest roots in their communities.

Whatever the future holds, it is clear that, collectively, the passion, power, and productivity of America's regional theater has, by virtue of its mere existence, mainstream popularity, and creative roots, emerged as the national theater of the United States of America. There's still a lot of excitement on Broadway, but as the first decade of the 21st century indicates, a lot of the Broadway thrills are emanating from the coast-to-coast artistic initiatives of America's regional theaters.

PART III

CAREER PLANNING

CAREER-PLANNING NEEDS

This book offers a "self-education, self-help" guide and your "instructors" include some of the most knowledgeable professionals in the business. Still, if you are currently a student, there's nothing like working with someone who knows you, knows your work, and can offer specific, personalized counsel to supplement your research. A list of the types of assistance you might expect from your faculty or the career-planning professionals on your campus is included below. Talk to your faculty, search your school's Web site and phone directory for professional assistance, and ask each person and office you talk to if they have any samples, publications, or advice.

Check your institution for a career planning office, placement office, internship office, mentoring program, job fair, study-abroad program, or counseling center that may offer tests, tools, and publications to help you.

Even if you're not a student, check out the libraries of neighboring colleges or universities for career information and services. Specifically, as an emerging professional, it is crucial to seek out assistance related to:

Arts Résumés, Photographs, and Cover Letters

Generic résumé skills won't work here—it must be a specialized workshop or individualized seminar focusing on résumés for actors, musicians, dancers, directors, designers, etc.

Interview and Audition Skills

Again, if these skills aren't being covered in your classes, seek out specially tailored workshops, training sessions, or seminars specific to your area of interest—theater auditions, dance auditions, design portfolio presentations, and actor auditions.

Time Management for Artists

Review the time- and life-management section of this book and develop a lifelong process that works for you.

Career Counseling Resources Overview

Protect your budget by checking at your school library or the library in your institution's career center for theater magazine subscriptions and job search publications. Every serious university library and career center should have copies of *American Theatre*, *ARTSEARCH*, *TCG Profiles*, *TCG Theatre Directory*, access to the online TCG profiles, and at least most of the books in the "10 Challenging Books to Power Your Acting Career" mentioned on page 130.

Entrepreneurial Assertive Personal Marketing

Every school and every library should have computers available for students and community members to research or conduct an Internet job search. Check out the "10 Web Sites to Open Up Your Web World" detailed on page 128. Career counselors should be available to advise students on the targeted use of direct mail, agent mailings, and developing telephone/tele-marketing skills, recommendations for employment and graduate school, and a network of mentors.

Financial Survival Tips: Budgeting a Career in the Arts

Workshops or seminars that address the basic financial realities of a life in the arts (such as applying/budgeting for graduate schools, planning a move to New York or Los Angeles, standard arts tax deductions, etc.) should be developed in every serious theater program.

Securing an Agent and Union Basics

The basic strategies are generally outlined in most theater career books and publications. "10 Pertinent Publications" (page 125) is a great place to start. These should all be available for perusal in your school's library, career center, or departmental office.

Conquering Performance Anxiety

There are special counseling and therapeutic ways to counter, adapt, or overcome performance anxiety (auditions, public speaking, design presentations, director conferences, etc.), and your school's faculty or counseling staff may be of assistance if you suffer from this common concern.

Stress Management

The theater is a highly collaborative, often competitive field where unemployment runs rampant for actors, directors and designers. Check out the stress section on page 352 ("12 Tips for Stress Reduction: Staying Fit for Life"), but seek help if your stress is impacting your health (and your choice of careers).

NETWORKING SURVIVAL SKILLS FOR THEATER PROS YOUNG AND OLD

"He that won't be counseled can't be helped," explained Ben Franklin, and in the spirit of "counseling and sharing," a group of artistic directors, managing directors, Equity actors, and non-Equity actors was asked to trade tips on surviving the highly competitive and financially perilous profession of theater. The generally wise, occasionally wacky, sometimes anonymous tips include:

Why Can't I Be Rich, Famous, *and* Happy?

Right out of school, try to take an audition trip across the country, schedule auditions in advance, and plan not only to see theater and audition for it, but to see the country as well. A well-traveled actor is a smart actor. Also, my dad says, "The goal in life is to be happy, not necessarily rich and famous."

Cindy Gold, Equity Actress and Northwestern University Professor

Be a Raging Bull

I recall, while on National Tour with *The Sound of Music*, seeing the tall, reedy fellow playing Max in the wings, preparing for an entrance, taking on the mannerisms of a raging bull, pawing the earth (the boards) with a twinkle in his eye. I invoke this memory/image to my students whenever I teach, because no matter how large or small the city or town on our tour, he prepped like a bull in the wings. Wherever you perform, do it with all your heart and all your might.

Tad Ingram, Equity Actor/Broadway Original Cast of *Parade*

Look Out—He's Flatlining!

One of my favorite quotes is, "It is not brain surgery. Let me make this production happen and get on with our lives." I would also say that you will be most successful when you can comfortably admit that you don't know something and can still learn from someone else. As a leader of one of this country's regional theaters, I can say without hesitation that there is always room for continued learning.

R. Scott Phillips, Managing Director, Utah Shakespearean Festival

Recognize Human Behavior

I'm always saying to actors, "Recognizable human behavior." I think that encompasses the entire human experience, but it also keeps a toehold in reality no matter what the situation. It has always been my experience as an audience member that the moment I see/hear something that doesn't seem psychologically possible, I check out of the moment. Even in the most extremely absurd situations, there is always a human being lurking beneath the lines and the circumstance. Only the desire to discover and present recognizable human behavior makes each moment rich and real.

Sidonie Garrett, Producing Artistic Director, Heart of America Shakespeare Festival

Believe in Instant Karma

What goes around will come around. Treat others exactly as you would like to be treated. Be kind and courteous. The tech person you step on today could be your producer/director tomorrow.

Avoid People Who Suck Energy

These people only give you permission to procrastinate. You are not the person who is losing if you miss a few social gatherings in order to work.

To Read or Not to Read?

That is the question. The only answer? Read as many plays as possible. Be familiar with all types of writing. The more familiar you are with a play, the better your audition will be. The better the audition, the better the part.

Leave Your Worries at the Door!

Remember, the people you work with are not your therapists. Don't be so wrapped up in your personal problems that you let your frustrations impact your work.

Don't Be a Dropout!

My students are often eager to move on to the professional world, many times before finishing even their undergraduate degree, but they come back later and say how important their education is, and they are glad they finished their degrees. They have also noted how an advanced degree opens doors that had been closed.

Cindy Melby Phaneuf, Producing Artistic Director,
Nebraska Shakespeare Festival/Isaacson Professor of Theatre,
University of Nebraska, Omaha

Think Twice Before Volunteering

Nobody likes an Equity Deputy. Actors are suspicious when an actor volunteers and it's tough when you are caught between *your* union and *your* theater's management.

Respect the Clock

Be on time. Punctuality shows that you respect and value a person's time. Being late is rude. Show up ready to work. Endure the process of auditions. Learn to reject the rejection before it rejects you.

Include Time for Yourself Every Day

Treat yourself to a walk, a trip to the local nursery, or a hot bath—you know, experience one of those international coffee moments that can change your life.

It's a Small World After All

This is not an Orlando joke, even though I am near Disney World: "It's a small world after all . . ." The regional theater scene, though spread across the country, is a close-knit circle. Do your best work, always. Contribute to whatever theater community you are in to the best of your best ability. The theater world stays in touch with each other, especially the regional theater artistic and managing directors. Your talent is important, but just as important is your attitude and positive energy.

Kate Ingram, Equity Actress,
Orlando Shakespeare Festival/Professor of Theater,
University of Central Florida

"We'll Always Have Utah!"

Falling for someone you work intimately with and for such a long time may be inevitable, especially in the veil of drama and "make believe." But rarely do these romances go beyond the run of the show.

Keep Your Pants On!

Never get too big for your britches. Be kind and considerate to everyone—you are part of an artistic team . . . today's stage manager may be tomorrow's director or producer.

David Heath, President, Heath Associates, Inc.

Who Died and Made *You* King?

Nobody likes to hear a scolding "ssh!" from another actor. Let the stage manager or director handle admonishing the parties involved. If they aren't present, remember that you catch more flies with honey and be diplomatic.

Who Died and Made *You* Elia Kazan?

Never, ever, ever, ever, ever direct another actor in your show.

Be Kind to Your Dressers

Actors need to worship costume designers, staff, and dressers. They make or break how you look every day on stage.

Make Makita Part of Your Method

Offer to help with strike if it's not mandatory as part of your non-Equity contract. If it's mandatory, do not whine. Be a good sport. You will be remembered for what kind of person you are to work with, not the believability of your page 26 speech on Thursday night.

Know Thyself

Avoid making life-changing decisions under stress, pressure, or on the spot. Make your decisions on your own time. Be clear in your own mind about what you want and what you are willing to do to get it—before you go in!

Stress Check!

Don't panic. Stay organized and learn when to say "no."

Prepare for the Worst, Hope for the Best

Go beyond basic preparation of the required or expected workload. Anticipate possible negative outcomes and have contingency plans.

Finally, A Story of Almost Pure Joy!

I'm going to be perfectly honest—sometimes I fantasize about going back to waiting tables. That's what I was doing five years ago, in my "starving artist" period. I spent long hours on my feet, got no breaks during my shift, and had to endure a boss who had little respect for women. However, most nights I walked out of there with over a hundred dollars in my pocket, and left everything else at the door. There was no reason to think about the job outside the building; I had plenty of time for friends and other activities. As an emerging artist, I have a perfect blend of artistic responsibilities and classroom contact with K-12 children. I get to direct, and I get to teach. Sometimes I can't believe how lucky I got.

But, there are sacrifices, too. I had to take out a graduate school loan that far exceeds my yearly salary. I had to uproot myself to St. Louis, a place so far from my closest friends and family that I sometimes feel I'm stranded on a deserted island. I am the administrator, program designer, marketing specialist, graphic designer, registrar, grant writer, and lead teacher for nearly all our education programs, and it's exhausting. Because of my choices, I am thirty-something and still single, without children, and a long, long way from owning a home.

So, on the difficult days, I suffer a little bit of nostalgia for the old, care-free days of spare time and expendable income. But, then I remember that I am madly in love with my job, and madly in love with Theater for Young Audiences. Joy is the reason I stay, and when Theater for Young Audiences is at its most potent and meaningful, joy thrives. For now, the frequent experience of joy is enough reason for me to keep hanging on.

Emily Petkewich, Education Director, Metro Theater Company

Uncredited tips by Krystal Allan, Brooke Aston, Evelyn Carol Case, Noelle Forestal, Kathy Hardoy, Amber Howard, James Hunt, Michelle Martinez, Melissa Maxwell, Erin McReynolds, Aleia Melville, Josh Miller, Justin Milley, and Pamela Woo.

STRATEGIC TIME AND LIFE MANAGEMENT SKILLS FOR SAVVY REGIONAL THEATER ARTISTS

"Listen, everyone is entitled to my opinion."

Madonna

As anyone who has ever auditioned, acted, stage managed, crewed, directed, or produced a show knows, time management is really life management, people management, money management, and, all too often, stress management. Whether you are an extra in a movie, a spear carrier in a Shakespeare play, a standup comic striving to land a movie, or a star at the largest regional theater in town, this chapter will help you get organized and may even change your life.

This chapter provides many tools that may help you organize your career, your romantic relationships, your family, and other aspects of your personal life. Still, *you* have to decide to use them. There are some tough life management questions that only you can answer, questions that are crucial to your use of time management as a strategic tool. At the very least, time management calls for deciding *who* you are, *where* you want to be, *how* you want to get there, and then tackling *your* agenda with ferocity.

Ask the Right Questions!

For example, ask yourself: "Where do I want to be at the end of this year (in terms of personal relationships? financial planning? work projects?) In five years? At retirement?" If you choose to plunge into time management as a strategic planning tool, these questions are your homework for the next two weeks. Sometimes, there's just no reason to reinvent the wheel. When it comes to your life, you deserve to be treated with dignity, you have the opportunity to learn from the mistakes of others, and as Sondheim so sardonically maintains in *Assassins*, "Everybody has the right to be happy."

Now, work to set your goals and plot out how to achieve them. My suggestion is that you organize your strategy on your calendar. Goal setting is freeing—it can improve your personal relationships, enhance your business relationships, and wildly increase your productivity. Time management may indeed change your life! Aldous Huxley said, "Ye shall know the truth and the truth shall make you mad!" Mad that you didn't get organized sooner.

Time and life management sometimes requires a different way of looking at yourself and the world. What time of day are you at peak performance? What tasks do you absolutely dread doing? Are you comfortable delegating? Do you have a quick temper? I'm not going to get into the "Zen of Time Management," but suffice to say that it is important that you know yourself and, as Shakespeare would say, "to thine own self be true."

Clarify What You Value

Time management often leads to values clarification—knowing what is most important to you and why. Do you value your career over family? Are you a team player? How important is money and fame vs. job satisfaction and competency? For the harried artist, craftsperson, or administrator, time management involves assertiveness training, interpersonal skills, and organizational savvy. Passive artists tend to get run over and aggressive artists often alienate key collaborators, but assertive artists usually manage to achieve their goals without stepping on people or violating the rights of others. When clear values, a strategic mind, and an assertive character merge in the arts or business, artists are generally successful at finding a *graceful* approach to the *ruthless* pursuit of one's goals.

There are many different approaches to time, life, and office management; I'm going to share just one. It's the system I use and it's a combination of many systems and starts with setting aside part of one day—you could pick any day (perhaps on your next long plane trip or next Saturday)—during which you hide away, do some soul searching, and spell out your short- and long-range goals and how you plan to achieve them. Your findings don't have to be profound—but they should be specific, should be in priority order, and should be attainable. Mine are listed on my to-do list as a constant reminder:

- Nurture Family
- Exercise
- Publish
- Generate Income
- Position for Retirement
- Excel as a Teacher/Administrator/Consultant

These items represent the most important things in my life, remind me that my career is not my entire life, and inspire me to do my best at work and at home.

Let's review this tool. At the top of any good to-do list are "priority" projects. At the bottom of my list are "To Do Today" tasks, which acknowledge the need to accomplish smaller timely tasks but don't allow me to stray too far from my first priority.

In the middle of this to-do list are the telephone, account numbers, or other numbers I use most frequently and those I may need for an emergency. This saves tons of time searching through phone books, calling assistants or family members for telephone numbers, health insurance numbers, driver's license numbers, etc. It also means I have crucial numbers with me when I travel and leave my Rolodex behind. For financial security, make sure you "code" or "disguise" confidential numbers!

Most important, this list is all on one sheet, corresponds to my working calendar and file system, is in priority order in regard to "Major Tasks/Minor Tasks," and can be updated on a daily basis in two minutes. This master list and my organizational planning calm me down, keep me from worrying, and propel me along each day. Ironically, they also allow me to be more spontaneous as surprise pockets of "found time" inevitably surface as a result of a carefully organized schedule.

Let's look at a sample working calendar. I prefer a *Week At A Glance Professional Appointments* book for three major reasons:

- It allows users to break up the day into 15-minute segments;
- It is large enough to accommodate $8^{1}/_{2} \times 11$ papers (the going size for most arts and business correspondence);
- It is large enough to be easily found, yet small enough to carry around discreetly.

Finally, to complete the "Time Management Ensemble," I heartily suggest a binder with a zipper that can hold a half-dozen computer disks, pens, pencils, a wallet, a calendar, a checkbook, and, most important, key files related to your priority to-do list, and a "Distribution Folder," a file folder where everything goes that needs to be mailed or given to someone else. The zippered binder, available in office supply and department stores everywhere, protects you from losing things and allows you to toss it in the back seat of your car with confidence.

Okay, enough about the tools that you can hold in your hand to make you feel better—let's talk about the strategies that use your brain power!

10 TIMELY TIPS
FOR SAVVY REGIONAL
THEATER ARTISTS

"Life is short, the art long."

Hippocrates

Timely Tip #1

Schedule the time it takes to prepare for an audition/interview/appointment, as well as the appointment, plus the time needed to follow up on the appointment. My experience is that this will cut your hurried, crisis-oriented scrambling in half. It will save you from running late for meetings, allow you to show respect for others by keeping your appointments on time, and enable you to complete projects at a time that is best for you—preferably when conversations and meetings are fresh on your mind.

"Decide exactly what you want to achieve. Do you want to help people, or do you want to be powerful?"

Mario Cuomo

Timely Tip #2

Authorize, empower, and delegate partners to facilitate your time management. Don't complain, don't blame, don't shame—simply explain the importance of your time to your friends, your coworkers, and/or your family. Make it personal and let them know you will respect their time and their thoughts on how to maximize productivity. Enlist their support, understanding, and help—and use it.

"Progress may have been all right once, but it has gone on too long."

Ogden Nash

Timely Tip #3

Be proactive and maintain control over your schedule. Publish your goals, objectives, meetings, and remarkably tight schedule and put your goals on your calendar. Schedule blocks of time each week when you will work on your major goals. Schedule 90 minutes of "do not disturb" time each day to tackle priority goals. "Punch a hole" in tough projects by committing to a 10-minute outline that will get you started. If you need to get a haircut, put air in the tire of your car, pick up the children from day care, or hide behind a *USA Today* and drink a café mocha—put it on your calendar! Make an appointment with an important person today: *you*!

> "Beware of the danger signals that flag problems: silence, secretiveness, or sudden outburst."
>
> Sylvia Porter

Timely Tip #4

Walk the streets. By increasing visibility, you often serve as your own best agent by meeting people, stimulating your career through personal contact, and creating an awareness of what a great person you are. One friendly lunch, quick meeting, or warm handshake is worth a hundred generic letters and résumés that you spend hours typing, printing, and stuffing. You can head off many problems, inspire loyalty, show personal interest, and gain people's confidence through visibility and outreach. Go see other people's shows and let them know how much you enjoyed their work!

> "Always put off until tomorrow what you shouldn't do at all."
>
> Anonymous

Timely Tip #5

Instruct your answering machine or service to take clear telephone messages with the full name, telephone number, date, time, and purpose of the call. Consider divulging your e-mail on your answering machine or marketing materials to facilitate contact with people you want to be able to contact you. Plan on interruptions. Emergencies happen; just expect them and manage them. Don't let them derail your plans—the rule of the "worst-case scenario" should be planned for and greeted with a calm sense of inevitability.

> "There is never enough time, unless you're serving it."
>
> Malcolm Forbes

Timely Tip #6

Screen all calls and e-mails and return phone calls and e-mails en masse at specified intervals each day at times that are convenient for *you*. This will eliminate two of the major time-wasters for most regional theater artists and will put you in control of your "e-mail" and "phone life." This also allows you to prepare and be ready for negotiations, concerns, and problems, and to gather the necessary data so that it is in front of you when you place the call or e-mail. It also prevents ongoing disturbance of your work on priority goals and saves a lot of time (since it is more appropriate for you to quickly end a call that you initiated). A good voice-mail system or excellent answering machine is worth its weight in gold. Practice appropriate telephone etiquette and keep your phone messages professional.

> "A man with one watch knows what time it is. A man with two watches is never sure."
>
> John Peer

Timely Tip #7

Write it down! Don't rely on your memory. Discipline yourself to jot down notes on important commitments or carry a small tape recorder that may be used for transcription later. Ask your friends and coworkers to commit important requests in writing or on e-mail so that you have a record of them and don't forget about them.

> "I don't say we all ought to misbehave, but we ought to look as if we could."
>
> Orson Welles

Timely Tip #8

Get the details on all rehearsals, production meetings, training sessions, or any other commitments that you have or make. Be aware of the who, what, where, when, and why of each commitment. This will hopefully keep you from wasting time looking for meetings or attending rehearsals, costume fittings, or photo calls that you don't really need to attend. Be on time for your commitments and don't bring surprises into meetings, rehearsals, or work sessions. Paraphrasing the former president of Avon Products: "Bring me your problems early and you have a partner in solving the problems; bring them to me late (or surprise me with them), and you have a judge!"

> "You're never too old to do goofy stuff."
>
> Ward Cleaver, *Leave It to Beaver*

Timely Tip #9

Get to know yourself. Goethe said, "He who seizes the right moment, is the right man." When are you at your best? When are your performing/ writing/memorizing/welding/sewing skills ready for peak performance? When are your analytical skills clearly accessible? When do your creative skills tend to blossom? Matching your goals and tasks to your highs and lows will keep you from spinning your wheels and will help you make the most of your time. How do you procrastinate? (When I reach for my fourth cup of coffee and it's not yet 9 a.m., I know I'm avoiding the day. And when I rearrange my to-do list more than once a day, I know I'm in serious trouble!)

"What one has to do usually can be done."

Anna Eleanor Roosevelt

Timely Tip #10

The future is now. Choose to spend time doing what you will remember 10 years from now and what you want other people to remember your doing. Learn to "Just Say No" based on your own priorities and the priorities of your theater. For example, I am often called on by my colleagues to sit on yet one more board or committee, or to deliver a speech or host a visiting VIP. Generally speaking, I usually sit down with the requesting party and review the Priority Projects I have selected or been previously assigned. We don't fight—Kafka reminds us that "In a fight between you and the world, bet on the world." *Together*, we explore options and usually tend to agree that my time is much better spent on previously assigned strategic planning, fund-raising, community outreach, teaching, audience development, and/or writing assignments.

19 TERRIBLE DISTRACTIONS THAT ERODE PRODUCTIVITY

"We haven't the time to take our time."

Eugene Ionesco

1 **Procrastination**
Solution: Force yourself to get the job done and reward yourself for completing priority tasks.

2 **Overcommitment/Poor Delegation Skills**
Solution: Just say no, or if you feel it's impossible to say no, review your business or personal priorities with those closest to you and seek their help in establishing a reasonable schedule. Endeavor to work with people you respect and trust and give them the opportunity to shine by delegating responsibility.

3 **Perfection Problems**
Solution: Give each task your best shot for the amount of time you have to work on it and move on knowing you did your best under the circumstances.

4 **Endless Firefighting**
Solution: Plan for normal interruptions, deal with them quickly, and get back to work. Always finish thoughts before dealing with interruptions and quickly outline where you plan to go with a rehearsal, report, budget plan, or production requirement before you leave it.

5 Shortsightedness/Inflexibility

Solution: Don't be so wed to your schedule that you are unable to perceive and grab hold of opportunities that relate to your key life and career goals. Realize that change is inevitable and that, as Charles Kettering once said, "If you have always done it that way, it is probably wrong."

6 Lack of Preparation

Richard Nixon used to say, "Always be prepared to negotiate, but never negotiate without being prepared."

Solution: To avoid straying from your work, and other distractions, bring to the table all the tools you need to finish the product.

7 Not Choosing the Right Place and the Right Time

Solution: Do easy tasks during high interruption times in your day and "priority difficult tasks" at a site and during a time when interruptions are minimal.

8 Open-door Policies

An open door (at work or home) says, "I am available to you and I'm not working on a priority project." An open door for a short and consistent time per day may work for you, your friends, neighbors, coworkers, or employees who know they can catch you daily between 2 and 3 p.m.

Solution: The aforementioned "Walk the streets" tip allows you to choose the place of your accessibility much more efficiently than keeping your door open.

9 The Waiting Game: Losing Time Just Hanging Out

Tired or irritated by bank lines, traffic, or the DMV?

Solution: With your organizational binder, you have myriad projects just waiting for you! Save your mail to read when you are standing in lines, stuck in traffic, or waiting for meetings to begin.

10 Searching for Addresses, Telephone Numbers, Etc.

Solution: Type all your important numbers into your computer and reduce the type so they can easily be fit into and found in your notebook.

This should include birthdays, anniversaries, holidays, etc. Important Note: Code any financial numbers to prevent theft.

11 Instant Gratification Syndrome

Solution: Reward yourself only when priority projects are completed, and chastise yourself for dealing with little tasks just to get them off your list.

12 Listening and Reacting to the Squeaky Wheel

Solution: Reward individuals who respect your time and work plan, and penalize individuals who waste your time.

13 Bad Attitude, Fear of Failure, Jealousy, Anger, and Depression

Solution: Let go of the past, look to the future, forgive, forget, and seize the joy that is available to you. Inventory your strengths and blessings and be grateful for all you have accomplished. Consider seeking professional assistance and outside support for persistent emotional problems.

14 Mealtime Madness

So often, your prime time for working on priority projects is preempted by long, unproductive breakfast, lunch, or dinner engagements or meetings that don't challenge or relax or involve you for more than a few minutes.

Solution: Avoid lunch dates and meal meetings that can drag on unproductively for hours without any graceful means of escape. Delegate!

15 Busy Work, Reading Contracts, Proofreading . . .

Solution: Read *every word* of any contracts you sign (including riders), proofread your own correspondence and edit materials appropriately. Save busy work for quiet TV or vegetation times, and for times when you are waiting for meetings to begin, when waiting in line, etc.

16 Handling the Same Projects, Papers, and Memos Over and Over and Over and Over and Over and Over and ...

Solution: Strive to handle each piece of paper just once before acting on it, delegating it, or trashing it. If you can't do this, put "#1" at the top of each new piece of paper that crosses your desk and add "#2," "#3," etc., each time you rehandle this paper. Resolve to complete the project, delegate the project, or toss the project the third time you handle it.

17 Handling Correspondence on a Piecemeal Basis

Solution: Resolve to save up minor correspondence and respond to it all during preset times during the week. Utilize the fastest means of dispensing with bureaucratic correspondence (fax, phone call, letter, e-mail, etc.) and don't waiver. Delegate whenever possible.

18 The Black Hell of TV

Solution: Use the time you must spend in front of a television to review casting notices or job openings, catch up on sit-ups and push-ups, clean-up your to-do list, or compose correspondence.

19 Reading Junk Mail

Solution: Don't do it (but be careful not to throw away important financial statements, residual checks, or timely bills)!

29 WONDERFUL WAYS TO SEIZE CONTROL OF YOUR OWN LIFE

1   Enjoy the Time Off
Never fret, worry, or fume about "waiting" for anything. Consider the extra minutes an absolute gift that may be used to pursue activities you enjoy (such as reading a newspaper, sipping a cup of coffee, or working on your to-do list).

2   You Are Special!
Take advantage of computer "mail-merge" capabilities to keep in contact with friends and colleagues. Personalize letters but use a consistent body of text as appropriate.

3   Way to Go!
Send thank-you notes and congratulatory notes as a way of showing appreciation, nurturing subordinates, encouraging cooperation, and sharing credit. As one smart team player notes, "It's amazing how much may be accomplished when we don't care who gets the credit." Richard Nixon would say it in a different way: "Always do as much for our friends as our adversaries would do for our enemies."

4   Teamwork Pays Off
When assembling a cast or work force, consider the whole ensemble along with the individual players.

5   Massage Time?

Avoid stressful situations or unpredictable traffic byways prior to rehearsals, performances, or important community meetings.

6   Stay Fit for Life

Reduce stress by exercising regularly, playing soothing music to drown out office distractions, dressing comfortably, and taking a break from the grind.

7   A Little Perspective, Please!

Ask yourself: What will matter most to me, my family, and/or my colleagues a week from now? At the end of the year?

8   This Is Really Important Work!

Consider ethical "codes" when scheduling on your calendar. For example, "stress reduction management" could serve as a calendar listing for a basketball game, a picnic on the beach, a mid-afternoon nap, or time to finish a new play from *American Theatre*. "Professional Development Hour" could be a code for listening to your favorite symphony or watching an important opera on video. Long-range planning provides the time and opportunity to read the latest journals and articles that shape your planning and learning process. The strategy is that an individual perusing your calendar will be more likely to barge in on your reading or attempt to usurp your picnic than to bother your "stress reduction" or "artistic planning" sessions.

9   Lead by Example

Demand ethical standards and make sure you set the pace in the way you treat co-workers, board members, and janitorial staff. Columnist Ann Landers suggested that "the standard by which you will be judged is how you treat the people who can't do anything for you."

10 Those Dang Dilemmas

When faced with a difficult dilemma or a confusing ethical decision, ask yourself: 1) Is it legal? 2) Is it fair? 3) Does it fall within the guidelines of my theater or business? 4) How would I feel if my decision were printed on the front page of my hometown newspaper tomorrow morning?

11 Pick Up the Phone and Talk to Me!

Surround yourself with positive-thinking, competent people. Here's a test: Call your home or office. How many rings before someone picks up? Does the individual who answers represent the professional image you want for your career? Does the person take careful messages? Is anyone even answering the phones or do you have an oftentimes frustrating voice-mail system or poorly functioning answering machine? How can you be well organized if those individuals (or machines) who represent you aren't well trained and organized?

12 Way to Go . . . and You're Fired?

Help your director, guest director, stage manager, or staff build their personnel files and feel better about their work by sending short notes of congratulations or a thank-you note on their production work. Put good news in writing . . . deliver bad news in person!

13 Read the Newspaper and Follow Up

A leadership and community outreach tip: Scan theater or arts publications and local newspapers and send notes of congratulations to directors, designers, or others who are positively reviewed. It's a very small world, and someone you congratulate today will most likely be interviewing or auditioning you next week.

14 Leave My Family Alone!

Instead of asking yourself, "Is it fair or appropriate for me to assertively end this nonproductive meeting or cut off this rambling, inconsiderate individual who pushed their way into my house or office?," ask yourself: "Is it fair for me to deprive my children of their mother/father, my spouse/partner of my companionship, or my theater of this crucial planning time because of this individual's lack of foresight or planning?"

15 Write It Down, or Just Forget It!

Let those closest to you (spouse/partner, children, faculty, staff, etc.) know that you need key tasks and requests in writing—even scribbled on a Post-it note. This saves you from forgetting, and having to deal with guilt and the wrath of others when you forget hasty requests screamed over balconies, on your way to work, in the hallways, when pulling out of the driveway, etc.

16 Watch Where You Grab Me!

Remind individuals who "grab you in hallways" that personal matters and personnel issues should be discussed behind closed doors and not in front of other company members and the world at large.

17 Don't Put Your Clothes On, Just Pull Them Out!

Begin your morning the evening before. Pack up everything you need to take to work and put it in the same place each night. Pull out your clothes the night before and consider a programmable coffeemaker.

18 Just File It Under "T" for Trash

Experts insist we spend 20 to 30 percent of our time looking for things. Toss out clothes you haven't worn in the last year, store everything in your desk that you haven't used in the past year, sift out files that are no longer necessary and move them out of your office (preferably into a garbage can).

19 But I Spent 88 Hours Building This Flat!

Work smarter, not harder. Remember that results count—not the time you spend on a project.

20 Welcome and Get Out Now!

When interrupted in the office, do a half-standing, uncomfortable-looking crouch in front of your desk, and ask, "What can I do for you?" Don't remain seated with a friendly smile—it's an invitation for the other party to sit down.

21 Why Am I Talking to You?

When you inadvertently end up on the phone with someone you have no interest in talking to, let the caller speak for a moment and quickly let him/her know you are "in the middle of a project" or "surrounded by people" and ask for the number so that the call may be returned. Then delegate it if you can.

22 Make Memos Count

When writing e-mails or memos, place your main point before your rationale, unless you feel your reader will disagree with you or lacks understanding of the issue and needs an explanation first. If you desire a response or a course of action, be specific and set a deadline. Never commit to letter, e-mail, or memo form what should be discussed face-to-face.

23 Boo! Your Letters Are Haunting You Again!

Letters, e-mails, and memos should be used to confirm new plans or policy, not to surprise, irritate, or announce a new policy. Consider the consequences of the letters you write and understand that they may come back to haunt you.

> "Everybody gets so much information all day long that they lose their common sense."
>
> Gertrude Stein

24 We Are So Good!

Consider writing an "annual report letter" to your director or supervisor to list your key work success stories, above-and-beyond-the-call-of-duty work, achievements, and progress. Being proactive enhances your image and saves valuable time defending your programs or work later. Keep it simple: short paragraphs and lists are fine. A personal annual report detailing your own achievements for your direct supervisor positions you more effectively for merit increases and future contract negotiations.

25 What Would You Do?

Always approach your supervisor with solutions, as well as with the problem. Ask those who report to you to do the same. As Richard Moran explains in *Never Confuse a Memo with Reality*, "you are getting paid to think, not to whine." Moran also advises, "Don't get drunk at the company holiday party; never in your life say, 'It's not my job,' and always have an answer to the question, 'What would I do if I lost my job tomorrow?'" I don't even want to begin to tell you the problems with alcohol I've seen at cast parties with the community present.

26 Here's What I Want from You! Please?

Artists who bring out the best in people treat their colleagues and employees with respect and dignity while communicating clear-cut expectations.

27 And You Think You Have Storage Problems Now?

Take a world view and plan ahead. Stockpile birthday and Christmas/Hanukkah/holiday presents in an empty closet, have generic greeting cards on hand, call stores and businesses before driving across town to find out they are closed, and stock up on groceries and office items you use a lot to save seemingly endless shopping trips. Use your assistant or a mail house to wrap and send mail and packages.

28 Could You Repeat That?

Listen carefully! Time, energy, and massive frustration (for you and others) may be saved if you pay attention the first time. For example, have a pencil in hand when listening to telephone messages so you don't have to listen to the entire message just to retrieve the phone number. Writing down travel instructions will save you from missing appointment times or having to stop and call for new directions.

29 Don't You Dare Knock on My Door!

Put a sign on your door that says "In Conference," "Timely Work Session," or "Available 1-2 p.m. Today" to discourage interruptions.

UNDERSTANDING HUMAN BEHAVIOR IS THE KEY TO SUCCESSFUL WORK IN THE ARTS

"Personal qualities/skills include being capable of striving in solitude and in community; a sense of independence; willingness to collaborate; readiness to accept work as it comes while seeking the ideal job; perseverance; networking, written and verbal communication skills; social skills . . . although you may work in a *regional theater*, your knowledge and aesthetic should be informed by the *national* and *global* models of theatrical practice."

Kathleen F. Conlin, Utah Shakespearean Festival Associate Artistic Director

The ridiculous rate of theater unemployment coupled with the sheer ferocity of a life in the American theater should be an obvious indicator of the need for careful and consistent organizational, life, and career planning. Producers and artistic directors are often amazed that the same individuals who spend many years and a small fortune on actor training, voice work, singing lessons, and dance training have trouble investing a few days and a modest amount of money to organize and/or polish their career skills. In a similar vein, actors are sometimes dumbfounded to discover that individuals who have risen to the executive ranks of arts organizations are sometimes rude, noncommunicative, poorly organized "leaders" with unpolished people skills, erratic behavioral traits, and modest expertise in either the arts or organizational planning.

Professional trade publications brim with offers to train the perfect actor, to recreate lips, eyes, busts, thighs, chins, and cheeks, and then to snap the definitive photograph to mail to a brilliant agent list in hopes of securing the breakthrough audition. Unfortunately, few publications, support organizations, or universities train actors, directors, designers, production personnel, or administrators in the realities of the nonprofit world and the terrifying myriad tasks that they will be expected to accomplish the first year on the job. In the same way that young actors quickly grow to realize that the person with the cutest nose and thinnest thighs is not necessarily the one who wins the role, arts personnel in all areas soon discover that prestigious schools, MBAs, and a warm smile don't guarantee survival in the deficit-laden, tough-to-conquer world of the arts. Whether training actors, directors, or producers, it is clear that interpersonal communications skills, group-process understanding, and savvy strategic skills are every bit as important as training in acting, directing, design, and theater history.

There's a reason that producers and artistic directors joke that the closest anyone comes to perfection is when they are applying for a job. Smart artists and executives know to take care with their cover letters, résumés, recommendations, and support materials. Experienced artists and administrators understand that nurturing directors, area heads, board members, or other potential employers is the most important step leading to an audition or an interview. So how does this nurturing process happen?

"Acting is a matter of giving away secrets," hints actress Ellen Barkin. The same is true of the artist, craftsperson, or administrator's career planning process—and in order to fully comprehend the rigors of the field, it is important to understand theater psyches, performing egos, employer needs, and the changing trends in the ever-evolving American arts environment. Speaking for myself, even after 30 years of career planning, four college degrees, attending or conducting over 12,000 auditions, working as an executive search consultant for nonprofit clients, studying over 100,000 résumés, conducting countless personal interviews, and talking to many of America's arts leaders, only now am I beginning to grasp the intricacies of the process.

For the past 26 years, I have taught seminars at national conventions, in professional theaters, and on college campuses, titled "Assertive Personal Marketing," "The Business of Acting," and "Introduction to Regional Theater." Almost every session begins with counselor basics: teaching actors and administrators how to establish a rapport, make connections, and carry on a conversation outside the interview or audition. Seminar participants are prodded to risk establishing a more personal relationship by reaching out to potential employers with a sense of humor and disarmingly, honest, straightforward talk that is appropriate to the situation. To help with this, participants are encouraged to identify the basic traits that attract them to people. For example, when questioned about first impressions and friendships, many participants acknowledge that they tend to like people who are kind to them—flattery! In addition, "warmth," "unselfishness," "friendliness," and "a giving, fun-loving personality" always top the "people we like most" list.

With this in mind, doesn't it follow that harried, overworked producers, artistic directors, and production managers might admire and respect similar traits if they were communicated in a phone call, letter, or interview? Knowing this, doesn't it make sense to learn how to communicate positive personality traits through an enjoyable conversation and even rehearse, role-play, or otherwise prepare for one of the most important parts of career building? Can you look someone straight in the eye, deliver a firm hand-shake, stand up straight, dress appropriately, make someone laugh, comfortably conduct a one-on-one interview, and participate in a group dis-cussion? Do you understand the difference between assertive, passive, and aggressive behavior? Answer these questions and integrate them into your institutional leadership and career planning and you will stand out in any pool of artists.

The bane of one's existence in most arts environments centers on petty politics, gossip, and innuendo. Understanding that the kind of people pro-ducers and directors wish to work with have all the personality traits of a faithful dog may propel you to the front of the employment line. Individuals with integrity, honesty, loyalty, warmth, and a sensitivity to others stand out in a crowd. A strong sense of ethics offers a comprehensive personal frame-work for living a professional life *worth* living. Mark Twain said it best: "Always do right . . . this will surprise some people and astonish the rest."

Ego and a remarkably fatalistic attitude regarding employment are two major obstacles for many administrators. "If I'm right for the job, they'll hire me," explains one staff member. "They know who I am and what I can do and if they don't want me, it's their loss," complains another longtime regional theater actor. These naive comments fail to acknowledge the incredibly busy and complex lives of most artistic directors, producers, and managing directors who respond favorably to friendly, consistent correspon-dence that reminds them that a potential employee is alive, still interested, and available.

Another artistic hiring roadblock is ignorance—simply not realizing that employers are human beings who may indeed have the sensibilities, inter-ests, concerns, and motivations of other living, breathing, thinking, feeling creatures. Many perceive the job search as a humiliating battle that they usually lose, while others seize employment contacts as an opportunity to endear themselves to a director, production manager, artistic director, or fellow actor or stage manager, and, perhaps even make a friend. Many direc-tors and producers I know are quick to fondly remember the individual who remembers *their* opening night—or better yet, their daughter's birthday. Producers' desks are lined with the photographs of actors who stuck by them through a life crisis, sent a bottle of wine to celebrate a particularly brilliant review, or let them know how much they enjoyed their production (*after* the critics savaged it).

Of course, inspiring company members, strategic planning, and career sensitivity is more than sending birthday cards, nurturing egos, and making friends. A commitment to polishing personnel skills, understanding artistic needs, attaining communications basics, and contributing to company morale is a must for the savvy actor, director, craftsperson, designer, or administrator. Preparing the total career package *and* working to understand human nature and the forces that guide the actions of executives and non-profit board members is exciting and rewarding work that will hopefully lead to an increased world perspective, personal satisfaction, and ongoing employment. Of course, if you are heading into theater production areas such as production management, technical direction, costumes, props, scenery, or scene painting, many more doors and arms are open to embrace your entry into the field. For almost everyone else, it may be best to remember the words of Nelson Mandela: "The greatest glory in living lies not in never falling, but in rising every time we fall." The chapters that follow offer insights into the process of striving, rebounding, learning, and developing your career.

"They say that time changes things, but you actually have to change them yourself."

Andy Warhol

ADVICE TO REGIONAL THEATER WORKERS EVERYWHERE

16 Wonderful Ways to Improve
Your Life in the Theater

"One day Alice came to a fork in the road and saw a Cheshire cat in a tree. 'Which road do I take?' she asked. 'Where do you want to go?' was his response. 'I don't know,' Alice answered. 'Then,' said the cat, 'it doesn't matter.'"

Lewis Carroll

1   Know Where You Want to Go and Stay Positive

Keep your eye on your goals, remember that you chose a creative but difficult profession, and approach your work with enthusiasm. Don't sabotage yourself! Henry Ford hit it on the head when he said, "Whether you think you can or whether you think you can't, you're right."

2   Plan Ahead for the People You Love

Don't forget you have a *life* as well a *career* to plan! Go ahead and plan something special for someone you love. Don't allow your life to turn into one big casting call or late-night rehearsal. Send flowers, book a reservation at that fabulous restaurant, or find a loved one something unique on eBay.

3   Be a Collaborator

Whether you're a director, designer, assistant stage manager, or property assistant, you'll accomplish so much more if you nurture, inspire, motivate, empower, support, thank, and show you're a willing part of your theater's team.

4 Hide from the Madness!

Avoid stressful situations prior to performances, key meetings, or work sessions. Schedule aggravating situations and meetings with people at times that are best for you (and schedule time after the session to unwind and regain perspective). For example, if you're a stage manager, don't schedule a meeting with an angry actor just prior to opening night; if you're a director, separate salary negotiations and artistic discussions. Find the right time for every important job. Balzac said it best when he observed, "Power is not revealed by striking hard or often, but by striking true."

5 Put the Madness in Perspective

Try prioritizing these items: Audition, Money, Chekhov, Chocolate, Health, Happiness, Mom. Ask yourself: Where do my true priorities lie?

6 Ask for Advice

People may look to you for leadership and to promote "ownership" or "buy-in" for your theater. When it is appropriate, consider asking your fellow workers or supervisor for advice or guidance or the benefit of their history with the organization. You don't have to take the advice, but people appreciate being asked. "You ain't gonna learn what you don't wanna know," says Jerry Garcia.

7 Just Say No to Defensive Behavior

Stay open to constructive suggestions and graciously ignore the rude remarks of ignorant people. An old Indian proverb says, "Call on God, but row away from the rocks."

8 Stay Out of Trouble

Racist remarks, sexist behavior, crude gestures, off-color jokes, and obnoxious banter may be fascinating on stage in a Joe Orton play. They are less than fascinating and potentially devastating if they impact your working relationships with your peers, your employer, or your community.

9 Take Risks

"Imagination will often carry us to worlds that never were. But without it we go nowhere," counsels Carl Sagan. Remember why the nonprofit theater movement was founded in the first place?

10 Put Your Personal Stamp on your Work

"Individuality is either the mark of a genius or the reverse. Mediocrity finds safety in standardization," writes Frederick E. Crane. You don't have to be outrageous, just don't be consistently derivative.

11 Prove Emerson Wrong

Pay attention to the people you love. The arts are demanding, but they don't need to rob you of your humanity. "Art is a jealous mistress," explains Ralph Waldo Emerson. "If a man has a genius for painting, poetry, music, architecture, or philosophy, he makes a bad husband and an ill provider." Prove Emerson wrong.

12 But When We Get Behind Closed Doors . . .

"Three may keep a secret if two of them are dead," quipped Benjamin Franklin. Joking or not, old Ben certainly knew what he was talking about. Discuss salaries, grievances, and official business behind closed doors and not in front of other theater folks and the world at large. Remember the Spanish proverb, "Whoever gossips to you will gossip about you."

13 Do a Good Deed Today

Bring honor to your institution and satisfaction to your family as an ongoing "good-deed doer." Look around your company and change someone's life for the better. As a respected artist, you have the power to brighten days with a kind word, warm gesture, or expression of interest. Ben Jonson said it best: "When a virtuous man is raised, it brings gladness to his friends, grief to his enemies, and glory to his posterity."

14 Dream On!

Take time to daydream, stay healthy, sleep well, and give yourself a fighting chance to tackle your dreams! "All men of action are dreamers," explains James G. Huneker. Consider sporadic five-minute "dream breaks" during the day.

15 Focus on Your Vision and Embrace the Future

"If art is to nourish the roots of our culture, society must set the artist free to follow his vision wherever it takes him," notes John F. Kennedy. If you focus on your vision, you can free yourself from society's negativity and live a life in which you are true to your own spirit. Try it for a day, a week, a month, or a lifetime.

16 Climb a Mountain and See the World

Take a world view and plan ahead. Take time each year to take stock of your life, pat yourself on the back for your progress and accomplishments, and thank those who have helped you along the way.

> "Doing the best at this moment puts you in the best place for the next moment."
>
> Oprah Winfrey

5 TIPS
FOR STARTING
A NEW JOB

First impressions are essential in every field and here are five proven suggestions for making a strong first impression (and a powerful ongoing impression) when starting a new job in the theater.

1 When you start a new job, shake the hand of your producer, director, or boss. Look that person in the eye and make it clear that you are excited about your work, loyal, trustworthy, industrious, and really happy to be working together on his or her agenda. Employers need to know that they can count on you.

2 Always arrive at work *at least* a half-hour to an hour early *every day* the first six months, and be the last person to leave the office. Be there on a weekend or a holiday if you can contribute in some significant (and, hopefully, visible) way. Be productive. Results count more than effort.

3 Leave a paper trail. Document your successes and failures. Let your successes be known with great subtlety. Own up to your failures and take responsibility . . . but don't dwell on them!

4 Asking for advice is a way of creating mentors, allies, and potential partners in your success. Be humble, quiet, and easygoing in your approach and generous with your gratitude. Write short, sincere thank-you notes.

5 Inspire . . . motivate . . . understand your boss and coworkers. What motivates them? What are their interests and career plans? Look at the big picture: *their* lives and *your* career.

A SHORT CAST OF CHARACTERS: PEOPLE YOU NEED TO KNOW IN THE THEATER

The Artistic Director and the Artistic Team

Certainly, the *artistic director* is the individual charged with crafting the vision, shaping seasons, hiring artistic personnel, and fully realizing the artistic mission of the institution. The title *producing artistic director* typically means that the artistic director is also heavily involved in and essentially responsible for overall strategic decision-making and is heavily involved in the financial and fund-raising aspects of the theater.

In most nonprofit theater operations, the following areas or individuals directly report to the artistic side of the institution (artistic director/producing artistic director, etc.):

- Directors
- Associate artistic directors
- Choreographers
- Musical direction (including composers, musicians, etc.)
- Designers (scenery, costumes, lights, sound, etc.)
- Actors
- Stage management
- Dramaturgy/literary management
- Production/technical direction (production manager, technical director, production crews, stage operations crews, etc.)

Since many of the standard theater positions are outlined on the Sample Organizational Chart for Regional Theaters at the end of this chapter, I won't repeat them all here. However, three key individuals who have strong connections to both the artistic direction of the theater and the management, budget, and income side of the theater deserve special mention and clarification:

THE PRODUCTION MANAGER

The *production manager* of larger professional theaters works closely with the artistic director, directors, designers, and craftspeople, and usually supervises all production and technical areas of the theater. On the management side, the production manager is also crucial in budgeting, personnel hiring and supervision, and financial controls. Aside from the expense of salaries and benefits, production (scenery, costumes, lights, sound, properties, etc.) tends to be the highest annual budget allocation. With these realities in mind, it is recommended that the production manager report to the artistic director on artistic matters and work closely with the managing director on financial and personnel matters. Technical directors and costume, scenery, lighting, makeup, stage operations, and other technical and production crews and personnel are typically considered production staff.

THE COMPANY MANAGER

Company managers are most often involved with the coordination and implementation of travel, housing, and contract commitments with an emphasis on meeting union agreements with the Actors' Equity Association (AEA), the Society for Stage Directors and Choreographers (SSDC), United Scenic Artists (USA), and other out-of-town independent contractors. In many theaters, the company manager is also encouraged to assist with company communications, company morale, and special events for the company. Since the bulk of the work is usually artist-related (even though the day-to-days are largely management oriented), it's recommended that the company manager maintain very strong ties and reporting responsibilities to both the artistic and management sides of the theater.

THE DIRECTOR OF EDUCATION

The *director of education* is often called on to conduct artistic research, tie productions to educational outreach efforts, and represent the artistic side of the theater. At the same time, the director of education is often considered a pivotal player in group ticket sales, consumer relations, and the development of earned income. With these dual responsibilities, it's recommended that the director of education nurture strong relationships and report to both the artistic and management sides of the theater.

The Managing Director

The *managing director* of most professional theaters is generally charged with the financial, fund-raising, marketing, and front-of-house and general day-to-day management of the theater. Working in partnership with the artistic director, the managing director is often called on to take the lead in community relations, personnel management, media relations, budget planning, and board of trustee development and planning.

In most nonprofit theater operations, the following areas directly report to the management side of the institution (executive director/managing director/general manager, etc.):

- Development (fund-raising, advancement, unearned income)
- Marketing (audience development, sales, earned income)
- Finance (business management, accounting, contracts, financial reporting)
- Front of house (box office, house management, concessions, gift shops, etc.)

The Sample Organizational Chart that follows offers an overview of areas of responsibility and general reporting lines for most regional theaters.

Sample Organizational Chart for Regional Theaters

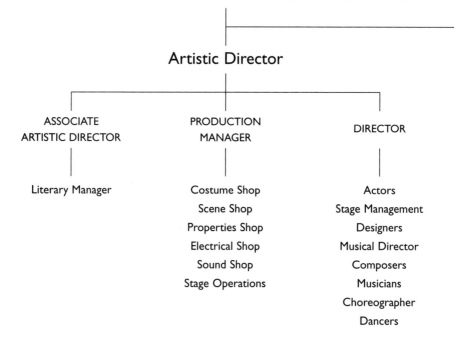

BOARD OF TRUSTEES

Board of Trustee Committees

(Executive Committee, Finance/Legal Committee, Nominating/Recruitment Committee, Fund-raising Coordination Committee, Governmental Relations Committee, Marketing/Volunteers Committee, Strategic Planning Committee)

Artistic Director

ASSOCIATE ARTISTIC DIRECTOR	PRODUCTION MANAGER	DIRECTOR
Literary Manager	Costume Shop	Actors
	Scene Shop	Stage Management
	Properties Shop	Designers
	Electrical Shop	Musical Director
	Sound Shop	Composers
	Stage Operations	Musicians
		Choreographer
		Dancers

Managing Director

GENERAL MANAGER/ FINANCE DIRECTOR	MARKETING DIRECTOR	DEVELOPMENT/ FUND-RAISING DIRECTOR
Finance	Audience Development	Annual Campaign
Box Office	Media	Grants
Front of House	Sales	Corporate
Office	Public Relations	Foundation
Facilities	Touring/Outreach	Volunteers
	Publications	Endowment

NOTES:

1 It's recommended that the artistic director and managing director both have strong ties and reporting lines to the production manager, company manager, and education director to protect both artistic and fiscal integrity.

2 Volunteers deserve top-level support.

PART IV

THE REGIONAL THEATER EMPLOYMENT UNIVERSE

100+ PRIME SOURCES

Information Equals Power

In a mad fit of institutional dedication and loyalty, I once auditioned 700 actors in three days when I was on the Board of Directors of the Southeastern Theatre Conference. This may seem like a bizarre way to get to know actors but, believe it or not, hundreds of artistic leaders subject themselves to this craziness (and worse) on an annual basis!

My advice is to attend auditions and conferences, get to know the business, consult many "experts" (whether it be through publications, personal interviews, or discussions with your career mentors), and *turn yourself into an expert on* YOUR *life and career!* This will empower you to make your own informed decisions and take responsibility for the decisions you make and the life you create.

The Truth (and More) Is Out There

There was a time when job seeking and career building seemed a mysterious enterprise. Today, thanks to the sweeping communications potential of the World Wide Web, the efficiency and availability of e-mail, and the clarity of theater and service organization Web sites, the information is generally out there if one knows where to start.

Certainly, the major publications of the industry are useful tools and so much career information is accessible on each publication's Web site, as well as on local newsstands (or in local bookstores). Spend time paging through these publications or surfing these Web sites and you'll be rewarded with timely job-search information, hiring tips, interview suggestions, audition and photography advice, networking guidance, agent submission details, professional development opportunities, arts advocacy lessons, class and training endorsements, and a whole host of other information that may be absolutely useful or sheer propaganda.

Thousands of publications and Web sites offer theater information—way too many to mention or list in this book. However, here are a few of my favorites on which you will find hundreds of resources that will help you narrow to your specific field of interest.

10 PERTINENT
PUBLICATIONS

AMERICAN THEATRE

www.tcg.org

American Theatre is the national monthly magazine for the American professional not-for-profit theater, informing readers about groundbreaking international work, providing state-by-state listings of professional theater seasons and offering ongoing reports and surveys of the field. Masterfully edited by Jim O'Quinn, with must-read musings by Theatre Communications Group (TCG) executive directors, *American Theatre* should be required reading for every theater professional and serious high school, college, and university theater student. Check the Web site to delve in and to track down subscription information.

ARTSEARCH

www.tcg.org

Also published by the Theatre Communications Group, *ARTSEARCH* is a fabulous regional theater resource and provides the opportunity for online job hunting for full-time, part-time, seasonal, year-round, and internship opportunities, from entry level to upper management. Listings include openings in administration, artistic, production, design, career development and education in theaters, performing arts centers, summer festivals, universities, arts councils, and related arts organizations. Check out the Web site for hard copies, online subscriptions, or both.

BACK STAGE EAST and BACK STAGE WEST

www.backstage.com

This site makes it possible to access content from *Back Stage East* (New York/National/International theater news) and *Back Stage West* (Southern California emphasis), including exclusive online content, advance casting notices before they appear in print, and regional casting notices for every state in the US, not to mention from Canada and worldwide. Subscriptions range in price. Check the Web site for details. Weekly editions are available in bookstores and newsstands nationwide and offer job notices, theater reviews, advice columns, savvy career information, and a host of other practical information. The production charts, casting ads, and updated theater addresses and contact information are worth the price of a subscription.

DRAMATICS

www.edta.org/publications/dramatics.asp

Dramatics is the Educational Theatre Association's magazine for theater students and teachers containing practical articles on acting, directing, design, and other facets of theater; sage advice from working professionals; new plays; and book reviews. Two special issues each year offer directories of college theater programs (December) and summer theater work and study opportunities (February). Check the Web site to delve in or for subscription information.

LIVE DESIGN

www.livedesignonline.com

Live Design offers a comprehensive look at the art and technology of show business with sound, lighting, scenery, production, and design articles; listings of Broadway master classes in production; industry resources; and articles related to unions and service organizations, including United States Institute for Theater Technology (USITT) news. Check the Web site to explore or for subscription information.

THE HOLLYWOOD REPORTER

www.hollywoodreporter.com

The Hollywood Reporter is a longtime entertainment industry information source focusing on film, television, and digital media, and is an excellent resource for theater folks looking to expand their horizons. Subscriptions range in price. Check the Web site for details.

QUARTO

www.staaonline.org

At last count, there were over 250 Shakespeare festivals in America; *quarto* offers practical advice on working in the field and a host of other ongoing features including "Weird William," "Shakespearean Snippets," and "Season of Shakespeare." Published by the Shakespeare Theatre Association of America (STAA), *quarto* is available to STAA associate members. Check the Web site for membership information.

STAGE DIRECTIONS

www.stage-directions.com

Stage Directions magazine focuses on production planning and implementation; theater resources; theater book, CD, and play reviews; theater profiles; and many other areas of the theater. Check the Web site to delve in or for subscription information.

THEATER MAGAZINE and TECHNICAL BRIEF

www.yale.edu/drama/publications

Theater Magazine is described by playwright Tony Kushner as "an indispensable publication for anyone seriously concerned with the art of theater in the world today." The magazine focuses "primarily, but not exclusively, on experimental theater—American and international—and theater that touches on political and cultural debates." Check out the Web site for subscription information or back issues.

Technical Brief, a publication of the Yale School of Drama Technical Design and Production Department, is a self-proclaimed "indispensable publication for technical managers in theater. Written by professionals for professionals, its purpose is simple: communication." Check the Web site for subscription information.

VARIETY

www.variety.com

Variety has covered film, television, international entertainment, and myriad other areas of show business since 1905. *Variety* prides itself on "timely, credible and straightforward news and analysis." Check the Web site to investigate or for subscription information.

10 WEB SITES
TO OPEN UP YOUR
WEB WORLD

AMAZON

www.amazon.com

Everyone knows this Web site, but few understand what a great resource it can be for theater professionals. The site offers quick script mailings and "how to" book purchases, out-of-print books and theater biographies, inexpensive used books, sections where theater books and magazines are rated, and quick links to what books theater people are buying. Check it out!

AMERICANTHEATER WEB

www.americantheaterweb.com

The AmericanTheater Web site invites you to browse a database of over 3,000 theaters and 7,000 productions. The Web site menu directs visitors to daily clippings from papers throughout the country and announcements about theater throughout the United States, and includes callboards and chat rooms.

BACKSTAGEJOBS

BackstageJobs.com

This free job listing service for behind-the-scenes positions in the "live entertainment industry" strives to detail information on "everything but acting."

CULTUREVULTURE

www.culturevulture.net/Theater/TheaterIndex.htm

This "somewhat haphazard and pronouncedly idiosyncratic sharing of matters cultural" lists theaters and productions throughout the US.

CURTAIN RISING

www.curtainrising.com

Curtain Rising offers 8,100 links to live theater, organizing the connections by touring companies, cities, states, Shakespeare Festivals, and live theater around the world. A quick, dandy resource!

EPERFORMER

www.eperformer.com

This national Web site profiles theaters and provides many links to pertinent information related to theater training and industry news, but the audition notices were wildly out of date the last time we checked.

PLAYBILL

www.playbill.com

Playbill magazine has served theater audiences since 1884. Today *Playbill*'s Web site offers listings for Broadway, Off-Broadway, regional, tours, London, summer stock, international news, ongoing features and statistics, and job listings. Check the Web site to delve in or for member services.

ROSS REPORTS

www.rossreports.com

Ross Reports Online offers entertainment industry listings of casting directors and agents with downloading features to create your own mailing labels. Subscriptions range in price. Check the Web site for details.

STAGEAGENT

www.stageagent.com

Focusing on dramas, musicals, and operas, StageAgent is a Web service dedicated to performers and producers, and endeavors to provide "useful information for the people who make theater magic happen." For more information, e-mail info@stageagent.com or check out the Web site.

ARTSLYNX INTERNATIONAL ARTS RESOURCE

www.artslynx.org/theatre/jobs.htm

This marvelous site lists jobs in multiple theater areas including acting, design, drama therapy, fight direction, education, production, stage management, and technical theatre.

10 CHALLENGING BOOKS TO POWER YOUR ACTING CAREER

ACTING FOR THE CAMERA: REVISED EDITION by Tony Barr
Regional theater may be the place to work, but film and television is a way to make money to subsidize your classical repertory career. The *Los Angeles Times* calls Tony Barr's writings "A first-class book for the beginner and refreshing review for any pro." New York: HarperPerennial, 1997.

ACTING PROFESSIONALLY by Robert Cohen
A straightforward guide to the business of acting, offering counsel on actor training approaches, career positioning, finding an agent, auditioning, interviewing, and making long-range career decisions. New York: McGraw-Hill, 2004.

AN ACTOR BEHAVES: FROM AUDITION TO PERFORMANCE by Tom Markus
The title says it all and producer/director Tom Markus has a witty, wonderful way of speaking the truth, spinning a yarn, and sharing a life in the theater. New York: Samuel French, 1992.

AN ACTOR SUCCEEDS by Terrance Hines and Suzanne Vaughan
Interviews with casting directors, writers, managers, accountants, publicists, agents, and attorneys make this a unique book full of actor tools and specialized advice. New York: Samuel French, 1990.

AUDITION: EVERYTHING AN ACTOR NEEDS TO KNOW TO GET THE PART by Michael Shurtleff
Over 20 years old and still useful! New York: Bantam Books, 1980.

AUDITIONING: AN ACTOR-FRIENDLY GUIDE by Joanna Merlin with a foreword by Harold Prince
Award-winning casting director, actor, and educator Joanna Merlin covers acting choices, the audition space, and comprehensive instruction on how actors can improve their auditions—this is my students' favorite! New York: Vintage, 2001.

MICHAEL CAINE—ACTING IN FILM: AN ACTOR'S TAKE ON MOVIE MAKING
Movies are being made all over America—maybe even near a regional theater in your neighborhood! This popular film actor's overview on the movies is worth reading if you are contemplating a trip to Hollywood or anywhere where movies are made. (Also available as a CD.) New York: Applause, 2000.

RESPECT FOR ACTING by Uta Hagen
Uta Hagen's profound book offers readers insights into the passion, joy, and craft of acting. New York: Wiley, 1973.

SANFORD MEISNER ON ACTING by Sanford Meisner
A founding member of the Actors Studio (with Lee Strasberg, Stella Adler, and Harold Clurman), Meisner developed his own unique lessons based on his understandings of Stanislavski, and influenced theater training in profound ways. New York: Vintage, 1987.

THE BACK STAGE ACTOR'S HANDBOOK: THE HOW-TO AND WHO-TO CONTACT REFERENCE FOR ACTORS, SINGERS, AND DANCERS (FOURTH EDITION) Compiled and Edited by Sherry Eaker
Back Stage editor Sherry Eaker draws on her vast network of writers and her immense personal experience to cover everything from résumés, headshots, negotiations, voice-overs, jingles, soaps, radio drama, commercials, children's theater, cabarets, stand-up comedy, film, theme parks, showcases, touring, and most every other area of the theater. New York: Back Stage Books, 2004.

10 BOUNTIFUL BOOKS ON DIRECTING, DESIGN, PRODUCING, AND PRODUCTION

A DIRECTOR PREPARES: SEVEN ESSAYS ON ART AND THEATER by Anne Bogart
A thought-provoking treatise on creating theater, by the artistic director of the SITI Company, an ensemble-based theater company that the author founded with Tadashi Suzuki. New York: Routledge, 2001.

A SENSE OF DIRECTION by William Ball
It may be out of print, but it's worth tracking down on the used-book market. It is indeed a rare book as it represents the life's work of one of America's theater pioneers: William Ball, founder and general director of the acclaimed American Conservatory Theatre (ACT) in San Francisco. New York: Drama Book Publishers, 1984.

BACKWARDS AND FORWARDS: A TECHNICAL MANUAL FOR READING PLAYS
by David Ball
Simply put, reading this short text will help you to analyze scripts, understand playwrights, and succeed as a director, actor, or producer. Carbondale, Illinois: Southern Illinois University Press, 1998.

HOW TO RUN A THEATER: A WITTY, PRACTICAL AND FUN GUIDE TO ARTS MANAGEMENT by Jim Volz
"Required reading for anyone working in the field of arts management—be they artists or managers," writes actress-choreographer-educator-manager Suzanne Celentano in the international *Arts Management Network Newsletter*. TCG's Ben Cameron called it, "A joy, not a chore, to read!" New York: Back Stage Books, 2005.

LIFE IS A CONTACT SPORT: TEN GREAT CAREER STRATEGIES THAT WORK
by Ken Kragan and Jefferson Graham

Personal manager, television producer, talent adviser, and supreme negotiator, Ken Kragen has been called "the most successful behind-the-scenes operator in show business." This book outlines his strategies for career success, and it's brilliant. New York: William Morrow, 1994.

MANAGEMENT AND THE ARTS by William J. Byrnes

This book offers an excellent overview of how the arts are structured, with marvelous tools for budgeting, fund-raising, financial management, personnel management, and arts organization with career-planning advice and examples. Burlington, Massachusetts: Focal Press, 2003.

MY LIFE IN ART by Konstantin Sergeevich Stanislavski

This wise book penned by one of the theater's great men ranks right up there with the author's three other books that should be on your bookshelf for ongoing reference: *An Actor Prepares, Building a Character, Creating a Role.* New York: Theatre Arts Books, 1996.

THE ARTISTIC HOME: DISCUSSIONS WITH ARTISTIC DIRECTORS OF AMERICA'S INSTITUTIONAL THEATRES by Todd London

First published in 1988, *The Artistic Home* still packs a punch and offers a giant dose of artistic empowerment, institutional vision, and theater history. New York: Theatre Communications Group, 1988.

THE DRAMATIC IMAGINATION: REFLECTIONS AND SPECULATIONS ON THE ART OF THEATRE by Robert Edmond Jones

This is the man who helped countless theater artists discover the importance of theatrical design. Scenery and lighting would never be the same. New York: Theatre Arts Books, 1969.

THE EMPTY SPACE: A BOOK ABOUT THE THEATRE: DEADLY, HOLY, ROUGH, IMMEDIATE by Peter Brook

Brook's 1968 book is a theater classic—read it and find out why—it might change the way you view the theater. New York: Touchstone, 1996.

10 LARGEST AMERICAN CITIES IN ORDER OF SIZE*

If you are planning a career in the theater, doesn't it make sense to go where the people are . . . or at least where there are potential audiences? If only it were that easy! With that strategy, no one would ever have created a theater in the tiny towns of Ashland, Oregon (Oregon Shakespeare Festival); Stratford, Canada (The Stratford Festival); or the midsize city of Montgomery, Alabama (Alabama Shakespeare Festival) where over 1.2 million people attended productions last year! Marvelous theaters have turned up in unlikely places (Hailey, Idaho; Creede, Colorado; Rochester, New York; West Liberty, Ohio; Jackson, Mississippi; Anchorage, Alaska; Skokie, Illinois; and Fish Creek, Wisconsin-to name a few).

The US population increase between 1990 and 2000 was the largest in American history, with the West growing the fastest and the South reaching 100 million people. All states increased in population, Nevada most rapidly (thanks to Las Vegas), and the majority of Americans were living in the 10 most populous states.

The 2000 census counted 281.4 million people in the United States, a 13.2 percent increase from the 1990 Census population of 248.7 million. Eight of the 10 largest cities in 2000 gained population in the 1990s (while Philadelphia and Detroit declined in size). New York remained the country's largest city with over 8 million people. Phoenix is hot in more ways than one—up by 34 percent over the decade.

* Source: Census Bureau, July 1, 2004, Estimates

City and State	Population April 1, 1990	Population April 1, 2000	Change Number	%
New York, NY	7,322,564	8,008,278	685,714	9.4
Los Angeles, CA	3,485,398	3,694,820	209,422	6
Chicago, IL	2,783,726	2,896,016	112,290	4
Houston, TX	1,630,553	1,953,631	323,078	19.8
Philadelphia, PA	1,585,577	1,517,550	-68,027	-4.3
Phoenix, AZ	983,403	1,321,045	337,642	34.3
San Diego, CA	1,110,549	1,223,400	112,851	10.2
Dallas, TX	1,006,877	1,188,580	181,703	18
San Antonio, TX	935,933	1,144,646	208,713	22.3
Detroit, MI	1,027,974	951,270	-76,704	-7.5

Source: U.S. Census Bureau, Census 2000; 1990 Census,
Population and Housing Unit Counts, United States (1990 CPH-2-1).

The 1990s was the first decade since the 1930s that New York City led in city population growth; Los Angeles was the leader in each of the decades from the 1940s through the 1990s (except for the 1970s, when Houston reigned supreme).

In 2005, San Jose replaced Detroit in the top ten and San Antonio outgrew Dallas to claim the eighth-largest city spot. As a June 29, 2005, *USA Today* report indicates, key factors in recent city growth trends have to do with changing immigration patterns (big-city housing costs are no longer a bargain) and "high housing costs in cosmopolitan cities that have almost no vacant land for construction." Conversely, "smaller less glamorous places have plenty of room to grow."

New York

There's nowhere on earth quite like the Big Apple, but it's hard to know where to start if you decide on NYC as your home base. Here's one fine resource to consider: The Alliance of Resident Theatres/New York, founded in 1972, includes around 400 not-for-profit theaters "who serve over 6 million theatergoers annually, constitute the single largest source of new work entering the American repertory, and have produced 15 winners of the Pulitzer Prize for Drama." The Web site, www.offbroadwayonline.com, is the "official Web site of Off Broadway" and lists internships and not-for-profit jobs in its online "Career Center."

Of course, there are these other theaters known as "Broadway theaters," and www.broadway.com is an excellent site for online theater ticketing, editorial coverage of theater events, interviews with actors and playwrights, theater reviews, and video features. Broadway.com also offers current box office results, show synopses, credits and biographies, and an in-depth Tony Awards area. The League of American Theaters and Producers sponsors the "official Web site of Broadway," www.livebroadway.com, which offers dozens of links detailing the history, productions, and commercial supporters of the Broadway theatre. If these sites don't answer your questions, head to the bookstore and pickup a few of the 10 Challenging Books to Power Your Acting Career (mentioned on page 130) or Google "Broadway Theater" and you'll have your choice of over 41,500,000 other Web sites.

Los Angeles

There's an amazing array and seemingly endless stream of world premieres, experimental theater, reinvented classical theater, musical theater, and straightforward drama on Los Angeles stages. Over two hundred theaters are operating at any given time in the Los Angeles area. Unfortunately, only a few pay a living wage and a lot of the theater is miserable, although many hold out the promise of résumé building, professional development, Hollywood networking, and/or sitcom heaven.

There are institutional theaters (The Geffen Playhouse, Mark Taper Forum, Pasadena Playhouse, Ahmanson, etc.) and there are "membership theaters" (nearly four dozen theaters whose company members generally pay dues for special services and to defray producing expenses), including The Antaeus Company, the Celtic Arts Center, Company of Angels, Knightsbridge Theatre, Theatre Banshee, Sacred Fools Theater Company, Son of Semele Ensemble, and Theatre of Note, to name a few. Helping to sort through the morass of theaters is the LA Stage Alliance (www.lastagealliance.com), which ably serves the Los Angeles performing arts community by increasing advocacy, awareness, and audience attendance on behalf of the 210 performing arts organizations in Los Angeles County. The organization has advocacy and ticket services and offers student and individual memberships. Member organizations span the distance from Ventura to La Mirada, California.

Chicago

The Midwest seems to have opened its arms and embraced aspiring theater producers, actors, and craftspeople, as more than 250 theaters representing a wide range of artistic ambitions and play-filled dreams exist in the Chicago area. There are the giants in town (the Goodman Theater, Chicago Shakespeare Theater on the Navy Pier, the Court Theatre, Northlight Theatre, Victory Gardens Theater, Steppenwolf Theatre Company, etc.) But theaters also surface every season, including Dog and Pony (2005), Congo Square Theatre (2000), The Hypocrites (1997), and About Face Theatre (1996). Founded in 1979, the League of Chicago Theatres (www.chicagoplays.com) works to promote awareness and visibility for live theater in the Chicago area and "provides services that strengthen the operations of more than 170 member theaters." *PerformInk* also provides online and in-print news on the theater industry in Chicago (www.performink.com) and *The Reader* is a good print source for theater news and auditions. All of these resources can serve as a good starting point for your research and potential move to the Windy City.

One of Chicago's most successful producers, the Goodman Theatre's Roche Schulfer, explains it this way:

> In Chicago, people not only believe that the arts are the fabric of society, they put their money where their mouth is as audience members, patrons and advocates. All of that makes Chicago a great place to start a new theater company. Relatively speaking, space, audiences, press coverage and money are available. The League of Chicago Theatres has created a very collaborative atmosphere among local producers. This is particularly true because the membership embraces Equity, non-Equity, not-for-profit, commercial, and educational theaters. As a result more and more young people are coming to Chicago to start theaters. Some may last only a few years but the long term success stories are well known: Steppenwolf, Victory Gardens and Chicago Shakespeare among many others were created out of whole cloth by the imagination of artists.

Houston

The big oil city of Houston has diversified over the years and the arts have generally prospered. The Houston Theater District Web site (www.houstontheaterdistrict.org) offers links to performance calendars and the big guys in town, including the Alley Theatre, Theatre Under the Stars, the Houston Grand Opera, Broadway in Houston, and Uniquely Houston (dedicated to nurturing small and mid-sized arts groups including theaters). Theatreport (www.theatreport.com) is a dandy online theater service with free registration, area theater news, job listings, audition notices, a theater directory, newsletters, polls, and forums to help you get the scoop from area residents and professionals. Along with the Alley and the large musical theaters, The Houston Shakespeare Festival, Stages Repertory Theater, Infernal Bridegroom Productions, The Ensemble Theater, Main Street Theater, Actor's Theater, Actor's Workshop, A.D. Players, Radio Music Theater, The Company Onstage, Country Playhouse, Theater Southwest, Theater Suburbia, and Curtains offer diverse employment or, at least, interview or audition opportunities.

Philadelphia

The "City of Brotherly Love" features more than Independence Hall, the Liberty Bell, over 90 museums, colonial churches, row houses, the 76ers, and history simply oozing from the streets. It may be hard to focus on just your career in Philadelphia, but the best place to start might be the Theatre Alliance of Greater Philadelphia (www.theatrealliance.org) as it provides member programs and services and lists jobs, auditions, discount tickets, and area news. You can also e-mail questions to info@theatrealliance.org. And check out the Greater Philadelphia Cultural Alliance at www.philaculture.org.

If you really want to plunge in, you can pick up Irvin R. Glazer's record of 813 theaters constructed in Philadelphia since 1724, *Philadelphia Theatres, A–Z*, but for a look at what's happening today, stick with the Theatre Alliance or the Philadelphia Theatre Web site at www.philadelphia.com/theater. The Walnut Street Theatre, the Wilma Theater, the Philadelphia Theatre Company, the Arden Theatre Company, and the Prince Music Theater may offer the best audition and employment bets, but there's plenty of other theater in and around town, including Act II Playhouse, Brat Productions, Azuka Theatre Collective, The Brick Theatre, Bristol Riverside Theatre, Bushfire Theatre of the Performing Arts, 1812 Productions, Freedom Repertory Theatre, Hunger Theatre, McCarter Theatre Center for the Performing Arts, Merriam Theater, People's Light and Theatre Company, The Philadelphia Shakespeare Festival, Philadelphia Theatre Company, Pig Iron Theatre Company, Random Acts of Theater, Inc., Society Hill Playhouse, and Venture Theatre.

Phoenix

It's more than one of the fastest-growing retirement centers in the United States! While discovering Phoenix's pioneering beginnings at the Museum of History, the fabulous Native American exhibits at the Heard Museum, and the must-see Museo Chicano, you can be planning your next career move before you take the educational "First Friday Art Walk." The Arizona Commission on the Arts (www.azarts.gov) has a well-organized Web site and support system that lists opportunities, tools, programs, theaters, and arts organizations in the state (including Phoenix, of course), and links to all of the theater Web sites. You can also e-mail: info@azarts.gov.

The unique and well-respected Arizona Theatre Company, founded in 1966, certainly leads the way as a major LORT theater (profiled elsewhere in this book), the Actors Theatre of Phoenix (founded in 1985), "strives to be a major voice in the cultural conversation of the Valley of the Sun," and the Phoenix Theatre (1920) describes itself as "the oldest arts institution in the State of Arizona and one of the oldest continuously operating arts organizations in the country." There's also the Arizona Jewish Theatre Company, the Arizona Opera Company, the Black Theatre Troupe, Inc., the Great Arizona Puppet Theater, the Improbable Theatre Company, and more theaters on the horizon.

San Diego

There's a reason that San Diego is the seventh-largest city in America. It's hard to resist the sun, the beaches, the culture, the museums, the zoo, and the easygoing lifestyle of southern California. The venerable theater The Old Globe, built for $20,000 as part of the California Pacific International Exposition in Balboa Park, has been around since 1935 and is profiled elsewhere in this book. San Diego Repertory Theatre, founded in 1976, is also a major theater force in the city. Located in historic Horton Plaza, the company operates two theaters as a multi-cultural, multi-disciplinary arts complex. Another theater known to pack a punch is the Sledgehammer Theatre, founded in 1986.

Two strong sources of information are the San Diego Performing Arts League (www.sandiegoperforms.com) and the SD Theatre Scene (www.sdtheatrescene.com). The latter lists auditions and employment opportunities, and offers a "Who's Who in San Diego Theatre," play listings, theater listings, and a host of other handy information and contacts for fifty or so theater companies, including the Asian American Rep, Backyard Productions, Black Rabbit, Center Stage Players, Cygnet Theatre, Full Circle Theatre, Lamb's Players Theatre, Nonsense Productions, N Park Vaudeville, OnStage Playhouse, Peter Pan Jr. Theater, Playwrights Project, Poorplayers Theatre, Women's Rep, and Instant Theatre. Of course, the award-winning La Jolla Playhouse and artistic director Des McAnuff (original director of *The Who's Tommy* and *Big River*) are just up the coast.

If you are contemplating a move to or a career in San Diego, check out www.sandiegoplaybill.com, which lists over 100 theaters stretching from Carlsbad to Oceanside and beyond.

San Antonio

A crossroads for the Wild West and a fascinating blending of Native Americans, Germans, Old Mexico, and the Deep South, San Antonio welcomes nearly 20 million annual visitors for the culture, the River Walk, the food, the Spurs, the missions, the largest Mexican marketplace outside of Mexico (Market Square), and, of course, The Alamo. The gorgeous Majestic Theatre, built in 1929, and the Charline McCombs Empire Theatre, built in 1913 (with arts roots dating back to 1879), are used as Broadway tour houses, etc. The Office of Cultural Affairs for the City of San Antonio supports arts and cultural organizations, individual artists, and community groups, and has a helpful Web site (www.sanantonio.gov/art/website/dir_theater.asp) that lists services, arts groups, calendars, and other information pertinent to your research.

Area theaters include the Actor's Theatre of San Antonio at the Woodlawn Theatre, Alamo Street Theatre, Alameda Theater, Carver Cultural Center, Guadalupe Theater, Harlequin Dinner Theatre, Sheldon Vexler Theatre, Josephine Theater, Jump-Start Performance Co., The Magik Children's Theatre, San Antonio Living History Association, San Pedro Playhouse, Spotlight Theatre & Arts Group, and Steven Stoli's Playhouse. The San Antonio Theatre Coalition, (www.satheatre.com), will be a terrific asset if you are considering San Antonio. The coalition shares audition information, season listings, maps to theaters, and a lot of other information. Check out the Web site or e-mail satheatre@satheatre.com. The Web site provides detailed information and links to more than 30 of member theaters.

Dallas

Currently the ninth-largest city in America, Dallas is #1 in Texas as a visitor destination spot and the 384 square miles of rolling prairie have been developed into a sophisticated, cosmopolitan Southwest wonder. Margo Jones started her theater here and helped launch the whole regional theater movement. She wanted it to always stay current, so the theater's name changed annually (Theatre '47, Theatre '48, Theatre '49—get the picture?). Read "A Brief History of Regional Theater in America" on page 39 for the longer story! The Dallas Theater Center (page 216) and Dallas Children's Theater (page 312) are the old stalwarts and are mentioned elsewhere in this book. The

Kitchen Dog Theatre, founded in 1990, and the Undermain Theatre, founded in 1984, have had a local impact, while Dallas is also home to a surprising array of new theaters, including four companies that have surfaced in the new millennium: Uptown Players, (2001), Contemporary Theatre of Dallas (2002), Second Thought Theatre (2003), and the Classical Acting Company (2003).

A great place to start your research is The Dallas Theatre League (www.dallastheatreleague.com), a professional association of all kinds of theaters. It encourages "cooperation between theaters and artists to promote common interests and better business methods; as well as to celebrate the expansive diversity of the Dallas theater community . . ." The League provides information on health insurance, performance calendars, theater companies, and direct links to more than 30 theaters, including Act I Productions, Risk Theater Initiative, Blacken Blues: Theater of African American Life, KD Studios, Rover Dramawerks, Lyric Stage, Shakespeare Festival of Dallas, Echo Theatre, Pegasus Theatre, ProgreXssive Arts Productions, Wing Span Theatre Company, and It's About Time Productions.

San Jose

It's not a bedroom community for San Francisco anymore. San Jose is a charming, progressive, coffeehouse-on-every-corner California city that's overshadowed by the Silicon Valley folks who have driven up housing prices astronomically. The computer boom has propelled San Jose into number 10 on the 2005 census list and it's a great city (if you can afford to live there).

Founded in 1980, the San Jose Repertory Theatre is home to a wonderfully designed theater, brilliantly run by artistic director Timothy Near. To research other theaters, Arts Council Silicon Valley (www.artscouncil.org) is a fine resource, listing more than 130 small- to mid-size arts organizations and artists countywide. There's also the Artsopolis Web site (www.artsopolis.com), which bills itself as "All Arts. Online. Anytime." It's definitely worth a look.

San Jose area theaters include the ABC Theatre Company, Actors Theatre Center (Sunnyvale), Affordable Theater (Los Altos), American Musical Theatre of San Jose, Belmont Professional Actor's Conservatory & Theatre (Belmont), Black Canvas Theatre Productions, Center Stage Productions, Children's Musical Theater San Jose, City Lights Theater Company, Company One, Contemporary Asian Theatre Scene, Dimension Performing Arts, Easy Street Theatre Company, Enad, Jaliya Inc., Teatro Visión, Tabard Theatre Company, Tabia African-American Theatre Ensemble, The National Puppet Theatre, ZigZag Rail Road Theatre Company, and the Mostly Irish Theatre Company, to name a few of the 90 or so theaters in the area.

10 OF THE FRIENDLIEST AMERICAN THEATER CITIES FOR YOUR CONSIDERATION

First of all, let's note that this is a wildly subjective list and that, as the regional theater history section of this book points out, great theater can happen virtually anywhere. Your best opportunities may be in the theaters closest to your home while your heart may yearn for theater companies in more exotic American cities such as Boulder, Colorado; Honolulu, Hawaii; Sedona, Arizona; Lenox, Massachusetts; Hilton Head Island, South Carolina; or Horse Cave, Kentucky! The important point is to research the American theater, keep your options open, and network like crazy. Here's a start on your research.

Atlanta, Georgia

Atlanta is generally the epitome of Southern hospitality, but don't let all the graciousness lull you—the ever-evolving downtown area can be dangerous, traffics snarls to a crawl during busy times of day, and all that fried food can wreak havoc with your cholesterol count. Still, the home of *Gone with the Wind* boasts affordable housing and a diverse and ambitious theater scene. The Atlanta Coalition of Performing Arts (www.atlantaperforms.com) comprises nearly 150 groups and almost 400 individual members. The Web site lists job openings, training programs, auditions, events, and performances.

The Alliance Theatre Company (detailed in Part V of this book) is the major LORT theater in town, while Georgia Shakespeare Festival, 7 Stages, The Shakespeare Tavern, Actor's Express, the Academy Theatre, Dad's Garage Theatre Company, the New Jomandi Productions, and Theatrical Outfit all have substantive and impressive artistic histories and visions. All told, in the area are over 80 theater operations, a lot of community theater, interesting family theater, thriving university theater, and a compelling spectrum of culturally diverse theaters.

Austin, Texas

Forbes Magazine has listed Austin as the third-best place for singles in America; *Men's Journal* deemed it the fourth-smartest city in America, Child.com listed it 27th in the "best cities for families" category, and *Sperlings BestPlaces* listed Austin 32nd in its list of the top fiscally fit places to live. How can you go wrong? Austin is the state capital of Texas and dang proud of it!

So where do you go to find out about the theater scene? The Austin Circle of Theaters (www.acotonline.org) is a nonprofit arts service group that's been helping theaters and theater folks since 1974. It provides marketing, ticketing, career information, e-mail updates to members, and hosts Austin's premiere theater industry awards event: the annual B. Iden Payne Awards.

The Rude Mechanicals may be the best known of the Austin groups but there are many others, including Austin Cabaret Theater, Austin Children's Theater Festival, Austin Playhouse, Austin Scottish Rite Theater, Austin ScriptWorks, Austin Shakespeare Festival, Austin Theater Alliance, Austin TheaterWorks!, Biscuits & Gravy Productions, Blue Theatre, Championship Theatre Group, Coda Theatre, Hyde Park Theatre, Mainline Theatre Project, OnstageTheater Company, One World Theater, Oracle Theatre Company, Salvage Vanguard Theater, Teatro Humanidad, Teatro Vivo, Theater Action Project, and the Zachary Scott Theater Center to name a few. To help with your research, About Austin Texas (www.austin.about.com/od/theater) is a good way to get a feel for the area.

Boston, Massachusetts, and Surrounding Areas

With so many historical stories of adventure on the streets of Boston, it's a wonder anyone goes to the theater. With the Boston Harbor, immigrant trails, freedom trails, the Black Heritage Trail, live renditions of the Battle of Bunker Hill, battleships, and over a hundred museums and attractions, you may have to work a bit to discover Boston's quality stages (such as Huntington Theatre Company, Boston Theatre Works, and The Lyric Stage Company of Boston) or nearby stages in Cambridge (including Harvard's American Repertory Theatre and The Shúgán Theatre Company). The world-renowned Williamstown Theatre Festival, founded in 1954, is also nearby, The Berkshire Theatre Festival has provided fond theater memories for Stockbridge visitors since 1928, and The Monomoy Theatre has been producing in Chatham/Cape Cod for almost 50 years.

StageSource (www.stagesource.org), the Alliance of Theatre Artists and Producers, is definitely worth checking out, as it hosts regional auditions and job expos, posts position openings, provides group health insurance for freelance theater artists, maintains headshot/résumé files, and publishes a fine resource guide to the theater community of Greater Boston. In the alliance's own words, "Theater, film and casting companies get access to thousands of theater artists and to support services, audience development, advocacy . . . theater performers, directors, playwrights, designers, technicians, and administrators get access to programs for professional and aspiring theater artists including access to job information, networking, resources, and more!" Since 1975, ArtsBoston (www.artsboston.org), a nonprofit audience development organization, has served as a collective voice for Boston's diverse arts community and growing audiences. ArtsBoston lists over 90 theaters on its Web site, ranging from ACT Roxbury, Actors' Shakespeare Project, Actors' Workshop, American Classics, and Animus Ensemble to the Blue Hair Troupe, Boston Playwrights' Theatre, Centre Stage Theatre, Chelsea Theater Works, Ubiquity Stage, and the Underground Railway Theater.

Denver, Colorado

Colorado is a heavenly spot for hiking, climbing, fishing, and sports, but is it really a place to pursue a career in the theater? You bet! The Denver Center Theatre Company is the Tony Award–winner in town, but much more is in the Great Denver Area that includes Arvada, Boulder, Golden, Fort Collins, Westminster, and a multitude of growing communities that crave the gorgeous backdrop of the Rocky Mountains. There are dozens of companies to approach, including the kooky Buntport Theatre, the Community Artists' Theatre, Curious Theatre Company, Denver Civic Theatre, Hunger Artists Ensemble Theatre, Impulse Theatre, Paragon Theatre, Rattlebrain Theatre Company, Su Teatro, The Bug Theatre, Arvada Center for the Arts and Humanities Theatre, and the Germinal Stage.

"OnStage" is the *Rocky Mountain News* overview on area theater and it can be accessed at www.rockymountainnews.com/drmn/on_stage. It's filled with news features and helpful information including play listings. The *Denver Post*'s theater news (www.denverpost.com/theater) is also clever, comprehensive, and enjoyable to read, and should be a part of your research if you plan to make the Rocky Mountain area your new home. Denver area theater receives a nice overview on the Denver.com Web site (www.denver.com/theater), and Colorado Arts Net (www.coloradoarts.net) lists dozens of theaters in the metropolitan Denver/Boulder/Evergreen area, providing addresses, phone numbers, and direct links to Web sites. It is a very helpful and comprehensive site. Finally, Artslynx Colorado (www.artslynx.org/colorado) provides instant access to over 130 arts groups in Colorado and can save you tons of research time. Boulder, Colorado, is just down the road and home to the Colorado Shakespeare Festival, the Nomad Theater, the Upstart Crow Theater Company, and others.

Minneapolis, Minnesota

If you travel to Minneapolis, you might think that you're in the New York of the Midwest—it's cold in the winter and the people talk funny! No, no, I mean the great selection of theaters, the four distinct seasons, the terrific shopping (the Mall of America), and the beauty of the city. Minneapolis.org (www.minneapolis.org) offers a fine overview on theater in the land of the lakes, noting that the city has more than 30 venues and nearly 100 theater groups. The mighty Guthrie Theater and much-revered The Children's Theatre Company reign in Minneapolis, but few folks realize how many other theaters grace the Minneapolis–St. Paul area.

Curtain Rising (www.curtainrising.com), a national Web site, offers a good starter list of 70 or more theaters in the Minneapolis area. These include 15 Head Theatre Lab, CalibanCo Theatre, Council of Doom Theatre Co., Cromulent Shakespeare Company, Fifty Foot Penguin Theater, Great American History Theatre, Gremlin Theatre, GTC Dramatic Dialogues, Illusion Theater, The Jungle Theater, Minnesota Fringe Theater and Performance Festival, Minnesota Jewish Theatre, Mixed Blood Theatre Company, Pangea World Theatre, Penumbra Theatre, Pigs Eye Theatre Company, Teatro del Pueblo, Theatre de la Jeune Lune, Theater Latte Da, Theater Mu, and Theatre Unbound. The City of Minneapolis Arts Commission helps foster the development of the arts and lists arts options and theater links at www.ci.minneapolis.mn.us/leisure.

Orange County, California

If you're independently wealthy or don't mind living with four, five, or six of your best buddies, Orange County is a ripe spot for homegrown theater nestled between the ocean, the mountains and the quickly vanishing orange groves, strawberry farms, and horse ranches. The median housing prices are among the highest in the nation, you must have a car to survive, and the area has more than its fair share of earthquakes, fires, and mudslides. Still, if you can find a spot with one of America's premier theaters, South Coast Repertory (Costa Mesa), or with one of America's most savvy, producing theaters, the Laguna Playhouse (Laguna Beach), you might be able to make ends meet. Otherwise, artistic and production opportunities abound in the myriad 99-seat and smaller theaters where few get paid but most everyone is mightily entertained.

The industrious Arts Orange County (www.artsoc.org) will help open up communications to the theaters with directories, workshops, advocacy, and a friendly, caring core of diligent, determined, and intelligent executives. There's the Vanguard Theatre, The Maverick Theatre, and Hunger Artists Theatre Company, Fullerton Civic Light Opera and others in Fullerton, Grand Central Theatre and the Rude Guerrilla Theater in Santa Ana, Shakespeare Orange County in Garden Grove, and over 50 other producing theaters in the county. Many artists make ends meet working at Disneyland, Knotts Berry Farm, or one of the other higher-budget entertainment venues in the area and create their own work at a friendly neighborhood theater during their down time.

Orlando, Florida

This area blossomed when Walt Disney World emerged and a host of other entertainment parks, arts-related businesses, and theater people followed (along with traffic, pollution, rising real estate, and crime). Still, despite the heat and humidity, Orlando is a quick drive to the Gulf of Mexico and the Atlantic Ocean and an ever-growing home to myriad theater groups including the very hot Orlando–UCF Shakespeare Festival and The Orlando Repertory Theatre. Of course, the remarkable Cirque du Soleil, the reliable Disney folks, Busch Gardens, Cypress Gardens, Universal Studios Florida, Gatorland, and all the other entertainment parks offer opportunities in a vast array of performance and related fields, and the cost of living in Florida is still reasonable.

Definitely, the best place to start is the Central Florida Performing Arts Alliance (www.orlandoperforms.com), which represents individuals, theaters, and businesses, and creates publications, provides facilities, organizes workshops, and advocates on behalf of the arts. The Alliance also lists grant opportunities, workshops and classes, job announcements and casting calls, and produces Unified Auditions to attract artistic and casting directors from around Central Florida. There are over 80 theater operations of various sizes in Central Florida including the Winter Park Playhouse, Moonlight Players, LA Acting Workshop, Celebration Players, Hispanic Theatre Project, Red Moon Theatre Joint, Mother J Productions, Inc., Poison Pixie Productions, RDC Productions, Empty Spaces, Phoenix Production Company, Orlando Black Essential Theatre, Sons of Thunder Theatre Company, Empowerments Theatre, Burry Man Productions, Naked Orange Theatre Company, Orlando Theatre Project, Mad Cow Theatre Company, Titusville Playhouse, Southern Winds Theatre, Women Playwrights Initiative, and Kangagirl Productions.

The Orlando International Fringe Theatre Festival, modeled after Edinburgh, Scotland's famous festival, typically involves over 50 companies involved that offer "10 Days of Theatre, Art, Music, and Madness!" The Orlando, Florida, Guide (www.orlandofloridaguide.com) also offers a theater section and terrific links to all the wonders of the city and state.

San Francisco, California

There's an unrivaled fusion of culture, art, theater, and thrilling American history in San Francisco that is much more than Alcatraz, Chinatown, the American Conservatory Theater, and the Golden Gate Bridge.

San Francisco's nonprofit Theatre Bay Area (TBA) has been telling the story for three decades and it is a good place to start your research. TBA's mission is to unite, strengthen, and promote theater in the region and it serves more than 300 member theater companies and 2,900 individual members in the San Francisco Bay Area and Northern California. Check out the Web site (www.theatrebayarea.org) and the remarkable theater scene that surrounds one of America's most exhilarating (and expensive) cities. Of course there are theaters with a rich history, including the Magic Theatre, Inc., founded in 1967, A Traveling Jewish Theatre, founded in 1979, and nearby Berkeley Repertory Theatre, founded in 1968. The San Francisco Shakespeare Festival and California Shakespeare Theater are also major forces in the area. Berkeley Rep, the American Conservatory Theatre, California Shakespeare, and San Francisco Shakespeare are all featured in section V of this book and the Web site will open the doors to the hundreds of other avant-garde, musical, contemporary, classic, and comedy stages.

Seattle, Washington

There was a time it seemed that everyone in the theater (outside of New York anyway) wanted to move to Seattle or Chicago to launch their regional theater careers. Dozens of exciting new theaters were opening, rent and real estate were reasonable, and, with all the rehearsals and performances, prospective theater professionals thought that they would barely notice the rain. Actually, given the lakes, mountains, ocean, Starbucks, and native beauty of the area, who cares about a little rain? Soon, however, the massive influx of Californians sent real estate sky high, the actor migration to Seattle resulted in many out-of-work performers, the harsh economics threatened the financial status of many performing arts groups, and today the city may only be a great place to live versus a mind-blowing, theatrical dream world. The best way for you to check out this wet and wonderful world is to hit SeattleActor.com (www.seattleactor.com), a well-managed and attractive Web site that offers audition information, actor tips, theater links, advice on the area, reviews, and other convenient information. "From auditions to reviews, photographers to voice teachers, SeattleActor.com strives to make the most of all of the resources available on the web," states the Web site— which does it astonishingly well! Also, for everyone in the business, the City of Seattle's Office of Cultural Affairs (www2.seattle.gov/arts) is worth perusing, and its Web site links to theaters and forums and discusses arts funding and workshops. Seattle Shakespeare Company's Stephanie Shine encourages actors to go to Theatre Puget Sound (www.tpsonline.org) for bi-annual unified audition information.

Finally, Seattle Performs (www.seattleperforms.com) lists daily perform-ances, reviews, and good links to over one hundred Seattle producers and presenters, including the prestigious ACT Theatre, historic Seattle Repertory Theatre, spunky Seattle Shakespeare Company, dedicated Intiman Theatre, legendary The Empty Space Theatre, delightful Seattle Children's Theatre, and many others, ranging from the Akropolis Performance Lab and Book-It Repertory Theatre to Macha Monkey Productions, One Lump Or Two Productions, Pork Filled Players, and Printers Devil Theatre. Other companies to watch out for are The 5th Avenue Theatre Association, the Village Theatre in Issaquah, Washington Ensemble Theatre, Capital Hill Arts Center, and Theater Schmeater.

Washington, D.C.

Of course, you could spend the better part of a lifetime simply learning about the theater and related arts by visiting the National Theatre Archive, the Smithsonian, the Kennedy Center for the Performing Arts, Ford's Theatre, the Washington Area Archive of the Performing Arts, and other historical sites in the area. This is one proud, wild, busy city with a very active and engaged theater community led by some of the best artists and producers in the business. Fortunately, there are helpful groups to assist you in researching or getting settled in Washington, D.C., and one of the best is WashingtonDC.com (www.washingtondc.com/theater), which has helpful listings of everything in the city, including the theater. Both this Web site and the DC Registry (dcregistry.com/theater.html) offer quick links to many area theaters.

Established in 1982, the League of Washington Theatres (www.lowt.org) is an association of nonprofit professional theaters for the Washington metropolitan area. It supports theater and helps create audience awareness and appreciation. The league lists annual auditions, training opportunities, and provides many useful links to the community. The Arena Stage and the Shakespeare Theatre Company generally garner the most attention and theater awards and have a rich history (detailed later in this book) to back up all the kudos. Still, there's the African Continuum Theatre Co., the GALA Hispanic Theatre, Theater J, the Round House Theatre, the Folger Theatre, The Studio Theatre, the Woolly Mammoth Theatre Company, The Signature Theatre, and over 50 other theaters to research in the nation's capital.

10+ SERVICE ORGANIZATIONS

AMERICAN ALLIANCE FOR THEATRE & EDUCATION (AATE)

7475 Wisconsin Avenue, Suite 300A, Bethesda, MD 20814
PHONE: (301) 951-7977; FAX: (301) 968-0144
E-MAIL: info@aate.com
WEB SITE: www.aate.com

Theater educators and theater artists are well served by the American Alliance for Theatre & Education (AATE), the leading national professional organization for those who use drama in the classroom. Perhaps the best feature of the site for employment seekers is the resources page that details links to influential arts organizations, funding opportunities, playwriting information, professional theater for youth, professional training and universities, and more.

THE AMERICAN THEATRE WING (ATW)

570 Seventh Avenue; New York, NY 10018
PHONE: (212) 765-0606; FAX: (212) 307-1910
E-MAIL: mailbox@americantheatrewing.org
WEB SITE: www.americantheatrewing.org

ATW is dedicated to supporting excellence and education in theater and, among its many activities, the ATW supports scholarship programs, theatrically related radio and television programs, a theatre intern group, video archives of theater seminars and discussions, and the annual presentation of the Tony Awards.

NEW DRAMATISTS

424 West 44th Street, New York, NY 10036-5298
PHONE: (212) 757-6960; FAX: (212) 265-4738
E-MAIL: newdramatists@newdramatists.org
WEB SITE: www.newdramatists.org

Founded in 1949 and located in the heart of New York City's Theater District, New Dramatists is, in its own words, "the nation's oldest nonprofit center for the development of talented playwrights." A membership organization devoted to cultivating the work of playwrights, New Dramatists provides career support, offers play readings, and develops workshops to help members "fulfill their potential and make lasting contributions to the theater." Over 500 writers have benefited from more than five decades of support. In 2001, the American Theatre Wing and the League of American Theatres and Producers awarded New Dramatists with a special Tony honor for its work.

New Dramatists has over 40 current resident playwrights and provides services ranging from the *Scriptshare* program (which links playwrights with theaters and film companies across the country) to a variety of international exchange programs that foster communication with theater communities around the world. The many past members who have received Tony Awards for writing include John Patrick in 1954 for *The Teahouse of the August Moon*, Joseph Masteroff in 1967 for *Cabaret*, August Wilson in 1987 for *Fences*, and John Patrick Shanley in 2005 for *Doubt*. Among other alumni are Israel Horovitz, John Guare, William Inge, Lanford Wilson, Suzan-Lori Parks, Paula Vogel, Donald Margulies, Nilo Cruz, and Doug Wright.

Membership applications and additional information about New Dramatists is available on line at www.newdramatists.org.

New Dramatists offers full- and part-time internships that are provided with small weekly stipends. College credit may be available. Check the Web site for details.

UNITED STATES CENTER FOR THE INTERNATIONAL ASSOCIATION OF THEATER FOR CHILDREN AND YOUNG PEOPLE

Association of Theater for Children and Young People (ASSITEJ/USA)
724 Second Avenue South, Nashville, TN 37210
PHONE: (615) 254-5719; FAX: (615) 254-3255
E-MAIL: usassitej@aol.com
WEB SITE: www.assitej-usa.org

ASSITEJ/USA is the national service organization that, in its own words, promotes "the power of professional theater for young audiences through excellence, collaboration and innovation across cultural and international boundaries." The Web site lists the latest news, links, and information about its member theaters.

ASSOCIATION FOR THEATRE IN HIGHER EDUCATION (ATHE)
P.O. Box 1290, Boulder, CO 80306-1290
PHONE: (888) 284-3737, (303) 530-2167; FAX: (303) 530-2168
E-MAIL: info@athe.org
WEB SITE: www.athe.org

The Association for Theatre in Higher Education is an organization of 1,800 or so individuals and institutions that, in its own words, "provides vision and leadership for the profession and promotes excellence in theater education."

Membership dues benefits include the online newsletter *ATHENEWS*, the quarterly journal *Theatre Journal*, and a semiannual journal, *Theatre Topics*. Members of ATHE can also join one or more of 23 focus groups to communicate with other members with similar interests. An annual conference brings everyone together for professional development, workshops, seminars, and myriad sessions of importance to the field.

THE DRAMA LEAGUE
520 Eighth Avenue, Third Floor, Suite 320, New York, NY 10018
PHONE: (212) 244-9494, Outside NYC (877) NYC-PLAY; FAX: (212) 244-9191
E-MAIL: info@dramaleague.org
WEB SITE: www.dramaleague.org

With over 3,000 members, The Drama League is, in its own words, "a service organization for theater lovers interested in enhancing their understanding and experience of live theater, and . . . unparalleled training program for emerging theater artists." Member benefits include discounted Broadway, Off-Broadway, and regional theater tickets, and workshops and seminars with leading figures in the theater. The league supports new initiatives for young artists through The Directors Project, "encouraging and training young talents while providing much-needed exposure and essential connections to the professional theatrical community."

LEAGUE OF HISTORIC AMERICAN THEATRES
616 Water Street, Suite 320, Baltimore, MD 21202
PHONE: (410) 659-9533, Toll-free (877) 627-0833; FAX: (410) 837-9664
E-MAIL: info@lhat.org
WEB SITE: www.lhat.org

The League of Historic American Theatres (LHAT) has been around since 1976, and is made up of a marvelous group of folks who "appreciate the cultural and architectural heritage of historic theaters and who work locally and nationally to rehabilitate them." Theater operators, managers, preservation activists, architects, structural engineers, design and acoustical consultants, urban planners, restorationists, booking and artist management firms, fund-raising consultants, and others are involved, and the Web site offers insights into the historic theaters that produce around America. Some services, such as the membership list/directory, are benefits available only to dues-paying members, but other services are available to all. If you are seeking a career in theater management, the LHAT Job Bank may be the perfect resource for you and you can view posted listings without cost. Check the Web site for details.

NATIONAL DINNER THEATRE ASSOCIATION (NDTA)

NDTA Audition Office/Charles Carnes, 3925 Sherman Blvd., Des Moines, IA 50310
PHONE: (515) 252-1942; FAX: (515) 252-1942
E-MAIL: goodone@mac.com
WEB SITE: www.ndta.com

Founded in 1978, the NDTA holds auditions and conferences annually and, in its own words, "includes some of the top theatrical producers in the country (both union and non-union)." NDTA provides information and networking potential and holds conferences twice a year. The annual auditions are held at the spring conference with performers from across the United States.

NATIONAL ALLIANCE FOR MUSICAL THEATRE (NAMT)

520 Eighth Avenue, #301, New York, NY 10018
PHONE: (212) 714-6668; FAX: (212) 714-0469
E-MAIL: info@namt.org
WEB SITE: namt.org

Founded in 1985, NAMT is a national service organization dedicated to musical theater, with a membership that includes theater institutions, universities, and independent producers. In its own words, NAMT advances musical theater by "nurturing the creation, development, production, presentation and recognition of new musicals and classics; providing a forum for the sharing of resources and information relating to professional musical theater through communications, networking and programming; and, advocating for the imagination, diversity, and joy unique to musical theater."

NON-TRADITIONAL CASTING PROJECT, INC. (NTCP)

1560 Broadway, #1600, New York, NY 10036
PHONE: (212) 730-4750; FAX: (212) 730-4820
E-MAIL: info@ntcp.org
WEB SITE: www.ntcp.org

Created in 1986 "to address and seek solutions to the problems of racism and exclusion in film, television, and theater," NTCP serves "as an expert advocate and educational resource for full inclusion in theater, film, television, and related media. Our current focus is to increase the participation of artists of color and artists with disabilities in the industry. NTCP's aim is to achieve a theater, film, and television industry that more accurately reflects our populace; where each artist is considered on her/his merits as an individual; where the stories being told reflect our communities; and where our individual humanity and forms of expression can be celebrated."

NTCP holds conferences and provides a national resource of 3,500 actors' résumés-photographs and résumés of writers, directors, choreographers, designers, and stage managers in its Artist Files & Artist Files Online (AFO), made available to producers, directors, and casting directors. Check out the Web site for details on services.

UNITED STATES INSTITUTE FOR THEATRE TECHNOLOGY (USITT)

6443 Ridings Road, Syracuse, NY 13206-1111
PHONE: (800) 938-7488; FAX: (866) 398-7488
E-MAIL: info@office.usitt.org
WEB SITE: www.usitt.org

Founded in 1960, USITT is the association of design, production, and technology professionals in the performing arts and entertainment industry. USITT's mission is, in its own words, "to actively promote the advancement of the knowledge and skills of its members." Its over 3,600 members are from throughout the United States, Canada, and 40 other countries. The membership includes scenery, costume, sound, and lighting designers; scenery, costume, sound, and lighting technicians; properties, makeup, and special effects craftpersons; stagehands, architects, theatrical consultants, acousticians, and performing arts educators; and staff and performing arts manufacturers, suppliers, and distributors.

The USITT Annual Conference & Stage Expo attracts over 3,800 folks to a different host city each year and generally offers more than 175 sessions featuring design, technology, costume, sound, architecture, management, engineering, and production. Of particular note from a career-planning point of view, the conference offers professional development workshops and a Theatre Conference Employment Service linking employers and applicants by providing computerized job listings, posting of résumés, and scheduled interviews. Also, portfolio reviews provide members with the opportunity to meet individually with professionals in their fields to discuss their portfolios, résumés, and careers with separate sessions for scenery, lighting, costume design, costume technology, props, and technical production. Other marvelous programs include the Stage Management Mentor Project, the Student Volunteer Program, the Tech Olympics, Tech Expo and Stage Expo, and a Young Designers Forum. Check out the comprehensive Web site for conference information and member services.

10 REGIONAL/NATIONAL AUDITION AND JOB SITES

CALIFORNIA EDUCATIONAL THEATRE ASSOCIATION (CETA)

WEB SITE: www.cetaweb.org

For more than 50 years, CETA has provided opportunities in theater production, teaching and scholarship and for over 20 years, CETA has held auditions and interviews that include professional theaters, colleges and universities. This annual audition and interview opportunity for students pursuing a career in theater, television, and film is "a next step for actors and designers to meet casting directors, agents, graduate programs and theaters." Long associated with the Kennedy Center/American College Theatre Festival (KCACTF), CETA's auditions and interviews are now based in Hollywood, California, the entertainment capital of the world.

FLORIDA PROFESSIONAL THEATRES ASSOCIATION

P.O. Box 2922, West Palm Beach, FL 33402-2922
PHONE: 561-848-6231; FAX: 561-848-7291
E-MAIL: fpta2000@aol.com
WEB SITE: www.fpta.net

This statewide service organization represents professional theater, entertainment, and production companies, as well as individual theater professionals, by coordinating annual statewide auditions for professional companies looking to hire Equity and non-Equity actors and conducting professional workshops for actors and staffs of professional companies.

FPTA also puts together a statewide professional theater directory, maintains job-bank files and résumé files on theater professionals, and provides other benefits. State auditions typically include over a dozen companies that have included the Actors' Playhouse (Coral Gables), American Stage (St. Petersburg), Asolo Theatre Company (Sarasota), Caldwell Theatre

Company (Boca Raton), Florida Repertory Theatre (Fort Myers), Florida Stage (West Palm Beach), Gorilla Theatre (Tampa), Hippodrome State Theatre (Gainesville), Tampa Bay Performing Arts Center (Tampa), and The Schoolhouse Theater (Sanibel Island).

INSTITUTE OF OUTDOOR DRAMA (IOD) NATIONAL OUTDOOR DRAMA AUDITIONS

Auditions Coordinator, Institute of Outdoor Drama
1700 Martin Luther King Jr., Blvd., CB #3240, UNC-Chapel Hill, NC 27599-3240
PHONE: (919) 962-1328; FAX: (919) 962-4212
E-MAIL: outdoor@unc.edu
WEB SITE: www.unc.edu/depts/outdoor/auditions

More than 50 original plays throughout the country (based on historical events and performed where they occurred) employ 3,000 actors, singers, dancers, and technicians each summer and these auditions are a way to discover them all. The Institute of Outdoor Drama (see the IOD section on page 322) sponsors the only combined auditions bringing outdoor historical dramas, performers, and technicians to one place. Approximately 15 outdoor historical dramas from across the country typically hold auditions at the University of North Carolina at Chapel Hill for summer jobs as performers and technicians. The auditions are open to anyone 18 or older with previous theater experience. Jobs require a 9- to 12-week commitment, including 2 weeks of rehearsal. Although most jobs are non-union, some companies will hire union actors and offer contracts leading toward union membership through the Actors' Equity Association Membership Candidacy Program. Outdoor historical drama is rich in opportunities for performers and technicians to hone their skills. The productions need the expertise of stunt or combat professionals, pyrotechnicians, horseback riders, historians, and others. Staff skilled in design, installation, and maintenance of equipment for sound, electronic vocal reinforcement, special effects, and lighting are also in demand. Companies that have attended in the past include the Pennsylvania Renaissance Faire, New Mexico's *Black River Traders*, North Carolina's *Horn in the West* and *The Lost Colony*, and Ohio's *Tecumseh!* Check the Web site for additional information and applications.

MIDWEST THEATRE AUDITIONS (MWTA)

PHONE: (314) 968-6937; FAX: (314) 968-6945
E-MAIL: mwta@pop.webster.edu
WEB SITE: www.webster.edu/depts/finearts/theatre/mwta/

The MWTA auditions are Equity and non-Equity combined auditions that typically attract over 600 actors and 100 design/tech/stage management interviewees to the 3-day session. Somewhere between 50 and 70 theater companies attend the annual meeting and past attendees have included everyone from the Utah Shakespearean Festival, Wisconsin's Milwaukee Repertory Theater, and Kentucky's Stephen Foster Story to Montana's Bigfork Summer Playhouse, South Dakota's Black Hills Playhouse, Ohio's Cedar Point Live Entertainment, and Montana's Missoula Children's Theatre.

NEW ENGLAND THEATRE CONFERENCE (NETC)

New England Theatre Conference, Inc., 215 Knob Hill Drive, Hamden, CT 06518
PHONE: (617) 851-8535; FAX: (203) 288-5938
E-MAIL: mail@netconline.org
WEB SITE: www.netconline.org

The New England Theatre Conference serves Connecticut, Maine, Massachusetts, New Hampshire, Rhode Island, and Vermont; provides professional services, career development, and recognition awards; and nurtures and promotes new theater activity. Boston drama critic Elliot Norton founded NETC in 1952. Recently, 700 performers auditioned for 60 or so companies at the annual conference. NETC publications include the quarterly *NETC News*, the scholarly *New England Theatre Journal*, mailing lists, and an *Annual Directory and Resource Book*.

NORTHWEST DRAMA CONFERENCE

WEB SITE: www.kcactf.org (Click on Region VII and click again on the Web site)

The Northwest Drama Conference encourages the highest possible standards of theater throughout the Pacific Northwest and facilitates the interchange of theater groups, persons and ideas through an annual conference. Check the Web site for annual information on and downloadable applications about the conference.

ROCKY MOUNTAIN THEATRE ASSOCIATION

WEB SITE: www.rmta.net (Check the Web site for state contacts, addresses, phone numbers, and e-mail addresses.)

Star Trek's William Shatner and *All in the Family*'s Carroll O'Connor are just two of the Rocky Mountain Theatre Association members who have gone on to fame and fortune. The RMTA region includes Colorado, Idaho,

Montana, Utah, and Wyoming; and represents over 30 organizations, including high schools, colleges, universities, and theatrical businesses. There are around 1,000 members. Founded in 1951, RMTA is one of the oldest regional theater organizations in America. Students, artists, theater professionals, and others gather annually at Festivention, a convention that includes workshops, performances, competitions, scholarships, employment opportunities, and informal gatherings. Also, RMTA Scholarship Auditions are conducted for college and university scholarships, and RMTA Employment Auditions are for professional summer stock positions at theaters throughout the Rocky Mountain region.

SOUTHEASTERN THEATRE CONFERENCE (SETC)

P.O. Box 9868, Greensboro, NC 27429

PHONE: (336) 272-3645; FAX: (336) 272-8810

E-MAIL: setc@setc.org

WEB SITE: www.setc.org

SETC is the regional theater organization for the southeastern US, with a membership of 4,000. It hosts the largest theater convention in the United States, with over 4,000 attendees at the annual March convention. SETC sponsors professional auditions every spring and fall for actors, singers, and dancers. More than 1,000 companies seek performers for both summer and year-round roles at the Spring Convention, where approximately 900 actors audition. Attendees also interview for other theater positions, attend workshops and theater festivals, and network with peers, university leaders, and industry professionals. Over the years, this has been a grand place for professionals and university students to seek jobs in all areas of theater, including acting, production, management, summer internships, and apprenticeships.

Founded in 1949, SETC's member states include Alabama, Florida, Georgia, Kentucky, Mississippi, North Carolina, South Carolina, Tennessee, Virginia, and West Virginia, but participants in the auditions and activities journey from throughout America and overseas. Many professional companies return annually, including representatives from the Actors Theatre of Louisville, Alabama Shakespeare Festival, Barter Theatre, Berkshire Theatre Festival, and Georgia Shakespeare Festival to Big Fork Summer Playhouse, Williamstown Theatre Festival, Springer Opera House, North Carolina Shakespeare Festival, Naples Dinner Theatre, Walt Disney Entertainment, Universal Japan, Blue Man Group, Dixie Stampede, The Lost Colony, Mill Mountain Theatre, Santa Fe Opera, Trumpet in the Land, and Missoula Children's Theatre.

The Fall Professional Auditions in September offer employment opportunities at over 30 theater companies for 250 to 300 auditionees. The Web site provides helpful, instant links to the member companies so you can look them over prior to auditions or interviews. SETC's endowment funds sponsor approximately $15,000 annually in academic scholarships for theater students. Membership in SETC includes *Southern Theatre*, a quarterly magazine; and *Job Contact Bulletin*, a web posting of technical, academic, administrative and design positions.

STRAWHAT AUDITIONS

#315, 1771 Post Road East, Westport, CT 06880
E-MAIL: info@strawhat-auditions.com
WEB SITE: www.strawhat-auditions.com

StrawHat assists non-Equity actors and production personnel "looking to start and continue their professional careers in the theater." The StrawHat Auditions are held in New York every spring and over 750 actors and production personnel usually attend while staff from more than 40 theaters conduct interviews and auditions. Actors audition for summer seasons while potential production personnel have their résumés posted online for phone or onsite interviews. In the company's own words, over one million visitors checked out www.strawhat-auditions.com "to learn more about summer stock theaters, review the thousands of actor and technical résumés on our site and to take advantage of casting and information services. The theaters that attend the auditions produce everything from melodrama to plays, history fairs to musicals. Most are summer stock theaters, but some are regionals that run almost year round." Check the Web site for registration fees, services and additional information.

UNIFIED PROFESSIONAL THEATRE AUDITIONS (UPTA)

51 S. Cooper Street, Memphis, TN 38104
PHONE: (901) 725-0776; FAX: (901) 272-7530
E-MAIL: upta@upta.org
WEB SITE: www.upta.org

Recently, 939 registered actors and production personnel and 99 companies registered for the annual UPTA auditions that "offer you access to quality, paying theaters, as well as offering theaters access to quality talent." Michael Detroit, UPTA's audition coordinator, notes that "UPTA is a set of auditions and interviews organized for actors, production personnel, and producers so that the greatest number of quality actors and production personnel who are available year-round can be seen by quality professional theater companies. These auditions are national in scope." The theaters that attend are offering paid year-round employment, paid jobbed-in employment, or paid internships. Note the word "*paid*"! For the regular auditions, actors need to be available for employment throughout the year and meet at least one of the audition requirements (post-graduate degree, Equity or EMC Program member, previous attendee, or endorsement from UPTA or TCG member). For the pre-professional auditions, actors must have an undergraduate degree by a certain date, be available for year-round work, and have their registration signed by their university department chair.

Production personnel must be available for employment throughout the year and meet the same requirements as the actors (except substituting Equity stage manager for Equity/EMC member). See the Web site for the complete details, requirements, testimonials, and application forms. The conference is held at the long-standing (since 1969) Playhouse on the Square in Memphis, Tennessee. Past company members include everyone from the Alaska Cabin Nite Dinner Theatre, Arkansas Repertory Theatre, Minnesota's Chanhassen Dinner Theatres, and New York's Disney Theatrical Productions to Ohio's Johnny Appleseed Outdoor Drama, Montana's Missoula Children's Theatre, Colorado's Rocky Mountain Repertory Theatre, and Blowing Rock, North Carolina's Tweetsie Railroad, Inc.

10+ CITY AND SURROUNDING AREA WEB SITES

Your geographical needs, interests, and plans will determine which of the Web sites listed below will be of use to you. The Web sites detail services, programs, auditions, and interviews offered by each organization. The theater artists, educators, craftspeople, and administrators who comprise these groups have all gotten their acts together and found collaborative ways to organize their careers as well as their productions!

ATLANTA COALITION OF PERFORMING ARTS (GEORGIA)
www.atlantaperforms.com

AUSTIN CIRCLE OF THEATERS (TEXAS)
www.acotonline.org

BALTIMORE THEATRE ALLIANCE (MARYLAND)
www.baltimoreperforms.org

CENTRAL FLORIDA PERFORMING ALLIANCE
www.orlandoperforms.com

CLEVELAND THEATER COLLECTIVE (OHIO)
www.clevelandtheater.com

ILLINOIS THEATRE ASSOCIATION
www.iltheassoc.org

LEAGUE OF WASHINGTON THEATRES (WASHINGTON, D.C.)
www.lowt.org

NEW JERSEY THEATRE ALLIANCE
www.njtheatrealliance.com

OHIO THEATRE ALLIANCE
www.ohiotheatrealliance.org

SACRAMENTO AREA REGIONAL THEATRE ALLIANCE (CALIFORNIA)
www.sarta.com

THEATRE ALLIANCE OF GREATER PHILADELPHIA (PENNSYLVANIA)
www.theatrealliance.org/auditions

THEATRE AUDITIONS IN WISCONSIN
www.dcs.wisc.edu/LSA/theatre/auditions.htm

THEATRE BAY AREA (CALIFORNIA)
www.theatrebayarea.org

10+ UNIONS/ ALLIANCES/SOCIETIES/ GUILDS/AGENCIES

ACTORS' EQUITY ASSOCIATION (AEA)

National Headquarters/Eastern Region
165 West 46th Street, New York, NY 10036
PHONE: (212) 869-8530; FAX: (212) 719-9815
WEB SITE: www.actorsequity.org

Orlando
10319 Orangewood Boulevard, Orlando, FL 32821
PHONE: (407) 345-8600; FAX: (407) 345-1522

The Central Region/Chicago
125 S. Clark Street, Suite 1500, Chicago, IL 60603
PHONE: (312) 641-0393; AUDITIONS: (312) 641-0418; FAX: (312) 641-6365

The Western Region/Los Angeles
Museum Square, 5757 Wilshire Boulevard, Suite One, Los Angeles, CA 90036
PHONE: (323) 634-1750; FAX: (323) 634-1777

San Francisco
350 Sansome Street, Suite 900
San Francisco, CA 94104
PHONE: (415) 391-3838; FAX: (415) 391-0102

Actors' Equity Association is the labor union representing more than 45,000 American actors and stage managers working in the professional theater. In its own words, "Equity has negotiated minimum wages and working conditions, administered contracts, and enforced the provisions of our various agreements with theatrical employers across the country" for over

90 years. "The time-honored Equity card is the symbol of a commitment to a theatrical career and represents the highest standards and responsibilities of professionalism. Those who choose to become members implicitly pledge to represent the theater, the union, and themselves, with integrity and dignity." From the AEA Web site you can download a free brochure that describes benefits, membership, and services, or you can write to any of the above addresses. Also, the AEA Web site provides applications, contract information, and explanations of three of the most misunderstood big-city agreements, under which actors are paid "stipends" vs. "salary." These Actors' Equity Association showcase agreements include the "Los Angeles 99-Seat Plan" agreement for smaller LA County Equity–approved theaters that perform no more than six performances a week with unsalaried actors. New York City's "Basic Showcase Code" allows Equity actors to participate in approved productions without salary if the total production budget is limited to $20,000 and performances are limited to twelve within a four-week period. Tickets are limited to $15 and seating is limited to 99. The "Seasonal Showcase Code" in New York City is for nonprofit theaters with ticket prices limited to $19, seating limited to 99 seats, and varying stipends.

Most of AEA's efforts are focused on collective bargaining and negotiating appropriate salary and working conditions that simply wouldn't have been possible without the diligent work of the Equity management and membership.

AMERICAN FEDERATION OF TELEVISION AND RADIO ARTISTS (AFTRA)

National Office—New York
260 Madison Avenue, New York NY 10016-2401
PHONE: (212) 532-0800; FAX: (212) 532-2242

National Office—Los Angeles
5757 Wilshire Boulevard, Ninth Floor, Los Angeles CA 90036-0800
PHONE: (323) 634-8100; FAX: (323) 634-8194

MEMBERSHIP DEPARTMENT: (866) 855-5191
E-MAIL: membership@aftra.com
WEB SITE: www.aftra.org

The American Federation of Television and Radio Artists (AFTRA) represents almost 80,000 performers, journalists, and other artists, as the national labor union for those working in the entertainment and news media.

According to AFTRA publications, its "scope of representation covers broadcast, public and cable television (news, sports and weather; drama and comedy, soaps, talk and variety shows, documentaries, children's programming, reality and game shows); radio (news, commercials, hosted programs); sound recordings (CDs, singles, Broadway cast albums, audio books); non-broadcast and industrial material as well as Internet and digital programming." AFTRA's membership includes a wide array of performers and talent, among them, pop, rock, country, classical, folk, jazz, comedy, Latin, hip hop, rap, and R&B artists; and others in television and radio advertising, non-broadcast video, audio books and messaging, and individuals who provide their skills for developing technologies such as interactive games and Internet material. The union negotiates and enforces over 300 collective bargaining agreements that guarantee minimum salaries, safe working conditions, and health and retirement benefits. The Web site directs professional performers or broadcasters who wish to join AFTRA to their local AFTRA offices or to the national membership department at (866) 855-5191, or by e-mail at membership@aftra.com to find out about AFTRA, the services it provides, and how to join.

AMERICAN GUILD OF MUSICAL ARTISTS (AGMA)
1430 Broadway, 14th Floor, New York, NY 10018
PHONE: (212) 265-3687; FAX: (212) 262-9088
E-MAIL: AGMA@MusicalArtists.org
WEB SITE: www.musicalartists.org

In its own words, AGMA is "the labor organization that represents the men and women who create America's operatic, choral and dance heritage," including the soloist, chorister, dancer/choreographer, and stage manager/stage director. Audition notices for members are published on the Web site and the AGMA Hotline.

AMERICAN GUILD OF VARIETY ARTISTS (AGVA)
184 Fifth Avenue, 6th Floor, New York, NY 10010
PHONE: (212) 675-1003
WEB SITE: americanguildofvarietyartistsagva.visualnet.com

AGVA represents live performers in variety shows, touring productions, and theme parks, and certain performers in Broadway, Off-Broadway, and cabaret productions, as well as various live performers in variety shows and touring productions.

THE DRAMATISTS GUILD OF AMERICA, INC.

1501 Broadway, Suite 701, New York, NY 10036
PHONE: (212) 398-9366; FAX: (212) 944-0420
WEB SITE: www.dramatistsguild.com

Over 6,000 dramatic writers are members of The Dramatists Guild of America, the professional association of playwrights, composers, and lyricists. The DGA has categories of membership that include active members, associate members, and student members, with a wide array of benefits and services including contract negotiation advice, access to the business affairs office (with model contracts and agreements), and subscription to *The Dramatist*, the bi-monthly DGA magazine. The members list is a virtual Who's Who in American Theater.

INTERNATIONAL ALLIANCE OF THEATRICAL STAGE EMPLOYEES (IATSE)

1430 Broadway, 20th Floor, New York, NY 10018
PHONE: (212) 730-1770; FAX: (212) 730-7809
WEB SITE: www.iatse-intl.org

IATSE is the labor union representing technicians, artisans, and craftspersons in the entertainment industry, including live theater, motion picture and television production, and trade shows. In its own words, "The International Alliance of Theatrical Stage Employees, Moving Picture Technicians, Artists and Allied Crafts of the United States, its Territories and Canada was originally chartered by the American Federation of Labor as the National Alliance of Theatrical Stage Employees in 1893. Our name has evolved over the course of 110 years of geographic and craft expansion as well as technological advancement. The current title, adopted in 1995, more accurately reflects the full scope of our activities in the entertainment industry.

"Since the birth of our organization, the stage hands and projectionists have been joined by a great variety of other craftspersons in the numerous branches of the entertainment industry, including motion picture and television production, product demonstration and industrial shows, conventions, facility maintenance, casinos, audio visual, and computer graphics."

NATIONAL ENDOWMENT FOR THE ARTS

The Nancy Hanks Center, 1100 Pennsylvania Avenue, NW, Washington, DC 20506
PHONE: (202) 682-5510
WEB SITE: www.arts.gov

The NEA has awarded more than 120,000 grants to artists and arts organizations throughout America. The recent Shakespeare in American Communities project marked the largest theatrical tour of Shakespeare in US history. A public agency dedicated to supporting excellence in the arts, the NEA strives to bring the arts to all Americans and provide leadership in arts education. Undergraduate and graduate students and other volunteers may apply for ongoing NEA Internships. Guidelines and application forms for grants and internships are available on line.

SCREEN ACTORS GUILD (SAG)

National Contact Information—Hollywood

5757 Wilshire Blvd., Los Angeles, CA 90036-3600
PHONE: (323) 954-1600 Main Switchboard; (323) 549-6648 for Deaf Performers
    Only: TTY/TTD; 1-800-SAG-0767 for SAG Members outside Los Angeles
WEB SITE: www.sag.org

New York

360 Madison Avenue, 12th Floor, New York, NY 10017
PHONE: (212) 944-1030 Main Switchboard; (212) 944-6715 for Deaf Performers
    Only: TTY/TTD

In the union's own words, "Screen Actors Guild is the nation's premier labor union representing actors. Established in 1933, SAG has a rich history in the American labor movement, from standing up to studios to break long-term engagement contracts in the 1940s to fighting for artists' rights amid the digital revolution of the 21st century. With 20 branches nationwide, SAG represents nearly 120,000 actors in film, television, industrials, commercials and music videos. The Guild exists to enhance actors' working conditions, compensation and benefits and to be a powerful, unified voice on behalf of artists' rights. SAG is a proud affiliate of the AFL-CIO."

SOCIETY OF STAGE DIRECTORS AND CHOREOGRAPHERS (SSDC)

1501 Broadway, Suite 1701, New York, NY 10036-5653
PHONE: (800) 541-5204; in NYC (212) 391-1070; FAX: (212) 302-6195
E-MAIL: info@ssdc.org
WEB SITE: www.ssdc.org

SSDC represents members throughout the US and abroad and is a national independent labor union. SSDC has jurisdiction over the employment of directors and choreographers working in Broadway and National tours, Off-Broadway, Off-Off-Broadway, resident theater/LORT, resident summer stock companies/Council of Resident Stock Theatres (CORST), summer stock and civic light opera, Council of Stock Theatres (COST), Dinner Theatres (DTA), Regional Music Theatre (RMT), Outdoor Musical Stock (OMS), and non-Equity tours. In its own words, SSDC "also provides a special contract to protect members who wish to work for theaters not covered by one of the above mentioned Collectively Bargained Agreements."

UNITED SCENIC ARTISTS, L.U. USA-829

29 West 38th Street, New York, NY 10018
PHONE: (212) 581-0300; FAX: (212) 977-2011
E-MAIL: usa829@usa829.org
WEB SITE: www.usa829.org

USA is the union for designers and artists in the entertainment industry. It has offices in New York, Chicago, Los Angeles, Miami, and New England. According to Larry Robinson, USA-829 historian, the American Society of Scenic Painters, formed in 1891, "had as its members the foremost scenic designers and artists of the United States," and, in 1918, became United Scenic Artists, Local 829. Collectively bargained agreements include Broadway, LORT, opera and dance, film, television, and special projects.

PART V

---

10 MAJOR EMPLOYERS
TOTALING OVER
1,000 THEATER COMPANIES

99+ MAJOR AMERICAN THEATERS

Including League of Resident Theaters (LORT),
Non-LORT Theaters Operating on the LORT Contract,
and Other Professional Theaters in the US

Many of the most prestigious and artistically ambitious nonprofit professional theaters in the US belong to a national association called the League
of Resident Theatres (LORT), and operate under LORT contracts. For
various reasons, other large professional theaters operate under special agreements with the unions. LORT companies are listed alphabetically, beginning
on the next page; companies with special agreements are listed on page 175;
and both types are combined in the alphabetized section of select company
profiles beginning on page 176. Many more Equity regional theaters operate
under Small Professional Theatre contracts (SPT) or Letters of Agreement
(LOA), and many of these theaters can be found elsewhere in this book.

LEAGUE OF RESIDENT THEATRES (LORT)

LORT Counsel: Harry H. Weintraub, Esq.
1501 Broadway, Suite 2401; New York, NY 10036
For general inquiries, contact Adam Knight, LORT Management Associate
PHONE: (212) 944-1501, ext. 19; FAX: (212) 768-0785
E-MAIL: adam@lort.org
WEB SITE: www.lort.org

The League of Resident Theatres includes many Tony Award–winning
companies. Through the member institutions, it includes many of the playwrights, producers, artists, managers, and company members who have
created and sustained theater throughout the United States, as well as the
creative forces who continue to drive the future of the American theater.

A few of the numerous principle objectives of LORT include promoting
"the general welfare of resident theaters," promoting "community interest in
and support of resident theaters," acting "in the interest and on behalf of its
members in labor relations and related matters," and serving "as bargaining
agent for its members in bargaining collectively with unions representing
employees of its members."

According to LORT documents, the criteria for new membership to LORT include assurances that the theater is "incorporated as a nonprofit IRS-approved organization; that each self-produced production must be rehearsed for a minimum of 3 weeks; that the theater must have a playing season of 12 weeks or more; and that the theater will operate under a LORT-Equity contract." Additional information is available on the LORT Web site.

LORT counsel Harry H. Weintraub, Esq., is one of America's unsung theater heroes and a gentleman who has helped many of America's theater producers and artists in their quest to produce at the highest levels of the theater. He helps guide and advise the LORT Executive Committee, made up of elected officials from the executive ranks of the membership.

LORT Member Theaters

ACT THEATRE, Seattle, WA

ACTORS THEATRE OF LOUISVILLE, Louisville, KY

ALABAMA SHAKESPEARE FESTIVAL, Montgomery, AL

ALLEY THEATRE, Houston, TX

ALLIANCE THEATRE COMPANY, Atlanta, GA

AMERICAN CONSERVATORY THEATER, San Francisco, CA

AMERICAN REPERTORY THEATRE, Cambridge, MA

ARDEN THEATRE COMPANY, Philadelphia, PA

ARENA STAGE, Washington, DC

ARIZONA THEATRE COMPANY, Tucson/Phoenix, AZ

ARKANSAS REPERTORY THEATRE, Little Rock, AR

ASOLO THEATRE COMPANY, Sarasota, FL

BARTER THEATRE, Abingdon, VA

BERKELEY REPERTORY THEATRE, Berkeley, CA

BERKSHIRE THEATRE FESTIVAL, Stockbridge, MA

CAPITAL REPERTORY THEATRE, Albany, NY

CENTERSTAGE, Baltimore, MD

CENTER THEATRE GROUP, Los Angeles, CA

CINCINNATI PLAYHOUSE IN THE PARK, Cincinnati, OH

CITY THEATRE COMPANY, Pittsburgh, PA

CLARENCE BROWN THEATRE, Knoxville, TN

THE CLEVELAND PLAY HOUSE, Cleveland, OH

COCONUT GROVE PLAYHOUSE, Miami, FL

COURT THEATRE, Chicago, IL

DALLAS THEATER CENTER, Dallas, TX

DELAWARE THEATRE COMPANY, Wilmington, DE

DENVER CENTER THEATRE COMPANY, Denver, CO

FLORIDA STAGE, Manalapan, FL

FORD'S THEATRE, Washington, DC

GEFFEN PLAYHOUSE, Los Angeles, CA

GEORGE STREET PLAYHOUSE, New Brunswick, NJ

GEORGIA SHAKESPEARE FESTIVAL, Atlanta, GA

GEVA THEATRE CENTER, Rochester, NY

GOODMAN THEATRE, Chicago, IL

GOODSPEED MUSICALS, East Haddam, CT

GREAT LAKES THEATER FESTIVAL, Cleveland, OH

GUTHRIE THEATER, Minneapolis, MN

HARTFORD STAGE COMPANY, Hartford, CT

HUNTINGTON THEATRE COMPANY, Boston, MA

INDIANA REPERTORY THEATRE, Indianapolis, IN

INTIMAN THEATRE, Seattle, WA

KANSAS CITY REPERTORY THEATRE, Kansas City, MO

LAGUNA PLAYHOUSE, Laguna Beach, CA

LA JOLLA PLAYHOUSE, La Jolla, CA

LINCOLN CENTER THEATER, New York, NY

LONG WHARF THEATRE, New Haven, CT

MALTZ JUPITER THEATRE, Jupiter, FL

MANHATTAN THEATRE CLUB, New York, NY

MCCARTER THEATRE CENTER, Princeton, NJ

MERRIMACK REPERTORY THEATRE, Lowell, MA

MILWAUKEE REPERTORY THEATER, Milwaukee, WI

NORTHLIGHT THEATRE, Skokie, IL

THE OLD GLOBE, San Diego, CA

PASADENA PLAYHOUSE, Pasadena, CA

PEOPLE'S LIGHT & THEATRE COMPANY, Malvern, PA

PHILADELPHIA THEATRE COMPANY, Philadelphia, PA

PITTSBURGH PUBLIC THEATER, Pittsburgh, PA

PLAYMAKERS REPERTORY COMPANY, Chapel Hill, NC

PORTLAND CENTER STAGE, Portland, OR

PORTLAND STAGE COMPANY, Portland, ME

PRINCE MUSIC THEATER, Philadelphia, PA

THE REPERTORY THEATRE OF ST. LOUIS, St. Louis, MO

ROUNDABOUT THEATRE COMPANY, New York, NY

SAN JOSE REPERTORY THEATRE, San Jose, CA

SEATTLE REPERTORY THEATRE, Seattle, WA

SHAKESPEARE THEATRE COMPANY, Washington, DC

SOUTH COAST REPERTORY, Costa Mesa, CA

STUDIO ARENA THEATRE, Buffalo, NY

SYRACUSE STAGE, Syracuse, NY

THEATRE FOR A NEW AUDIENCE, New York, NY

THEATREWORKS, Palo Alto, CA

TRINITY REPERTORY COMPANY, Providence, RI

VIRGINIA STAGE COMPANY, Norfolk, VA

THE WILMA THEATER, Philadelphia, PA

YALE REPERTORY THEATRE, New Haven, CT

25+ Select Theaters Operating Under Special LORT Contracts

THE ACTING COMPANY, New York, NY

AMERICAN PLAYERS THEATRE, Spring Green, WI

ARROW ROCK LYCEUM THEATRE, Arrow Rock, MO

ARVADA CENTER FOR THE ARTS AND HUMANITIES THEATRE, Arvada, CO

BAY STREET THEATRE, Sag Harbor, NY

BUSHFIRE THEATRE OF PERFORMING ARTS, Philadelphia, PA

CALIFORNIA SHAKESPEARE FESTIVAL THEATER, Berkeley, CA

THE CHILDREN'S THEATRE COMPANY, Minneapolis, MN

CONTEMPORARY AMERICAN THEATER FESTIVAL, Shepherdstown, WV

THE FOOTHILL THEATRE COMPANY, Nevada City, CA

FREEDOM REPERTORY THEATRE, Philadelphia, PA

THE HUMAN RACE THEATRE COMPANY, Dayton, OH

MILL MOUNTAIN THEATRE, Roanoke, VA

THE NEW HARMONY THEATRE, New Harmony, IN

THE OREGON SHAKESPEARE FESTIVAL, Ashland, OR

ORLANDO-UCF SHAKESPEARE FESTIVAL, Orlando, FL

THE PHOENIX THEATRE, Indianapolis, IN

PIONEER THEATRE COMPANY, Salt Lake City, UT

THE PUBLIC THEATER/NEW YORK SHAKESPEARE FESTIVAL, New York, NY

THE SAN FRANCISCO SHAKESPEARE FESTIVAL, San Francisco, CA

SEATTLE CHILDREN'S THEATRE, Seattle, WA

SEVEN ANGELS THEATRE, Waterbury, CT

THE SHAKESPEARE THEATRE OF NEW JERSEY, Madison, NJ

SHAKESPEARE FESTIVAL/LA, Los Angeles, CA

THE SITI COMPANY, New York, NY

UTAH SHAKESPEAREAN FESTIVAL, Cedar City, UT

WALNUT STREET THEATRE, Philadelphia, PA

THE ACTING COMPANY

P.O. Box 898, New York, NY 10108-0898

630 Ninth Avenue, Suite 214, New York, NY 10036

ADMINISTRATION: (212) 258-3111; FAX: (212) 258-3299

E-MAIL: mail@theactingcompany.org

WEB SITE: www.theactingcompany.org

Perhaps the *New York Times* says it most succinctly: "The Acting Company endures as the major touring classical theater in the United States." For three decades and nearly 100 productions, The Acting Company has been touring and teaching in America's cities with a touring repertory of classical productions, enjoyable young actors, and teaching artists. The company generally tours to over 50 cities and 70,000 patrons (including more than 25,000 students). The company was founded in 1972 by John Houseman and current producing director Margot Harley with members of the first graduating class of Juilliard's Drama Division. Company alumni include Kevin Kline and Patti LuPone, and past honors include the Obie Award and two Tony Award nominations.

GENERAL EMPLOYMENT OPPORTUNITIES, INTERNSHIPS

Check the Web site for audition and employment opportunities or e-mail: mail@theactingcompany.org. The Acting Company often needs development, marketing, and production interns and there's a direct link on the Web site.

ACT THEATRE

A Contemporary Theatre, Kreielsheimer Place, 700 Union Street,
    Seattle, WA 98101-4037

ADMINISTRATION: (206) 292-7660; BOX OFFICE: (206) 292-7676;
    FAX: (206) 292-7670

E-MAIL: act@acttheatre.org

WEB SITE: www.acttheatre.org

There's more than great coffee, computers, and the Seattle Repertory Theatre in Seattle. Despite some tough financial times, ACT has managed to hold on to a loyal and dedicated subscriber base, produce the work of many emerging playwrights, and garner numerous awards including Shubert, NEA, AT&T, and Kennedy Center recognition. ACT was established in 1965 by Gregory and Jean Falls as the first theater dedicated to new plays in Seattle. After a $30 million renovation in 1996, ACT Theatre opened as Kreielsheimer Place, a blossoming cultural center with four performance spaces, administrative offices, rehearsal spaces, and scene and costume shops. ACT's mission of "presenting great contemporary stories told through the voices of the uniquely talented community of Seattle actors, designers and artisans" has resulted in artistic productions of the highest caliber and the staging of more than eighty contemporary plays at Kreielsheimer Place including the work of Philip Glass, Donald Margulies, Randy Newman, Joyce Carol Oates, Neil Simon, Stephen Sondheim, Lanford Wilson, David Hare, and Theresa Rebeck.

CAREER OPPORTUNITIES OVERVIEW

ACT Theatre posts historical information, a season overview, and information regarding job opportunities, internship programs, auditions, and playwright submissions on its Web site: www.acttheatre.org.

CASTING

ACT holds general auditions for the first 30 non-Equity actors to sign up for the first Thursday of each month. Only one audition is allowed each actor in a six-month period. To participate, actors may schedule an appointment in person, in advance, by coming to the box office lobby of ACT at 700 Union Street. Bring a headshot and résumé. Check out the Web site for more details. The theater requests that you not call to schedule or cancel an appointment. To be included in ACT's Actor database, mail one headshot and résumé along with a cover letter to: Casting/ACT Theatre, 700 Union Street, Seattle, WA 98101-4037.

SCRIPT SUBMISSIONS

ACT accepts scripts solicited by the literary manager or artistic director and scripts sent by agents and/or other theater professionals. Northwest playwrights can submit a synopsis of their play and a 10-page sample of their work. ACT does not accept unsolicited scripts. Scripts for The Women Playwrights and FringeACT Festivals are considered through nomination only.

INTERNSHIPS

ACT's internship program "is committed to fostering the growth and development of dedicated students of theater in the Seattle area," offering unpaid internships year-round in development, marketing, literary, and artistic areas. Internship application packets should include a résumé, cover letter highlighting your interest in and prior experience with ACT, and two letters of recommendation. Application materials may be sent via e-mail to act@acttheatre.org or by mail to: ACT Theatre, Internships, 700 Union Street, Seattle, WA 98101-4037. See the Web site for more instructions.

ACTORS THEATRE OF LOUISVILLE

316 West Main Street, Louisville, KY 40202-4218

ADMINISTRATION: (502) 584-1265; BOX OFFICE: (502) 584-1205 or (800) 4ATL-TIX;
FAX: (502) 561-3300

WEB SITE: www.actorstheatre.org

The Kentucky Derby may have a lock on the equestrian crowd, but when it comes to new plays, theater critics and artistic leaders love Louisville. Actors Theatre of Louisville was created in 1964 and designated the State Theatre of Kentucky ten years later. In 1976, then–artistic director Jon Jory started the internationally celebrated Humana Festival of New American Plays, and for 30 years Actors Theatre of Louisville and Humana have been almost household words for professional theater folk. Today, artistic director Marc Masterson leads the company. In its own words, "Actors Theatre provides insight into the human experience through live theater that invigorates minds and emotions," while its "vision is to build a home for inspired collaboration where great art sets new standards in excellence that will shape the future of the American theater. We seek discovery by embracing the artistic spirit in everything we do. We will build a better community by bringing people together to participate in the power of collective imagination." Annually, nearly 600 performances of about 30 plays lure over 200,000 annual audience members to this phenomenon.

Originally housed in a tiny loft (formally the Gypsy Tea Room) and later a railroad station, the theater eventually settled in a merging of the old Bank of Louisville and the adjacent Myers-Thompson Display Building. The 637-seat Pamela Brown Auditorium opened in 1972 and the 159-seat Victor Jory Theatre opened in 1973. In 1994, a $12.5 million expansion and renovation project included the new 318-seat Bingham Theatre. The venues are funky, the city is welcoming and the combination has produced over 300 Humana Festival plays that have been celebrated in theaters throughout America. Humana Festival premieres include the Pulitzer Prize–winning plays *Dinner with Friends* (Donald Margulies), *Crimes of the Heart* (Beth Henley), and *The Gin Game* (D.L. Coburn). In 1980, Actors Theatre became the fifth company to receive the Regional Theatre Tony Award. Actors Theatre's international touring program has included more than 1,500 invitational performances in over 29 cities in 15 foreign countries.

AUDITIONS AND INTERVIEWS

Individual auditions and interviews are held at Actors Theatre of Louisville (ATL) and information is generally posted on the Web site. ATL strongly encourages interested candidates to visit the city and audition or interview in Louisville. ATL often attends University/Resident Theatre Association (U/RTA) auditions in New York, Chicago, and San Francisco. Other auditions sites often include Los Angeles, Seattle, the Southeastern Theatre Conference (SETC), and the Northeastern Theatre Conference (NETC).

CASTING

Equity auditions are held in New York, Chicago, or Los Angeles. Auditions are arranged through agent submissions, and scheduled by a casting director in one of those cities. Actors are encouraged to send a photo and résumé to Casting, Actors Theatre, 316 West Main Street, Louisville, KY 40202-4218.

Local auditions include annual open calls for actors of all ages and are held in order to meet actors from the Louisville community. These auditions are generally not for specific roles in productions, but for introductory purposes. To schedule an appointment, call (502) 584-1265 ext. 3005.

General auditions for Equity actors from the region and across the nation are generally held in Louisville twice a year. For details, send a self-addressed stamped envelope to Casting, Actors Theatre of Louisville, 316 West Main Street, Louisville, KY 40202-4218. For a general audition, prepare two monologues of no more than four minutes in combined length. See the Web site for specifics.

ACTING APPRENTICE/INTERNSHIP PROGRAM

The theater offers an apprentice/intern training program designed to help recent college graduates make the transition from academic to professional theater. This competitive program results in excellent employment placement for its talented participants. The apprentices, an ensemble of 22 actors, attend regular classes in movement, scene study, text analysis, and audition technique. Apprentices participate in master classes with distinguished artists and administrators, who include agents and casting directors, visiting guest directors, and actors. Apprentices also observe rehearsals, perform in projects throughout the season and work with technical and stage management staff as crew support on mainstage productions. The apprentice season concludes with an acting showcase for industry professionals in New York City. Additional information is on the theater's Web site.

OTHER INTERNSHIPS

Professional interns work directly with department managers and staff, receiving hands-on training in either administration or technical theater.

Internships are available on a full-time seasonal basis (late August to late May) with possible exceptions on a project or summer intern basis. These are vital staff positions that give practical experience in the intern's desired field.

Interns are selected by application and interview. It is possible to arrange course credit with the intern's academic institution. Internship areas include apprentice/intern company administration, arts administration/company management, communications, costumes, development, festival management, lighting, literary management, properties, scenic artistry, sound design, stage management, and technical direction.

ALABAMA SHAKESPEARE FESTIVAL

One Festival Drive; Montgomery, AL 36117
ADMINISTRATION: (334) 271-5300; BOX OFFICE: (334) 271-5353 or
    Toll Free (800) 841-4ASF (4273)
E-MAIL: info@asf.net
WEB SITE: www.asf.net

Shakespeare, Southern writers, and rotating repertory in the Heart of Dixie? The Alabama Shakespeare Festival (ASF), located in the state capital, Montgomery, is the sixth-largest Shakespeare festival in the world and attracts more than 300,000 annual visitors from all 50 states and over 60 countries.

ASF was founded by Martin Platt in 1972 as a summer theater festival in an un-air-conditioned old high school auditorium and blossomed in a 250-acre park and a new two-theater, 100,000 square-foot, $21.5 million complex in 1985. ASF operates year-round, producing over a dozen productions and 400 annual performances in the 750-seat Festival Stage and 225-seat Octagon.

The Southern Writers' Project (SWP) was founded by longtime artistic director Kent Thompson in 1991 as an exploration of the South's rich cultural heritage and is dedicated to creating a theatrical voice for Southern writers and topics. Geoffrey Sherman, ASF's new producing artistic director, "is delighted to work with a company that is devoted, as I am, to producing theatrical classics as well as new works. I am dedicated to leading this theater in continued service to Montgomery, the surrounding community, and all of Alabama," says Sherman. "ASF is one of the best theaters in the country! Every element of the theater from technical support through design and performance is superb!"

SCRIPT SUBMISSIONS

The Southern Writers' Project accepts original scripts and adaptations, not professionally produced, that meet certain criteria posted on the Web site. Submissions that meet these criteria are considered for the Southern Writers' Project Festival of New Plays, an annual weekend of readings of new work. These plays are then considered for production in subsequent ASF seasons.

CASTING, GENERAL EMPLOYMENT OPPORTUNITIES, INTERNSHIPS

Casting, employment, and internship information may be obtained by writing the theater, e-mailing info@asf.net, or through the Web site, www.asf.net.

MASTERS OF FINE ARTS GRADUATE PROGRAMS

In partnership with the University of Alabama, the Alabama Shakespeare Festival is home to a unique Professional Actor Training Program and graduate programs in costume design and production, scene design/technical production, stage management, and theatre management/arts administration. Graduate scholarships and stipends are available and additional information can be found on the ASF Web site, www.asf.net.

ALLEY THEATRE

615 Texas Avenue, Houston, TX 77002
ADMINISTRATION: (713) 228-9341; BOX OFFICE: (713) 228-8421;
    FAX: (713) 222-6542
WEB SITE: www.alleytheatre.org

Some legends seem too good to be true, but the Alley Theatre's beginnings have been retold in so many historical documents and LORT Conference bar rooms that they deserve a quick synopsis. In 1947, high school teacher and regional theater pioneer Nina Vance mailed 214 penny postcards asking, "Do you want a new theater for Houston?" Over 100 friends, neighbors, and interested parties gathered in an 87-seat dance studio hidden at the end of an alley . . . such were the beginnings of The Alley Theatre. Don't believe it? Call me and I'll send you a copy of the postcard! Today, The Alley is one of the few companies in the US that still maintains a resident acting company and tours nationally and internationally.

Recipient of the 1996 Regional Theatre Tony Award, the Alley now performs year-round as a professional resident theater company in its two-theater complex in downtown Houston. The Alley has also toured 40 American cities and abroad, most recently nurturing relationships with composer Frank Wildhorn and with Vanessa and Corin Redgrave's The Moving Theatre of London. Three Alley productions debuted on Broadway in the 1990s: Tennessee Williams's rediscovered *Not About Nightingales* and Frank Wildhorn's *The Civil War* and *Jekyll & Hyde*. These creative relationships are tied to Gregory Boyd's arrival as artistic director in 1989. Boyd has produced more than 130 productions at the Alley, including two productions in one season at the Venice Biennale and at New York's Lincoln Center. Dean Gladden was appointed managing director in 2006.

The 824-seat Hubbard Stage and the "up to 310-seat" Neuhaus Stage are home to "a wide range of plays, embracing classic, new, and neglected plays."

The Alley has grown tremendously from its humble beginnings and the complex now houses its own costume, scenic and properties, and lighting and sound departments; rehearsal studios; and administrative offices. The Alley maintains a company of more than 100 individuals.

GENERAL EMPLOYMENT OPPORTUNITIES
The Alley Theatre does not accept unsolicited résumés, and résumés are only accepted for specific job openings. Job openings are usually advertised on the company's Web site, in the *Houston Chronicle*, or in TCG's *ARTSEARCH*. Check the Web site for current information.

CASTING
The Alley Theatre maintains a resident company of actors. When casting productions, the Alley looks first to its company to fill key roles, then auditions on an as-needed basis. The Alley announces auditions on its Web site as well as through the local media. The Alley maintains a database of select actors seen in auditions or in performance in the past two years. The staff does not keep or return unsolicited headshots and résumés of actors that it has not seen in audition or in performance.

ALLEY THEATRE PRODUCTION DEPARTMENT
For production positions, write to: Production Manager, Alley Theatre, 615 Texas Avenue, Houston TX, 77002. Apply by e-mail or fax: (713) 228-0527. The theater does not accept phone calls for positions.

INTERNSHIPS
The Alley Theatre's internship program provides college- and graduate school–level students the chance to participate in and observe a professional theater environment and meet regularly to share experiences and learn about other areas of the theater. Applicants to the program must be at least 18 years old and have a minimum of 12 hours of college credit.

Intern applicants should possess basic computer literacy, excellent team-work and communication skills, initiative, and flexibility. The Alley doesn't offer internships in design, acting, or directing, although students are encouraged to learn about these areas from their experience in any of the other Alley internships. Intern applications are available online at www.alleytheater.org. Internships at the Alley are non-paying although other employee perks exist such as free parking and complimentary tickets to Alley productions.

Production internships are available in costumes, lighting and sound, production management, properties, scenery (carpentry and painting), and stage management. Theater Administration Internships are available in company management, development, education and community outreach, marketing, and dramaturgy/artistic office.

ALLIANCE THEATRE COMPANY

1280 Peachtree Street NE, Atlanta, GA 30309

ADMINISTRATION: (404) 733-4650; BOX OFFICE: (404) 733-5000; FAX: (404) 733-4625

E-MAIL: info@alliancetheatre.org

WEB SITE: www.alliancetheatre.org

If Atlanta's many innovative theaters have their say, the South will indeed rise again! Home to many American premieres, the Alliance Theatre Company's mission "sets the highest artistic standards, creating the power-ful experience of shared theater for diverse people." Pearl Cleage's *Blues for an Alabama Sky*, Sandra Deer's *So Long on Lonely Street*, and Alfred Uhry's *The Last Night of Ballyhoo* all premiered at the Alliance.

As a resident of the Robert W. Woodruff Arts Center in Atlanta, the Alliance Theatre produces ten productions annually, with performances in the 750-seat Alliance Stage and the 200-seat Hertz Stage, and Theatre for Young Audiences offerings in the 14th Street Playhouse. Richard Dreyfuss, Paul Winfield, Morgan Freeman, and Jane Alexander all appeared on the Alliance Theatre stage. National foundations including the Shubert Foundation, the National Endowment for the Arts, and the Lila Wallace Reader's Digest Fund awarded major funding to the Alliance during the 1990s. The theater celebrated its 30th anniversary in 1998-99 with the world premiere of Elton John and Tim Rice's *Elaborate Lives: The Legend of Aida*, produced by special arrangement with Walt Disney Theatrical Productions. Current artistic director Susan V. Booth has a strong commit-ment to the creation of new works for the American theater, coupled with fresh explorations of classical works.

CASTING

Check the Web site for audition information as it is updated often. The Alliance Theatre generally holds two invited casting calls for each of its Alliance Stage and Hertz Stage productions—the first in Atlanta and the second in New York. Additional calls are conducted in other cities on an as-needed basis. Alliance Children's Theatre productions usually feature adult actors and are cast solely out of Atlanta. All open calls held in Atlanta are listed on the Alliance Audition Information Phone Line at (404) 733-4622 and on the Atlanta Coalition of Performing Arts (ACPA) Hotline at (770) 521-8338. New York calls are based primarily on agent submissions through New York casting agencies. Open calls are listed in *Backstage*. The Alliance Theatre participates in the ACPA Unified General Auditions held each spring in Atlanta. For information call ACPA at (770) 521-8338. Actors living in the Atlanta area are encouraged to send headshots and résumés to Casting Director, Alliance Theatre, 1280 Peachtree Street NE, Atlanta, GA 30309.

SCRIPT SUBMISSIONS

The Alliance Theatre accepts submission of full scripts only from literary agents (professional representation). Please note that lawyers and law firms do not qualify as "professional representation" at this venue. Due to the high volume of submissions and the theater's desire to respond with care and relative promptness to each one, it is not able to accept unsolicited full manuscripts directly from authors. Playwrights without professional representation may submit a one-page synopsis telling the play's entire story and listing any past productions, a complete list of characters, and up to ten pages of sample dialogue. See the Web site for additional information or contact the Alliance Theatre Literary Department, by e-mailing ATCLiterary@woodruffcenter.org or writing to: Alliance Theatre Literary Department, 1280 Peachtree Street NE, Atlanta, GA 30309.

INTERNSHIPS

The Alliance Theatre offers many exciting internship opportunities in acting, administration, artistic, education, literary, and production.

GENERAL EMPLOYMENT OPPORTUNITIES

Located in midtown Atlanta, Woodruff Arts Center employs over 500 people, is in the heart of Atlanta's Arts District, and includes the Alliance Theatre Company, High Museum of Art, Atlanta Symphony Orchestra, 14th Street Playhouse and the Atlanta College of Art. More information is available through the Woodruff Center Job Hotline, (404) 733-4323.

ACT/AMERICAN CONSERVATORY THEATER

30 Grant Avenue, Sixth Floor, San Francisco, CA 94108-5800

ADMINISTRATION: (415) 834-3200; BOX OFFICE: (415) 749-2ACT; FAX: (415) 433-2711

E:MAIL: Casting: ghubbard@act-sf.org; MFA PROGRAM: mfa@act-sf.org;

  SUMMER TRAINING CONGRESS: studioact@act-sf.org

WEB SITE: www.act-sfbay.org

So many of America's current artistic leaders and acting company members still point to the American Conservatory Theater's early inspiration as the driving force for their careers in the theater. Founded in 1965 by William Ball, ACT opened its first San Francisco season at the Geary Theater in 1967.

Many performances were broadcast nationally on PBS, the theater was awarded the prestigious Regional Theatre Tony Award for outstanding theater performance and training in 1979, and in 1996 ACT's efforts to develop creative talent for the theater were recognized with the prestigious Jujamcyn Theaters Award. Today, under the leadership of artistic director Carey Perloff, "American Conservatory Theater nurtures the art of live theater through dynamic productions, intensive actor training in its conservatory, and an ongoing dialogue with its community." The conservatory serves over 1,800 students every year and Danny Glover, Annette Bening, Denzel Washington, Benjamin Bratt, and Winona Ryder are among former students. To quote ACT materials, "With its commitment to excellence in actor training and to the relationship between training, performance, and audience, the ACT Master of Fine Arts Program has moved to the forefront of America's actor training programs, while serving as the creative engine of the company at large."

CASTING

The casting office at ACT casts ACT's mainstage and second-stage shows, as well as new-play development workshops and readings throughout the season. The staff holds yearly general auditions for Equity actors on a show-by-show basis by invitation only. Check the Web site for more complete information, but ACT looks for actors "with significant classical training and performing experience." ACT works under LORT A and LORT D contracts with Actors' Equity. ACT reps attend both the Equity and non-Equity portions of the Theater Bay Area (TBA) general auditions, which are held yearly in the Bay Area during the winter. For more information about TBA's auditions, call (415) 430-1140 or visit its Web site at www.theatrebayarea.org. Auditions in New York and Los Angeles are also scheduled. Audition announcements are listed on the Web site and on the Actors' Equity Web site. Local auditions are also listed in *Theatre Bay Area* magazine and on the local Equity hotline; out-of-town auditions are listed in such publications as *Back Stage East* and *Back Stage West*. Casting of actors 18 years old and under is coordinated through ACT's Young Conservatory, which can be reached at (415) 439-2444. ACT accepts submissions of headshots and résumés via mail only (no e-mails): Casting Office, American Conservatory Theater, 30 Grant Avenue, Sixth floor, San Francisco, CA 94108-5800.

GENERAL EMPLOYMENT OPPORTUNITIES
Check the Web site or contact: ACT, Attn: Human Resources, 30 Grant Avenue, San Francisco, CA 94108-5800 or via e-mail at hr@act-sf.org.

INTERNSHIPS
ACT's internship program provides advanced training in both theater production and administration. ACT interns have access to a variety of benefits designed to integrate them into the artistic life of the company. A monthly series of intern roundtables with guest speakers provides an overview of the creative work throughout the organization. The two general categories of ACT internships include artistic and administrative internships and production department internships.

AMERICAN PLAYERS THEATRE
P.O. Box 819, Spring Green, WI 53588
ADMINISTRATION: (608) 588-7401; BOX OFFICE: (608) 588-2361; FAX: (608) 588-7085
E-MAIL: aptmaster@americanplayers.org
WEB SITE: www.americanplayers.org

American Players Theatre is a grand, classical theater in a lovely natural amphitheater on 110 acres of woods and meadow just off the Wisconsin River in Spring Green, Wisconsin. The 1,148-seat venue is committed to the plays of Shakespeare and other works ranging from the Greeks to British comedies. When in full production, the company comprises approximately two dozen actors and 120 other staff who produce five plays in rotating repertory. Founded in 1979, the theater notes that "our first obligation is to tell a gripping story, our next is to make dramatic poetry the necessary and unpretentious expression of those intimate and otherwise inexpressible moments of human consciousness that great plays explore."

CASTING, GENERAL EMPLOYMENT OPPORTUNITIES
Generally, APT assembles 13 to 15 Equity actors and 14 to 16 non-union actors (including four to six interns). Actors must have classical experience and/or a deep appreciation for poetic text. Interested actors should submit

a photo and résumé in October to be considered for the following season. Auditions are held November through January with the season completely cast by February 1 (except for interns). Specific dates and locations are posted in the fall and APT generally auditions in Chicago, Milwaukee, and New York. Check the Web site for more details. APT hopes to have its full production staff hired by March each year and a variety of production positions are often open.

AMERICAN REPERTORY THEATRE

Loeb Drama Center, Harvard University, 64 Brattle Street,
   Cambridge, MA 02138
ADMINISTRATION: (617) 495-2668; BOX OFFICE: (617) 547-8300;
   FAX: (617) 495-1705
E-MAIL: information@amrep.org
WEB SITE: www.amrep.org

The American Repertory Theatre (ART) is a complex combination of a resident acting company and an international training conservatory, operating in association with Harvard University. Recipient of a Pulitzer Prize, a Regional Theatre Tony Award, and a Jujamcyn Award, ART has performed in over 81 cities in 22 states since 1980, and internationally in 21 cities in 16 countries on four continents. Founded in 1980 by Robert Brustein and Robert J. Orchard, ART is in residence at Harvard University's Loeb Drama Center. In 2002, Robert Woodruff became the ART's artistic director. In the company's own words, "ART provides a home for artists from across the world, whose singular visions generate and define the theater's work. The company presents a varied repertoire than includes new plays, progressive productions of classical texts, and collaborations between artists from many disciplines. The ART is also a training ground for young artists. The theater's artistic staff teaches undergraduate classes in acting, directing, dramatic literature, design, and playwriting at Harvard, and in 1987 the ART founded the Institute for Advanced Theater Training. In conjunction with the Moscow Art Theatre School, the Institute provides world-class training for graduate-level actors, directors, and dramaturgs."

The ART's American and world premieres include works by Christopher Durang, Elizabeth Egloff, Jules Feiffer, Dario Fo, Carlos Fuentes, Philip Glass, David Mamet, Marsha Norman, Han Ong, David Rabe, Paula Vogel, Derek Walcott, Naomi Wallace, and Robert Wilson. The company launched a year-long national and international tour of

The King Stag that wrapped up with a three-week residency at London's Barbican Centre in the summer of 2001.

CASTING

The American Repertory Theatre is a LORT B theater. The company's Web site generally lists Boston Equity Principal auditions for each season. Most recent instructions were to prepare two contrasting two-minute monologues, one contemporary and one classical, and to bring a picture and résumé stapled together. Call (617) 496-2000 ext. 8840 to schedule an appointment. The address for mailing résumés is: Artistic Coordinator, American Repertory Theatre, 64 Brattle Street, Cambridge, MA 02138.

There is a separate application/audition process for the Institute for Advanced Theatre Training. See the Institute home page on ART's Web site for the specifics.

GENERAL EMPLOYMENT OPPORTUNITIES

Staff positions, when available, are posted via the Harvard University Web site at http://jobs.harvard.edu. On that page, select "American Repertory Theatre (Loeb)" from the list of "Institutions."

INTERNSHIPS

ART internships are open to any interested person and are directed toward undergraduate and graduate students as well as young professionals. College credit is available for certain internships through the intern's sponsoring institution. Administrative internships are often available in these areas: artistic, box office, financial, fundraising, house management, literary, marketing/PR, and production. Production internships are available in stage management, crew, scene, shop, paint, costumes, props, lighting, and sound.

ARDEN THEATRE COMPANY

40 N. 2nd Street, Philadelphia, PA 19106
ADMINISTRATIVE: (215) 922-8900; BOX OFFICE: (215) 922-1122; FAX: (215) 922-7011
E-MAIL: info@ardentheatre.org
WEB SITE: www.ardentheatre.org

The Arden Theatre Company is, in its own words, "dedicated to bringing to life the greatest stories by the greatest storytellers of all time. We draw from any source that is inherently dramatic and theatrical—fiction, nonfiction, poetry, music, and drama. The Arden presents programs for the diverse greater Philadelphia community that arouse, provoke, illuminate, and inspire."

The Arden has produced over 24 world premieres, has a full-time paid staff of around 30, boasts the second-highest attendance among Philadelphia's nonprofit producing theaters, and has a budget of around $3 million. Founded in 1988 by Terrence J. Nolen, Amy Murphy, and Aaron Posner, the Arden began producing at the 70-seat Walnut Street Theatre Studio, later co-founded the St. Stephen's Performing Arts Center to provide the company with a larger theater, and in 1995 purchased a 50,000-square-foot building in Philadelphia's Old City neighborhood. This building includes the 175-seat Arcadia Stage and the 360-seat F. Otto Haas Stage. The Arden operates under an agreement between LORT and Actors' Equity Association. The scenic, costume, lighting, and sound designers in LORT theaters are represented by United Scenic Artists Local USA-829, IATSE.

CASTING

The Arden's casting representatives participate in the annual Equity and non-Equity Theatre Alliance of Greater Philadelphia auditions. Additional Arden auditions are held throughout the year by invitation only. To be considered for an upcoming role, please submit your headshot and résumé to: Attention: Casting, Arden Theatre Company, 40 North Second Street, Philadelphia, PA, 19106. Materials sent via e-mail will not be opened.

SCRIPT SUBMISSIONS

The Arden accepts agent submissions and professional recommendations. Playwrights without agents must submit plays following these guidelines: Send 20 pages of sample dialogue, a synopsis and character breakdown, the play's production and workshop history, and the playwright/creative team biographies via e-mail to dsmeal@ardentheatre.org. The theater does not accept unsolicited scripts and only materials submitted as indicated above will be given consideration. See the Web site for additional details.

GENERAL EMPLOYMENT OPPORTUNITIES

The Arden accepts résumés and letters of introduction to: Attention: Human Resources, Arden Theatre Company, 40 North Second Street, Philadelphia, PA 19106. Fax: (215) 922-7011. E-mail: jobs@ardentheatre.org.

APPRENTICES

The Arden's Professional Apprentice (APA) program provides work in every aspect of the Arden's operations, including artistic direction, marketing, box office, development, production (load-in/strike, run crew, prop/set/costume building, etc.), stage management, finance, and general management. Graduates of the apprentice program include the founders of several new Philadelphia-based theater companies, a Grammy Award-winning singer/songwriter, and an NEA/TCG Career Development Directors Fellow.

INTERNSHIPS

Internships at the Arden are designed to provide insight and hands-on experience for a specific technical or administrative area of the theater. Intern applicants should send a copy of their current résumé, including two references, a cover letter discussing their specific areas of interest, and available time commitments to: Internships, Arden Theatre Company, 40 North Second Street, Philadelphia, PA 19106, E-mail: jobs@ardentheatre.org.

ARENA STAGE

1101 Sixth Street, SW, Washington, DC 20024

ADMINISTRATION: (202) 554-9066; BOX OFFICE: (202) 488-3300;
    FAX: (202) 488-4056

E-MAIL: info@arenastage.org

WEB SITE: www.arenastage.org

Entering the Arena Stage complex, one can sense the excitement of the audience and experience the sublime history of one of America's most dynamic cultural institutions. Arena Stage is a theater of firsts—the first regional theater to transfer a production to Broadway, the first invited by the US State Department to tour behind the Iron Curtain, and the first to receive a Tony Award. Founded in 1950 by Edward Mangum, Zelda Fichandler, and Thomas C. Fichandler, Arena Stage is one of America's oldest, most revered theater companies. The mission of Arena Stage, in the words of artistic director Molly Smith, is "to produce huge plays of all that is passionate, exuberant, profound, deep, and dangerous in the American spirit. We are interested in plays of the Americas—North and South—with a special emphasis on living writers. On occasion we may dip into the European canon or other bodies of work for contrast, but for now we are interested in plays associated with American themes, history, culture, and literary traditions."

From humble beginnings in a former movie house (The Hippodrome Theatre), 1950-55, to the converted hospitality hall of the Old Heurich Brewery in 1956-61, Arena Stage emerged as an industry leader. By the time the company mounted its first production in its new Arena Stage in 1961, Zelda Fichandler's vision and leadership were already the stuff of legend. She helped set the pace for the American regional theater and contributed to the field for 40 seasons (through 1991) as Arena Stage's producing director.

Today, in the theater's own words, "Our legacy of world-class productions includes vast epics, charged dramas, rousing musicals, and probing profiles. From the monumental to the developmental, we've helped build the canon of American theater."

CASTING

Submit to: Casting Director, Arena Stage, 1101 6th Street, SW, Washington, DC 20024. Audition requests are evaluated "based on training and experience and résumés will become permanent in our casting files and should only be updated upon request or if there are additions to credits, or a new photo." Additional information is available on the Web site.

SCRIPT SUBMISSIONS

Arena Stage only accepts scripts directly from writers with "bona fide professional representation." The literary manager does accept queries from writers without representation in the form of a cover letter, résumé, one-page synopsis, and (no more than) ten consecutive pages of sample dialogue. These submissions can be mailed to: Literary Manager, Arena Stage, 1101 Sixth Street, SW, Washington, DC, 20024.

GENERAL EMPLOYMENT OPPORTUNITIES

Check the theater Web site at www.arenastage.org for information.

ARIZONA THEATRE COMPANY

P.O. Box 1631, Tucson, AZ 85702

ADMINISTRATION/PHOENIX: (602) 256-6899; ADMINISTRATIVE/TUCSON: (520) 884-8210;
  BOX OFFICE/PHOENIX: (602) 256-6995; BOX OFFICE/TUCSON: (520) 622-2823;
  FAX/PHOENIX: (602) 256-7399; FAX/TUCSON: (520) 628-9129

E-MAIL: info@arizonatheatre.org

WEB SITE: www.arizonatheatre.org

This is indeed a tale of two cities! The Arizona Theatre Company is unique among LORT theaters in that it operates at the Temple of Music and Art in Tucson and in the Herberger Theater Center in Phoenix, playing to about 150,000 annually. The Santa Rita Hotel in Tucson, Arizona, provided a home, and Sandy Rosenthal led the way for the Arizona Civic Theatre's first production in 1967. Five years later, in 1972, the troupe developed into a professional company and was soon attracting a number of America's most sought-after directors and managers (including Mark Lamos and David Hawkanson). Christened the Arizona Theatre Company in 1978, it added a Phoenix presence with productions of *Vanities* and *Equus*, produced full seasons in both cities in 1983-84, was commended by President Ronald Reagan for innovative operations, and was deemed the State Theatre of Arizona in 1990.

Today, according to artistic director David Ira Goldstein, ATC "seeks to honor the diversity, intelligence and good will of our audience through producing a wide-ranging repertoire of both new and classic works." Together with Jessica Andrews, who took over as managing director in 1995, the company has attracted new plays and world premieres while developing significant relationships with American playwrights.

CASTING

Arizona Theatre Company holds general season auditions for Equity and non-Equity actors in Tucson and Phoenix. Consult the Web site for dates and details. Appointments are required and audition announcements can usually be downloaded from the site. ATC also conducts production-specific auditions throughout the year in various cities including New York, Los Angeles, Seattle, and San Francisco. Headshots and résumés may be mailed to: Attention: Casting, Arizona Theatre Company, 40 E. 14th Street, Tucson, Arizona, 85701. Do not e-mail headshots or résumés.

SCRIPT SUBMISSIONS

ATC accepts unsolicited play submissions from Arizona writers only. In the submission, Arizona writers must include the full play script, a production history, if any, a brief autobiography of the playwright, and a stamped self-addressed envelope for a reply.

Submissions from out of state must include a synopsis of the play, ten pages of sample dialogue, a production history, if any, a brief autobiography of the playwright, and a stamped self-addressed envelope for a reply. Send all submissions to: Attention: Literary Department, Arizona Theatre Company, 40 E. 14th Street, Tucson, Arizona, 85701.

INTERNSHIPS

ATC's internship program provides students with training in both theater administration and production. Many interns have gone on to become successful staff members at Arizona Theatre Company and other professional theaters throughout the country, including the Alley Theatre, Huntington Theatre Company, and Chicago Shakespeare Theater. Administration internships are available in theater management, artistic, development, marketing/public relations, and company management. Production internships are available in costumes, props, electrics/lighting, sound, scenic, stage management, scenic painting, and production management. See the Web site for more specifics. Students must be enrolled in a course of study and receive college credit throughout the duration of the internship in order to participate in the professional internship program.

To apply or to request additional information regarding ATC's professional internship program, mail a résumé and letter of interest to: Arizona Theatre Company, Professional Internship Program, P.O. Box 1631, Tucson, AZ 85702.

ARKANSAS REPERTORY THEATRE COMPANY—THE REP

601 Main Street, P.O. Box 110 Little Rock, AR 72201
ADMINISTRATION: (866) 378-0445; BOX OFFICE: (501) 378-0405 or
    Toll Free (866) 684-3737; FAX: (501) 378-0012
E-MAIL: info@therep.org
WEB SITE: www.therep.org

Bill and Hillary Clinton used to live just around the corner from this ambitious, engaging company and even turned up in the audience from time to time. Cliff Fannin Baker founded the The Rep in 1976 and dazzled crowds with passionate storytelling and artistic standards that often rivaled the best in American theater. Today, in its own words, Arkansas Repertory Theatre "exists to create a diverse body of theatrical work . . . with a focus on dramatic storytelling that illuminates the human journey. The Rep entertains, engages, and enriches local and regional audiences of all ages and backgrounds." The Rep moved into a new downtown performing arts center in 1988 and was one of the few companies that toured both regionally and nationally. Current producing artistic director Robert Hupp heads the company, which operates under an AEA Letter of Agreement.

CASTING, GENERAL EMPLOYMENT OPPORTUNITIES, INTERNSHIPS

Arkansas Rep's Web site, www.therep.org, lists audition sites and positions that are currently open. Additional information is available via e-mail at info@therep.org.

ARROW ROCK LYCEUM THEATRE

P.O. Box 14, Arrow Rock, MO 65320
ADMINISTRATION: (660) 837-3311; FAX: (660) 837-3112
E-MAIL: lyceumtheatre@lyceumtheatre.org
WEB SITE: www.lyceumtheatre.org

A small white church stands up on the hill on Main Street in Arrow Rock, Missouri, and it's listed as a National Historic Landmark. The 130-year-old church is also billed as "the oldest professional regional theater in Missouri" and home to the Arrow Rock Lyceum Theatre. Quin Gresham is the artistic director and the theater produces musicals and plays for five months out of every year. Check the Web site for employment and audition information. A recent expansion included a 408-seat air-conditioned venue for the forty-year-old company.

ARVADA CENTER FOR THE ARTS AND HUMANITIES THEATRE

6901 Wadsworth Boulevard, Arvada, CO 80003-9985

BOX OFFICE/ADMINISTRATION: (720) 898-7200; FAX: (720) 898-7204

WEB SITE: www.arvadacenter.org

Dedicated on July 4, 1976, the Arvada Center for the Arts and Humanities has grown to become the seventh-largest cultural attraction in the Denver metro area. The center is home to an Equity theater and features children's theater and six mainstage shows. It is a past *Denver Post* Ovation Award–winner and a Colorado favorite for families, according to *Colorado Parent Magazine*, which voted the theater "Best of the Best" in 2005 for its children's theater programming. Deborah L. Ellerman is the executive director and Rod Lansberry is the artistic producer.

GENERAL EMPLOYMENT OPPORTUNITIES

Employment opportunities at the Arvada Center are generally advertised in either the *Denver Post* or the *Rocky Mountain News*. The Arvada Center is a division of the City of Arvada, and all job postings are listed on the city's job line, which can be reached by calling (720) 898-7850. Dial 453 for job listings.

ASOLO THEATRE COMPANY

5555 North Tamiami Trail, Sarasota, FL 34243

ADMINISTRATION: (941) 351-9010; BOX OFFICE: (941) 351-8000 or
    Toll Free (800) 361-8388; FAX: (941) 351-5796

E-MAIL: asolo@asolo.org

WEB SITE: www.asolo.org

The long, rich history of the Asolo Theatre Company has almost fairytale beginnings. In the 1950s, circus leader John Ringling moved a gorgeous eighteenth-century court theater from Asolo, Italy, to Sarasota, Florida. This building provided a summer home to a Florida State University company in 1960 and the seasonal event became known as the Asolo Theatre Festival. In 1966, the company became a year-round, professional LORT Theatre and in 1973, the entire graduate actor-training program from Florida State University was shifted from the main campus in Tallahassee to Sarasota. The FSU/Asolo Conservatory was born and America's theater world was almost instantly a better place. The Asolo was founded by Eberle Thomas, Robert Strane, Richard G. Fallon, and Arthur Dorlag.

Following 30 years in the original Asolo Theatre, the acclaimed Asolo Theatre Company moved into the stunning, palm tree–laden FSU Center in 1990, where it currently performs in rotating repertory in the delightful 500-seat Harold E. and Esther M. Mertz Theatre—a former opera house built in 1903 in Dunfermline, Scotland. This building, which had been rescued from a planned razing, was shipped in crates over the ocean and reconstructed piece by piece within the FSU Center. In 1994, the 161-seat Jane B. Cook Theatre was built for the performance of the Conservatory season and for smaller productions of the Asolo Theatre Company.

In the theater's own words, "The Asolo performs primarily in a rotating repertory with a resident company to celebrate the actor-artist, to attract regional, national and international audiences and to provide a training ground for FSU graduate students. The Asolo is dedicated to work which moves, enlightens, entertains, and educates individuals of all ages and backgrounds."

To quote producing artistic director Howard J. Millman, "Putting a season together is one of the most challenging, frightening, and exhilarating experiences I face every year. I always wonder if I have chosen a mix of plays exciting enough to attract our audience. I wonder if I have enough great roles for our resident artists, and I wonder if there are enough significant roles for our students who are about to step out into the professional world."

CASTING

The Asolo generally holds auditions in Sarasota between May and July for the upcoming season and also attends the May Florida Professional Theatre Association (www.fpta.net) and the Florida West Coast Theatre Alliance auditions. For the Asolo Sarasota auditions, check the Web site, local newspapers, and other media for updated information.

THE CONSERVATORY

Florida State University/Asolo Conservatory for Actor Training is a three-year graduate program culminating in a Master of Fine Arts degree through the Florida State University School of Theatre. Every Florida State University/Asolo Conservatory MFA candidate receives a full tuition waiver from Florida State University and an assistantship to help defray living expenses, supported by Asolo Scholarship donors. The Asolo Theatre Company and Florida State University together fund the second-year students' study in London. All students graduate with Equity eligibility through work with the Asolo Theatre Company, as understudies in their first year and as associate members of the acting company in their third year.

The FSU/Asolo Conservatory for Actor Training is a member of the University/Resident Theatre Association, Inc. (U/RTA) and is accredited by the National Association of Schools of Theatre.

GENERAL EMPLOYMENT OPPORTUNITIES, INTERNSHIPS

Check the Asolo Web site or contact: Personnel, Asolo Theatre Company, 5555 N. Tamiami Trail, Sarasota, FL 34243 or e-mail: asolo@asolo.org.

BARTER THEATRE

127 West Main Street, Abingdon, VA 24210
MAILING ADDRESS: P.O. Box 867, Abingdon, VA 24212
ADMINISTRATION: (276) 628-2281; BOX OFFICE: (276) 628-3991; FAX: (276) 619-3335
E-MAIL: barterinfo@bartertheatre.com
WEB SITE: www.bartertheatre.com

"Imagine a live hog or a dead rattlesnake for the price of admission. We are a theater of curiosity. And endurance." So reads the introduction to the Barter Theatre and it's no wonder! The Barter is one of America's oldest theaters and its remarkable beginnings are an integral part of early American theater history lore. Actor Robert Porterfield attacked the Depression head on when he arrived in southwest Virginia with an audience development approach that would make subscription guru Danny Newman proud. Bartering farm produce for play tickets seemed a logical way to make ends meet and on June 10, 1933, Barter Theatre opened its doors charging 40 cents or an equal amount of vegetables, milk, eggs, pigs, chickens, or whatever might be found for trade.

To quote Barter historians, "At the end of the first season, the Barter Company cleared $4.35 in cash, two barrels of jelly, and a collective weight gain of over 300 pounds. Today, at least one performance a year celebrates the Barter heritage by accepting donations for an area food bank."

The Barter is a founding member of LORT, a charter member of TCG, and was a major force behind the creation of ANTA, the American National Theatre Association.

In 1946, the Barter was designated the State Theatre of Virginia, and in 1948, the company was awarded the Tony Award for Regional Theatre. The Barter is home to two theaters, the Barter Theatre (507 seats) and the more intimate Barter Stage II (167 seats). One of artistic director Richard Rose's favorite quotes is from John Eldredge's *Wild at Heart*: "Don't ask what the world needs. Ask yourself what makes you come alive, and go do that, because what the world needs is people who have come alive."

CASTING

Barter Theatre generally employs a resident company of actors year-round. The company is made up of eight to ten Equity actors and six to seven non-Equity actors (Player Company). Usually Barter Theatre holds local auditions once a year, almost always during the month of December. To attend one of the local auditions, call (276) 619-3338 or consult the Web site sometime near the middle of November to schedule an audition in December. These auditions usually take place over the course of two days. Also, Barter Theatre occasionally casts in New York City using Paul Russell Casting, is represented at the LORT auditions every year, and at Unified Professional Theatre Auditions and Southeastern Theatre Conference.

Résumés may also be sent to Associate Director, Barter Theatre, P.O. Box 867 Abingdon, VA, 24212-0867.

INTERN/APPRENTICE AUDITIONS

Those interested in Barter's Player Company or the Barter Intern/Apprentice program should check the Web site for a contact name and number or send their résumés to: The Barter Player Company Artistic Director, Barter Theatre, P.O. Box 867, Abingdon, VA, 24212-0867.

GENERAL EMPLOYMENT OPPORTUNITIES

Open positions are posted on the company Web site.

INTERNSHIPS

For information on other internships, contact: The Barter Player Company Artistic Director, Barter Theatre, P.O. Box 867, Abingdon, VA, 24212-0867

BAY STREET THEATRE

P.O. Box 810, Sag Harbor, NY 11963
ADMINISTRATION: (631) 725-0818; BOX OFFICE: (631) 725-9500; FAX: (631) 725-0906
E-MAIL: mail@baystreet.org
WEB SITE: www.baystreet.org

Sybil Christopher and Emma Walton are co-artistic directors for this 299-seat professional theater on the Long Wharf in Sag Harbor. Founded in 1991, Bay Street is dedicated to "presenting new, classic, and contemporary works of the highest professional quality, which challenge as well as entertain, speak to our diverse community, and champion the human spirit. It is our mission to create an artistic haven, where an extended family of established and emerging artists may flourish in an atmosphere free from commercial pressures."

Bay Street operates from March through December, and many of its past premieres or shows in development have moved to Broadway, Off-Broadway, or other venues, including *Swingtime Canteen* and *Three Hotels*. Year-round programs include play readings, cabarets, performances and programs for young people, an internship program, acting and playwriting workshops, and the Young Playwrights Festival.

CASTING, SCRIPT SUBMISSIONS, GENERAL EMPLOYMENT OPPORTUNITIES

Bay Street Theatre accepts scripts by agent submission only. Casting is by agent submission to the casting director for each production. Check the Web site for audition information, internship overviews, and part-time and full-time positions.

BERKELEY REPERTORY THEATRE

2025 Addison Street, Berkeley, CA 94704
ADMINISTRATION: (510) 647-2900; BOX OFFICE: (510) 647-2949 or
   Toll Free (888) 427-8849; FAX: (510) 647-2976
E-MAIL: info@berkeleyrep.org
WEB SITE: www.berkeleyrep.org

BERKELEY REP SCHOOL OF THEATRE

The Nevo Education Center, 2071 Addison Street
MAILING ADDRESS: 2025 Addison Street, Berkeley, CA 94704
ADMINISTRATION: (510) 647-2972; FAX: (510) 647-2979
E-MAIL: school@berkeleyrep.org

Berkeley, California, in the mid-1960s was the place to be and Berkeley Repertory Theatre founder Michael Leibert made the most of the converted storefront theater he established in 1968 as the East Bay's first resident professional theater. In 1980, the company moved into a new complex in downtown Berkeley. Sharon Ott succeeded Leibert in 1984 and Tony Taccone took the helm in 1997. Susan Medak, current LORT president, has been managing director since 1990.

Recipient of the 1997 Regional Theatre Tony Award, Berkeley Rep has attracted the world's most prestigious theater artists, including Tony Kushner, Mabou Mines, Anna Deavere Smith, Tadashi Suzuki, Culture Clash, Theatre de la Jeune Lune, George C. Wolfe, and Mary Zimmerman, and has produced premieres of plays by Neal Bell, Philip Kan Gotanda, Lillian Groag, Naomi Iizuka, Heather McDonald, and José Rivera, to mention just a few.

In 2001, the company added the Roda Theatre, a 600-seat proscenium space to the already existing 400-seat thrust stage. A theater school in the adjacent Nevo Education Center opened soon after. In the company's own words:

> Berkeley Repertory Theatre seeks to set a national standard for ambitious programming, engagement with its audiences, and leadership within the community in which it resides. We endeavor to create a diverse body of work that expresses a rigorous, embracing aesthetic and reflects the highest artistic standards, and seek to maintain an environment in which talented artists can do their best work. We strive to engage our audiences in an ongoing dialogue of ideas, and encourage lifelong learning as a core community value. Through productions, outreach and education, Berkeley Rep aspires to use theater as a means to challenge, thrill and galvanize what is best in the human spirit.

CASTING

Berkeley Rep is a LORT B theater. It hires Equity actors and, every once in a while, local non-union actors for large-cast shows. Actors are hired on a show-by-show basis during the season and auditions for individual shows are by invitation only. Auditions are held annually in the late spring and are announced on the Actors' Equity hotline and the *Theater Bay Area* hotline and magazine. Berkeley Rep also attends the Theatre Bay Area general auditions, which are usually held in February. Out-of-town Equity actors who may be visiting the Bay Area are seen on the third Monday of every month. Members of Equity who plan to be in the Bay area and would like to schedule auditions should check the Web site for instructions.

SCRIPT SUBMISSIONS

Berkeley Rep accepts script submissions only from writers, agents, and theater artists with whom it has an existing professional relationship. Berkeley Rep is not able to accept unsolicited scripts. The only exception to this policy is for writers whose permanent address is within the Bay Area. Those scripts will be read and assessed. To quote the theater's materials: "To determine the kinds of plays in which Berkeley Rep has an interest, you might profitably consult the history page of our Web site. We are attracted to plays that explore the complexity of contemporary society, that demand the theater as their form of expression and that compel our audience toward a significant examination of how and why we live our lives as we do. We are partial toward work in which the language is used for expressing multifaceted ideas in a complex way rather than simply as a vehicle for human psychology."

INTERNSHIPS

Interns accepted into the program generally begin work in August or September and conclude their residency in June or July. See the Web site for more information. Internships in artistic and administrative areas include assisting the artistic director, working with the casting director, development and fund-raising, education, graphics/web/publications, literary/dramaturgy, company/theater management, and marketing/box office.

Production internships include stage management, production management, scenic construction, scenic art, sound, lighting/electrics, properties, and costumes. Applications are accepted no earlier than January 1 and materials must be received by April 1 for positions beginning the following August. Application forms and additional information are available on the Web site. All materials should be submitted to: Berkeley Repertory Theatre, Attention: Internship Coordinator, 2025 Addison Street, Berkeley, CA, 94704.

BERKSHIRE THEATRE FESTIVAL

P.O. Box 797, Stockbridge, MA 01262
ADMINISTRATIVE: (413) 298-5536; BOX OFFICE: (413) 298-5576;
    FAX: (413) 298-3368
E-MAIL: info@berkshiretheatre.org
WEB SITE: www.berkshiretheatre.org

The Berkshire Theatre Festival is one of the oldest and most respected in the United States. Executive director Kate Maguire notes that "the theater's access to its past translates into a vivid sense of what it means to be a participant in today's diverse and ofttimes unsettling world." Between Memorial Day and Labor Day, Berkshire Theatre Festival generally produces four Equity Main Stage productions, four to five Unicorn Theatre productions, and one BTF PLAYS! production for young audiences.

Designed and constructed by Stanford White, the Stockbridge Casino opened in 1888 and soon emerged as the center of social and cultural life in Stockbridge. Membership declined in the early 1900s and by 1927 the casino faced demolition. Mabel Choate, the wealthy daughter of one of the casino's founders, bought it for $2,000 and sold it to a group known as the Three Arts Society. Reborn as the Berkshire Playhouse, the 415-seat theater opened in 1928 with *The Cradle Song*, starring Eva Le Gallienne. Forty-odd years later, the Three Arts Society sold the Playhouse, which was renamed the Berkshire Theatre Festival. The theater is listed on the National Register of Historic Places. In the 1970s, the Unicorn Theatre was created as a second stage. In the company's own words, the Berkshire Theatre Festival's mission "is to sustain, promote, and produce theater for the community through performance and educational activities. BTF remains dedicated to producing theater that recognizes its venerable past as well as providing a home for the next generation of the American theater's creative artists."

GENERAL EMPLOYMENT OPPORTUNITIES

BTF is in the far western corner of Massachusetts in the heart of the Berkshires. Résumés are reviewed between December and April and production positions that are often available include assistant to the production manager, Equity stage managers, non-Equity stage managers, technical director, assistant technical director, master carpenter, carpenters, scenic charge, painters, prop master, props, carpenter, prop artisan, costume shop manager, assistant costume shop manager, drapers, first hand, stitchers, wardrobe supervisors, master electricians, electricians, sound engineer, and assistant sound engineer. Administrative positions include box office clerks, company manager, assistant company manager, and house managers. To apply, check the Web site for updated information and send a cover letter, résumé, and three references to: General Manager, Berkshire Theatre Festival, P.O. Box 797, Stockbridge, MA, 01262.

APPRENTICES

Descriptions and an application are available on the company Web site and should be mailed with a cover letter, résumé, and three references to: Administrative Director of Education, Summer Performance Training Program, Berkshire Theatre Festival, P.O. Box 797, Stockbridge, MA 01262-0797. Candidates range in age from 18 to 25 and are interested in pursuing a career in theater. The program runs from June to September, is tuition based, and the fee covers room and board. Students may apply for financial assistance from the Betsey McKearnan Scholarship Fund. The program includes training in acting, voice, movement, strength building, and various styles of text work with an emphasis on ensemble work. College credit is available. Apprentices are encouraged to participate at all levels of production, sharing both backstage and onstage responsibilities.

INTERNSHIPS

Each season the Berkshire Theatre Festival offers between 20 and 25 internships. Length of internship varies from three to four months, depending on the position and intern's availability. However, generally from mid-May to Labor Day, interns will work on four mainstage Equity productions and four productions on the Larry Vaber Stage in the Unicorn Theatre. Room and board are included. Internships are often available in public relations, marketing, development, accounting, company management, audience services, and general administration. Production internships are often available in scenic art, carpentry, props, costumes, electrics, sound, stage management, general production, and production management.

BUSHFIRE THEATRE OF PERFORMING ARTS

224 South 52nd Street, Philadelphia, PA 19139
ADMINISTRATION: (215) 747-9230; BOX OFFICE: (215) 747-9230; FAX: (215) 747-9236
E-MAIL: thebushfire@earthlink.net
WEB SITE: www.bushfiretheatre.org

The Bushfire Theatre Company was founded by a group of actors interested in creating theater opportunities for African American actors. In 1977, Al Simpkins developed the Bushfire Theatre of Performing Arts to produce theater "that depicts the African-American experience." This work includes a wide-ranging repertory of original work, dramas, comedies and musicals. An old vaudeville theater, The Locust, was renovated into a working theater and the company has also developed other spaces to make room for a café, the SanKofa Puppet Theatre, a Children's Literary Club, reception spaces, and offices. The complex includes a 419-seat mainstage theater, a 90-seat workshop space, and a 90-seat café theater.

CALIFORNIA SHAKESPEARE THEATER

701 Heinz Avenue, Berkeley CA 94710
ADMINISTRATION: (510) 548-3422; BOX OFFICE: (510) 548-9666; FAX: (510) 843-9921
E-MAIL: info@calshakes.org
WEB SITE: www.calshakes.org

Founded in 1974, the California Shakespeare Theater is known for its innovative Shakespeare productions, other re-imagined classics, occasional contemporary work, and the beautiful Bruns Memorial Amphitheatre in the East Bay Hills between Berkeley and Orinda in a protected watershed. Under the leadership of artistic director Jonathan Moscone, managing director Debbie Chinn, and associate artistic director Sean Daniels, Cal Shakes is committed to "being a leading community citizen by nourishing the imaginations of audiences, artists, and learners of all ages." "Artistic

Learning" programs offer a diverse constituency of Bay Area patrons a series of educational experiences as well as the four-play season from May to October.

CASTING, GENERAL EMPLOYMENT OPPORTUNITIES
The theater posts information regarding jobs and auditions on its Web site and makes audition information available through *Back Stage West* and the *Theatre Bay Area* magazine. To be included in the actor database, mail one headshot and résumé along with a cover letter to: Casting/California Shakespeare Theater, 701 Heinz Avenue, Berkeley, CA, 94710.

APPRENTICESHIPS
The theater offers year-round apprenticeships in the administrative offices and production apprenticeships during the season. See the Web site or e-mail the theater for details.

CAPITAL REPERTORY THEATRE
III North Pearl Street, Albany, NY 12207
ADMINISTRATION: (518) 462-4531; BOX OFFICE: (518) 445-7469; FAX: (518) 465-0213
E-MAIL: info@capitalrep.org
WEB SITE: www.capitalrep.org

Founded in 1980 by Michael Van Landingham and Oakley Hall III, Capital Rep is a LORT company working in the Market Theatre, a 254-seat thrust stage. Located near New York City, the theater attracts quality artists and takes great pride in its ambitious production history and connection to its community.

In the company's own words, "The mission of Capital Repertory Theatre is to create a meaningful theater generated from an authentic link to the community. Capital Repertory Theatre serves as a safehouse for the cultural lives of both artists and the community at large. It fosters the belief that the theater must serve as an advocate and caretaker of the common threads that bind the American culture together in a world that is defined more and more by diversity. Capital Repertory Theatre strives to bring to life those works that speak to our common cultural heritage as well as new work that expands our perceptions of ourselves and explores new horizons of thought through the medium of theater."

Capital Rep artistic director Maggie Mancinelli-Cahill notes that "the theater must have an authentic connection to its community to be meaningful. As an advocate and caretaker of a culture defined more and more by diversity, Capital Repertory Theatre strives to bring to life works that speak to the commonality of our heritage. Rather than be bound by any specific aesthetic agenda, the theater at its best entertains, cajoles, and inspires; it enlists its community by providing a wide scope of work drawn from classics, vintage comedy, and drama, as well as from new horizons of human thought and expression. It recognizes the mind and imagination as its most powerful ally."

GENERAL EMPLOYMENT OPPORTUNITIES
Capital Rep posts openings on its Web site. Production and stage management apprentice applicants should contact the production manager for job descriptions and more details about the positions: Production Manager, Capital Repertory Theater, 111 North Pearl Street, Albany, NY 12207; e-mail to prodmgmt@capitalrep.org.

CENTERSTAGE
700 North Calvert Street, Baltimore, MD 21202
ADMINISTRATION: (410) 986-4000; BOX OFFICE: (410) 332-0033; FAX: (410) 539-3912
E-MAIL: info@centerstage.org
WEB SITE: www.centerstage.org

Baltimore's leading theater was founded in 1963 by a community arts committee and operates under a LORT contract in the 541-seat Pearlstone Theatre and 150- to 350-seat Head Theatre. Playing to more than 100,000 annual audience members, this award-winning theater resides in Baltimore's historic Mt. Vernon Cultural District. In the theater's own words:

> CENTERSTAGE is an artistically driven institution, producing and developing an eclectic repertory in collaboration with leading theater artists for a diverse audience, interested in challenging, bold, thought-provoking work. Values central to our mission are the centrality of the artistic vision to all institutional decision making, a rigorous pursuit of excellence in all we do, the courage to take risks, and a commitment to diversity. Simply put, artistry—in service both to our artists and our audiences—is CENTERSTAGE's top priority."

Artistic director Irene Lewis and company are "collectively committed to developing and producing the broadest possible range of theater" as CENTERSTAGE's annual program typically includes a six-play mainstage season that encompasses "re-imagined classical work, new plays, and a music theater piece." First Look is a developmental workshop series designed to nurture the artist and to expose audiences to the early stages of new plays.

Three First Look readings of plays commissioned by CENTERSTAGE, and two additional workshopped plays, have led to subsequent mainstage productions: Warren Leight's *No Foreigners Beyond This Point* and Lynn Nottage's *Intimate Apparel* (2002-'03), James Magruder's new version of Molière's *The Miser* (2003-'04), Thomas Gibbons's *Permanent Collection* (2004-'05), and Motti Lerner's *The Murder of Isaac* (2005-'06).

CASTING

CENTERSTAGE generally auditions local actors twice a year at general auditions held by the theater each fall and as part of the Baltimore Theatre Alliance (BTA) area-wide auditions held in June. For more information on the BTA auditions, visit www.baltimoreperforms.org or call (410) 662-9945. CENTERSTAGE also participates in annual general Actors' Equity auditions in New York City (posted with AEA). For additional information or questions, check the Web site or try the company e-mail address.

SCRIPT SUBMISSIONS, NEW PLAY COMMISSIONS

CENTERSTAGE presents new works on the mainstage and has worked with many of America's most exciting emerging playwrights. The company has "a revitalized play commissioning program" as well as First Look, a workshop/play-reading series. The First Look series offers each script a week-long workshop with professional actors and directors, with a reading for the general public.

INTERNSHIPS

Theater production, arts administration, and dramatic literature are all internship areas and full-time interns must commit to an entire season at CENTERSTAGE (usually August/September to May/June). Academic credit is available but arrangements must be made by the intern. Interns may be able to supplement internship stipends by working in the box office, as a child wrangler, or as a bartender in one of the theater's three cafés. Production interns are usually in electrics, props, scenic art, sound, stage management, costume, or carpentry; and administrative and artistic interns are usually in audience development, company management, development, community programs, front of house, publications, and dramaturgy. To apply for an internship at CENTERSTAGE, see the Web site for the internship form and send it via mail to Internship Coordinator, CENTERSTAGE, 700 North Calvert Street, Baltimore, MD 21202 or via fax to (410) 986-4091. Review the Web site for other information and options.

CENTER THEATRE GROUP: AHMANSON THEATRE, MARK TAPER FORUM, KIRK DOUGLAS THEATRE

Company Offices at the Music Center Annex,
    601 W. Temple Street, Los Angeles, CA 90012
ADMINISTRATION AND BOX OFFICE: (213) 628-2772; FAX: (213) 972-4360
E-MAIL: taper_manager@ctgla.org
WEB SITE: www.taperahmanson.com

Mark Taper Forum & Ahmanson Theatre at the Music Center
135 N. Grand Avenue
Los Angeles, CA 90012

Kirk Douglas Theatre
9820 Washington Blvd.
Culver City, CA 90232

Center Theatre Group is the umbrella for the Mark Taper Forum, Ahmanson Theatre, and Kirk Douglas Theatre. The group's identity will always be linked to the groundbreaking regional theater entrepreneur Gordon Davidson, who founded the Mark Taper Forum in 1967 and worked for decades to develop the intimate Kirk Douglas Theatre before handing over the reins to Michael Ritchie in 2005. Mr. Davidson talked of "enlightening, amazing, challenging, and entertaining our audience" and predicted that the "future of Mark Taper Forum lies in the pursuit of artistic excellence, aesthetic daring, and community service." Indeed, Mr. Davidson helped pave the way for America regional theaters. In discussing his first season as artistic director in 2005-2006, Michael Ritchie hinted at his future priorities: "I'm pleased that this—my first season at the Taper—represents what I think is best about an entertaining season of theater: a wide range of compelling stories to tell, a broad spectrum of theatrical styles in which to tell these stories, and the creativity and artistry of the playwrights, directors, actors, and designers who serve as our guides through these stories."

According to its historical documents, the Center Theatre Group "exists to nurture artists by placing the creative process at the foundation of its commitment and by initiating programming that identifies, encourages, and supports these artists and the development of new work; to expose theater to a wide range of audiences; to enlighten young people, by encouraging their appreciation of theatergoing as a lifelong experience; and to provide artists and a diverse community an unparalleled educational and emotional encounter for generations to come."

The Music Center opened in 1964 and has been the home for the Mark Taper Forum, Ahmanson Theatre, Los Angeles Opera, Los Angeles

Philharmonic, and the Los Angeles Master Chorale. CTG/Ahmanson Theatre productions have garnered Tony Awards and the 1990 Pulitzer Prize for Drama (August Wilson's *The Piano Lesson*). The Mark Taper Forum Pulitzer Prize–winning productions include *The Shadow Box* by Michael Cristofer in 1977, *The Kentucky Cycle* by Robert Schenkkan in 1991, and *Angels in America Part One—Millennium Approaches* by Tony Kushner in 1992. It has also been celebrated with a host of Tony Awards, including the Regional Theatre Award in 1977.

CASTING, GENERAL EMPLOYMENT OPPORTUNITIES

It's probably best to check the Web site for updates to this process as recent artistic changes have been sweeping through the company.

SCRIPT SUBMISSIONS

At press time, the company requested a brief description of the work and from 5 to 10 sample pages along with a résumé, audio tape, and/or reviews. Playwrights may also want to check in with the Literary Department, Mark Taper Forum, 135 N. Grand Avenue, Los Angeles, CA, 90012.

THE CHILDREN'S THEATRE COMPANY

2400 Third Avenue South, Minneapolis, MN 55404-3597
ADMINISTRATION: (612) 874-0500; BOX OFFICE: (612) 874-0400;
   FAX: (612) 874-8119
E-MAIL: info@childrenstheatre.org
WEB SITE: www.childrenstheatre.org

Hailed as America's flagship theater for young people and families, CTC is a nationally respected, award-winning institution founded in 1965. In the institution's own words, "The Children's Theatre Company exists to create extraordinary theater experiences that educate, challenge, and inspire young people." Artistic director Peter C. Brosius joined CTC in 1997 and managing director Teresa Eyring signed up in 1999. The company produces six mainstage shows annually. These productions include original plays, classic tales, and work from around the globe. Winner of the 2003 Regional Theatre Tony Award, CTC is the first theater for young people to receive this honor. CTC's production of *A Year with Frog and Toad* received substantial critical acclaim and was nominated for three Tony Awards. Leading playwrights who have worked at the theater include Kevin Kling, Kari Margolis, Carlyle Brown, Ruth MacKenzie, Nilo Cruz, Jeffrey Hatcher, and Kia Corthron. CTC is based on a campus in south Minneapolis along with the Minneapolis Institute of Arts and the Minneapolis College of Art and

Design. It operates on a budget of over $8 million in a 60,000-square-foot facility built in 1974 and has a 746-seat performance space. CTC operates under an AEA Special Agreement contract.

CASTING, GENERAL EMPLOYMENT OPPORTUNITIES, INTERNSHIPS

Casting, employment, and internship information may be obtained by writing the theater, e-mailing info@childrenstheatre.org, or through the Web site.

CINCINNATI PLAYHOUSE IN THE PARK

962 Mt. Adams Circle, Cincinnati, OH 45202-1593

MAILING ADDRESS: P.O. Box 6537, Cincinnati, OH 45206-0537

ADMINISTRATION: (513) 345-2242; BOX OFFICE: (513) 421-3888, (800) 582-3208
    (toll-free in Ohio, Kentucky and Indiana); FAX: (513) 345-2254

E-MAIL: administration@cincyplay.com

WEB SITE: www.cincyplay.com

Perched high on a hill near the rambling Ohio River, the Cincinnati Playhouse in the Park overlooks downtown Cincinnati and thrives as a professional regional theater that combines artistic excellence and wide-ranging productions for diverse audiences. Producing artistic director Edward Stern, who joined the Playhouse in 1992, rejuvenated the subscriber base, provided a warm home, and midwestern hospitality for artists and emerging playwrights, and led his company to a Regional Theatre Tony Award in 2004. "Theater must do a better job of developing future audiences," advises Mr. Stern, who is certainly doing his part, producing nearly year-round to more than 200,000 people. The 626-seat Robert S. Marx Theatre and the 225-seat Thompson Shelterhouse are surrounded by Eden Park.

Meyer Levin's *Compulsion*, directed by David Marlin Jones, the theater's first artistic director, opened the then 166-seat Shelterhouse theater in 1960. Over the years, everyone from Scott Bakula, Roscoe Lee Browne, Patty Duke, Bonnie Franklin, and Swoosie Kurtz to Cleavon Little, Donna McKechnie, Estelle Parsons, Anthony Perkins, Charlotte Rae, Lynn Redgrave, Mercedes Ruehl, Susan Stroman, Daniel J. Travanti, Cicely Tyson, and Henry Winkler have touched audiences with their work. The Robert S. Marx Theatre opened in 1968, enabling the theater to produce in two spaces. In 1973, Harold Scott joined the Playhouse as the first African American artistic director in the history of American regional theater. To quote Playhouse historical materials:

> The Playhouse always has contributed to the national stage. Ever since the U.S. premiere of Henry Livings' *Eh?* in 1966, which subsequently played to great success Off-Broadway, the American theater

has benefited greatly from the vision and craftsmanship now synonymous with the Playhouse. Among its many other premieres are *Caravaggio* in 1971, directed and produced by Word Baker; *Sing Hallelujah!*, which enjoyed huge acclaim when it moved to Off-Broadway's Village Gate in 1987; *Tapestry: The Music of Carole King* (1988), which ran Off-Broadway five years later; and *The Notebook of Trigorin* (1996), a newly discovered work by Tennessee Williams which garnered international attention.

Over the past two decades, the Playhouse has typically produced at least one world premiere production each season, including *In Walks Ed* by Keith Glover in 1997 (nominated for the Pulitzer Prize) and *The Love Song of J. Robert Oppenheimer* by Carson Kreitzer, honored as the runner-up for the 2004 American Theatre Critics/Steinberg New Play Award. Edward Stern and executive director Buzz Ward head a company of more than 75 people, not to mention a board of about 54 trustees, nearly 1,000 volunteers, and more than 19,000 season subscribers.

CASTING

The Cincinnati Playhouse in the Park generally participates in the League of Cincinnati Theatres Unified Auditions. For more information or to download an application, visit www.leagueofcincytheatres.com. Check the Web site or information line for additional audition information.

THE MICKEY KAPLAN NEW AMERICAN PLAY PRIZE

To quote prize materials: "The Mickey Kaplan New American Play Prize was established in 2004 in support of Cincinnati Playhouse in the Park's longstanding commitment to the development and production of new works by both established and emerging playwrights and to the introduction of powerful and inventive new voices to the American stage . . . The play selected as the Kaplan winner receives a full production at Cincinnati Playhouse in the Park as part of the theater's annual season and is given regional and national promotion. The playwright receives a $15,000 award, as well as travel and residency expenses for the Cincinnati rehearsal period. Plays must be full-length in any genre: comedy, drama, musical, etc." See the Web site for details. Submissions go to The Mickey Kaplan New American Play Prize, Cincinnati Playhouse in the Park, P.O. Box 6537, Cincinnati, OH, 45206.

THE MACY'S NEW PLAY PRIZE FOR YOUNG AUDIENCES

A $5,000 commission fee will be granted to the winner of the Macy's New Play Prize for Young Audiences. The play will receive a full production as part of the Playhouse's outreach program. The play should be 50 to 55 minutes in length, written for an audience of elementary, middle, or high school students, able to tour in a van, and be suitable for a cast of three to five actors (actors can play multiple roles). No musicals. The play cannot have been produced previously. See the Web site for other guidelines and information.

CITY THEATRE COMPANY

1300 Bingham Street, Pittsburgh, PA 15203
ADMINISTRATION: (412) 431-4400; BOX OFFICE: (412) 431-CITY;
    FAX: (412) 431-5535
E-MAIL: theatre@citytheatrecompany.org
WEB SITE: www.citytheatrecompany.org

City Theatre Company specializes in new plays and has developed work by such national playwrights as Adam Rapp, Christopher Durang, and Jeffrey Hatcher. City Theatre's mission is "to provide an artistic home for the development and production of contemporary plays of substance and ideas that engage and challenge a diverse audience." A 270-seat mainstage and the 100-seat Lester Hamburg Studio are the two key performance spaces and, in 2004, City Theatre purchased a former steel rolling plant for development into parking and other creative uses.

City Theatre opened in 1975 as the City Players sharing its renovated performance space with the newly formed Pittsburgh Public Theater. Unfortunately, by 1978, Pittsburgh Public Theater's schedule necessitated its occupying the space year-round, and the City Players soon moved into a residency with the University of Pittsburgh's Theatre Arts Department and changed its name to the City Theatre. They continued touring, as well as working with the newly formed Three Rivers Shakespeare Festival. The company restructured in 1981, and in 1987 the troupe found a new complex on Pittsburgh's South Side: the former Bingham United Methodist Church. In 1991, the renovated space became City Theatre's new home. In 2000, Marc Masterson, City Theatre producing director for 20 years, took the job of artistic director of Actors Theatre of Louisville and Tracy Brigden began as artistic director in 2001. Typically, City Theatre produces seven plays along with MOMENTUM: new plays at different stages (a new works festival), and the Young Playwrights Festival (seventh- to twelfth-grade playwrights from the region).

CASTING

For casting information, check out the Web site, set up an appointment at casting@citytheatrecompany.org, and be aware of the audition policies: "General Equity and non-Equity auditions for City Theatre are held in

June. If you are an actor visiting or moving to the Pittsburgh area, and would like to audition, appointments are available at the discretion of the artistic staff." Headshots and résumé submissions are accepted throughout the year. Send a headshot and résumés to: City Theatre, 1300 Bingham Street, Pittsburgh PA 15203, Attention: Casting.

SCRIPT SUBMISSIONS

City Theatre Company commissions new plays, though commissioned playwrights are not chosen through a formal submission or application process. City Theatre approaches writers it has an interest in but "we are always seeking unproduced work, and we accept full-length original plays, adaptations, translations, musicals, and solo plays." City Theatre Company does not accept unsolicited scripts, nor does it accept submissions by e-mail. For consideration, playwrights should mail a query letter, along with a résumé, a complete synopsis of the play, a character breakdown, a 15- to 20-page dialogue sample (and demo cassette or CD for musicals), and the development and production history of the play to: Literary Manager & Dramaturg, City Theatre Company, 1300 Bingham Street, Pittsburgh, PA, 15203. See the Web site for additional information.

CLARENCE BROWN THEATRE

206 McClung Tower, Knoxville, TN 37996
ADMINISTRATION: (865) 974-6011; BOX OFFICE: (865) 974-5161;
    FAX: (865) 974-4867
E-MAIL: cbt@utk.edu
WEB SITE: www.clarencebrowntheatre.com

This theater was founded by Anthony Quayle and Ralph G. Allen on the campus of the University of Tennessee in 1974. The university's historical records document theater on campus "as early as 1840." Unfortunately, there weren't any decent facilities on campus for play production and, over the years, the program improvised with use of the university's Ayres Hall, Tyson House, the downtown Bijou Theatre, Tyson Junior High School, and, in the summer of 1951, a tent (named the Carousel Theatre because of its arena design).

The summer experiment was very successful, and it became clear that a permanent theater could fill community and university needs. Plans were made, and in December 1951, UT trustees approved the financing for a building designed on the basis of the Carousel tent. During the next two decades the Carousel Theatre program expanded to include thirteen productions annually. The department produced over 200 shows and total attendance was in excess of 70,000 people. The Children's Carousel, a series of plays for school children, began in 1953. The tremendous success of "Kiddie Carousel," as it was frequently called, is credited by many with helping to create a strong theater audience in Knoxville.

In 1973, Clarence Brown and his wife, Marian Spies Brown, donated $12 million as a permanent endowment fund to guarantee a high level of support for professional theater and theater study. Using this support and NEA grants, Ralph Allen and Sir Anthony Quayle founded the Clarence Brown Theater Company and toured throughout the Southeast with a 1976 production of *Rip Van Winkle* (starring Quayle and directed by Joshua Logan), even touring to Washington, DC's Kennedy Center. Over the years, Zoe Caldwell, Dame Judith Anderson, Mary Martin, Earl Hyman, and Eva Le Gallienne joined the company, and Ralph Allen's Broadway hit, *Sugar Babies* was developed at the theater.

In the 1980s, Thomas Cooke instituted an international exchange and the department hosted and co-sponsored the International Theatre Festival, world premieres, and an actor training conference with attendees from more than 17 countries. The new producing artistic director of the theater is Calvin MacLean.

CASTING, SCRIPT SUBMISSIONS, GENERAL EMPLOYMENT OPPORTUNITIES
Check the Web site for audition information or call (865) 974-6725 for additional information.

THE CLEVELAND PLAY HOUSE
8500 Euclid Avenue, Cleveland, OH 44106
ADMINISTRATION: (216) 795-7000; BOX OFFICE: (216) 795-7000 x4; FAX: (216) 795-7005
WEB SITE: www.clevelandplayhouse.com

One of my favorite regional theater moments was standing outside the historic, monumental Cleveland Play House complex in the 1980's and watching a group of LORT leaders and regional theater founders (including the joyous and irascible Peter Zeisler) try to hail a taxi after dark in Cleveland, Ohio! Being a good Ohio boy, I was the guy who "was volunteered" to go out and explain the ways of the Midwest (meaning you had to call for a taxi in Ohio) to this group of big-city producers. Considered one of the oldest of America's regional theaters (founded in 1915 by Raymond O'Neill), the Cleveland Play House has been key to developing new works for the American theater while producing a wide-ranging repertoire "celebrating the creative impulse of the artist," and creating educational programs for the community. Distinguished artistic director Michael Bloom produces the classics and original work in the 612-seat Kenyon C. Bolton Theatre, the 503-seat Francis E. Drury Theatre, the 159-seat Charles S. Brooks Theatre, and the 125-seat Studio One. The mission of The Cleveland Play House is "to produce plays of the highest professional standards that inspire, stimulate, and entertain our diverse audiences and to conduct training and educational programs that enhance the quality of life for those we serve and help to insure the future of theater."

CASTING

The Cleveland Play House generally conducts an open call for all union and non-union actors from the local area. Check the Web site for specific information. Following the open call, individuals may be called in to read for specific productions during the course of the season. For actors outside the Cleveland area, the theater uses Paul Fouquet of Elissa Myers Casting, 333 West 52nd Street, #1008, New York, NY, 10019. Actors from out of town who are passing through may call for a general audition, depending on staff availability. All interested actors may send a picture-résumé to Casting, Cleveland Play House, 8500 Euclid Avenue, Cleveland, OH, 44120.

GENERAL EMPLOYMENT OPPORTUNITIES, INTERNSHIPS

Check the Web site, www.clevelandplayhouse.com.

SCRIPT SUBMISSIONS

Cleveland Play House is committed to commissioning plays, developing them in a Next Stage Festival, and producing them on the main stage. The Next Stage Festival generally includes six to eight playwrights, including members of the Playwrights' Unit (a group of Cleveland-area playwrights who meet in a supportive environment to receive constructive criticism and encouragement) and early-career writers who have submitted their work to the director of New Play Development during the course of the previous year. While The Cleveland Play House does not accept unsolicited manuscripts, it does accept a synopsis and 10-page sample. See the Web site for details. Send your proposal to: The Cleveland Play House, Attention: Play Submissions, 8500 Euclid Avenue, Cleveland, OH, 44106-0189.

COCONUT GROVE PLAYHOUSE

3500 Main Highway, Miami, FL 33133
WEB SITE: www.cgplayhouse.com

To quote the theater's Web site, "Over the course of nearly a score of years . . . Coconut Grove Playhouse has touched the lives of close to two million children and adults with its enriching and entertaining programming, made possible with the aggregate support of numerous individuals, corporations, foundations, and government agencies." The Coconut Grove Playhouse was founded in 1961 to serve South Florida's diverse community using a LORT B and D contracts for productions that usually run between October and June.

As of August, 2006, the theater's phones were disconnected and the Web site sported a "Currently Closed" notice. The headline of a *Miami Today* article, dated August 3, 2006, asked the question: "Opening night or final curtain for Coconut Grove Playhouse?" Writer Michael Lewis noted that "it would be a shame if directors failed to get the Coconut Grove Playhouse's doors open again after 50 years as Miami's marquee theater." An earlier article by the *South Florida Sun-Sentinel* reported that a deficit "threatens to sink the theater as it celebrates its 50th season." Keep an eye on the Web site.

CONTEMPORARY AMERICAN THEATER FESTIVAL AT SHEPHERD UNIVERSITY

P.O. Box 429, Shepherdstown, WV 25443

ADMINISTRATION/BOX OFFICE: (800) 999-CATF or 304-876-3473;

    FAX: (304) 876-5443

E-MAIL: info@catf.org

WEB SITE: www.catf.org

The Contemporary American Theater Festival is, in its own words, "dedicated to producing and developing new American theater." Producing director Ed Herendeen founded the company in 1991 and has produced over a dozen world premieres and commissioned a number of new plays for production in historic Shepherdstown, West Virginia. The Festival also hosts special events including "Under the Tent" lectures. In recent years, playwrights Lee Blessing and Keith Glover have worked on new shows with the Festival.

GENERAL EMPLOYMENT OPPORTUNITIES, APPRENTICESHIPS, INTERNSHIPS

The Festival lists openings on the Web site and often hires for a two-month period (June and July). CATF also provides intern- and apprenticeships in all areas of the theater. These positions are usually listed on the Web site in December.

SCRIPT SUBMISSIONS

The Festival generally accepts agent submissions only. To submit a play for consideration, send a one-page synopsis and your biography to: Play

Submissions, The Contemporary American Theater Festival, P.O. Box 429 Shepherdstown, WV, 25443.

COURT THEATRE

5535 S. Ellis Avenue, Chicago, IL 60637
ADMINISTRATION: (773) 702-7005; BOX OFFICE: (773) 753-4472;
   FAX: (773) 834-1897
E-MAIL: info@courttheatre.org
WEB SITE: www.courttheatre.org

For over 50 years, the Court Theatre has been reinventing the classics with a long line of impressive artists and directors. Between September and June, the theater generally produces five productions in the 250-seat theater located on the University of Chicago campus, for around 35,000 patrons. The theater also plays to 4,000 area students through its high school matinee and in-school residencies programs. Charles Newell has been artistic director of Court Theatre since 1994. He has directed more than 20 productions and embraced the mission of "discovering the power of classic theater" along with the vision "to be the nationally celebrated professional center of excellence for classic theater at the University of Chicago." The theater states its top three strategic goals as being to "produce provocative, emotive, disciplined, and irreverent classic theater that attracts national recognition; define and create an environment that is a locus for the finest classic theater artists; and create opportunities for artists to develop skills in classic theater that draw the best early-career and established artists to Court."

CASTING

Send headshot-résumé and inquiries to: Casting Director, Court Theatre, 5535 S. Ellis Avenue, Chicago, IL, 60637. Non-Equity general auditions are generally listed on the theater Web site along with Actors' Equity national and local generals. Watch the Equity Web site for information or contact info@courttheatre.org.

GENERAL EMPLOYMENT OPPORTUNITIES

Check the Web site, www.courttheatre.org.

INTERNSHIPS

Paid theater internships exist for University of Chicago students in casting, dramaturgy, directing, production management, theater administration, arts education, development, box office, marketing, and front-of-house management. Descriptions and application guidelines are available on the Web site.

DALLAS THEATER CENTER

3636 Turtle Creek Blvd, Dallas, TX 75219-5598

ADMINISTRATION: (214) 526-8210; BOX OFFICE: (214) 522-8499;

    FAX: (214) 521-7666

E-MAIL: comments@dallastheatercenter.org

WEB SITE: www.dallastheatercenter.org

Frank Lloyd Wright designed the theater; the brilliant Paul Baker established the company and stayed for 23 years, Texas-native Adrian Hall left an indelible mark, Ken Bryant embraced the community, and Richard Hamburger has led the way since 1992. Committed to reinterpreting the classics, the Dallas Theater Center produces old plays, contemporary plays, and premieres, endeavoring to "create communal experiences that inspire new ways of thinking and living." The company ambitiously seeks to nurture and help shape the future of the American theater. The 466-seat Kalita Humphreys Theater is a thrust theater that melds with the trees on a steep slope above Turtle Creek, while the 500-seat Arts District Theater provides a flexible space.

CASTING

Dallas Theater Center general auditions are posted on the Web site. Questions can be directed to the local casting director, Jaynie Saunders, at jaynie.saunders@dallastheatercenter.org, and headshots and résumés may be submitted by mail at any time to: Casting, Dallas Theater Center, 3636 Turtle Creek Blvd., Dallas, TX, 75219

GENERAL EMPLOYMENT OPPORTUNITIES

Specific employment opportunities are listed on the Web site in great detail. The theater's production department occasionally requires qualified short-term people for scenic construction, costume construction, electrics load-ins, sound load-ins, etc. If this interests you, send your résumé with a cover letter expressing your field(s) of expertise and interest to: Production Manager. Dallas Theater Center, 3636 Turtle Creek Blvd., Dallas, TX 75219-5598.

DELAWARE THEATRE COMPANY

200 Water Street, Wilmington, DE 19801-5048

ADMINISTRATION: (302) 594-1104; BOX OFFICE: (302) 594-1100;

    FAX: (302) 594-1107

E-MAIL: dtc@delawaretheatre.org

WEB SITE: www.delawaretheatre.org

Here's a company that originally produced in an old firehouse before building and moving into its current location on Wilmington's Riverfront in 1985. Mixing the classics with contemporary and new work, the Delaware Theatre Company recruits heavily from New York and throughout the nation. The annual audience of around 40,000 enjoys productions in the theater's 389-seat proscenium stage. Founded in 1979 by Cleveland Morris and Peter DeLaurier, DTC is the Brandywine Valley's only resident professional theater.

In its own words, the Delaware Theatre Company "is a cultural, educational and community-service organization whose purpose is to create theater of the highest professional quality in Delaware and thereby enrich the cultural life of the area." Producing director Anne Marie Cammarato shepherds an operating budget of over $2 million. The theater has been a critical part of the community's plans to revitalize Wilmington's waterfront and pioneer a master cultural-tourism plan for the Brandywine Valley.

DTC's award-winning educational programs include the Delaware Young Playwrights Festival, theater classes, a summer theater camp, and valuable programs using theater to combat teen addictions and the spread of HIV/AIDS among adolescents, as well as specialized programs for at-risk children who are mentally challenged, hearing impaired, chronically ill, autistic, incarcerated, and/or who live in group homes.

CASTING, GENERAL EMPLOYMENT OPPORTUNITIES

Casting for actors is conducted by Delaware Theatre Company's through its general call and by casting agents. Notices are submitted to breakdown services and posted on the Web site. Send pictures and résumés to the Associate Artistic Director, Delaware Theatre Company, 200 Water Street, Wilmington, DE, 19801. Other positions are posted on the very well-organized employment section of the company Web site.

DENVER CENTER THEATRE COMPANY

1101 13th Street, Denver, CO, 80204

ADMINISTRATION: (303) 893-4000; BOX OFFICE: (303) 893-4100 or
    Toll Free (800) 641-1222; FAX: (303) 825-2117

E-MAIL: webmaster@dcpa.org

WEB SITE: www.denvercenter.org

One of my favorite theater moments was watching a spaceship fly onto the stage during artistic director Edward Payson Call's Denver Center production of Shakespeare's *The Tempest* in the early 1980s. A lot of theatrics have taken place in the Rocky Mountains since that time and DCTC has led the way. Founded in 1979 by Donald R. Seawell and helmed by artistic director

Donovan Marley for over two decades, the Denver Center Theatre Company celebrated its 25th anniversary, 77 world premieres, and a Tony Award before welcoming incoming artistic director Kent Thompson to the mile-high city in 2005. The four stages in the Helen Bonfils Theatre Complex include the 778-seat thrust Stage Theatre, the 450-seat Space Theatre in the round, the 250-seat proscenium Ricketson Theatre, and the smaller thrust 200-seat Jones Theatre. DCTC world premieres include *Quilters* (six Tony nominations), *The Immigrant* (both a 1986 play and a 2002 new musical), *Black Elk Speaks*, *It Ain't Nothin' but the Blues* (four Tony Award nominations), *Tantalus* (critically acclaimed in its Denver world premiere and six-city United Kingdom tour), and *The Laramie Project* (a critically acclaimed New York run followed by an Emmy-nominated HBO Film).

CASTING, GENERAL EMPLOYMENT OPPORTUNITIES, INTERNSHIPS

Audition and job information is posted on the Web site and internship opportunities are available in Denver Center Media (film production), the Denver Center Theatre Company, development, graphic design, the National Center for Voice and Speech, public affairs, and public relations.

DCTC NATIONAL THEATRE CONSERVATORY

The National Theatre Conservatory provides students with the opportunity to develop their talents and skills "within the challenging environment of a performing arts center and to prepare them for active careers in the American theater and in the film and television industries." The MFA training program is designed to "bring all students closer to the realization of their potential while steadily developing insights, attitudes, standards, and disciplines that will nourish them for the rest of their creative lives." Check out the Web site for requirements and applications.

FLORIDA STAGE

Plaza del Mar, 262 South Ocean Boulevard, Manalapan, FL 33462

ADMINISTRATION: (561) 585-3404; BOX OFFICE: (561) 585-3433 (Inside Palm Beach County); BOX OFFICE: (800) 514-3837 (Outside Palm Beach County); FAX: (561) 588-4708

E-MAIL: info@floridastage.org

WEB SITE: www.floridastage.org

Florida Stage's mission is "to engage its audiences through the presentation of a literature of the theater that deals with issues, ideas and the innovative use of language, structure, and style" and "welcomes and encourages each audience member to meet its work with intellect and imagination." The company is committed to providing a "creative working environment that nurtures theater professionals from Florida and across the United States, and promotes the highest levels of artistic quality and achievement."

The theater was founded as the Learning Stage in 1985 by actor/director Louis Tyrrell. In 1991, the company had moved to an intimate, three-quarter thrust 250-seat space in nearby Manalapan and had become the Pope Theatre Company. In 1997, the group changed its name to Florida Stage. The company has produced over 15 world premieres including works by William Mastrosimone, Peter Sagal, Nilo Cruz, and Lee Blessing.

CASTING

Florida Stage holds general auditions each year for professional actors during the summer months and callbacks throughout the season as needed. For more information, checkout the Web site and postings on the Actors' Equity Hotline for South Florida. Florida Stage also attends the annual Florida Professional Theatre Association auditions in the early fall. Equity actors visiting the area can call the theater and the company "will make every effort to arrange an audition during your stay in South Florida."

SCRIPT SUBMISSIONS

Florida Stage no longer accepts unsolicited play submissions. Agents are asked to e-mail Florida Stage producing director Louis Tyrrell before submitting. Playwrights are asked to work through agents and not submit directly.

INTERNSHIPS

Hands-on training is offered in the areas of administration, costumes, stage management, and in general technical areas. Interns work with Florida Stage professionals as crew, shop labor, and staff assistants. Administration interns are concentrated in the areas of company management, dramaturgy, and general administration. Internships span the production season (October–June). A salary is paid to each intern and housing may be provided for those who live outside Palm Beach County, Florida. For more information, contact the production manager.

THE FOOTHILL THEATRE COMPANY

P.O. Box 1812, Nevada City, CA 95959

Business Office, 404 Spring Street, Nevada City, CA 95945

ADMINISTRATION: (530) 265-9320; BOX OFFICE: (530) 265-8587 or

Toll Free (888) 730-8587; FAX: (530) 265-9325

E-MAIL: info@foothilltheatre.org

WEB SITE: www.foothilltheatre.org

FTC is heading into its third decade. Artistic director Scott Gilbert and executive director Sharyn Cleary produce theater "within the context of a professional artistic ensemble" and endeavor "to bring together people of diverse beliefs through the shared experience of live theater, offering high-quality theater in multiple venues." Complementing the company's wide-ranging work during the core season is its summer Sierra Shakespeare Festival set in the tall pines of the Fred Forsman Amphitheatre at the Nevada County Fairgrounds. FTC has also produced many seasons for the Lake Tahoe Shakespeare Festival.

FORD'S THEATRE

511 10th Street, NW, Washington, DC 20004
ADMINISTRATION: (202) 638-2941; BOX OFFICE: (202) 347-4833;
    FAX: (202) 347-6269
E-MAIL: onstage@fordstheatre.org
WEB SITE: www.fordstheatre.org

Ford's Theatre, John Wilkes Booth, and Abraham Lincoln will always be darkly linked in America's history, but the theater itself stands today as a symbol of President Lincoln's love of the performing arts, and is an American treasure visited by schoolchildren and worldwide visitors. Guided by producing director Paul R. Tetreault, Ford's Theatre is also a working venue committed to producing many of this country's most gifted playwrights. Ford's has hosted Mark Lamos's production of Thornton Wilder's *The Matchmaker*, Marshall W. Mason's production of Carson McCullers' *The Member of the Wedding*, and Deaf West Theatre's groundbreaking, Tony-nominated *Big River*. Located in Downtown, Ford's Theatre re-opened its doors in 1968 (following 103 years of closure). Frankie Hewitt was the driving force for nearly three decades, establishing the new producing organization and the in-house museum, while preserving the national theatre landmark.

CASTING, GENERAL EMPLOYMENT OPPORTUNITIES, INTERNSHIPS

Employment and internship opportunities are posted on the company Web site.

FREEDOM REPERTORY THEATRE

1346 North Broad Street, Philadelphia, PA 19121
ADMINISTRATION: (215) 765-2793; BOX OFFICE: (215) 978-8497;
    FAX: (215) 765-4191
WEB SITE: www.freedomtheatre.org

Rooted in the African American tradition, this North Philadelphia institution is "dedicated to achieving artistic excellence in professional theater and performing arts training." The theater's home is an historic mansion that once belonged to actor Edwin Forrest. Founded in 1966 by John Allen, the theater's producing artistic director is Walter Dallas. The 299-seat theater has attracted a remarkable array of artists, including Grover Washington, Jr., August Wilson, Ntozake Shange, and Lynn Nottage. Freedom Repertory also serves "as a learning laboratory and a model of excellence" for the Performing Arts Training Program which has provided over 10,000 students with "a safe, challenging environment in which to learn acting, dance, and vocal arts." Freedom Rep produces four annual productions each year in the John E. Allen, Jr. Theatre.

GENERAL EMPLOYMENT OPPORTUNITIES, APPRENTICESHIPS, INTERNSHIPS
Check the Web site at www.freedomtheatre.org or call the theater for additional information.

GEFFEN PLAYHOUSE

10886 Le Conte Avenue, Los Angeles, CA 90024-3021
ADMINISTRATION: (310) 208-6500; BOX OFFICE: (310) 208-5454;
    FAX: (310) 208-0341
E-MAIL: boxoffice@geffenplayhouse.com
WEB SITE: www.geffenplayhouse.com

Recently renovated, the warm and intimate main stage of the Geffen Playhouse is a grand spot to experience contemporary plays and the classics, while the new Audrey Skirball-Kenis Theater at the Geffen Playhouse is set to house and develop new works for Los Angeles. The Geffen's ambitious 10-year project of producing a "Festival of American Originals" is underway and audiences continue to flock to the cutting-edge work produced on the fringe of the UCLA campus. Past artists read like a Who's Who of the Theater, including Marcel Marceau, Uta Hagen, David Hyde Pierce, Frank Langella, Steve Martin, John Mahoney, Jason Alexander, Peter Falk, Debbie Allen, Annette Bening, Donald Margulies, Neil Simon, and many more. The experienced producing duo of producing director Gilbert Cates and Artistic Director Randall Arney have established the Geffen as one of Los Angeles' premier theaters.

CASTING, GENERAL EMPLOYMENT OPPORTUNITIES, INTERNSHIPS
Check the Web site or drop a note to the Geffen for updated employment information.

GEORGE STREET PLAYHOUSE

9 Livingston Avenue, New Brunswick, NJ 08901

ADMINISTRATION: (732) 846-2895; BOX OFFICE: (732) 246-7717; FAX: (732) 247-9151

WEB SITE: www.georgestplayhouse.org

In 2003, *American Theatre* magazine noted that three of the top fifteen plays produced in America's regional theaters were developed at the George Street Playhouse. That's a great start to the 21st century! Founded in 1974 by Eric Krebs and currently helmed by artistic director David Saint, George Street Playhouse is committed to the production of new and established plays. The Playhouse serves an audience of approximately 140,000 through a Main Stage Series (in a 367-seat proscenium/thrust stage), education, and outreach initiatives with a staff of approximately 50 artists, technicians, and administrators. The mission of George Street Playhouse is "to enrich people's lives by producing world-class theater" and the Playhouse seeks to produce the "highest quality of intellectually and emotionally challenging new works, re-imagined classics, and educational programming that speak with relevance to society; to serve as a vital cultural institution in New Jersey and a creative force nationally; to positively shape and be shaped by the diverse character of our community; and to create a nurturing home for the highest level of professional in the arts."

CASTING

George Street currently uses McCorkle Casting, Ltd. for Equity actor casting needs. For non-Equity actors, auditions are held at the annual New Jersey Theatre Alliance Combined Auditions. Contact the Alliance for more information or visit its Web site at www.njtheatrealliance.org. Check the George Street Web site for updates.

SCRIPT SUBMISSIONS

George Street doesn't accept unsolicited scripts but will consider "inquiry packets" which contain a synopsis of a play, a character breakdown, set requirements and sample pages (no more than ten) along with a self-addressed envelope. Check the Web site for specific information. Mail the inquiry packets to: George Street Playhouse, 9 Livingston Avenue, New Brunswick, NJ, 08901, Attn: Literary Associate.

SUMMER ACADEMY INTERNSHIPS & TEACHERS

Academy interns provide teaching assistance and administrative support to instructors teaching a wide variety of theater classes and performance programs to students ranging in age from 5 to 17. Bachelor's degree preferred (minimum of one year of college required) with a background in theater, education or a related field. Theater teachers teach acting skills, direct projects, and act as summer counselors. Teachers work Monday through Friday, 8:30 A.M. to 4:30 P.M. Theater teaching experience is recommended, with a degree in theater, education, or related fields required. Check the Web site for additional information. To apply, send a cover letter, résumé, and contact information for three references to: Director of Education, George Street Playhouse, 9 Livingston Ave., New Brunswick, NJ, 08901 or fax to 732-247-9151.

GENERAL EMPLOYMENT OPPORTUNITIES, INTERNSHIPS
Open positions are detailed on the company Web site.

GEORGIA SHAKESPEARE FESTIVAL
4484 Peachtree Road, NE, Atlanta, GA 30319
ADMINISTRATION: (404) 504-3400; BOX OFFICE: (404) 264-0020; FAX: (404) 504-3414
E-MAIL: Audition Information: companymanager@gashakespeare.org;
    General Information: boxoffice@gashakespeare.org
WEB SITE: www.gashakespeare.org

This is one terrific theater company and it's come a long way since the days of performing in a large circus tent. In its own words, "Georgia Shakespeare Festival exists to delight and inspire audiences with the excitement, mystery, and fun of live theater. While William Shakespeare shall be our primary playwright, we shall also explore other perspectives, stimulating and enduring authors. Georgia Shakespeare Festival, a not-for-profit organization, shall unite local and national artists to produce for our audience a lively and imaginative Festival. An integral part of the Festival's purpose shall be to provide educational opportunities for our audiences, young and old alike, through pre- and post-production activities. We shall be committed to the theater as a viable profession and shall utilize an apprentice program for both actors and technicians to further the education of aspiring theater professionals. The Festival shall be managed within a sound and stable plan." Founded in 1986, Georgia Shakespeare Festival is one of the oldest and most active Shakespeare Festivals in the Southeast. Producing artistic director and GSF co-founder Richard Garner and managing director Robert Fass lead the company with passion and finesse. It performs in the lovely 509-seat Conant Performing Arts Center, surrounded by a forest and the vibrant Oglethorpe University campus community, modeled after England's Oxford University. GSF's mainstage season runs from June through November.

CASTING, GENERAL EMPLOYMENT OPPORTUNITIES, INTERNSHIPS
Check the Web site and write the theater for information.

GEVA THEATRE CENTER

75 Woodbury Boulevard, Rochester, NY 14607
ADMINISTRATION: (585) 232-1366; BOX OFFICE: (585) 232-4382; FAX: (585) 232-4031
E-MAIL: gevatalk@gevatheatre.org
WEB SITE: www.gevatheatre.org

Founded in 1972, Geva attracts over 174,000 patrons annually to the 552-seat
Elaine P. Wilson Mainstage. Productions range from musicals to reinvigo-
rated American and world classics. The Ron & Donna Fielding Nextstage,
Geva's 180-seat second stage, features contemporary theater and is home to
Geva Comedy Improv. Geva Theatre Center offers educational, outreach,
and literary programs "designed to enrich and deepen the theatergoing
experience for our current audience and provide access and affordable
theater to the Rochester community including thousands of area students."
Geva is also committed to developing new plays and playwrights and nurturing "audiences and artists of the next generation."

CASTING

Geva's casting is coordinated by casting director Paul Fouquet in New York
City. Address all résumés-headshots to his attention at: Elissa Myers
Casting, 333 West 52nd Street, Suite 1008, New York, NY, 10019. Geva
Theatre Center also holds general auditions for Equity members, plus non-
Equity adults and children. Check the Web site for updates.

SCRIPT SUBMISSIONS

American Voices New Play Readings are one-day workshops (three per
season) of previously unproduced scripts with little or no development
history. After rehearsal, the script is presented in a public reading followed
by a talkback with the playwright. Hibernatus Interruptus: A Winter
Festival of New Plays is Geva Theatre Center's annual, two-week new play
workshop cluster. Geva selects and/or commissions two to four new and/or
unproduced plays, tailors the length and focus of each workshop to the
playwright's needs, and usually presents the works-in-progress as staged
readings, followed by talkbacks with the playwrights. Unproduced scripts
submitted to Geva are considered for the new play programs listed above.
Geva does not accept unsolicited scripts from writers without professional representation. Geva welcomes submission inquiries, including cover
letter, synopsis, résumé or production history, and 10 sample pages of dialogue, which may be sent to New Plays Coordinator, Geva Theatre Center,
75 Woodbury Blvd., Rochester, NY, 14607. Other playwright opportunities
and specifics on submissions are listed on the Web site or by e-mailing
gevatalk@gevatheatre.org.

GENERAL EMPLOYMENT OPPORTUNITIES
Checkout the Web site or write the theater for employment and intern opportunities.

GOODMAN THEATRE

170 N. Dearborn Street, Chicago, IL 60601-3205

ADMINISTRATION: (312) 443-3811; BOX OFFICE: (312) 443-3800; FAX: (312) 443-7448

E-MAIL: info@goodman-theatre.org

WEB SITE: www.goodman-theatre.org

The rich and vibrant history of the Goodman Theatre may be traced back to 1925 when it was founded as a tribute to playwright Kenneth Sawyer Goodman. Originally a repertory company and drama school connected to the Art Institute of Chicago, the theater took a giant leap forward 75 years later in 2000—as the company moved from the old Goodman to its glorious new 170,000-square-foot home in the heart of Chicago's North Loop. The 856-seat Albert Ivar Goodman Theatre's inaugural show, August Wilson's *King Hedley II*, was followed by Alan Ayckbourn's *Garden* in the flexible 335- to 467-seat Owen Bruner Goodman Theatre. Artistic director Robert Falls and executive director Roche Schulfer have led the Goodman Artistic Collective (including Frank Galati, Mary Zimmerman, and Regina Taylor) to the Regional Theatre Tony Award, to Broadway productions, and to myriad world premieres (including notable works by David Mamet, August Wilson, and Rebecca Gilman).

CASTING
The Goodman casts primarily Chicago-based actors. Auditions for specific productions throughout the season are by invitation only. If you have interest in a particular production, mail your picture, résumé, and letter of interest to the attention of the Casting Director at the Goodman Theatre.

The Goodman holds general auditions each year in the summer months. Once Equity general audition dates have been announced, Equity performers can either make an appointment in person at the Equity Office or call the Chicago Equity audition hotline. Non-Equity performers should request an audition in writing by sending one picture, résumé (with address and phone number), and SASE. Written requests should be postmarked between May 1st and July 15th. Do not call the Goodman to schedule an audition. See the Web site for additional information. Actors planning on moving to the Chicago area may send in a picture and résumé upon arrival and try to set up a general audition appointment. For more specific questions, contact the Casting office at (312) 443-3817 or e-mail CastingInfo@goodman-theatre.org.

SCRIPT SUBMISSIONS

The Goodman does not accept unsolicited manuscripts from playwrights. Only an agent may submit unsolicited scripts. The Goodman requests that playwrights without agents first send the following: a professional résumé, a professional letter of recommendation, a brief synopsis, an optional 10-page dialogue sample, and a self-addressed stamped envelope. Allow six to eight weeks for submissions to be read and processed. The literary department will contact you if it wishes to solicit the full manuscript. Materials should be sent to Literary Manager, Goodman Theatre, 170 North Dearborn Street, Chicago, IL, 60601.

INTERNSHIPS

The Goodman Theatre Internship Program is for qualified college students and recent college graduates who are preparing for careers in professional theater. Goodman interns have the opportunity to refine their practical and critical thinking skills through close interaction with Goodman staff and artists, and through independent exploration of Chicago's legendarily large and diverse theater community. Internships are offered in the following areas: casting, costumes, development, dramaturgy, education and community programs, general management, literary management, marketing/PR/press, production management, sound, and stage management. Stipends are available for all internships. Stage management interns are also eligible to receive Equity membership points. The awarding of academic credit is at the discretion of the intern's college or university. Internship applications and information are detailed on the Web site.

GENERAL EMPLOYMENT OPPORTUNITIES

For general employment, check the Web site and address inquiries to: Human Resource Manager, Goodman Theatre, 170 N. Dearborn St., Chicago, IL, 60601. Fax: (312) 553-7234.

GOODSPEED MUSICALS

Norma Terris Theatre, 33 North Main Street, Chester, CT 06412
MAILING ADDRESS: P.O. Box A, East Haddam, CT 06423
ADMINISTRATION: (860) 873-8664; BOX OFFICE: (860) 873-8668;
    FAX: (860) 873-2329
E-MAIL: info@goodspeed.org
WEB SITE: www.goodspeed.org

So many grand musicals have been shaped and produced at the Goodspeed Opera House since Goodspeed Musicals was formed in 1959 to restore the 19th-century Goodspeed Opera House. Professional theater resurfaced in 1963 and artistic director Michael P. Price, who joined Goodspeed in 1968, has spent almost four decades building the theater's international reputation for production, preservation and advancement of musical theater and the development of new works. Over 25 world premieres have been produced in The Norma Terris Theatre, located in Chester, Connecticut. From April through December, Goodspeed produces three musicals at the Opera House in East Haddam, and three new musicals at the Terris Theatre. Sixteen Goodspeed productions have transferred to Broadway, receiving more than a dozen Tony Awards. William Goodspeed built the Opera House in 1876 for his bank and shipping operations and to provide a home for theater.

SCRIPT SUBMISSIONS
Goodspeed Musicals does not accept unsolicited submissions of new musicals and only accepts submissions from agents and professional recommendations. Materials from agents should be forwarded to: Producing Associate and Literary Manager, Goodspeed Musicals, Box A, East Haddam, CT, 06423. No phone calls, please.

GENERAL EMPLOYMENT OPPORTUNITIES
Casting and employment opportunity inquiries should be addressed to the theater, and production applications and internship requests may be submitted on the company Web site. There may be opportunities not published on www.goodspeed.org, but the Web site is a good place to start.

GREAT LAKES THEATER (SHAKESPEARE) FESTIVAL
1501 Euclid Avenue, Suite 300, Cleveland, OH 44115
ADMINISTRATION: (216) 241-5490; BOX OFFICE: (216) 241-6000;
    FAX: (216) 241-6315
E-MAIL: mail@greatlakestheater.org
WEB SITE: www.greatlakestheater.org

Shakespeare provided the earliest roots for this grand old theater, and great plays of all cultures and time periods currently find their way to the 1,001-seat Ohio Theatre. Founded in 1962, the mission of Great Lakes Theater Festival has evolved and includes bringing "the pleasure, power, and relevance of classic theater to the widest possible audience in northern Ohio" and "the occasional mounting of new works that compliment the classical repertoire." In its own words, this Cleveland theater company endeavors "to share such vibrant experiences with people across all age groups, creeds, racial and ethnic groups, and socioeconomic backgrounds."

In 1961, English professor and Shakespeare director Arthur Lithgow (actor John Lithgow's dad), who had founded a Shakespeare theater a decade earlier at Yellow Springs' Antioch College, was invited to produce in the Lakewood City Auditorium. On July 11, 1962, the Great Lakes Shakespeare Festival opened. Lawrence Carra, Vincent Dowling, Gerald Freedman, and James Bundy all followed as artistic directors and made their marks on the theater. Mr. Freedman brought Hal Holbrook, Olympia Dukakis, Jean Stapleton, Piper Laurie, and others to the Ohio stage. Producing artistic director Charles Fee joined the company in 2002 bringing a renewed vision for staging the classics. He currently produces five annual shows at the Playhouse Square Complex.

CASTING
Great Lakes Theater Festival and the Cleveland Play House conduct an open call for all union and non-union actors each year. The auditions are by appointment. To make an appointment to audition, call (216) 795-7000 ext. 967. Check the Web site for additional information.

AUDITIONS FOR ACTOR/TEACHERS
Great Lakes Theater Festival (GLTF) also auditions for non-Equity actor/teachers for its School Residency Program; actors of all cultural backgrounds are encouraged to audition for full-time, seasonal, paid positions.

Requirements include an undergraduate degree in any discipline, as well as previous stage experience or actor training. Teaching experience or prior work with elementary, junior high, or high school age students, a plus, but not required. Applicants must have use of a reliable automobile. Check the Web site for additional information.

INTERNSHIPS
Summer internships are generally available in production and company management, stage management, costuming and wardrobe, properties, and set construction. Internships are full-time, paid positions. To be eligible, you must be an entering, current, or graduating college student. Start and end dates are flexible. To apply provide a cover letter and résumé to Great Lakes Theater Festival. Check the Web site for deadlines and additional information. Send your letter to: Production Internships, Great Lakes Theater Festival, 1501 Euclid Avenue, Suite 300, Cleveland, OH, 44115.

GUTHRIE THEATER

725 Vineland Place, Minneapolis, MN 55403-1187

ADMINISTRATION: (612) 347-1100; BOX OFFICE: (612) 377-2224 or

   Toll Free (877) 447-8243; FAX: (612) 347-1188

E-MAIL: management@guthrietheater.org

WEB SITE: www.guthrietheater.org

The Guthrie Theater is one of the revered "grandfathers" of the American theater movement which, in its own words, "sees itself as a leader in American Theater with both a national and international reputation." The beginnings of the Guthrie date back to 1959 when Sir Tyrone Guthrie, Oliver Rea, and Peter Zeisler decided to create a theater with a resident acting company that was different from their Broadway experience. The company was formed in 1963 with the vision that actors performing the classics in rotating repertory would develop into an artistic family and that this intimacy would create a marvelous relationship between actors and audience members. Indeed, this is what happened during the early years. Actor George Grizzard (who played the title role in the opening season's *Hamlet*) tells marvelous stories of the opening season that included such noted actors as Jessica Tandy, Zoe Caldwell, and Hume Cronyn. Legendary artistic directors Douglas Campbell, Michael Langham, Alvin Epstein, Liviu Ciulei, and Garland Wright followed over the years. Current artistic director Joe Dowling, long associated with Ireland's Abbey Theatre, pursues the Guthrie Theater's mission to serve "as a vital artistic resource for the people of Minnesota and the region . . . to celebrate, through theatrical performances, the common humanity binding us all together. The Theater is devoted to the traditional classical repertoire that has sustained us since our foundation and to the exploration of new works from diverse cultures and traditions."

Today, the Guthrie employs more than 900 people per year. On June 24, 2006, the Guthrie opened a new multistage theater center on the banks of the Mississippi River including three stages: a classic thrust stage for the grand-scale classics of the centuries, a proscenium stage for the more intimate classics of this century, and a studio theater to nurture new plays.

CASTING

The theater mostly casts locally, although some out-of-town actors are hired for almost every Guthrie production. The majority of out of town casting is arranged through the Guthrie's New York City representative, McCorkle Casting (575 Eighth Avenue, 18th Floor, New York, NY, 10018). Auditions for specific productions are held in Minneapolis and in New York as needed throughout the year. Actors are advised to check the Sunday classified ads in the *Star Tribune* or *Pioneer Press*. Annual Twin Cities general auditions are usually scheduled in February or March. Occasionally, Guthrie auditions are held in other major cities (such as Los Angeles, Seattle, and Chicago). Actors may send pictures and résumés to: Casting, Guthrie Theater, 725 Vineland Place, Minneapolis, MN, 55403.

SCRIPT SUBMISSIONS

The Literary Department accepts new play submissions only from literary agents and does not accept unsolicited plays or request plays based upon reading synopses. The Guthrie Theater commissions, develops and produces new work, and is interested in new full-length plays, as well as adaptations and translations of classical plays. Response time varies from three to six months. Literary agents should address scripts to: Literary Manager, Guthrie Theater, 725 Vineland Place, Minneapolis, MN, 55403.

GENERAL EMPLOYMENT OPPORTUNITES

Check specific position openings and actual application forms on the company Web site and apply by mailing, faxing or e-mailing a cover letter, résumé, and job application form to: Human Resources, Guthrie Theater, 725 Vineland Place, Minneapolis, MN, 55403.

INTERNSHIPS

An extensive intern program exists for theater and college students. The type of internship for which a student can apply usually determines the length of that internship. Complimentary tickets are available to interns as well as a 50-percent discount on Guthrie classes. Internships are unpaid positions. To apply for an internship, review the Web site information and print and mail in the application form from the Web site. Internships are available in company management, costume shop, development, directing, dramaturgy/literary, education, marketing, stage management, and technical production. The theater does not offer internships in acting.

HARTFORD STAGE COMPANY

50 Church Street, Hartford, CT 06103
ADMINISTRATION: (860) 525-5601; BOX OFFICE: (860) 527-5151; FAX: (860) 525-4420
E-MAIL: administration@hartfordstage.org
WEB SITE: www.hartfordstage.org

Hartford Stage is a Regional Theater Tony Award–winner, a Margo Jones Award–winner for Development of New Works, and the proud owner of OBIE awards, a New York Critics Circle award, a Dramatists Guild/CBS Award, and an Elliot Norton Award. Jacques Cartier founded the theater in

1963 in an old grocery store warehouse and opened it with *Othello* in 1964. Paul Weidner took over in 1968, moving the company to the 489-seat John W. Huntington Theater. Mark Lamos became artistic director in 1980, bringing international recognition to Hartford Stage during his seventeen seasons. Michael Wilson came on board in 1998 and developed the Tennessee Williams Marathon, the annual Brand: NEW festival, and Summer Stage. Hartford Stage has premiered over 50 plays (world or American premieres), including works by Theresa Rebeck, José Rivera, Christopher Durang, Horton Foote, Eve Enlser, Edward Albee, Alfred Uhry, Beth Henley, Edwin Sànchez, and Tennessee Williams.

CASTING

General Equity and non-Equity auditions for each season are held in late July/early August. Children's auditions (ages six to thirteen) are held separately in early October. Additional auditions are held on an as-needed basis throughout the year. Notice of all auditions are posted on the Web site with specific instructions for making an appointment. Actors are welcome to send a headshot and résumé at any time during the year to: Casting, Hartford Stage, 50 Church Street, Hartford, CT, 06103. No phone calls.

SCRIPT SUBMISSIONS

Hartford Stage accepts scripts by agent submission or professional recommendation only. Response time is usually several months. The theater does not accept unsolicited material for review.

GENERAL EMPLOYMENT OPPORTUNITIES

Full-time, part-time, and seasonal opportunities exist from time to time in various areas of the theater. Available positions are often updated on the Web site and are generally advertised in *The Hartford Courant* and *ARTSEARCH*. To be considered for employment at Hartford Stage, send a résumé and cover letter to Hartford Stage, 50 Church Street, Hartford, CT, 06103, or stop by the box office at the same address to fill out an application.

THE HUMAN RACE THEATRE COMPANY

126 North Main Street, Suite 300, Dayton, OH 45402-1710
ADMINISTRATION: (937) 461-3823; BOX OFFICE: (937) 228-3630 or
    Toll Free (888) 228-3630; FAX: (937) 461-7223
E-MAIL: contact@humanracetheatre.org
WEB SITE: www.humanracetheatre.org

The Human Race Theatre Company is one of Dayton, Ohio's many welcome surprises, as the Humana Loft Series provides audiences with edgy contemporary plays, new works, and American classics. The Musical Theatre Workshop offers original work or seldom-performed musicals, while the company's education and outreach programs are ambitious, exciting, and important to the Miami Valley community. The company makes its home in the Metropolitan Arts Center in downtown Dayton and from time to time, offers work in the historic Victoria Theatre and the glitzy Schuster Center. Youth-training programs, including Adventures in Theater classes, residencies, in-school tours, youth summer stock, and Theater in Context, allow the company to connect with over 30,000 students and teachers annually. In the troupe's own words, "The Human Race Theatre Company works to affect the conscience of our community, to see our audiences as our partner in the creative experience, to provide a platform for our artists to evolve and explore, and to be an educational resource for our community. As our name suggests, we present universal themes that explore the human condition and startle us into a renewed awareness of ourselves." Marsha Hanna is the theater's artistic director and Kevin Moore is the executive director.

CASTING

The Human Race holds general auditions in the spring and early summer in Dayton, Cincinnati, and Chicago. Specific dates and locations are announced in April. At these auditions, the company is usually casting roles for the Humana Loft Series productions (typically a combination of plays and musicals), one production on the Victoria Theatre's Fifth Third Broadway Series, an In-School Tour production and least one Musical Theater Workshop production. The Human Race works under a Small Professional Theater contract in The Loft Theatre, a 219-seat thrust stage. Other employment opportunities and internships are listed on the Web site when available.

HUNTINGTON THEATRE COMPANY

264 Huntington Avenue, Boston, MA, 02115-4606
ADMINISTRATION: (617) 266-7900; BOX OFFICE: (617) 266-0800; FAX: (617) 353-8300
E-MAIL: jobs@huntingtontheatre.org
WEB SITE: www.huntingtontheatre.org

Founded in 1982, the Huntington Theatre Company is now over two decades old, still enjoying its residence at Boston University, and continuing to grow with artistic director Nicholas Martin and managing director Michael Maso at the helm. The company works in both the 890-seat Boston University Theatre and the Stanford Calderwood Pavilion at the Boston Center for the Arts (which houses the 360-seat Virginia Wimberly

Theatre and the 200-seat Nancy and Edward Roberts Studio Theatre). Over 17,000 subscribers attest to the artistic quality of the company, which has received three Tony Award nominations for Broadway transfers. The Huntington has produced nearly fifty New England, American, or world premieres, including works by Tom Stoppard, Brian Friel, Christopher Durang, Donald Margulies, and Horton Foote, to mention a few. The Breaking Ground Festival of new play readings and the Stanford Calderwood Fund for New American Plays are part of the Huntington's efforts to commission and develop new works from emerging and established writers.

CASTING
The Huntington holds general casting sessions. Send résumés to: Casting, Huntington Theatre Company, 252 Huntington Avenue, Boston MA, 02115-4606.

SCRIPT SUBMISSIONS
The Huntington Theatre Company does not generally accept unsolicited submissions from writers without agents but will accept unsolicited submissions from agencies in the United States, Canada, and the UK. In efforts to support the work of area writers, the literary department will accept unsolicited scripts from playwrights without agents who are residents of the Greater Boston region. For these purposes, the Boston region includes all of Massachusetts and Rhode Island. See the Web site for additional information.

GENERAL EMPLOYMENT OPPORTUNITIES
Check the Web site for opportunities, e-mail jobs@huntingtontheatre.org or check with: Personnel Administrator, Huntington Theatre Company, 264 Huntington Avenue, Boston, MA, 02115.

INDIANA REPERTORY THEATRE
140 West Washington Street, Indianapolis, IN 46204
ADMINISTRATION: (317) 635-5277; BOX OFFICE: (317) 635-5252; FAX: (317) 236-0767
E-MAIL: indianarep@indianarep.com
WEB SITE: www.indianarep.com

The Indiana Repertory Theatre (IRT) is a gem that in its own words, "values live theater as an entertaining and educational event created by professional artists especially for our audience. We believe theater provides a unique opportunity for audiences and artists to share experiences that can be enjoyable, uplifting, thought-provoking, even life-changing. The IRT is the place that creates and perpetuates programs to make these experiences available to all segments of our community."

Founded by Edward Stern, Gregory Poggi, and Benjamin Mordecai in 1972 and designated the State of Indiana's "Theater Laureate" in 1991, the historic Indiana Theatre is a cultural landmark now led by artistic director Janet Allen and managing director Daniel Baker. IRT is the only fully professional resident not-for-profit theater in the state, attracts audiences of over 139,000 annually and plays to more than 49,000 students from 59 of Indiana's 92 counties. Generally, a staff of more than 100 seasonal and year-round employees creates nine productions in the 1927 Indiana Theatre, which houses the 607-seat Mainstage, 269-seat Upperstage, and 150-seat Cabaret theaters.

CASTING
General auditions are conducted every year in May or early June for Equity and experienced non-Equity actors. IRT also auditions actors on a show-by-show basis by invitation only in Indianapolis, Chicago, and New York. IRT encourages actors to send a cover letter, headshot, and résumé to Casting, IRT, 140 West Washington Street, Indianapolis, IN, 46204. Check the Web site for dates, times and procedures.

SCRIPT SUBMISSIONS
Submit plays to the Resident Dramaturg, Indiana Repertory Theatre, 140 West Washington Street, Indianapolis, IN, 46204.

GENERAL EMPLOYMENT OPPORTUNITIES
Check the Web site for general hiring information and submit applications and résumés to: Human Resources, Indiana Repertory Theatre, 140 West Washington Street, Indianapolis, IN, 46204.

INTERNSHIPS
IRT doesn't have a formal internship program, but informal internships are available in most production areas. Internships are unpaid, are for students only, and must be taken for credit. Interested students should check the Web site for details.

INTIMAN THEATRE
201 Mercer Street, Seattle, WA 98109
MAILING ADDRESS: P.O. Box 19760, Seattle, WA 98109
ADMINISTRATION: (206) 269-1901; BOX OFFICE: (206) 269-1900; FAX: (206) 436-7895
E-MAIL: intiman@intiman.org
WEB SITE: www.intiman.org

One of the best theaters in the Pacific Northwest is the Intiman, founded in 1972, and committed to developing new work including the world premiere of Joan Holden's *Nickel and Dimed* and the Tony Award–winning musical *The Light in the Piazza*, by Craig Lucas and Adam Guettel. Under the leadership of artistic director Bartlett Sher and managing director Laura Penn, Intiman produces classics and contemporary plays, and in its own words, "produces engaging dramatic work that celebrates the intimate relationship among artist, audience, and language and, through the exploration of enduring themes, illuminates the shared human experience of our diverse community." Intiman is producing *The American Cycle* through 2008. It is a five-year series of classic American stories, civic dialogue, community partnerships, and educational programming for multigenerational audiences launched in 2004.

CASTING

The Intiman's "Actor Info-line" is (206) 269-1901, ext. 351, or information is also on Seattle's Equity hotline, (888) 266-1731, ext. 109. The Intiman holds two days of Equity local auditions per year and Equity generals are listed on the local Equity Hotline. Intiman also attends the general auditions organized by Theatre Puget Sound (TPS). TPS organizes two rounds of local generals per year. For more information, check out its Web site at www.tpsonline.org. Intiman maintains an active file of both local and out-of-town actors based on those auditions. The theater also maintains a select database of actors seen in general auditions or performance.

SCRIPT SUBMISSIONS

The Intiman accepts work from literary agents or by the recommendation of an artistic director, literary manager, or dramaturg affiliated with a professional theater. No unsolicited manuscripts are accepted. Check the Web site for more specifics. The Intiman produces from April through December, so the best submission time is from October through March.

GENERAL EMPLOYMENT OPPORTUNITIES

Check the Web site for general employment information.

KANSAS CITY REPERTORY THEATRE

4949 Cherry Street, Kansas City, MO 64110
ADMINISTRATION: (816) 235-2727; BOX OFFICE: (816) 235-2700; FAX: (816) 235-5367
E-MAIL: info@kcrep.org
WEB SITE: www.kcrep.org

Housed in the Performing Arts Center on the University of Missouri, Kansas City campus, The Rep produces six mainstage plays each season and employs more than 250 company members who mount plays for 100,000 annual patrons. Founded in 1964 as part of the UMKC Department of

Theater, the Rep works mostly in University facilities. The theater is dedicated to enhancing the training of UMKC's theater students who work with and understudy Rep artists. Peter Altman is the producing artistic director, George Keathley was artistic director from 1985 to 2000, and founder Dr. Patricia McIlrath guided the theater from 1964 until she retired in 1985.

CASTING

The Rep generally holds auditions in the spring of each year in Kansas City. Auditions are posted in the *Kansas City Star* and on the Equity Hotline (913) 248-8228. Auditions include one or two memorized monologues, one from a verse play, not to exceed four minutes total, an 8x10 glossy headshot, and a current theatrical résumé. The Rep selects both union and non-union actors through the audition process. The Rep also holds general casting auditions in Kansas City, New York and Los Angeles. Send a picture and résumé to Casting, Kansas City Repertory Theatre, 4949 Cherry Street, Kansas City, MO, 64110. Check the Web site for details.

GENERAL EMPLOYMENT OPPORTUNITIES

Check the Web site for openings.

INTERNSHIPS

Check the Web site for details on a new internship program.

LAGUNA PLAYHOUSE

Moulton Theater, 606 Laguna Canyon Road, Laguna Beach, CA 92652
MAILING ADDRESS: P.O. Box 1747, Laguna Beach, CA 92652
ADMINISTRATION: (949) 497-2787; BOX OFFICE: (949) 497-2787; FAX: (949) 497-6948
E-MAIL: box_office@lagunaplayhouse.com
WEB SITE: www.lagunaplayhouse.com

Just around the corner from the Pacific Ocean, this ambitious theater has a grand history and a network of professional artists to shape the future. It all started in a living room in 1920, when a group of Laguna Beach citizens sat down to establish a local theater. From private homes and storefronts, the Laguna Playhouse has blossomed into an impressive professional theater with ongoing west coast, American, and world premieres playing to over 110,000 patrons. In 1924, at a cost of $5,000, the Playhouse was built on Ocean Avenue. It was used to entertain the soldiers and was dressed up for USO dances during World War II. In 1969, the theater's current home, the Moulton Theatre, opened on Laguna Canyon Road. Richard Stein assumed the leadership of the Playhouse in 1990 as executive director, and was joined in 1991 by Andrew Barnicle as artistic director; a successful expansion ensued. An expansion site has been located next door to the Moulton Theatre and a recent $5 million pledge will assist the Playhouse with this long-anticipated development project. Plans call for an intimate, 225-seat, thrust-stage facility, with backstage facilities, classroom spaces, sound recording studio, function room and audience amenities. It will be physically connected to the present Moulton Theatre and together will form the centerpiece of the Laguna Beach Arts District.

CASTING
Actors seeking roles in mainstage season productions are invited to submit a photo and résumé to Casting, Laguna Playhouse, P.O. Box 4049, Laguna Beach, CA, 92652. Most productions are cast through agent submissions. Since the Laguna Playhouse operates under a LORT contract, few roles are cast with non-Equity performers. However, all actors are welcome to submit résumés. Audition information for adult and youth roles in the Youth Theater season is posted under the "Education" section of the Web site.

SCRIPT SUBMISSIONS
Scripts may be submitted to Laguna Playhouse, P. O. Box 4049, Laguna Beach, CA, 92652. The Playhouse does not encourage unsolicited manuscripts, and the review process may take up to one year.

GENERAL EMPLOYMENT OPPORTUNITIES, INTERNSHIPS
Check the Web site for openings. The theater also maintains a list of experience technicians interested in working in a "temporary overhire" situation to work load-ins and strike in the areas of carpentry, electrics, and sound.

LA JOLLA PLAYHOUSE
P.O. Box 12039, La Jolla, CA 92039
ADMINISTRATION: (858) 550-1070; BOX OFFICE: (858) 550-1010; FAX: (858) 550-1075
E-MAIL: information@ljp.org
WEB SITE: www.lajollaplayhouse.com

A number of Broadway shows were created at the La Jolla Playhouse (including *The Who's Tommy* and *Big River*), and artistic director Des McAnuff believes in advancing theater "as an art form and as a vital social, moral, and political platform by providing unfettered creative opportunities for the leading artists of today and tomorrow." In the theater's own words, "With our youthful spirit and eclectic, artist-driven approach we will continue to cultivate a local and national following with an insatiable appetite for audacious and diverse work." The Playhouse produces a mainstage season of six to eight new plays, classics, and musicals, many of which are world premieres, and supports the creation of new work through its "Page To Stage" play development program, which includes commissions, readings, and workshops. Two-time Tony Award–winner McAnuff and the Playhouse have produced over 40 world premieres, 24 West Coast premieres, and 7 American premieres. The theater received the 1993 Regional Theater Tony Award.

La Jolla Playhouse was founded in 1947 by Gregory Peck, Dorothy McGuire, and Mel Ferrer, and revived in 1983 under the leadership of Des McAnuff, who served as artistic director from 1983 to 1994. McAnuff was succeeded by Michael Greif, who served as artistic director from 1995 to 1999. La Jolla is currently led again by McAnuff. The Playhouse is in residence on the University of California, San Diego campus.

CASTING, SCRIPT SUBMISSIONS, GENERAL EMPLOYMENT OPPORTUNITIES
Check the Web site for ongoing information.

INTERNSHIP PROGRAM
The Playhouse offers full-time and part-time internships over a minimum of 12 weeks. The program runs all year, but can be extended or adjusted according to availability and departmental need. There is no stipend. Positions generally include public relations, graphics, general management, company management, costumes, fund-raising/special events, artistic, literary/dramaturgy, education, and outreach programs, production management, props, run/wardrobe crew, scene shop, scenic artist, stage management, and operations. Positions aren't offered in directing or acting.

College credit is available. An application, personal statement, résumé, and two letters of recommendation must be received prior to consideration. An online internship application should also be completed and sent to: La Jolla Playhouse, Attn: Internship Program, P.O. Box 12039, La Jolla, CA, 92039.

LINCOLN CENTER THEATER
The Vivian Beaumont and Mitzi E. Newhouse Theaters, 150 West 65th Street, New York, NY 10023
ADMINISTRATION: (212) 362-7600; BOX OFFICE: customerservice@lct.org or Telecharge: (212) 239-6210; FAX: (212) 873-0761
E-MAIL: info@lct.org
WEB SITE: www.lct.org

Founded by John D. Rockefeller and re-established in 1985 under the leadership of chairman John V. Lindsay, director Gregory Moshe, and executive producer Bernard Gersten, Lincoln Center has produced myriad award-winning plays for millions of audience members at the Vivian Beaumont Theater, the Mitzi E. Newhouse Theater, and other venues.

John D. Rockefeller's mandate that "the arts are not for the privileged few, but for the many" still thrives as the Lincoln Center Theater makes every effort to "keep admission prices low and its doors open to all." Ongoing activities include the literary journal, *Lincoln Center Theater Review*; the Playwrights Program; the Directors Lab; Open Stages, an arts-in-education program operated in cooperation with New York City public schools; and the Platform Series of free conversations with LCT artists. Currently, chairman John B. Beinecke, artistic director André Bishop, and executive producer Bernard Gersten oversee the 1,100-seat Vivian Beaumont Theater and the 299-seat Mitzi E. Newhouse Theater. Since 1985, the not-for-profit company Lincoln Center Theater has operated the Beaumont and Newhouse, producing world premieres and classics including *Marie Christine*, *Parade*, *Juan Darien*, *Arcadia*, *Contact*, *A New Brain*, *Pride's Crossing*, *Hapgood*, *The Sisters Rosensweig*, and *The Substance of Fire*.

CASTING, SCRIPT SUBMISSIONS, GENERAL EMPLOYMENT OPPORTUNITIES

Check the Web site and e-mail the theater at info@lct.org for ongoing information.

LONG WHARF THEATRE

222 Sargent Drive, New Haven, CT 06511

ADMINISTRATION: (203) 787-4284; BOX OFFICE: (203) 787-4282 or
  Toll Free (800) 782-8497; FAX: (203) 776-2287

E-MAIL: info@longwharf.org

WEB SITE: www.longwharf.org

So many great plays have found a home at the Long Wharf Theatre since two Yale University alumni created the institution in 1965. Jon Jory and Harlan Kleiman opened the theater with Arthur Miller's *The Crucible*. The venue was constructed in an old warehouse and named for the Long Wharf port along New Haven Harbor. Four decades later, the Tony Award–winning company boasts an annual audience exceeding 100,000 and, in its own words, produces "imaginative revivals of classics and modern plays, rediscoveries of neglected works, and a variety of world and American premieres." Broadway or Off-Broadway transfers include *Wit* (1999 Pulitzer Prize), *Hughie*, *Broken Glass*, *The Gin Game*, *Streamers*, *American Buffalo*, *Requiem for a Heavyweight*, and *Quartermaine's Terms*.

CASTING

Long Wharf Theatre works under a LORT/AEA contract and the union determines the number of non-Equity actors in any production. Equity auditions are held in New York, Chicago, or Los Angeles, depending on the needs of the production, and auditions are arranged through agent submissions, and scheduled by a casting director in each city. Actors may send a photo and résumé to Casting, Long Wharf Theatre, 222 Sargent Drive, New Haven, CT, 06511.

SCRIPT SUBMISSIONS

Long Wharf Theatre only accepts scripts received via agent submission or professional recommendation and does not accept unsolicited scripts.

GENERAL EMPLOYMENT OPPORTUNITIES

Check the Web site and e-mail the theater at info@longwharf.org for ongoing information. Freelance production artists are often in demand. The Long Wharf Theatre posts employment opportunities for experienced theater professionals. Check the Web site or send queries to Human Resources, Long Wharf Theatre, 222 Sargent Drive, New Haven, CT, 06511.

INTERNSHIPS

Internships offer recent college graduates and early-career professionals the opportunity to work extensively in their area of interest in a professional regional theater. Internship benefits include seminars and workshops led by guest artists and theater professionals, complimentary tickets to all Long Wharf productions, and the opportunity to attend other Connecticut theaters and special events, a weekly housing stipend, and affordable housing available through Long Wharf. Full-time, full-season internships are available, as well as part-time and semester-long internships. College credit may be arranged with academic institutions. Application forms are online, or e-mail: internships@longwharf.org for additional information.

MALTZ JUPITER THEATRE

1001 E. Indiantown Road, Jupiter, FL 33477

ADMINISTRATION: (561) 743-2666; BOX OFFICE: (561) 575-2223 or
    Toll Free (800) 445-1666
E-MAIL: info@jupitertheatre.org
WEB SITE: www.jupitertheatre.org

With productions ranging from world premieres to musicals to contemporary plays, the theater has undergone a dramatic $10 million renovation, recently opening as a 550-seat, nonprofit community-based regional theater. The theater also plans to produce classic plays with nationally renowned actors, as well as leading cabaret acts, concerts, and a play-to-film series. Phase II of the theater's development will include facilities to accommodate a Children's Theater Institute, expanded community programming, additional seating and workspace, and an new Art Deco exterior.

CASTING, GENERAL EMPLOYMENT OPPORTUNITIES, INTERNSHIPS

Check the Web site for general employment information or e-mail info@jupitertheatre.org

MANHATTAN THEATRE CLUB

311 West 43rd Street, 8th floor; New York, NY 10036
ADMINISTRATION: (212) 399-3000; FAX: (212) 399-4329
E-MAIL: questions@mtc-nyc.org
WEB SITE: www.mtc-nyc.org

MTC/Biltmore Theatre

261 West 47th Street, New York, NY 10036

Stages I and II at NY City Center

131 West 55th Street, New York, NY 10019
BOX OFFICE: CityTix: (212) 581-1212; Telecharge: (212) 239-6200

The revered Manhattan Theatre Club is, in its own words, "the creative and artistic home for America's most gifted theatrical artists, producing works of the highest quality by both established and emerging American and international playwrights." Manhattan Theatre Club nurtures and develops new and emerging talent in playwriting, musical composition, directing, acting, and design. Artistic director Lynne Meadow and executive producer Barry Grove have developed the theater from an Off-Off Broadway showcase into one of the country's leading theater institutions.

Founded in 1970, MTC has 20,000 subscribers and produces seven plays a year in Broadway's restored Biltmore Theatre on West 47th Street and at the historic City Center complex on West 55th Street. The company's three performance spaces include the 650-seat Biltmore Theatre and City Center's 299-seat Stage I and 150-seat Stage II. MTC's many awards include 11 Tony Awards and 3 Pulitzer Prizes.

CASTING

MTC accepts both agent and personal submissions. Individuals and agents should submit headshots and résumés along with a letter of interest. All submissions can be sent to: Manhattan Theatre Club, Attn: Casting, 311 West 43rd Street, 8th Floor, New York, NY, 10036.

DIRECTING FELLOWSHIPS

Manhattan Theatre Club offers Directing Fellowships for each of the Biltmore (Broadway), Stage I and Stage II (Off-Broadway) shows. These fellows are selected by letter-résumé submission and work closely with MTC staff and directors in assisting with the staging of each production. Experienced individuals should send a letter of interest and current résumé to MTC: Directing Fellows, Manhattan Theatre Club, 311 West 43rd Street, Eighth Floor, New York, NY, 10036 or to directingfellows@mtc-nyc.org

SCRIPT SUBMISSIONS

The literary department at MTC accepts only agent submissions for full-length plays. MTC does not accept unsolicited scripts, but interested parties can fax or mail MTC announcements of local readings and productions.

GENERAL EMPLOYMENT OPPORTUNITIES, INTERNSHIPS

Check the Web site for detailed production opportunities and artistic, business, casting, development, special events, education, executive producer, general management, information technology, marketing, literary, and production internships. Interns are provided a weekly stipend, free tickets to all MTC productions, invitations to readings of new plays and exciting special events, and free and discounted ticket offers to other companies' Broadway and Off-Broadway performances. Check the Web site for details and the MTC intern application form.

McCARTER THEATRE CENTER

91 University Place, Princeton NJ 08540

ADMINISTRATION: (609) 258-6500; TICKETS AND GENERAL INQUIRIES: (609) 258-2787 or (888) ARTSWEB; FAX: (609) 497-0369

E-MAIL: admin@mccarter.org

WEB SITE: www.mccarter.org

Emily Mann has led the Tony Award–winning McCarter Theatre with her unique vision "to create a theater of testimony, engaged in a dialogue with the world around it, paying tribute to the enduring power of the human spirit and scope of the imagination." Over twenty new plays and adaptations have had their world or American premieres at the McCarter since 1991 and more than 200,000 audience members journey to the theater annually. Recipient of the 1994 Tony Award for Outstanding Regional Theater, McCarter's five-play Theater Series is supplemented by broad-based outreach activities, including programs for students, the elderly, and persons with disabilities. The building was constructed in 1929 to provide a permanent home for Princeton University's Triangle Club. Daniel Seltzer founded the theater in 1972. It currently is supported by nearly 15,000 subscribers.

CASTING
Productions are cast through Alan Filderman Casting, The Bernard Telsey Agency, and Elissa Myers Casting in New York. Check the McCarter Web site for agency addresses. McCarter also participates in general audition calls required by Actors' Equity contract, and in the New Jersey Theatre Alliance lottery auditions (973) 593-0189; www.njtheatrealliance.com. For casting inquiries e-mail: casting@mccarter.org. For non-Equity casting for the annual *A Christmas Carol*, send a picture and résumé to McCarter Theatre, Attn. Christmas Carol Casting, 91 University Place, Princeton, NJ, 08540, or e-mail picture and résumé to casting@mccarter.org. Check the Web site for additional information on children's casting for boys and girls ages 5 to 13.

SCRIPT SUBMISSIONS
The McCarter accepts full-length scripts sent by agents or established theater professionals (director, artistic director, literary manager) who are familiar with the work produced at McCarter. The McCarter does not accept unsolicited scripts or e-mail submissions. All letters of inquiry should be sent to: McCarter Theatre, Attn: Literary Manager, 91 University Place, Princeton, NJ, 08540.

GENERAL EMPLOYMENT OPPORTUNITIES
Check the Web site for specific positions and send résumés to McCarter Theatre Center for the Performing Arts, 91 University Place, Princeton, NJ, 08540. Résumés are also accepted for freelance scenic artists, costume/wardrobe staff, and stage technicians with professional experience. Shop overhire is generally on a per-show basis. Stage work varies throughout the season: mostly one- to three-day electrics and scenery load-ins; occasional three-week run crew positions. Send letter, résumé, and references to the Production Manager, fax them to (609) 497-0369, or e-mail production@mccarter.org.

MERRIMACK REPERTORY THEATRE
50 East Merrimack Street, Lowell, MA 01852
ADMINISTRATION: (978) 654-7550; BOX OFFICE: (978) 454-3926;
    FAX: (978) 654-7575
E-MAIL: info@merrimackrep.org
WEB SITE: www.merrimackrep.org

Founded in 1979 by John Briggs, Mark Kaufman, D.J. Maloney, and Barbara Abrahamian, Merrimack Rep is one of only three League of Resident Theatres (LORT) in eastern Massachusetts. Located in historic downtown Lowell, the theater has an active September through May production season as well as a Young Artists at Play summer program and educational and community outreach programs.

CASTING
Send photos and résumés to Casting, Merrimack Repertory Theatre, 50 East Merrimack Street, Lowell, MA 01852. No phone calls.

INTERNSHIP OPPORTUNITIES
Internships at MRT are open to students with a serious interest in pursing a career in professional theater. For information or an application to MRT's internship program, e-mail at artadmin@merrimackrep.org. Internships are available in stage management, electrics, carpentry, dramaturgy, education/outreach, youth theatre (summer only), arts management, box office management, business management, development, and public relations.

MILL MOUNTAIN THEATRE
One Market Square SE, Second Floor, Roanoke, VA 24011-1437
ADMINISTRATION: (540) 342-5730; BOX OFFICE: (540) 342-5740 or
    Toll Free (800) 317-6455; FAX: (540) 342-5745
E-MAIL: mmtmail@millmountain.org
WEB SITE: www.millmountain.org

The Mill Mountain Theatre was founded in 1964, runs on a budget of around $2.5 million and plays to nearly 80,000 annual patrons, including 30,000 students. Performance spaces include the 400-seat Trinkle Main Stage and the 125-seat Waldron Stage. The newly-appointed artistic director is Patrick Benton and the year-round production company helped spur the renaissance of downtown Roanoke. Mill Mountain is nationally known for its world premieres, dramatic classics, vibrant musicals, youth-oriented productions, educational classes, and touring productions.

CASTING, SCRIPT SUBMISSIONS, GENERAL EMPLOYMENT OPPORTUNITIES
Check the MMT Web site for employment and audition information and mail play submissions to: Literary Coordinator, Mill Mountain Theatre, One Market Square SE, Second Floor, Roanoke, VA, 24011. MMT accepts unsolicited one-acts. Check the Web site for details. All other submissions for the Norfolk Southern Festival of New Works, ScriptTease, mainstage, second stage, and touring productions are by invitation only.

MILWAUKEE REPERTORY THEATER

108 E. Wells Street, Milwaukee, WI 53202

ADMINISTRATION: (414) 224-1761; BOX OFFICE: (414) 224-9490; FAX: (414) 224-9097

E-MAIL: mailrep@milwaukeerep.com

WEB SITE: www.milwaukeerep.com

In 1954, Milwaukee native Mary John founded the Fred Miller Theater on Oakland Avenue (named after the head of Miller Brewing Company). The company produced Broadway's current hits, often with star performers. A resident acting company and expanded repertoire (including the classics and new works) resulted in the Milwaukee Repertory Theater in a 1963 reorganization and in 1968, the Rep moved into a 504-seat theater in downtown Milwaukee. In 1987, the company moved to a new complex, across from Milwaukee's City Hall. The converted power plant is an artistic fortress and houses three theaters: the Quadracci Powerhouse Theater seating 720, the 218-seat flexible Stiemke, and the Stackner Cabaret (a 118-seat full-service restaurant and bar).

Nagle Jackson served as the Rep's artistic director for much of the 1970s, John Dillon signed on as artistic director in 1977, and Joseph Hanreddy took over the company's artistic leadership in 2003. The Rep has a history of international collaboration, maintains a resident acting company, and runs many community programs.

CASTING, GENERAL EMPLOYMENT OPPORTUNITIES

Check the company Web site and write the theater.

INTERNSHIPS

The Rep works with about 15 acting, directing, and literary interns who join the company full-time. Brochures and applications are available on the company Web site. Interns in the artistic department devote their time entirely to acting, directing, or dramaturgy.

THE NEW HARMONY THEATRE

University of Southern Indiana, 8600 University Boulevard, Evansville, IN 47712-3596

ADMINISTRATION: (812) 682-3115; BOX OFFICE (TOLL FREE): (877) NHT-SHOW;

   FAX: (812) 464-0029

E-MAIL: nhtheatre@usi.edu

WEB SITE: www.usi.edu/nht

New Harmony, Indiana, is a spiritual sanctuary that once thrived as a haven for international scientists, scholars, and educators who "sought equality in communal living." Tucked away on the banks of the Wabash River in southwestern Indiana, historic New Harmony is home to the New Harmony

Theatre (NHT), produced by the University of Southern Indiana and operating under a special LORT agreement. Founded in 1987, the theater itself is located on 419 Tavern Street and generally operates in the summer, producing contemporary plays, classics, and musicals. The artistic director is Scott LaFeber.

CASTING, GENERAL EMPLOYMENT OPPORTUNITIES

NHT conducts a national search for theater professionals. Casting occurs in New York and Los Angeles, at the Southeastern Theatre Conference, and regionally. Designers and technicians are hired chiefly in New York and Chicago, through national conferences, and distinguished colleges. Details for auditions and employment opportunities are generally listed on the Web site or can be obtained by e-mailing nhtheatre@usi.edu.

NORTHLIGHT THEATRE

9501 Skokie Blvd., Skokie, IL 60077
ADMINISTRATION: (847) 679-9501; BOX OFFICE: (847) 673-6300; FAX: (847) 679-1879
E-MAIL: bjjones@northlight.org
WEB SITE: www.northlight.org

With a budget near $3 million and attendance approaching 75,000, the Northlight Theatre continues to grow its overall community following a move from Evanston to Skokie (both Chicago suburbs). In its own words, Northlight "presents life-affirming theatrical works which reflect and challenge the values and beliefs of the community it serves and involves community members, young and old, in the theatrical experience." Over the more than 30 years since its founding by Greg Kandel in 1974, the theater has produced over 150 plays, including over 30 world premieres, and has received a bunch of Chicago's prestigious Joseph Jefferson Awards. Artistic director B. J. Jones notes that Northlight continues "to balance artistic risk with engaging and pleasurable evenings in the theater" and invites audiences to come to the theater "ready to think, to feel, to be challenged, and to enjoy. In return we will offer you thought-provoking, emotionally engaging work, flecked with humor and rich with the familiar ache of the human experience." Managing director Phil Santora notes that Northlight produces musicals, classics, world premieres—and, adds B.J. Jones—"freshly minted work from the New York and world stage."

CASTING

Northlight Theatre casts primarily from actors based in the Chicago area. Casting actors from outside this area depends specifically upon the demands of each individual production. General Equity auditions are held once a year and listings are made on the Northlight Web site, in *PerformInk*, and via the Equity hotline. General auditions for usually held in early summer for non-Equity performers. Announcements for non-Equity general auditions are made on the Northlight Web site and in *PerformInk*. Submit a headshot and résumé with your phone number, c/o Casting, Northlight Theatre, 9501 Skokie Blvd., Skokie, IL, 60077. No calls.

GENERAL EMPLOYMENT OPPORTUNITIES

Check the Web site for detailed employment information and openings.

INTERNSHIPS

Northlight Theatre offers a variety of internships to qualified applicants with an interest in professional theater and not-for-profit management. Internships are available in the artistic, administrative, and technical/production areas of the theater. Check the Web site for specifics. Internships are generally non-salaried and typically part-time for three months (summer), four months (fall), or five months (winter/spring). Stage management internships are approximately eight to ten weeks per production and stage management interns may be eligible for stipend positions.

SCRIPT SUBMISSIONS

Northlight does not accept unsolicited manuscripts. To have their scripts considered, playwrights should first send Northlight a letter of inquiry with a synopsis of the play and a few sample pages (a scene or less). Include a brief description of any unusual staging requirements, a cast breakdown, and any other such relevant information. If reviews of the play are available (workshop or full production) enclose them as well. Enclose a SASE in order to have your materials returned. Check the Web site for more detailed information. Northlight does accept submissions from bona fide literary agents and they should be sent to: Dramaturg & Literary Manager, Northlight Theatre, 9501 Skokie Blvd., Skokie, IL, 60077.

THE OLD GLOBE

P.O. Box 122171, San Diego, CA 92112-2171
ADMINISTRATION: (619) 231-1941; BOX OFFICE: (619) 234-5623 ext. 2;
    FAX: (619) 231-1036
E-MAIL: mailus@theoldglobe.org
WEB SITE: www.theoldglobe.org

The Old Globe is the theater many students and professionals dream of— a company with a savvy, joyous, warm-hearted artistic director with Broadway and international credits (Jack O'Brien), venues in a glorious park, surrounded by a world-class zoo and the Pacific Ocean, and productions that capture America's imagination, ranging from musical premieres to Shakespeare. Emerging from the California-Pacific International Exposition in Balboa Park in 1935, The Old Globe now boasts a subscription base over 40,000 and a reputation for terrific, audience-engaging theater. Craig Noel started as an actor at The Old Globe in 1937 and signed on as executive producer in 1981. His legacy is an inspiration and his hiring of Jack O'Brien as artistic director established what became a revered leadership triumvirate when Louis G. Spisto arrived as executive director.

The Old Globe premieres of *Dirty Rotten Scoundrels*, *Hairspray*, *The Full Monty*, *Damn Yankees*, *Into the Woods*, *Joe Turner's Come and Gone*, *Rumors*, *The Piano Lesson*, and *Two Trains Running* all went onto Broadway productions (to mention a few) and both the theater and Jack O'Brien have garnered well-deserved Tony Awards.

CASTING

Check the Web site for information and make casting inquiries to Casting Director Brendon Fox, The Old Globe, P.O. Box 122171, San Diego, CA, 92112-2171.

SCRIPT SUBMISSIONS

Submissions are accepted year-round from agents and by invitation only. No unsolicited scripts; rather, send a synopsis, dialogue sample, and letter of inquiry to The Old Globe, Artistic Dept., P.O. Box 122171, San Diego, CA, 92112.

GENERAL EMPLOYMENT OPPORTUNITIES

Check the Web site for opportunities and details and send a cover letter and résumé to: Human Resources, The Old Globe, P.O. Box 122171, San Diego, CA, 92112-2171 or e-mail: HR@TheOldGlobe.org.

INTERNSHIPS

While The Old Globe does not offer a formal internship program, individual departments sometimes have openings for non-paid interns for various projects. Old Globe materials encourage students to "contact the director of the area in which you wish to volunteer your services." Check the Web site for staff lists. The Old Globe occasionally accepts applications for internships in stage management, involving interns in daily rehearsals, technical rehearsals, production meetings, and understudy rehearsals. The stage management internship is a full-time commitment, six days a week. A typical internship would last eight weeks, though the length of internship could be adapted to fit school schedules. Interns are considered company members and receive perks such as complimentary tickets and free entrance to Balboa

Park attractions. For stage management internships, send a cover letter, résumé, and two letters of recommendation to: Internships, c/o Production Stage Manager, The Old Globe, P.O. Box 122171, San Diego, CA, 92112-2171, or check the Web site for other options.

OREGON SHAKESPEARE FESTIVAL

15 S. Pioneer Street, Ashland, OR 97520

ADMINISTRATION: (541) 482-2111; BOX OFFICE: (541) 482-4331; FAX: (541) 482-0446

E-MAIL: humanresources@osfashland.org

WEB SITE: www.osfashland.org

With roots firmly entrenched in the Chautauqua movement in the 1890s, the Oregon Shakespeare Festival's first production was a 1935 Angus L. Bowmer–produced *Twelfth Night*, part of a two-play "festival" with *The Merchant of Venice*. OSF has come a long way, now producing nearly a dozen annual productions, over 700 performances and myriad other events, tours, workshops, and classes for more than 360,000 visitors from throughout the world. Artistic director Libby Appel, executive director Paul Nicholson, producing director David A. Dreyfoos, and a company of over 450 remarkable artists and craftspeople keep OSF in the upper echelon of the world's theater elite. Bill Rauch succeeds Appel as artistic director when she retires at the end of the 2007 season. The Tony Award–winning institution is the largest nonprofit theater in the nation and its eight-and-a-half-month season in three theaters is produced with a budget exceeding $21 million. In the theater's own words, "the mission of the Oregon Shakespeare Festival, using Shakespeare as our standard and inspiration, is to create fresh and bold interpretations of classic and contemporary plays in repertory, shaped by the diversity of our American culture."

CASTING

To apply for an audition slot, actors should send a photo and résumé to OSF, Attn: Casting, P.O. Box 158, Ashland, OR, 97520. OSF asks that résumés include current mailing (or e-mail) addresses and phone numbers, and the names of directors with whom you have worked, as well as the theaters where you have performed. Audition information will then be sent to you. OSF does not offer internships in acting. The Oregon Shakespeare Festival operates on a special contract based on the LORT B+ tier. Contracts are either ten-month (January–October) or seven-month (April–October). Company members routinely perform in several productions, as well as understudying—auditions are for the company, not for specific roles. Check the Web site for additional details.

SCRIPT SUBMISSIONS

OSF does not accept unsolicited manuscripts—only submissions from literary agents. Playwrights who do not have an agent may send OSF a letter of introduction with a synopsis of the play, the first 10 pages of the script, and a character list with specifics about age, gender, and ethnicity. If the material interests OSF, they will respond with a request for the complete script. Send submissions or synopses to: Oregon Shakespeare Festival, Attn: Literary Assistant, P.O. Box 158, Ashland, OR, 97520.

GENERAL EMPLOYMENT OPPORTUNITIES

Check the OSF Web site for detailed openings (including fellowships, assistantships, internships, and residencies) and application information, or write or e-mail: Director of Human Resources at Oregon Shakespeare Festival, P.O. Box 158, Ashland, OR, 97520; e-mail: Jobs@osfashland.org.

ORLANDO-UCF SHAKESPEARE FESTIVAL

812 E. Rollins Street, Orlando, FL 32803
ADMINISTRATION: (407) 447-1700; BOX OFFICE: (407) 447-1700 ext. 1;
    FAX: (407) 447-1701
E-MAIL: info@shakespearefest.org
WEB SITE: www.shakespearefest.org

This rapidly developing company is one of the Southeast's best-kept artistic secrets. Orlando-UCF Shakespeare Festival produces top-notch professional theater, develops edgy new plays, and provides innovative educational and artistic experiences for Central Florida. The UCF in the title refers to the University of Central Florida, a strong Shakespeare supporter that has assisted the Festival in an innovative educational and professional theater journey first envisioned by founder Stuart Omans in 1989.

Artistic director Jim Helsinger's vision is "to create theater of extraordinary quality that encourages the actor/audience relationship, embraces the passionate use of language, and ignites the imagination. Our goal is to be a nationally recognized destination theater offering productions and education year-round for all audiences." Today the company's season typically includes six productions, a Theatre for Young Audiences Series, a workshop series for new plays called PlayLab, the ten-day Harriett Lake Festival of New Plays, two summer Shakespeare productions performed by local high school students in their TYC and SYC programs, summer camps for children, community and professional classes, and extensive teaching in K-12 schools. The John and Rita Lowndes Shakespeare Center includes a 324-seat theater, a 118-seat theater, the 70-seat Studio B, and the 100-seat

Studio D. Boldly situated on a lake on the edge of downtown Orlando is an amphitheater for the summer Shakespeare plays.

CASTING, GENERAL EMPLOYMENT OPPORTUNITIES
Direct links from the company Web site provide quick access to timely audition information and job openings.

PASADENA PLAYHOUSE
39 S. El Molino Avenue, Pasadena, CA 91101
ADMINISTRATION: (626) 792-8672; BOX OFFICE: (626) 356-7529; FAX: (626) 792-6142
WEB SITE: www.pasadenaplayhouse.org

There's a sense of history, a sense of Hollywood, and a sense of style that permeate the air of the Pasadena Playhouse, one of America's oldest regional theaters (dating back to 1917). Today, in its own words, "the Pasadena Playhouse remains committed to the development and presentation of a culturally diverse variety of theatrical productions at the highest level of artistry. By cultivating and utilizing the unique resources inherent in our greater community, the Pasadena Playhouse will preserve and amplify the powerful voice of theater, assuring its vitality for generations to come." Artistic director Sheldon Epps and executive director Lyla White have kept the Playhouse going strong with world premieres, unique versions of the classics, and powerful stagings of contemporary plays.

Gilmor Brown decided to produce a season of plays in an old burlesque house in 1917 and put together the Savoy Players. By 1925, a new theater had debuted on South El Molino Avenue and by the 1930s, the Playhouse was a Hollywood showcase. Named the State Theatre in 1937, it was eventually placed on the National Register of Historic Places. Over the years, the theater has attracted such stars as Dustin Hoffman, Gene Hackman, Linda Hunt, Hal Holbrook, Phylicia Rashad, Harry Groener, Carol Lawrence, Stacey Keach, Bea Arthur, Shirley Knight, Diahann Carroll, Brian Stokes Mitchell, and Rebecca De Mornay. In 2004, the Balcony Theater at the Playhouse reopened to feature the Furious Theatre Company, and a reading series called "Hothouse at the Playhouse" for the development of new work from diverse and emerging playwrights.

CASTING, GENERAL EMPLOYMENT OPPORTUNITIES, INTERNSHIPS
Check the theater's Web site and/or write the theater for ongoing openings and casting information.

SCRIPT SUBMISSIONS
"New-play development and the creation of material for the stage from the ground up is both a responsibility and a joyous opportunity for a theater of

our stature and reputation," notes artistic director Sheldon Epps. Check the Web site and write to the theater for submission information.

PEOPLE'S LIGHT & THEATRE COMPANY

39 Conestoga Road, Malvern, PA 19355

ADMINISTRATION: (610) 647-1900; BOX OFFICE: (610) 644-3500;

   FAX: (610) 640-9521

E-MAIL: pltc@peopleslight.org

WEB SITE: www.peopleslight.org

"Simply put," explain the folks at People's Light, the mission is to "to bring together theater artists of the highest caliber with large and diverse audiences in a welcoming environment to celebrate an increasingly complex world . . . we think that a diversity of age, race, cultural background, and aesthetic goals among artists and audiences is vital to artistic growth and to the strength of a united community. We maintain a resident company of artists because we feel that continuity is essential in order to stay closely connected with our community, and for artists, audiences, and neighbors to grow together."

Celebrating over thirty years of operation, The People's Light & Theatre is located in the heart of Chester County, Pennsylvania, and averages eight to nine plays per season, mixing world premieres, contemporary plays and fresh approaches to classic texts for a Main Stage Series and Family Discovery Series. Project Discovery is an arts education program serving more than 35,000 young people each year. Also, the year-round Theatre School at People's Light offers classes for adults and young people taught by the theater's resident artists.

"People's Light was founded in 1974 by four young theater artists who were committed to two ideals: long-term collaboration among artists with diverse aesthetics, and active participation in the life of the immediate community," notes artistic director Abigail Adams, who joined the company in 1975. The company's $4.5 million budget sustains the ongoing development of an ensemble that includes actors, directors, designers, playwrights, dramaturgs, and teaching artists who attract an annual audience of about 100,000 patrons. The physical spaces include two black box theaters, one with 375 seats, the other 180 seats. They have been home to over 300 plays and 100 world and/or regional premieres.

CASTING

People's Light has a resident company of over 20 actors, but also casts some Equity and non-Equity roles from outside the company. Those interested in auditioning for People's Light should send headshot and résumé to: Casting, c/o Management Associate, 39 Conestoga Road, Malvern, PA, 19355. People's Light is a member of the Theatre Alliance of Greater Philadelphia and participates in its Annual Auditions. For more information regarding these auditions, visit the web site at http://www.theatrealliance.org/.

SCRIPT SUBMISSIONS, GENERAL EMPLOYMENT OPPORTUNITIES, INTERNSHIPS
To send inquiries, check the Web site for detailed position descriptions and openings and for a list of staff.

PHILADELPHIA THEATRE COMPANY

Plays & Players Theater, 1714 Delancey Street, Philadelphia, PA 19103
MAILING ADDRESS: 230 South 15th Street, Fourth Floor, Philadelphia, PA 19102
ADMINISTRATION: (215) 985-1400; BOX OFFICE: (215) 985-0420;
 FAX: (215) 985-5800
WEB SITE: www.phillytheatreco.com

Philadelphia Theatre Company is "dedicated to presenting the Philadelphia and world premieres of major works by contemporary playwrights with an emphasis on American drama. We seek to develop an audience of open-minded theatergoers across cultural, ethnic, and social lines by producing drama that is at once challenging, entertaining, and imaginatively staged." Founded as The Philadelphia Company in 1974, PTC has produced over 100 world and Philadelphia premieres, including Terrence McNally's *Master Class*, Alan Zweibel's *Bunny Bunny*, David Ives' *Lives of the Saint*, J.T. Rogers' *White People*, John Henry Redwood's *No Niggers, No Jews, No Dogs*, Daniel Stern's *Barbra's Wedding*, Jeffrey Hatcher's *A Picasso*, and Bruce Graham's *According to Goldman*.

CASTING

PTC casts on a per-show basis and auditions are held in Philadelphia and New York. Audition notices are posted on this Web site as well as on the Philadelphia Actors' Equity hotline, the Theatre Alliance of Greater Philadelphia Web site, and elsewhere. If you are not already on file or have updated information, send photos and résumés to: Casting Director, Philadelphia Theatre Company, 230 S. 15th Street, 4th Floor, Philadelphia, PA, 19102. No phone calls or e-mail submissions.

SCRIPT SUBMISSIONS

PTC does not accept unsolicited scripts or inquiries; it directly solicits playwrights of interest and accepts agent submissions. Agents may submit work to: Literary Department, Philadelphia Theatre Company, 230 S. 15th Street, 4th Floor, Philadelphia, PA, 19102.

GENERAL EMPLOYMENT OPPORTUNITIES, INTERNSHIPS, FELLOWSHIPS
Check the Web site for ongoing listings. PTC Fellowships include the Career Development Initiative (CDI) in Directing and Production and applications and details are provided on the Web site. Inquiries may be e-mailed to careers@phillytheatreco.com.

THE PHOENIX THEATRE

749 N. Park Avenue, Indianapolis, Indiana 46202
ADMINISTRATION: (317) 635-2381; BOX OFFICE: (317) 635-7529; FAX: (317) 635-0010
E-MAIL: info@phoenixtheatre.org
WEB SITE: www.phoenixtheatre.org

Founded in 1983, The Phoenix Theatre is a year-round professional company focusing on new, diverse, and challenging plays. It produces in the 150-seat proscenium Mainstage and the 70- to 80-seat Underground Stage. The artistic mission of The Phoenix Theatre is to serve as a catalyst for social responsibility and enlightenment," notes producing director Bryan Fonseca.

GENERAL EMPLOYMENT OPPORTUNITIES, APPRENTICESHIPS, INTERNSHIPS
Check the Web site or e-mail info@phoenixtheatre.org for details.

PIONEER THEATRE COMPANY

University of Utah, Simmons Pioneer Memorial Theatre,
    300 South 1400 East #325, Salt Lake City, UT 84112-0660
ADMINISTRATION: (801) 581-6356; BOX OFFICE: (801) 581-6961;
    AUDITION HOTLINE: (801) 585-3927; FAX: (801) 581-5472
WEB SITE: www.pioneertheatre.org

Founded in 1962, Salt Lake's ambitious regional theater is in residence at the University of Utah. The company produces a seven-play season running from September through May that includes classics, musicals, and contemporary dramas and comedies. The theater prides itself on being the first in Utah to produce important works by contemporary playwrights, such as August Wilson's *Fences*, Tom Stoppard's *Arcadia*, David Auburn's *Proof*, and Wendy Wasserstein's *An American Daughter*. Charles Morey is the longtime artistic director and he doesn't shy away from large-scale productions.

CASTING, GENERAL EMPLOYMENT OPPORTUNITIES
Check the company Web site for quick access to timely audition information and job openings. PTC generally holds auditions for shows in Salt Lake City and New York City. For Salt Lake auditions, check the Web

site or call (801) 585-3927. New York audition appointments are through agent submissions only.

PITTSBURGH PUBLIC THEATER

621 Penn Avenue, Pittsburgh, PA 15222

ADMINISTRATION: (412) 316-8200; BOX OFFICE: (412) 316-1600; FAX: (412) 316-8216

E-MAIL: info@ppt.org

WEB SITE: www.ppt.org

This high-quality professional theater has been an important part of Pittsburgh's renaissance of the arts and the downtown area. Founded by Joan Apt, Margaret Rieck, and Ben Shaktman (chartered in 1974 and opened in 1975), the Pittsburgh Public Theater's mission is to "provide artistically diverse theatrical experiences of the highest quality." The 650-seat O'Reilly Theater was designed by world-renowned architect Michael Graves and is located in the heart of Pittsburgh's Cultural District. The venue was a $20 million project of The Pittsburgh Cultural Trust. The Hazlett Theatre, dedicated by President Benjamin Harrison in 1889, was the Public's first home (1974-99).

CASTING

Auditions are held on a show-by-show basis for Equity and non-Equity actors. Notices are placed in local newspapers, at local talent agencies, and on the Public Theater Web site. Actors may send a headshot and résumé to Pittsburgh Public Theater, Attn: Artistic, 621 Penn Avenue, Pittsburgh, PA, 15222.

SCRIPT SUBMISSIONS

PPT accepts full scripts only from literary agents or with a letter of recommendation from an artistic director or literary manager of an established professional theater or playwriting organization. PPT accepts unsolicited queries only. Queries should include a cover letter with the playwright's contact information, a one-page synopsis of the play, and a dialogue sample of up to ten pages. Response time for queries is two to four months. Include a SASE/SASP for a response. Check the Web site for details. Queries should be addressed to "Resident Dramaturg" at the PPT address.

GENERAL EMPLOYMENT OPPORTUNITIES, INTERNSHIPS

Check the Web site for specifics. Pittsburgh Public Theater offers internships on a show-by-show, semester, and/or seasonal basis. Hours vary depending on the need and range from 20 to 40 per week. All internships are unpaid; however, academic credit is available at the discretion of the intern's enrolled institution. Internships are generally offered in production management, technical administration, costume design and construction, literary and education, sound design, lighting design, scenic art, and administration and finance. Send a letter of interest indicating internship of choice, a résumé, and three references to: Education Department Internship, Program, Pittsburgh Public Theater, 621 Penn Avenue, Pittsburgh, PA 15222.

PLAYMAKERS REPERTORY COMPANY

CB# 3235, Center for Dramatic Art, UNC Campus, Chapel Hill, NC 27599-3235
ADMINISTRATION: (919) 962-1122; BOX OFFICE: (919) 962-PLAY; FAX: (919) 962-4069
WEB SITE: www.playmakersrep.org

A long legacy of theater excellence started in 1918 with the Carolina Playmakers at the University of North Carolina at Chapel Hill and developed into the PlayMakers Repertory Company, founded in 1975. In the theater's own words, "Our purpose is to provide a top-quality public arena for the professional implementation of the philosophy and aesthetics explored in the Department. Through the collaboration of guest artists, resident professionals, students, and audiences, we examine the theatrical event and the methods used for its realization in contemporary performance. We explore playmaking in our time." The theater's season generally runs from October through April, featuring five plays in the 500-seat Paul Green Theatre built in 1978. In 1998, the Center for Dramatic Art opened next door and includes the 208-seat Elizabeth Price Kenan Theatre.

CASTING, SCRIPT SUBMISSIONS, GENERAL EMPLOYMENT OPPORTUNITIES, INTERNSHIPS

Check out the Web site, www.playmakersrep.org, for contact numbers and information.

PORTLAND CENTER STAGE

1111 SW Broadway, Portland, OR 97205
ADMINISTRATION: (503) 248-6309; Ticket Information: (503) 274-6588;
   FAX: (503) 796-6509
E-MAIL: info@pcs.org
WEB SITE: www.pcs.org

Portland Center Stage "dares to make theater as ravishing, innovative and thought provoking as our wildest dreams," explains company publications.

PCS produces a blend of classical, contemporary, and premier works as well as a summer playwrights festival, Just Add Water/West. In residence at the Portland Center for the Performing Arts, PCS has nearly 8,000 subscribers and attracts an annual audience of more than 90,000 patrons. PCS began as the northern sibling of the Oregon Shakespeare Festival in Ashland and premiered in 1988 with *Heartbreak House*. In 1993, after five successful seasons, the company became an independent theater company and Elizabeth Huddle was selected as producing artistic director in 1994. Chris Coleman became the theater's fourth artistic director in 2000. PCS produces seven annual productions in the Winningstad and Newmark Theatres. In 2004, the company announced a $32.9 million capital campaign to build a new theater complex in the historic Portland Armory to house a 599-seat main stage theater, a smaller, 200-seat black box theater, administrative offices, a rehearsal hall and production facilities. They moved into their new space in September 2006.

CASTING
Check the Web site for Equity and non-Equity audition information, dates, and contact numbers.

SCRIPT SUBMISSIONS
Portland Center Stage accepts full-length scripts from literary agents. PCS also accepts scripts directly from writers when they are recommended by the artistic director or literary manager of a professional theater or playwright organization. Those without agents may query the theater for interest in a particular script. Check the Web site for the six major instructions for queries. Submissions or query letters may be sent to: Literary Manager, c/o: Portland Center Stage, 1111 SW Broadway, Portland, OR, 97205. E-mail questions to literary@pcs.org.

GENERAL EMPLOYMENT OPPORTUNITIES
Detailed job descriptions are often posted on the Web site. For more information contact PCS at jobs@pcs.org.

PORTLAND STAGE COMPANY
25A Forest Avenue, Portland, ME 04101
MAILING ADDRESS: P.O. Box 1458, Portland, ME 04104
ADMINISTRATION: (207) 774-1043; BOX OFFICE: (207) 774-0465; FAX: (207) 774-0576
E-MAIL: info@portlandstage.com
WEB SITE: www.portlandstage.com

This northern New England professional theater produces a wide range of artistic works and programs that, in the theater's own words, "explore basic human issues and concerns relevant to the communities served by the theater." The company uses the theater as a "catalyst for discussion, debate, interpretation, and exploring the human condition, historically and currently, in our society and in the global community." Founded in 1974 as a touring company, the Profile Theater, Portland Stage Company has an audience of around 40,000 annual patrons and produces two festivals. The *Little Festival of the Unexpected* connects young American playwrights with audiences in a week-long event devoted to the development of new plays and, in a collaboration with the University of Iowa's International Writing Program, *From Away* brings international writers to Portland to share ideas and perspectives from other cultures.

CASTING, SCRIPT SUBMISSIONS, GENERAL EMPLOYMENT OPPORTUNITIES
Check the Web site and write the theater for information.

INTERNSHIPS
PSC internships introduce recent college graduates to professional theater and generally accepts about a dozen interns in directing/dramaturgy, stage management, marketing/development, carpentry/props, costumes, and general production. Interns generally work full-time, receive housing and about a $70 per week stipend, and work from late August through May. Check the company Web site for applications, details, descriptions, and deadlines.

PRINCE MUSIC THEATER
1412 Chestnut Street, Philadelphia, PA 19103
BUSINESS OFFICE: 100 South Broad Street, Suite 650, Philadelphia, PA 19110
ADMINISTRATION: (215) 972-1000; BOX OFFICE: (215) 569-9700; FAX: (215) 972-1020
WEB SITE: www.princemusictheater.org

In its own words, the mission of the Prince Music Theater is "to nurture and develop the unique American art form of music theater of the highest artistic caliber over a wide aesthetic range—including opera, music drama, musical comedy, and experimental work. Above all, we are dedicated to artists of our time seeking to break new ground, while we also celebrate the legacy of the creative mavericks and pioneers who have forged the American musical theater." Founded in 1984 as the American Music Theater Festival, the company worked in over two dozen venues throughout Philadelphia until 1999 when it found a permanent home in the former Midtown Theater. Marjorie Samoff is the producing artistic director. The Prince Music Theater serves a diverse local audience and "a national community of artists and organizations dedicated to creating a body of contemporary American work as a legacy for the future."

CASTING

Audition notices are posted on the Theatre Alliance of Greater Philadelphia listserve, aka "T@GP Listserv." Please see the Web site www.theatrealliance.org for details on how to subscribe to the listserv. Actors/singers may also check the Web site for details or write to Prince Music Theater, ATTN: Casting Director, 100 South Broad Street, Suite 650, Philadelphia, PA, 19110. E-mail submissions to casting@princemusictheater.org.

SCRIPT SUBMISSIONS, GENERAL EMPLOYMENT OPPORTUNITIES

Check the Web site for specific opportunities or write the theater for information.

INTERNSHIPS

Internships are generally available in the administrative, marketing, or artistic departments. Applicants should send a résumé and letter of introduction to Personnel Dept., Prince Music Theater, 100 South Broad Street, Suite 650, Philadelphia, PA, 19110 or fax it to (215) 972-1020.

THE PUBLIC THEATER/NEW YORK SHAKESPEARE FESTIVAL

[See 250+ Shakespeare Festivals, beginning page 298]

THE REPERTORY THEATRE OF ST. LOUIS

P.O. Box 191730, St. Louis, Missouri 63119
ADMINISTRATION: (314) 968-7340; BOX OFFICE: (314) 968-4925; FAX: (314) 968-9638
E-MAIL: mail@repstl.org
WEB SITE: www.repstl.org

Founded in 1966, the Repertory Theatre of St. Louis has evolved into one of America's most exciting, productive, and respected regional theaters. Artistic director Steven Woolf has been at the helm since 1986; managing director Mark D. Bernstein arrived in 1987. The Rep has mixed the classics, musicals, new plays, and contemporary work in its 733-seat Mainstage theater, 125-seat Studio theater, and 75-seat Lab Space. "The Rep seeks to develop audiences which become strong advocates for live performance," notes Mr. Woolf. While the Rep operates under an Equity LORT contract, the its Imaginary Theatre Company operates under a TYA (Theatre for Young Audiences) contract.

CASTING

The Rep holds local, annual general auditions. Requirements vary from season to season but generally call upon actors to prepare two contrasting monologues (or a monologue and a song for musical auditions). Both Equity and non-Equity actors are invited to audition. Actors should check the Web site and/or the *St. Louis Post-Dispatch* and the *Riverfront Times* for additional information and opportunities. The Rep's New York casting director is Rich Cole, who can be reached through Rich Cole Casting, 648 Broadway, Suite 912, New York, NY 10012, (212) 614-7130. New York casting is handled through agent submissions and open casting calls in New York. These calls are posted as needed or as required by the Actors' Equity Association.

SCRIPT SUBMISSIONS, GENERAL EMPLOYMENT OPPORTUNITIES
Check the Web site for specific job openings and descriptions and/or e-mail (mail@repstl.org) for information regarding employment and play submissions.

INTERNSHIPS
Internship opportunities are posted on the company Web site when available.

ROUNDABOUT THEATRE COMPANY
231 West 39th Street, Suite 1200, New York, NY 10018
ADMINISTRATION: (212) 719-9393; BOX OFFICE: (212) 719-1300; FAX: (212) 869-8817
E-MAIL: info@roundabouttheatre.org
WEB SITE: www.roundabouttheatre.org

Located in the heart of New York's Times Square, the Roundabout is one of America's best placed and most beloved theaters. The company achieved an amazing turnaround, moving from near bankruptcy to nearly two-dozen Tony Awards over the years with artistic director Todd Haimes in the driver's seat. At the very heart of the Roundabout's work, in its own words, is the company's "commitment to teaming great theatrical works with the industry's finest artists to re-energize classic plays and musicals." The institutional mission was expanded in 1995 to include "the development and production of new works by today's great writers and composers. The production of these new works, alongside the production of classics, enables Roundabout to embody the crossroads of American theater." Playing to over 40,000 subscribers and a million patrons annually, the Roundabout operates the American Airlines Theatre, Studio 54, and the Harold and Miriam Steinberg Center for Theatre/ Laura Pels Theatre.

Founded in 1965 by Gene Feist and Elizabeth Owens, the Roundabout opened in a 150-seat theater in the basement of a supermarket in Chelsea before moving into a converted 299-seat movie theater on West 23rd Street in 1974. In 1984 Roundabout took up residence in Union Square's Tammany

Hall, then moved again in 1991 to a brief stay at the Criterion Center on West 45th Street. The 399-seat Laura Pels Theatre opened in 1995.

CASTING, SCRIPT SUBMISSIONS, GENERAL EMPLOYMENT OPPORTUNITIES
Check the Web site for specific opportunities in all areas or e-mail jobs@roundabouttheatre.org for information.

INTERNSHIPS
Roundabout internships are usually available in general management, development, marketing, ticket services, business, education, and production (including lighting, props, costume, and production management). Roundabout does not offer internships in acting or literary management. Persons interested in assistant director fellowships must apply through the Drama League's directing fellowship program. Application materials should be sent to: Education Program Associate, Roundabout Theatre Company, 231 West 39th Street, Suite 1200, New York, NY, 10018 or by fax to (212) 768-0776. Roundabout's Career Development program accepts high school students, undergraduate and graduate college students, and early-career professionals. Internships typically run from September to December, January to May, or June to September and may be full-time or part-time, depending on the department. Check the Web site for specifics.

THE SAN FRANCISCO SHAKESPEARE FESTIVAL
P.O. Box 460937, San Francisco CA 94146-0937
ADMINISTRATION/BOX OFFICE: (415) 558-0888 or Toll Free (800) 978-PLAY;
    FAX: (415) 865-4433
E-MAIL: sfshakes@sfshakes.org
WEB SITE: www.sfshakes.org

The San Francisco Shakespeare Festival's debut production was a triumphant *The Tempest* in Golden Gate Park in 1983. Today, the company is a major producer and arts education provider that includes "sister organizations" known as the Oakland–East Bay Shakespeare Festival and the Silicon Valley Shakespeare Festival. *Free Shakespeare in the Park* is produced every year for over 50,000 patrons in San Francisco, Oakland, Pleasanton, and Cupertino from July to October, and Shakespeare on Tour takes a 60-minute Shakespeare performance to students statewide. This includes around 300 annual performances to over 120,000 children.

The Bay Area Shakespeare Camps enable students age seven to eighteen to study Shakespeare. Midnight Shakespeare offers at-risk youth the opportunity to learn communication skills, performance skills, discipline, and teamwork through Shakespeare. The Shakespeare Festival employs over 200 educators, artists, actors, directors, designers. The much admired executive director is Toby Leavitt.

CASTING, GENERAL EMPLOYMENT OPPORTUNITIES

Check the company Web site for quick access to timely audition and job information. SFSF also offers production and administrative internships. Free Shakespeare in the Park and indoor mainstage productions operate under a LORT D, LOA contract, and employ a mix of Equity and non-Equity actors. Shakespeare on Tour is a non-Equity program. The Shakespeare Festival holds open auditions for both programs and posts upcoming auditions in regional trade publications. For information on upcoming auditions, call (415) 865-4434 ext. 5. Those interested in employment with the Shakespeare Festival should send a cover letter and résumé to The San Francisco Shakespeare Festival, P.O. Box 460937, San Francisco, CA, 94146.

SAN JOSE REPERTORY THEATRE

101 Paseo de San Antonio, San Jose, CA 95113

ADMINISTRATION: (408) 367-7266; BOX OFFICE: (408) 367-7255;

   FAX: (408) 367-7237

E-MAIL: help@sjrep.com

WEB SITE: www.sjrep.com

Perhaps one of America's best-kept regional theater secrets, San Jose Rep operates in a gorgeous complex in the heart of downtown San Jose, a booming community that has long emerged from the shadow of San Francisco. Artistic director Timothy Near has led the company to national stature by producing new plays and classics that, in her words, are "marked by innovative interpretations and a reflection and inclusion of our community and the world in which we live." Serving the Silicon Valley and the greater Bay Area, the rep generally produces seven mainstage shows and offers extensive community and educational outreach programs, including Red Ladder Theatre Company (for disadvantaged youth and other underserved groups) and creative dramatics classes. Founded in 1980 by James P. Reber, the company plays to over 120,000 patrons annually in its 500+-seat theater.

CASTING

San Jose Rep hires actors on a show-to-show basis, choosing Equity actors and local non-union actors (generally only for large-cast productions and as extras). Auditions are by invitation only and may include both Equity and non-Equity actors. Out-of-town actors who plan to be in the San Jose area may request an audition by contacting the casting office. San Jose Repertory Theatre holds annual auditions in late spring/early summer. Audition information is announced on the Equity Hotline, Theatre Bay Area Hotline, *Callboard* magazine, and on the Web site. The Rep's artistic staff also attends the Theatre Bay Area general auditions each year. Actors may submit a headshot-résumé and cover letter to: Casting Director, San Jose Repertory Theatre, 101 Paseo de San Antonio, San Jose, CA, 95113.

SCRIPT SUBMISSIONS, GENERAL EMPLOYMENT OPPORTUNITIES, INTERNSHIPS
E-mail (info@sjrep.com) the company for specific openings and opportunities.

SEATTLE CHILDREN'S THEATRE
201 Thomas Street, Seattle, WA 98109
ADMINISTRATION: (206) 443-0807; BOX OFFICE: (206) 441-3322;
    DRAMA SCHOOL: (206) 443-0807; FAX: (206) 443-0442
E-MAIL: sctpr@sct.org; SCHOOL E-MAIL: dramaschool@sct.org
WEB SITE: www.sct.org

Time magazine has hailed the Seattle Children's Theatre for its outstanding work and, in the theater's own words, SCT "offers the best in professional, thought-provoking performances for the entire family, from foot-stomping musicals like *Seussical* to classic adaptations like *Sleeping Beauty*." SCT produces from September through June in its two Seattle Center theaters. SCT also runs the SCT Drama School, offering theater arts classes for the public. Throughout its 30-year history, SCT has entertained over four million children and adults. Artistic director Linda Hartzell has been at SCT since 1985 and was joined by Kevin Maifeld, managing director, in 2001.

CASTING
To apply for an audition slot, send a picture, résumé, copy of Actors' Equity card and stamped, self-addressed envelope to: Auditions, Seattle Children's Theatre, 201 Thomas Street, Seattle, WA, 98109.

INTERNSHIPS
SCT internships often include work with the Drama School and Education Outreach program, as well as assistant teaching in a variety of classes. E-mail SCT at dramaschool@sct.org. Additional internships may also be available.

GENERAL EMPLOYMENT OPPORTUNITIES
Job postings are detailed on the company Web site.

SEATTLE REPERTORY THEATRE

155 Mercer Street, P.O. Box 900923, Seattle, WA 98109

ADMINISTRATION: (206) 443-2210; BOX OFFICE: (206) 443-2222; or Toll Free (877) 900-9285; FAX: (206) 443-2379

E-MAIL: feedback@seattlerep.org

WEB SITE: www.seattlerep.org

Founded in 1963 by Bagley Wright, the Seattle Repertory Theatre received the 1990 Regional Theatre Tony Award while producing in the 856-seat Bagley Wright proscenium theater and the 133-seat flexible PANCHO Forum. In its own words, "Seattle Repertory Theatre produces plays that excite the imagination and nourish a lifelong passion for the theater." Recent artistic directors include Sharon Ott and Daniel Sullivan, and Ben Moore is the current managing director. The Rep produces a season of plays, new play workshops, and educational programs that engage audiences of "diverse ages, cultures, and economic backgrounds."

CASTING

Seattle Repertory Theatre participates in the annual general auditions organized by Theatre Puget Sound. Auditions are announced in the *Seattle Times* and *P-I*, *Seattle Weekly*, and *The Stranger*, on the Equity Hotline; and on the Theatre Puget Sound Web page. Separate audition dates are set for Equity and non-Equity actors. Equity actors visiting from out of town are welcome to request an audition appointment by calling the theater: (206) 443-2210. Auditions are scheduled on a time-available basis. For the general audition, provide an 8x10 photo and a current résumé. Present one monologue—contemporary or classical—of no more than three minutes in length. The Seattle Rep artistic staff, in consultation with directors, invites individual actors to read for roles in specific productions. These auditions are held throughout the year on an invitation-only basis. See the Web site for more specifics. Seattle Rep also works with a variety of casting directors in New York, Los Angeles, Chicago, and the San Francisco Bay Area. Send résumés, cover letters, and photos to Seattle Repertory Theatre, Attn: Contact Information Update, 155 Mercer Street, P.O. Box 900923, Seattle, WA, 98109.

SCRIPT SUBMISSIONS

Seattle Rep welcomes scripts from literary agents and professional colleagues but does not accept unsolicited manuscripts. The Rep is "dedicated to maintaining strong relationships with playwrights we have worked with in the past and continue to develop relationships with emerging playwrights through literary agents and professional colleagues."

GENERAL EMPLOYMENT OPPORTUNITIES, INTERNSHIPS
Current job/internship listings are posted on the company Web site. The requested materials should be sent to: Human Resources, Seattle Repertory Theatre, 155 Mercer Street, P.O. Box 900923, Seattle, WA, 98109. E-mail inquiries may also be sent to: humanresources@seattlerep.org. No phone calls.

SEVEN ANGELS THEATRE
Hamilton Park Pavilion/Plank Road, Waterbury, CT 06705
MAILING ADDRESS: P.O. Box 3358, Waterbury, CT 06705
ADMINISTRATION: (203) 591-8223; BOX OFFICE: (203) 757-4676; FAX: (203) 757-1807
WEB SITE: www.sevenangelstheatre.org

Seven Angels Theatre is a professional Equity theater founded in 1990. The company notes that it's "the only major professional arts organization to emerge in Waterbury and the Greater Waterbury region in 60 years" and it has the region's largest subscriber base (around 2,000) with annual attendance of approximately 50,000 patrons. The company produces and presents up to 200 performances a year and has an active educational program that includes Young Angels, Bright Lights, Summer Theatre Camp, and StageArts School.

CASTING, GENERAL EMPLOYMENT OPPORTUNITIES, INTERNSHIPS
SAT hires Equity, non-Equity, and community talent and provides various internships. Send résumés and headshots to Seven Angels Theatre, P.O. Box 3358, Waterbury, CT, 06705.

SHAKESPEARE FESTIVAL/LA
1238 West 1st Street, Los Angeles, CA 90026
ADMINISTRATIVE/BOX OFFICE: (213) 481-2273; FAX: (213) 975-9833
WEB SITE: www.shakespearefestivalla.org

Producing artistic director Ben Donenberg founded Shakespeare Festival/LA in 1984. He describes the company as "driven by an underlying impulse that equates the creation of professional, award-winning theater with the performance of tangible human services. Our evolving programs reflect this impulse as they demonstrate, in form and content, a unique, effective, and artful response to the pressing need for community development." Shakespeare Festival/LA moved into a new home in downtown Los Angeles in 2000, which allowed the organization to create new institutional partnerships (including being a part of the NEA Shakespeare project) and boost programming for teachers and inner-city youth in Los Angeles.

In addition to its summer festival and educational programs, Shakespeare Festival/LA's youth employment program hires young people challenged by severe economic circumstances to "create and perform an adaptation of a Shakespeare play" while other initiatives help teachers find unique ways to tackle Shakespeare in the classroom. Highly lauded professional performances of Shakespeare's plays are offered free of charge.

SHAKESPEARE THEATRE COMPANY

450 7th Street NW, Washington, DC 20004-2207

ADMINISTRATIVE OFFICE: The Shakespeare Theatre, 516 8th Street SE, Washington, DC 20003-2834

ADMINISTRATION: (202) 547-3230; BOX OFFICE: (202) 547-1122 or Toll Free (877) 487-8849; FAX: (202) 547-0226

E-MAIL: web_admin@shakespearedc.org

WEB SITE: www.shakespearedc.org

The Shakespeare Theatre Company in Washington, D.C., under artistic director Michael Kahn's leadership since 1986, presents five plays by Shakespeare and other classical playwrights in its 451-seat performance space in the heart of Washington, D.C.'s Pennsylvania Quarter arts district, and two weeks of free Shakespeare at the Free For All each summer in Rock Creek Park. In its own words, the mission of The Shakespeare Theatre is "to become the nation's leading force in producing and preserving the highest quality of classic theater. The Theatre endeavors to strengthen the tradition of classic theater in America through productions that reflect its current world."

The Shakespeare Theatre Education Department includes Text Alive!, a curriculum enrichment program, Shakespearience student matinees, Classics in the Classroom, Theatre History Initiative, and a variety of other programs.

ACADEMY FOR CLASSICAL ACTING

Intended for professional actors, the Academy for Classical Acting is accredited through The George Washington University and involves 12 months of study in voice, speech, acting, text, mask, Alexander technique, movement, clown, and stage combat. Check the Web site for more details.

CASTING

TST has a small resident acting company and casts other roles (both Equity and non-Equity) on an ongoing basis throughout the year. Most auditions are by invitation only. TST also attends the Washington, D.C.–Baltimore Area Wide Auditions for Equity members each winter, and the League of

Washington Theatres general auditions every summer. General auditions are advertised in *Back Stage* for New York auditions and general auditions are held in D.C. each summer. TST also reviews photos and résumés received by mail, and contacts actors to schedule auditions based on their classical experience and training. New York casting director, Stuart Howard Associates coordinates all New York auditions. See the Web site for more details. Mail casting inquiries, photos and résumés to: Associate Director, The Shakespeare Theatre, 516 8th Street SE, Washington, DC, 20003.

GENERAL EMPLOYMENT OPPORTUNITIES
Check the Web site for specific openings, details and job descriptions, or e-mail inquiries to: jobs@shakespearedc.org. No calls.

INTERNSHIPS
Administrative internships are generally available in artistic administration, development, education, general management, graphic design, and public relations/marketing. Production internships often surface in costumes, lighting, production management, sound, stage management, stage properties, and technical direction.

ACTING FELLOWS
The Shakespeare Theatre provides opportunities for up to eight actors to join the Acting Fellows Company for a full season as part of established relationships with Vassar College and the Kennedy Center American College Theatre Festival. Actors who are not affiliated with a particular program may audition for remaining positions. Check the Web site for details.

THE SHAKESPEARE THEATRE OF NEW JERSEY
36 Madison Avenue, Madison, NJ 07940
ADMINISTRATION: (973) 408-3278; BOX OFFICE: (973) 408-5600;
FAX: (973) 408-3361
E-MAIL: information@shakespearenj.org
WEB SITE: www.shakespearenj.org

Founded in 1962, The Shakespeare Theatre of New Jersey (formerly the New Jersey Shakespeare Festival) plays to over 100,000 audience members annually and is New Jersey's only professional theater company dedicated to Shakespeare's canon and other classic masterworks. In its own words, the company "strives to illuminate the universal and lasting relevance of the classics for contemporary audiences." The vibrant artistic director, Bonnie J. Monte, has led the company since 1990. The mainstage season plays out in the F.M. Kirby Shakespeare Theatre in Madison and runs June through December. An outdoor stage production is presented each summer at The Greek Theatre, an open-air amphitheater located on the College of Saint Elizabeth campus in nearby Morris Township. The institution's staff of 22 full-time employees works year-round and is joined by more than 250 additional company members during the heart of the season.

CASTING, GENERAL EMPLOYMENT OPPORTUNITIES, INTERNSHIPS
Check the Web site or e-mail the theater for details.

THE SITI COMPANY
SITI Company Studio and Offices, 520 Eighth Avenue, Suite 310,
  New York, NY 10018
ADMINISTRATION: (212) 868-0860; FAX: (212) 868-0837
E-MAIL: inbox@siti.org
WEB SITE: www.siti.org

Artistic director Anne Bogart founded SITI with Japanese director Tadashi Suzuki in 1992. The ensemble-based theater company's three ongoing components are "the creation of new work, the training of young theater artists, and a commitment to international collaboration."

In its own words, the company was founded "to redefine and revitalize contemporary theater in the United States through an emphasis on international cultural exchange and collaboration." Originally envisioned as a summer institute in Saratoga Springs, New York, SITI has expanded to encompass a year-round program based in New York City with a summer season in Saratoga. SITI believes that "contemporary American theater must necessarily incorporate artists from around the world and learn from the resulting cross-cultural exchange of dance, music, art, and performance experiences." Two notable collaborations include *Reunion* (about eight aging, negative, still-angry Group Theater people who are reunited for a public symposium to discuss the story of the Group Theater in the 1930s) and *Hotel Cassiopeia*, a collage of images, events, songs, movie stars, and dances, written by Charles L. Mee.

SOUTH COAST REPERTORY
655 Town Center Drive, P.O. Box 2197, Costa Mesa, CA 92628-2197
ADMINISTRATION: (714) 708-5500; BOX OFFICE: (714) 708-5555; FAX: (714) 708-5576
E-MAIL: theatre@scr.org
WEB SITE: www.scr.org

David Emmes and Martin Benson make up one of the longest-running and most successful artistic teams in regional theater history, and the theater's work developing new plays is among America's most accomplished. South Coast Repertory was founded in the belief that "theater is an art form with a unique power to illuminate the human experience." As testimony to its success, the company was awarded the Regional Theater Tony Award in 1988. In the company's own words, "We commit ourselves to exploring the most urgent human and social issues of our time, and to merging literature, design, and performance in ways that test the bounds of theater's artistic possibilities. We undertake to advance the art of theater in the service of our community, and aim to extend that service through educational, intercultural, and outreach programs that harmonize with our artistic mission." The esteemed managing director is Paula Tomei.

Opening with *Tartuffe* in 1964 in the Newport Beach Ebell Club, South Coast Repertory rented a former marine hardware store on Balboa Peninsula that was developed into a 75-seat proscenium stage in 1965. Don Took, Martha McFarland, Art Koustik, Richard Doyle, Hal Landon Jr., and Ron Boussom were deemed the theater's founding artists and most still turn up 40 years later on South Coast Repertory stages. A variety store in Costa Mesa was converted into a 217-seat theater in 1967, and in 1978-'79, a new 507-seat mainstage and 161-seat second stage were built in Costa Mesa on donated land. A 336-seat stage and major renovations to the complex and existing theaters were completed in 2002. Pivotal to the theater's accomplishments over the years have been the NewSCRipts play readings, the Hispanic Playwrights Project, and the Pacific Playwrights Festival.

CASTING

South Coast Repertory operates its Segerstrom and Argyros Stage theaters under LORT contracts, and produces three Theatre for Young Audience productions and a yearly educational touring production under a LORT TYA contract. The company casts its season on a show-by-show basis. Photos and résumés from Los Angeles–area actors only may be submitted for specific productions. South Coast Repertory also hires non-union talent from time to time for specific projects. Submit photos and résumés with a cover letter and contact information clearly printed on the résumé to: Casting, South Coast Repertory, P.O. Box 2197, Costa Mesa, CA, 92628-2197. For more information, e-mail the casting office or check the Web site for details. South Coast Repertory participates in the Actors' Equity general auditions twice each season and actors wishing to attend these auditions should contact the Equity offices for dates and times.

GENERAL EMPLOYMENT OPPORTUNITIES

South Coast Repertory posts detailed position descriptions and openings on the company Web site (www.scr.org).

PLAYWRIGHT COMMISSIONS, COLLABORATION LABORATORY

Colab is an integrated play development program employing diverse strategies to aid playwrights in creating new work. Playwright commissions support writers and help the theater develop longterm relationships. Productions of *The Violet Hour* by Richard Greenberg, *Sight Unseen* by Donald Margulies, *Golden Child* by David Henry Hwang, and *The Beard of Avon* by Amy Freed were all successful South Coast Repertory commissions. Other recent commissioned playwrights include Nilo Cruz, David Lindsay-Abaire, Lynn Nottage, Howard Korder, and Annie Weisman.

NewSCRipts is a developmental staged reading series that allows playwrights to hear their work read in front of an audience, receive feedback, and work closely with the theater's literary staff for further development. The theater does not accept direct submissions to the NewSCRipts program or the Pacific Playwrights Festival. Participation is by invitation for projects submitted according to the procedures outlined on the Web site. The Pacific Playwrights Festival presents six to eight new plays in readings, workshops, and productions during a three-day period.

SCRIPT SUBMISSIONS

South Coast Repertory accepts submissions for full-length plays, translations, and adaptations. Submitted plays are considered for possible inclusion in the NewSCRipts series and the Pacific Playwrights Festival, as well as for production on SCR stages. Playwrights must submit their work either through established agents or by first sending a query letter, brief synopsis, and 10-page dialogue sample to: Literary Department, South Coast Repertory, P. O. Box 2197, Costa Mesa, CA 92628-2197. See the Web site for additional information.

STUDIO ARENA THEATRE

710 Main Street, Buffalo, NY 14202-1990

ADMINISTRATION: (716) 856-8025; BOX OFFICE: (716) 856-5650 or (800) 77STAGE;
    FAX: (716) 856-3415

WEB SITE: www.studioarena.org

In 1927, the institution was first chartered as a nonprofit theater and educational institution and developed into Studio Arena in 1965. As western New York's only professional resident theater, Studio Arena has produced over 40 world or American premieres and currently resides in Buffalo's Theater District on Main Street. Over the years, Studio Arena has attracted Christine Baranski, Kathy Bates, Betty Buckley, Glenn Close, Olympia Dukakis, John Goodman, James Whitmore, Celeste Holm, Kim Hunter, Swoosie Kurtz and many other prestigious actors to its stages.

CASTING, SCRIPT SUBMISSIONS, GENERAL EMPLOYMENT OPPORTUNITIES, INTERNSHIPS
Check the Web site for specific information and updates. Elissa Myers Casting (333 West 52nd Street, Suite 1008, New York, NY, 10019) receives headshots and résumés, and intern inquiries and submissions should be sent to Jana L. Blaha, Executive Assistant, at jblaha@studioarena.com.

SYRACUSE STAGE
820 East Genesee Street, Syracuse, NY 13210
ADMINISTRATION: (315) 443-4008; BOX OFFICE: (315) 443-3275;
　FAX: (315) 443-9846
E-MAIL: syrstage@syr.edu
WEB SITE: www.syracusestage.org

An exciting theater in a great university town, Syracuse Stage generally produces eight mainstage plays, a Young Playwrights Festival, a children's touring show, and educational programs as central New York's premier regional theater. In its own words, the theater's mission is "to enrich, empower, and entertain our community through the creation of professional theater." Over 90,000 annual patrons attend Syracuse Stage productions and the theater has produced a number of world premieres, including works by Tina Howe, Michele Lowe, and Cheryl West. Syracuse Stage was founded in 1974 by Arthur Storch, a Broadway director who arrived in town as chairman of the Syracuse University Drama program. Growing audiences prompted the 1979 conversion of an old movie theater into the flexible 499-seat John D. Archbold Theatre. In 1992 James A. Clark was appointed producing director and chairman of the Drama Department, and Tazewell Thompson was named artistic director. Robert Moss replaced Thompson as the theater's third artistic director in 1996. The actors, directors, and designers employed by Syracuse Stage are usually professionals working in New York and Los Angeles and at resident theaters around the country.

CASTING, GENERAL EMPLOYMENT OPPORTUNITIES, INTERNSHIPS
Check the Web site and e-mail the theater at syrstage@syr.edu for ongoing information.

SCRIPT SUBMISSIONS

To submit a play for consideration, send your résumé, the plot synopsis, and 10-page dialogue sample to Play Submissions, Syracuse Stage, 820 East Genesee Street, Syracuse, NY, 13210-1508.

THEATRE FOR A NEW AUDIENCE

154 Christopher Street, #3D, New York, NY 10014
ADMINISTRATION: (212) 229-2819; BOX OFFICE: (212) 229-2819, ext. 0;
    FAX: (212) 229-2911
E-MAIL: info@tfana.org
WEB SITE: www.tfana.org

Founded by artistic director Jeffrey Horowitz in 1979, Theatre for a New Audience states that its mission is "to help develop and vitalize the performance and study of Shakespeare and classic drama." Theatre for a New Audience produces for audiences Off-Broadway, tours nationally and internationally, and even presented a Shakespeare production at the Royal Shakespeare Company in England. In its own words, "Theatre for a New Audience finds the contemporary heart of the classics" with "a reverence for language, spirit of adventure and visual boldness." The company has worked with many of the world's best, including Julie Taymor, Sir Peter Hall, Robert Woodruff, and Bartlett Sher. Theatre for a New Audience produces at The Duke Theater in a 199-seat flexible space.

CASTING

All casting is through Deborah Brown Casting, 160 West End Avenue, Suite 15P, New York, NY, 10023. No calls.

GENERAL EMPLOYMENT OPPORTUNITIES

General employment opportunities are posted on Playbill.com and/or in TCG's *ARTSEARCH*. Administrative and stage management internship availability varies on a season-by-season basis. TFANA does not offer acting internships. Check the Web site for more information.

SCRIPT SUBMISSIONS

Theatre for a New Audience does not accept play submissions.

AMERICAN DIRECTORS PROJECT

The American Directors Project was established in 1997 to promote the development of American directors of Shakespeare. Through this program, TFANA invites six to eight young- to mid-career directors to work with a remarkable array of professionals. Check the Web site for annual information, but past participants have included Cicely Berry, Karin Coonrod, Scott Ellis, Bartlett Sher, Victor Garber, and Ron Rifkin.

THEATREWORKS

P.O. Box 50458, Palo Alto, CA 94303-0458

ADMINISTRATION: (650) 463-1950; BOX OFFICE: (650) 463-1960; FAX: (650) 463-1963

E-MAIL: info@theatreworks.org

WEB SITE: www.theatreworks.org

Founded in 1970 by artistic director Robert Kelley, TheatreWorks "is committed to being one of America's outstanding professional theaters . . . our work celebrates the human spirit through innovative premieres, productions, and programs inspired by our exceptionally diverse community." TheatreWorks employs over 300 artists annually, has a professional staff of 42, and plays to over 100,000 enthusiastic patrons each year. The company offers a year-round season of dramas, comedies, musicals, and world premieres and produces in 625-seat and 150-seat theaters in the Mountain View Center for the Performing Arts and in the 425-seat Lucie Stern Theatre complex in Palo Alto.

CASTING

TheatreWorks holds general auditions twice each year, typically in January and the summer. The company also attend the Theatre Bay Area regional auditions held each spring. Callbacks are by invitation for each production, throughout the year. The theater hires Equity and non-Equity actors. Check out the Web site for additional information. In the company's own words, "TheatreWorks has a long history of culturally specific and nontraditional casting." Auditions are listed in *Callboard* Magazine. Actors can also check the theater's voice-mail message at (650) 463-1950 ext. 610, e-mail (casting@theatreworks.org), or call (650) 463-7107.

SCRIPT SUBMISSIONS

TheatreWorks prefers "well-written, well-constructed plays that celebrate the human spirit through innovative productions and programs inspired by our exceptionally diverse community. There is no limit on the number of characters, and we favor plays with multi-ethnic casting possibilities." The theater accepts plays and musicals submitted by theaters and/or agents, including plays produced Off-Off Broadway and regionally other than the Bay Area, plays and musicals not produced in the Bay Area within the last five years, plays and musicals that have never been produced but have had some development, and plays and musicals looking for development. The theater does not accept unsolicited manuscripts, one-acts, or "plays with togas." For inquiries, send a cover letter, short synopsis, 10-page sample dialogue, submitted play's production history (including development), playwright's theater résumé, and a self-addressed, stamped return envelope. See the Web site for more details.

GENERAL EMPLOYMENT OPPORTUNITIES, INTERNSHIPS
Open full-time and part-time positions and internships are listed in detail on the Web site, along with contact names and e-mails. Internships are often available in marketing, development, scenic construction, and costume rentals.

TRINITY REPERTORY COMPANY
201 Washington Street, Providence, RI 02903
ADMINISTRATION: (401) 521-1100; BOX OFFICE: (401) 351-4242; FAX: (401) 521-0447
E-MAIL: info@trinityrep.com
WEB SITE: www.trinityrep.com

Trinity Repertory Company is the largest artistic organization in Rhode Island and is a professional theater that is "firmly rooted in and dedicated to the life of its community. Through its principal aesthetic of great stories, well told, Trinity Rep aspires to the continuous creation of a theater that represents all that is Rhode Island, all that is American, all that is human. With the unique performance style of a resident acting company, Trinity Rep nurtures the development of new work while keeping the classics alive and relevant to the new generation of theater audiences."

CASTING
Trinity Rep is a resident company of artists and does not audition specifically for company members. "One is invited to join after we have worked with you on a number of projects. We cast from the resident company as frequently as possible each season." Out-of-town auditions are for Equity only and are listed through Equity and the trade papers. Trinity Rep also uses casting directors in New York. Role-specific auditions for union and nonunion actors are listed on the company Web site, through the *Providence Journal*, and occasionally through the *Stagesource* hotline in Boston. Check the Web site for ongoing information.

SCRIPT SUBMISSIONS
Trinity Rep generally produces at least one premiere production a year, as well as readings and workshops of numerous new plays. Each year Trinity Rep's Mabel T. Woolley Literary Department reads and reviews hundreds of new scripts. To submit a new play for consideration at Trinity Rep, a

writer should first send a cover letter, a one-page synopsis of the play, and up to ten pages of dialogue from the play to: Mabel T. Woolley Literary Department, Trinity Repertory Company, 201 Washington Street, Providence, RI, 02903.

GENERAL EMPLOYMENT OPPORTUNITIES

Check the company Web site, where positions are listed as they become available. Send cover letter and résumé to Human Resources, Trinity Rep, 201 Washington Street, Providence, RI, 02903 or E-mail: hr@trinityrep.com.

INTERNSHIPS

Trinity Rep offers college students and recent college graduates the opportunity to receive intensive professional training in theater production and administration through its internship program. Internships are full-time positions, and interns are treated as members of the theater staff, with all the same responsibilities and expectations. Trinity Rep provides interns with housing (furnished apartments with basic utilities) as well as a $75 per week stipend. There may also be opportunities for interns to earn a small amount of overhire income at the theater. Check the Web site for more details and contact names and numbers. Internships are generally available in theater management, education, literary management, communications, marketing, development, production management, stage management, scenic carpentry, electrics, sound, costumes, and props.

UTAH SHAKESPEAREAN FESTIVAL
Cedar City, Utah
[See 250+ Shakespeare Festivals, page 301]

VIRGINIA STAGE COMPANY AT THE WELLS THEATRE
P.O. Box 3770, Norfolk, VA 23514
ADMINISTRATION: (757) 627-6988; BOX OFFICE: (757) 627-1234; FAX: (757) 628-5958
E-MAIL: cbauman@vastage.com
WEB SITE: www.vastage.com

The mission of Virginia Stage Company is "to develop and sustain a fully professional theater serving Southeastern Virginia, which enriches the region and the field through the production of theatrical art of the highest quality." Founded in 1979, the company currently plays to an audience of more than 100,000 patrons. VSC's Education Department tours to over 50,000 Hampton Roads students annually and participates as a partner in education by providing services such as performances, drama classes, production training, and workshops to Title One schools and others at no charge. The Tony Award–winning musical *The Secret Garden* was first produced at VSC in 1989. The company operates in the 677-seat Wells Theatre, named after baseball player-turned-vaudeville entrepreneur Jake Wells. Chris Hanna is Virgina Stage Company's artistic director.

CASTING, GENERAL EMPLOYMENT OPPORTUNITIES, INTERNSHIPS
Virginia Stage Company holds local auditions annually. Check the Web site for information and updates on employment and internships.

SCRIPT SUBMISSIONS
Virginia Stage Company is unable to consider unsolicited manuscripts for production. Letters of inquiry regarding potential submissions should be directed to artistic director Chris Hanna.

WALNUT STREET THEATRE
825 Walnut Street (at 9th), Philadelphia, PA 19107
PHONE: (215) 574-3550; FAX: (215) 574-3598
WEB SITE: www.wstonline.org

Over 50,000 subscribers and 300,000 patrons flock to the historic Walnut Street Theatre, considered by many to be the oldest theater in America. According to company officials, "it stands alone as the only theater operating continuously as a theater since it opened in 1809." Everyone from Edwin Booth and Helen Hayes to Houdini, George M. Cohan, and Katharine Hepburn have appeared on the Walnut Street Theatre stage. Originally opened for equestrian acts as The New Circus in 1809, Walnut Street can claim Thomas Jefferson attended its first theater production, *The Rivals*, in 1812. The Walnut Street Theatre has been designated both a National Historic Landmark and the State Theatre. Producing artistic director Bernard Havard returned the Walnut to a producing theater in 1983 when it was "reconceived as a nonprofit regional theater dedicated to the preservation and development of the art of theater." Since 1983, the company has produced over 20 world premieres and 10 American premieres. The Walnut Street Theatre School was added in 1985. Walnut Street Theatre employs over 600 people and the annual budget is near $10 million. Walnut Street operates under a special contract with Actors' Equity and related unions.

CASTING
Walnut Street Theatre is dedicated to the casting and employment of local, Philadelphia-based actors. Each mainstage and studio production begins with local auditions. The theater also participates in general auditions as part

of the Theatre Alliance of Greater Philadelphia. Send a photo and résumé for consideration to Assistant to the Producing Artisitic Director/Casting, Walnut Street Theatre, 825 Walnut Street, Philadelphia, PA, 19107. See the Web site for additional information.

GENERAL EMPLOYMENT OPPORTUNITIES
General employment information is listed in detail on the Web site.

APPRENTICESHIPS
Positions are generally open in acting, carpentry, casting/literary management, costumes, education, fundraising, general management, house management, marketing, production management, props, public relations, running crew/stage, scenic painting, stage management (mainstage and studio series), and subscriptions. The program is a full-time commitment with a weekly scholarship, individual HMO medical coverage, gym membership, and free tuition to Theatre School classes. The terms of scholarships vary. Check the Web site for details and applications.

THE WILMA THEATER
265 S. Broad Street, Philadelphia, PA 19107
ADMINISTRATION: (215) 893-9456; BOX OFFICE: (215) 546-STAGE;
    FAX: (215) 893-0895
E-MAIL: info@wilmatheater.org
WEB SITE: www.wilmatheater.org

In its own words, "The Wilma Theater exists to present theater as an art form, engaging artists and audiences in an adventure of aesthetic philosophical reflection of the complexities of contemporary life. We accomplish our mission by producing thoughtful, well-crafted productions of intelligent, daring plays that represent a range of voices, viewpoints, and production styles." Artistic/producing directors Jiri Zizka and Blanka Zizka "search for plays, as well as new adaptations and translations, to which creative visual and musical techniques add another dimension, allowing each play to evolve beyond the confines of immediate verbal meaning into the world of metaphor and poetic vision."

Founded in 1973 as The Wilma Project, the company engaged avant garde theater artists, including the Bread & Puppet Theatre, Mabou Mines, Charles Ludlam's Ridiculous Theatrical Company, The Wooster Group, Ping Chong & the Fiji Company, and Spalding Gray until 1979, when the Zizkas "forged a creative relationship with the Wilma as artists-in-residence." They assumed artistic leadership in 1981. The Wilma soon moved to a 100-seat theater and eventually a new 296-seat home in 1996. Over 500 students enrolled in The Wilma Studio School each year for theater training.

CASTING

The Wilma encourages actors to submit a headshot and résumé for the company's casting files and to "indicate the role and production in which you are interested." Wilma auditions are by invitation only. Send to Casting, The Wilma Theater, 265 South Broad Street, Philadelphia, PA, 19107.

SCRIPT SUBMISSIONS

The Wilma considers full-length plays, translations, adaptations, and musicals from an international repertoire with an emphasis on innovative, bold staging; world premieres; ensemble works; works with poetic dimension; plays with music; multi-media works; social issues. The preferred maximum cast size is 12; the stage measures 44' x 46'. Due to staffing and scheduling limitations, the Wilma is only able to accept unsolicited manuscripts from agents. However, if accompanied by a recommendation from a literary manager, dramaturg, or other theater professional, a query will be accepted by the theater. Queries should include a cover letter, a synopsis, and a writing résumé or description of your writing background, plus samples of the piece (optional). Check the Web site for other important details.

YALE REPERTORY THEATRE

1120 Chapel Street, P.O. Box 1257, New Haven, CT 06505
ADMINISTRATION: (203) 432-1515; BOX OFFICE: (203) 432-1234;
FAX: (203) 432-6423
E-MAIL: yalerep@yale.edu
WEB SITE: www.yale.edu/yalerep

The intimate and accomplished Yale Repertory Theatre is the 1991 recipient of the Regional Theatre Tony Award, having mounted over 90 world premieres, including four Pulitzer Prize winners. Yale Rep's close relationship with the Yale School of Drama has created a grand sharing of internationally prominent artists and together they are "committed to the rigorous, daring, and passionate exploration of our art form. We embrace a global audience." Artistic director James Bundy notes that "Our highest aim is to train artistic leaders—in every theatrical discipline—who create bold new works that astonish the mind, challenge the heart, and delight the senses." Victoria Nolan is the theater's seasoned, savvy managing director. Robert Brustein founded Yale Repertory Theatre in 1966 as the "Master Teacher" of the Yale School of Drama. Lloyd Richards served as Dean of the Drama

School and artistic director of Yale Repertory Theatre from 1979 to 1991. Stan Wojewodski Jr., served as dean and artistic director from 1991 to 2002.

CASTING

Yale Rep casts locally (mostly non-Equity) and in New York and Los Angeles. Check out the e-mail information line (yalerep@yale.edu) and the Web site (www.yale.edu/yalerep) for ongoing information.

SCRIPT SUBMISSIONS

Yale Rep accepts full-script submissions only from recognized literary agents. Unrepresented authors may send a letter of query, detailed synopsis, character breakdown, résumé, and 10-page dialogue sample to the literary office.

GENERAL EMPLOYMENT OPPORTUNITIES, INTERNSHIPS

Administration and production positions are generally listed in *ARTSEARCH* and through Human Resources at Yale University. Yale University offers internships at Yale Repertory but the theater doesn't offer internships.

400+ TCG THEATERS

THEATRE COMMUNICATIONS GROUP (TCG)

520 Eighth Avenue, 24th Floor
New York, NY 10018-4156
PHONE: (212) 609-5900; FAX: (212) 609-5901
E-MAIL: tcg@tcg.org
WEB SITE: www.tcg.org

Theatre Communications Group (TCG) is the world's best link to the American theater and "the national organization for the American not-for-profit professional theater." Founded in 1961 (the same year as New York's La MaMa Theatre and the Utah Shakespearean Festival), TCG has provided a national forum and communications network for a field that, in its own words, is "as aesthetically diverse as it is geographically widespread."

According to the Web site's *Theatre Profiles*—a grand collection of facts, artistic statements, contact information, and production overviews published by TCG, capturing over 250 of America's nonprofit theaters—TCG offers a "comprehensive support system that addresses concerns of the theater companies and individual artists that collectively represent our national theater."

TCG's mission is "to strengthen, nurture, and promote the not-for-profit American theater." Through its artistic, management, and international programs, advocacy activities, and publications, TCG seeks to increase the organizational efficiency of its member theaters, cultivate and celebrate the artistic talent and achievements of the field, and promote a larger public understanding of and appreciation for the theater field. At press time, TCG was searching to replace the exceptional Ben Cameron as executive director. Jim O'Quinn is the longtime editor of TCG's *American Theatre*, a monthly magazine that is a terrific tool for theater employees at every stage of their careers.

TCG's centralized services include publishing *American Theatre*, *ARTSEARCH* employment bulletin, the *TCG Theatre Directory* (a must for every theater office), the *Dramatists Sourcebook*, *Stage Writers Handbook*, *Stage Directors Handbook*, and much more. *Theatre Profiles* is an online compendium of information about TCG member theaters and their productions, going back to 1995. Perhaps most important to theater leaders and managers, TCG organizes, analyzes, and communicates pertinent, timely, factual information that is extremely useful to individuals and institutions in both their local concerns and national advocacy. TCG's artistic programs include career development programs and grants to theaters and theater artists. Management programs offer professional development opportunities for theater leaders.

Special advocacy alerts on lobbying efforts and legislative developments are also a key service of TCG. As mentioned in other areas of this book, every theater person and theater institution in America should have an ongoing collection of *American Theatre* magazines, the *ARTSEARCH* employment bulletin, and the *TCG Theatre Directory*, listing the names, addresses, phone numbers, Web sites, e-mails, and general information for the TCG membership. Why should everyone have these publications? Because they're the best way to keep on top of trends, key potential employers, theater innovations, creative explorations, and the activities of your profession.

TCG has more than 400 theater members in 47 states, and 17,000 individual members. You should consider becoming one of them.

Internships
Internships are available to qualified individuals interested in entering fields related to arts administration, management, editing, and journalism through hands-on experience. Check the Web site for details.

Theatre Communications Group/International Theatre Institute
TCG/ITI is a network of theater centers in 92 countries that serves as a clearinghouse of information and networking source between professionals and a resource for students. Check the Web site for details.

The Members
TCG's 437 member theaters (all available through direct links on the TCG Web site) are:

1812 PRODUCTIONS, Philadelphia, PA, www.1812productions.org
THE 52ND STREET PROJECT, New York, NY, www.52project.org
7 STAGES, Atlanta, GA, www.7stages.org

A NOISE WITHIN, Glendale, CA, www.anoisewithin.org

ABOUT FACE THEATRE, Chicago, IL, www.aboutfacetheatre.com

ACADEMY THEATRE, Avondale Estates, GA, www.academytheatre.org

ACT THEATRE, Seattle, WA, www.acttheatre.org

THE ACTING COMPANY, New York, NY, www.theactingcompany.org

ACTOR'S EXPRESS, Atlanta, GA, www.actorsexpress.com

THE ACTORS' GANG, Culver City, CA, www.theactorsgang.com

ACTORS GUILD OF LEXINGTON, Lexington, KY, www.actorsguildoflexington.org

ACTORS THEATRE OF LOUISVILLE, Louisville, KY, www.actorstheatre.org

ACTOR'S THEATRE OF CHARLOTTE, Charlotte, NC,
    www.actorstheatrecharlotte.org

ACTORS THEATRE OF PHOENIX, Phoenix, AZ, www.actorstheatrephx.org

ADIRONDACK THEATRE FESTIVAL, Glens Falls, NY, www.ATFestival.org

THE AFRICAN CONTINUUM THEATRE COMPANY (ACTCO), Washington, DC,
    www.africancontinuumtheatre.com

ALABAMA SHAKESPEARE FESTIVAL, Montgomery, AL, www.asf.net

ALLEY THEATRE, Houston, TX, www.alleytheatre.org

ALLIANCE THEATRE COMPANY, Atlanta, GA, www.alliancetheatre.org

AMAS MUSICAL THEATRE, INC., New York, NY, www.amasmusical.org

AMERICAN CONSERVATORY THEATER, San Francisco, CA, www.act-sf.org

AMERICAN FOLKLORE THEATRE, Fish Creek, WI, www.folkloretheatre.com

AMERICAN PLAYERS THEATRE, Spring Green, WI, www.playinthewoods.org

AMERICAN REPERTORY THEATRE, Cambridge, MA, www.amrep.org

AMERICAN SHAKESPEARE CENTER, Staunton, VA,
    www.americanshakespearecenter.com

AMERICAN STAGE, St. Petersburg, FL, www.americanstage.org

AMERICAN THEATER COMPANY, Chicago, IL, www.atcweb.org

AMERICAN THEATRE COMPANY, Tulsa, OK, www.americantheatrecompany.org

ARDEN THEATRE CO., Philadelphia, PA, www.ardentheatre.org

ARENA STAGE, Washington, DC, www.arenastage.org

ARIZONA THEATRE COMPANY, Tucson, AZ, www.arizonatheatre.org

THE ARKANSAS ARTS CENTER CHILDREN'S THEATRE, Little Rock, AR,
    www.arkarts.com

ARKANSAS REPERTORY THEATRE, Little Rock, AR, www.therep.org

ARTISTS REPERTORY THEATRE, Portland, OR, www.artistsrep.org

ARTS CENTER OF COASTAL CAROLINA, Hilton Head, SC,
    www.artscenter-hhi.org

ARVADA CENTER FOR THE ARTS AND HUMANITIES, Arvada, CO,
    www.arvadacenter.org

ASOLO THEATRE COMPANY, Sarasota, FL, www.asolo.org

ATLANTIC THEATER COMPANY, New York, NY, www.atlantictheater.org

AURORA THEATRE COMPANY, Berkeley, CA, www.auroratheatre.org

B STREET THEATRE, Sacramento, CA, www.bstreettheatre.org

BARKSDALE THEATRE, Richmond, VA, www.barksdaletheatre.org

BARRINGTON STAGE COMPANY, Sheffield, MA, www.barringtonstageco.org

BAY STREET THEATRE, Sag Harbor, NY, www.baystreet.org

BERKELEY REPERTORY THEATRE, Berkeley, CA, www.berkeleyrep.org

BERKSHIRE THEATRE FESTIVAL, Stockbridge, MA, www.berkshiretheatre.org

BILINGUAL FOUNDATION OF THE ARTS, Los Angeles, CA, www.bfatheatre.org

BLANK THEATRE COMPANY, Los Angeles, CA, www.theblank.com

BLOOMSBURG THEATRE ENSEMBLE, Bloomsburg, PA, www.bte.org

BOARSHEAD THEATER, Lansing, MI, www.boarshead.org

BOISE CONTEMPORARY THEATER, Boise, ID, www.bctheater.org

BOOK-IT REPERTORY THEATRE, Seattle, WA, www.book-it.org

BORDERLANDS THEATER, Tucson, AZ, www.borderlandstheater.org

BOSTON THEATRE WORKS, Boston, MA, www.bostontheatreworks.com

BRAT PRODUCTIONS, Philadelphia, PA, www.bratproductions.org

BRAVA THEATER CENTER, San Francisco, CA, www.brava.org

BRISTOL RIVERSIDE THEATRE, Bristol, PA, www.brtstage.org

BURNING COAL THEATRE COMPANY, Raleigh, NC, www.burningcoal.org

BUSHFIRE THEATRE OF PERFORMING ARTS, Philadelphia, PA,
    www.bushfiretheatre.org

CALIFORNIA REPERTORY COMPANY, Long Beach, CA, www.calrep.org

CALIFORNIA SHAKESPEARE THEATER, Berkeley, CA, www.calshakes.org

CALIFORNIA THEATRE CENTER, Sunnyvale, CA, www.ctcinc.org

THE CAPE COD THEATRE PROJECT, Falmouth, MA,
    www.capecodtheatreproject.org

CAPITAL REPERTORY THEATRE, Albany, NY, www.capitalrep.org

CASTILLO THEATRE, New York, NY, www.castillo.org

CENTER FOR NEW THEATER AT CAL ARTS, Valencia, CA, www.calarts.edu

CENTER FOR PUPPETRY ARTS, Atlanta, GA, www.puppet.org

CENTER THEATRE GROUP, Los Angeles, CA, www.taperahmanson.com

CENTERSTAGE, Baltimore, MD, www.centerstage.org

CENTRE STAGE-SOUTH CAROLINA, Greenville, SC, www.centrestage.org

CHARLESTON STAGE, Charleston, SC, www.charlestonstage.com

CHERRY LANE THEATRE, New York, NY, www.cherrylanetheatre.org

CHICAGO DRAMATISTS, Chicago, IL, www.chicagodramatists.org

CHICAGO SHAKESPEARE THEATER, Chicago, IL, www.chicagoshakes.com

THE CHILDREN'S THEATRE COMPANY, Minneapolis, MN,
    www.childrenstheatre.org

CHILDSPLAY, INC., Tempe, AZ, www.childsplayaz.org

THE CIDER MILL PLAYHOUSE, Endicott, NY, www.cidermillplayhouse.org

CINCINNATI PLAYHOUSE IN THE PARK, Cincinnati, OH, www.cincyplay.com

CINCINNATI SHAKESPEARE FESTIVAL, Cincinnati, OH, www.cincyshakes.com

CITY GARAGE, Santa Monica, CA, www.citygarage.org

CITY THEATRE, Miami, FL, www.citytheatre.com

CITY THEATRE COMPANY, Pittsburgh, PA, www.citytheatrecompany.org

THE CIVILIANS, New York, NY, www.thecivilians.org

CLARENCE BROWN THEATRE, Knoxville, TN, www.clarencebrowntheatre.org

CLASSICAL THEATRE OF HARLEM, New York, NY, classicaltheatreofharlem.org

CLASSIC STAGE COMPANY, New York, NY, www.classicstage.org

THE CLEVELAND PLAY HOUSE, Cleveland, OH, www.clevelandplayhouse.com

CLEVELAND PUBLIC THEATRE, Cleveland, OH, www.cptonline.org

COLLABORACTION, Chicago, IL, www.collaboraction.org

THE COLONY THEATRE COMPANY, Burbank, CA, www.colonytheatre.org

COLUMBUS CHILDREN'S THEATRE, Columbus, OH,
    www.colschildrenstheatre.org

COMMONWEAL THEATRE COMPANY, Lanesboro, MN,
    www.commonwealtheatre.org

COMPANY OF FOOLS, Hailey, ID, www.companyoffools.org

CONGO SQUARE THEATRE, Chicago, IL, www.congosquaretheatre.org

CONNECTICUT REPERTORY THEATRE, Storrs, CT, www.crt.uconn.edu

CONTEMPORARY AMERICAN THEATER FESTIVAL, Shepherdstown, WV,
    www.catf.org

CORNERSTONE THEATER COMPANY, Los Angeles, CA,
    www.cornerstonetheater.org

THE COTERIE THEATRE, Kansas City, MO, www.coterietheatre.org

COURT THEATRE, Chicago, IL, www.courttheatre.org

CREEDE REPERTORY THEATRE, Creede, CO, www.creederep.org

CURIOUS THEATRE COMPANY, Denver, CO, www.curioustheatre.org

CYRANO'S THEATRE COMPANY, Anchorage, AK, www.cyranos.org

DAD'S GARAGE, Atlanta, GA, www.dadsgarage.com

DALLAS CHILDREN'S THEATER, Dallas, TX, www.dct.org

DALLAS THEATER CENTER, Dallas, TX, www.dallastheatercenter.org

DEAF WEST THEATRE, North Hollywood, CA, www.deafwest.org

DELAWARE THEATRE COMPANY, Wilmington, DE, www.delawaretheatre.org

DELL'ARTE INTERNATIONAL, Blue Lake, CA, www.dellarte.com

DENVER CENTER THEATRE COMPANY, Denver, CO, www.denvercenter.org

DEPOT THEATRE, Westport, NY, www.depottheatre.org

DETROIT REPERTORY THEATRE, Detroit, MI, www.detroitreptheatre.com

DOBAMA THEATRE, Cleveland Heights, OH, www.dobama.org

DOUBLE EDGE THEATRE PRODUCTIONS, INC., Ashfield, MA,
www.doubleedgetheatre.org

EAST WEST PLAYERS, Los Angeles, CA, www.eastwestplayers.org

THE EMPTY SPACE THEATRE, Seattle, WA, www.emptyspace.org

ENSEMBLE STUDIO THEATRE, New York, NY, www.ensemblestudiotheatre.org

THE ENSEMBLE THEATRE, Houston, TX, www.ensemblehouston.org

ENSEMBLE THEATRE OF CINCINNATI, Cincinnati, OH, www.cincyetc.com

ENSEMBLE THEATRE COMPANY, Santa Barbara, CA, www.ensembletheatre.com

EUGENE O'NEILL THEATER CENTER, Waterford, CT, www.theoneill.org

EVERYMAN THEATRE, Baltimore, MD, www.everymantheatre.org

FIRST STAGE CHILDREN'S THEATER, Milwaukee, WI, www.firststage.org

FLORIDA STAGE, Manalapan, FL, www.floridastage.org

FLORIDA STUDIO THEATRE, Sarasota, FL, www.fst2000.org

FOLGER THEATRE, Washington, DC, www.folger.edu

THE FOOTHILL THEATRE COMPANY, Nevada City, CA,
www.foothilltheatre.org

FORD'S THEATRE, Washington, DC, www.fordstheatre.org

THE FOUNDRY THEATRE, New York, NY, www.thefoundrytheatre.org

FOUNTAIN THEATRE, Los Angeles, CA, www.fountaintheatre.com

FREE STREET PROGRAMS, Chicago, IL, www.freestreet.org

GABLESTAGE, Coral Gables, FL, www.gablestage.org

GAINESVILLE THEATRE ALLIANCE, Gainesville, GA, gainesvilletheatrealliance.org

GALA HISPANIC THEATRE, Washington, DC, www.galatheatre.org

GAMM THEATRE, Pawtucket, RI, www.gammtheatre.org

GAMUT THEATRE GROUP, Harrisburg, PA, www.gamutplays.org

GEFFEN PLAYHOUSE, Los Angeles, CA, www.geffenplayhouse.com

GEORGE STREET PLAYHOUSE, New Brunswick, NJ, www.georgestplayhouse.org

GEORGIA SHAKESPEARE FESTIVAL, Atlanta, GA, www.gashakespeare.org

GEVA THEATRE CENTER, Rochester, NY, www.gevatheatre.org

GOLDEN THREAD PRODUCTIONS, San Francisco, CA, www.goldenthread.org

GOODMAN THEATRE, Chicago, IL, www.goodman-theatre.org

GREAT LAKES THEATER FESTIVAL, Cleveland, OH, www.greatlakestheater.org

GREENBRIER VALLEY THEATRE, Lewisburg, WV, www.gvtheatre.org

GROWING STAGE THEATRE FOR YOUNG AUDIENCES, Netcong, NJ,
www.growingstage.com

GUTHRIE THEATER, Minneapolis, MN, www.guthrietheater.org

HANGAR THEATRE, Ithaca, NY, www.hangartheatre.org

HARLEQUIN PRODUCTIONS, Olympia, WA, www.harlequinproductions.org

HARTBEAT ENSEMBLE, Hartford, CT, www.hartbeatensemble.org

HARTFORD STAGE COMPANY, Hartford, CT, www.hartfordstage.org

HARWICH JUNIOR THEATRE AND HARWICH WINTER THEATRE,
    West Harwich, MA, www.hjtcapecod.org

HISTORY THEATRE, St. Paul, MN, www.historytheatre.com

HONOLULU THEATRE FOR YOUTH, Honolulu, HI, www.htyweb.org

HORIZON THEATRE COMPANY, Atlanta, GA, www.horizontheatre.com

THE HUMAN RACE THEATRE COMPANY, Dayton, OH,
    www.humanracetheatre.org

HUNTINGTON THEATRE COMPANY, Boston, MA, www.huntingtontheatre.org

THE HYPOCRITES, Chicago, IL, www.the.hypocrites.com

HYDE PARK THEATRE, Austin, TX, www.hydeparktheatre.org

IDAHO SHAKESPEARE FESTIVAL, Boise, ID, www.idahoshakespeare.org

ILLINOIS THEATRE CENTER, Park Forest, IL, www.ilthctr.org

ILLUSION THEATER, Minneapolis, MN, www.illusiontheater.org

IMAGINATION STAGE, Bethesda, MD, www.imaginationstage.org

INDIANA REPERTORY THEATRE, Indianapolis, IN, www.indianarep.com

INTAR THEATRE, New York, NY, www.intartheatre.org

INTERACT THEATRE COMPANY, Philadelphia, PA, www.interacttheatre.org

INTERNATIONAL CITY THEATRE, Long Beach, CA, www.ictlongbeach.org

INTIMAN THEATRE, Seattle, WA, www.intiman.org

INVISIBLE THEATRE, Tucson, AZ, www.invisibletheatre.com

IRISH CLASSICAL THEATRE, Buffalo, NY, www.irishclassicaltheatre.com

IRONDALE ENSEMBLE PROJECT, Brooklyn, NY, www.irondale.org

THE JEWISH THEATER OF NEW YORK, New York, NY, www.jewishtheater.org

JEWISH THEATRE OF THE SOUTH, Dunwoody, GA, www.jplay.org

THE JOHN DREW THEATER, East Hampton, NY, www.guildhall.org

THE JUNGLE THEATER, Minneapolis, MN, www.jungletheater.com

KANSAS CITY REPERTORY THEATRE, Kansas City, MO, www.kcrep.org

THE KAVINOKY THEATRE, Buffalo, NY, www.kavinokytheatre.com

KENNEDY CENTER-YOUTH AND FAMILY PROGRAMS, Arlington, VA,
    www.kennedy-center.org

KENTUCKY REPERTORY THEATRE AT HORSE CAVE, Horse Cave, KY,
    www.kentuckyrep.org

KENTUCKY SHAKESPEARE FESTIVAL, Louisville, KY, www.kyshakes.org

KITCHEN DOG THEATER, Dallas, TX, www.kitchendogtheater.org

KITCHEN THEATRE COMPANY, Ithaca, NY, www.kitchentheatre.org

L.A. THEATRE WORKS, Venice, CA, www.latw.org

LA JOLLA PLAYHOUSE, La Jolla, CA, www.lajollaplayhouse.com

LA MAMA E.T.C., New York, NY, www.lamama.org

LABYRINTH THEATER COMPANY, New York, NY, www.labtheater.org

LAGUNA PLAYHOUSE, Laguna Beach, CA, www.lagunaplayhouse.com

LANTERN THEATER COMPANY, Philadelphia, PA, www.lanterntheater.org

LARK PLAY DEVELOPMENT CENTER, New York, NY, www.larktheatre.org

LINCOLN CENTER THEATER, New York, NY, www.lct.org

LONG WHARF THEATRE, New Haven, CT, www.longwharf.org

LOOKINGGLASS THEATRE COMPANY, Chicago, IL, www.lookingglasstheatre.org

LORD LEEBRICK THEATRE COMPANY, Eugene, OR, www.lordleebrick.com

LOST NATION THEATER, Montpelier, VT, www.lostnationtheater.org

THE LYRIC STAGE COMPANY OF BOSTON, Boston, MA, www.lyricstage.com

MABOU MINES, New York, NY, www.maboumines.org

MAD RIVER THEATER WORKS, West Liberty, OH, www.madrivertheater.org

MADISON REPERTORY THEATRE, Madison, WI, www.madisonrep.org

MAGIC THEATRE, San Francisco, CA, www.magictheatre.org

MAIN STREET THEATER, Houston, TX, www.mainstreettheater.com

MANHATTAN ENSEMBLE THEATER, New York, NY, www.met.com

MANHATTAN THEATRE CLUB, New York, NY, www.manhattantheatreclub.com

MARIN SHAKESPEARE COMPANY, San Rafael, CA, www.marinshakespeare.org

MARIN THEATRE COMPANY, Mill Valley, CA, www.marintheatre.org

MARYLAND ENSEMBLE THEATRE, Frederick, MD, www.marylandensemble.org

MA-YI THEATER COMPANY, New York, NY, www.ma-yitheatre.org

MCCARTER THEATRE CENTER, Princeton, NJ, www.mccarter.org

MEADOW BROOK THEATRE, Rochester, MI, www.mbtheatre.com

MELTING POT THEATRE COMPANY, New York, NY, www.meltingpottheatre.com

MERRIMACK REPERTORY THEATRE, Lowell, MA, www.merrimackrep.org

MERRY-GO-ROUND PLAYHOUSE, INC., Auburn, NY, www.merry-go-round.com

METRO THEATER COMPANY, St. Louis, MO, www.metrotheatercompany.org

MILWAUKEE CHAMBER THEATRE, Milwaukee, WI, www.chamber-theatre.com

MILWAUKEE REPERTORY THEATER, Milwaukee, WI, www.milwaukeerep.com

MILWAUKEE SHAKESPEARE, Milwaukee, WI, www.milwaukeeshakespeare.com

MINT THEATER COMPANY, New York, NY, www.minttheater.org

MIRACLE THEATRE GROUP, Portland, OR, www.milagro.org

MIRROR REPERTORY COMPANY, New York, NY, www.mirrorrepertoryco.com

MIXED BLOOD THEATRE COMPANY, Minneapolis, MN, www.mixedblood.com

MONTANA REPERTORY THEATRE, Missoula, MT, www.montanarep.org

MONTGOMERY THEATER, Souderton, PA, www.montgomerytheater.org

MOVING ARTS, Los Angeles, CA, www.movingarts.org

MU PERFORMING ARTS, Minneapolis, MN, www.muperformingarts.org

MUM PUPPETTHEATRE, Philadelphia, PA, www.mumpuppet.org

NATIVE VOICES AT THE AUTRY, Los Angeles, CA, www.autrynationalcenter.org

NAUTILUS MUSIC-THEATER, St. Paul, MN, www2.bitstream.net/~iras/nautilus.htm

NEBRASKA REPERTORY THEATRE, Lincoln, NE, www.unl.edu/rep

NEVADA SHAKESPEARE COMPANY, Reno, NV, www.nevada-shakespeare.org

THE NEW AMERICAN SHAKESPEARE TAVERN, Atlanta, GA,
www.shakespearetavern.com

NEW AMERICAN THEATER, Rockford, IL, www.newamericantheater.org

THE NEW CONSERVATORY THEATRE CENTER, San Francisco, CA,
www.nctcsf.org

NEW DRAMATISTS, INC., New York, NY, www.newdramatists.org

NEW FEDERAL THEATRE, INC., New York, NY, www.newfederaltheatre.org

NEW GEORGES, New York, NY, www.newgeorges.org

NEW GROUND THEATRE, Davenport, IA, www.newgroundtheatre.org

THE NEW HARMONY THEATRE, Evansville, IN, www.newharmonytheatre.com

NEW JERSEY REPERTORY COMPANY, Long Branch, NJ, www.njrep.org

NEW PARADISE LABORATORIES, Philadelphia, PA,
www.newparadiselaboratories.org

NEW PROFESSIONAL THEATRE, New York, NY, www.newprofessionaltheatre.org

NEW REPERTORY THEATRE, Watertown, MA, www.newrep.org

NEW STAGE THEATRE, Jackson, MS, www.newstagetheatre.com

NEW THEATRE, INC., Coral Gables, FL, www.new-theatre.org

NEW WORLD THEATER, Amherst, MA, www.newworldtheater.org

NEW YORK STATE THEATRE INSTITUTE (NYSTI), Troy, NY, www.nysti.org

NEW YORK THEATRE WORKSHOP, New York, NY, www.nytw.org

NEXT ACT THEATRE, Milwaukee, WI, www.nextact.org

NEXT THEATRE COMPANY, Evanston, IL, www.nexttheatre.org

NORTH CAROLINA STAGE COMPANY, Asheville, NC, www.ncstage.org

NORTH COAST REPERTORY THEATRE, Solana Beach, CA,
www.northcoastrep.org

NORTH SHORE MUSIC THEATRE, Beverly, MA, www.nsmt.org

NORTH STAR THEATRE, Mandeville, LA, www.northstartheatre.com

NORTHERN STAGE, White River Junction, VT, www.northernstage.org

NORTHLIGHT THEATRE, Skokie, IL, www.northlight.org

NORTHWEST CHILDREN'S THEATER AND SCHOOL, Portland, OR,
www.nwcts.org

ODYSSEY THEATRE ENSEMBLE, Los Angeles, CA, www.odysseytheatre.com

THE OLD GLOBE, San Diego, CA, www.theoldglobe.org

OLNEY THEATRE CENTER FOR THE ARTS, Olney, MD, www.olneytheatre.org

OMAHA THEATER COMPANY FOR YOUNG PEOPLE, Omaha, NE, www.otcyp.org

ONTOLOGICAL-HYSTERIC THEATER, New York, NY, www.ontological.com

THE OPEN EYE THEATER, Margaretville, NY, www.theopeneye.org

OPEN STAGE OF HARRISBURG, Harrisburg, PA, www.openstagehbg.com

OPENSTAGE THEATRE & COMPANY, Fort Collins, CO,
www.openstagetheatre.org

OREGON CHILDREN'S THEATRE, Portland, OR, www.octc.org

OREGON SHAKESPEARE FESTIVAL, Ashland, OR, www.osfashland.org

ORLANDO-UCF SHAKESPEARE FESTIVAL, Orlando, FL, www.shakespearefest.org

OUT OF HAND THEATER, Atlanta, GA, www.outofhandtheater.com

PALM BEACH DRAMAWORKS, West Palm Beach, FL,
www.palmbeachdramaworks.org

PAN ASIAN REPERTORY THEATRE, New York, NY, www.panasianrep.org

PANGEA WORLD THEATER, Minneapolis, MN, www.pangeaworldtheater.org

PAPER MILL PLAYHOUSE, Millburn, NJ, www.papermill.org

PASADENA PLAYHOUSE, Pasadena, CA, www.pasadenaplayhouse.org

PASSAGE THEATRE COMPANY, Trenton, NJ, www.passagetheatre.org

PCPA THEATERFEST, Santa Maria, CA, www.pcpa.org

PEGASUS PLAYERS THEATRE, Chicago, IL, www.pegasusplayers.org

PENINSULA PLAYERS THEATRE, Fish Creek, WI, www.peninsulaplayers.com

THE PENNSYLVANIA SHAKESPEARE FESTIVAL, Center Valley, PA,
www.pashakespeare.org

PENOBSCOT THEATRE, Bangor, ME, www.penobscottheatre.org

PENUMBRA THEATRE COMPANY, St. Paul, MN, www.penumbratheatre.org

PEOPLE'S LIGHT & THEATRE COMPANY, Malvern, PA, www.peopleslight.org

PERFORMANCE NETWORK, Ann Arbor, MI, www.performancenetwork.org

PERISHABLE THEATRE, Providence, RI, www.perishable.org

PERSEVERANCE THEATRE, Douglas, AK, www.perseverancetheatre.org

PETERBOROUGH PLAYERS, Peterborough, NH, www.peterboroughplayers.org

PHILADELPHIA SHAKESPEARE FESTIVAL, Philadelphia, PA,
www.phillyshakespeare.org

PHILADELPHIA THEATRE COMPANY, Philadelphia, PA, www.phillytheatreco.com

PHOENIX THEATRE, Phoenix, AZ, www.phxtheatre.org

PHOENIX THEATRE, Indianapolis, IN, www.phoenixtheatre.org

PICK UP PERFORMANCE COMPANY, New York, NY, www.pickupperformance.org

PIG IRON THEATRE COMPANY, Philadelphia, PA, www.pigiron.org

PILLSBURY HOUSE THEATRE, Minneapolis, MN, www.pillsburyhousetheatre.org

PING CHONG & COMPANY, New York, NY, www.pingchong.org

PIONEER THEATRE COMPANY, Salt Lake City, UT, www.pioneertheatre.org

PITTSBURGH IRISH & CLASSICAL THEATRE (PICT), Pittsburgh, PA,
www.picttheatre.org

PITTSBURGH PUBLIC THEATER, Pittsburgh, PA, www.ppt.org

PIVEN THEATRE WORKSHOP, Evanston, IL, www.piventheatre.org

PLAYGROUND, San Francisco, CA, www.playground-sf.org

PLAYHOUSE ON THE SQUARE, Memphis, TN, www.playhouseonthesquare.org

PLAYHOUSE WEST, Walnut Creek, CA, www.playhousewest.org

PLAYMAKERS REPERTORY COMPANY, Chapel Hill, NC, www.playmakersrep.org

THE PLAYWRIGHTS' CENTER, Minneapolis, MN, www.pwcenter.org

PLAYWRIGHTS HORIZONS, New York, NY, www.playwrightshorizons.org

PLAYWRIGHTS THEATRE OF NEW JERSEY, Madison, NJ, www.ptnj.org

PLOWSHARES THEATRE COMPANY, Detroit, MI, www.plowshares.org

PORTLAND CENTER STAGE, Portland, OR, www.pcs.org

PORTLAND STAGE COMPANY, Portland, ME, www.portlandstage.com

PREGONES THEATER, Bronx, NY, www.pregones.org

PRIMARY STAGES, New York, NY, www.primarystages.com

PRINCE MUSIC THEATER, Philadelphia, PA, www.princemusictheater.org

PROARTS COLLECTIVE OF AUSTIN, Austin, TX, www.proarts.info

PROFILE THEATRE PROJECT, Portland, OR, www.profiletheatre.org

THE PUBLIC THEATER, New York, NY, www.publictheater.org

THE PUBLIC THEATRE, Auburn, ME, www.thepublictheatre.org

PUSHPUSH THEATER, Decatur, GA, www.pushpushtheater.com

RED BARN THEATRE, Key West, FL, www.redbarntheatre.com

REDMOON THEATER, Chicago, IL, www.redmoon.org

RENAISSANCE THEATERWORKS, Milwaukee, WI, www.r-t-w.com

THE REPERTORY THEATRE OF ST. LOUIS, St. Louis, MO, www.repstl.org

RIVER STAGE, Sacramento, CA, www.riverstage.org

RIVERLIGHT AND COMPANY, Battle Creek, MI, www.willard.lib.mi.us/npa/rlight/index.html

RIVERSIDE THEATRE, Iowa City, IA, www.riversidetheatre.org

ROADSIDE THEATER, Norton, VA, www.roadside.org

ROUND HOUSE THEATRE, Bethesda, MD, www.roundhousetheatre.org

ROUNDABOUT THEATRE COMPANY, New York, NY, www.roundabouttheatre.org

ROXY REGIONAL THEATRE, Clarksville, TN, www.roxyregionaltheatre.org

RUDE MECHANICALS (A K A RUDE MECHS), Austin, TX, www.rudemechs.com

SAINT MICHAEL'S PLAYHOUSE, Colchester, VT, www.saintmichaelsplayhouse.com

THE SALT LAKE ACTING COMPANY, Salt Lake City, UT, www.saltlakeactingcompany.org

SALVAGE VANGUARD THEATER, Austin, TX, www.salvagevanguard.org

SAN DIEGO REPERTORY THEATRE, San Diego, CA, www.sandiegorep.com

SAN JOSE REPERTORY THEATRE, San Jose, CA, www.sjrep.com

SEATTLE CHILDREN'S THEATRE, Seattle, WA, www.sct.org

SEATTLE PUBLIC THEATER AT THE HISTORIC BATHHOUSE, Seattle, WA, www.seattlepublictheater.org

SEATTLE REPERTORY THEATRE, Seattle, WA, www.seattlerep.org

SEATTLE SHAKESPEARE COMPANY, Seattle, WA, www.seattleshakespeare.org

SECOND STAGE THEATRE, New York, NY, www.secondstagetheatre.com

SHAKESPEARE & COMPANY, Lenox, MA, www.shakespeare.org

THE SHAKESPEARE FESTIVAL AT TULANE, New Orleans, LA,
www.neworleansshakespeare.com

SHAKESPEARE SANTA CRUZ, Santa Cruz, CA, www.shakespearesantacruz.org

SHAKESPEARE THEATRE COMPANY, Washington, DC,
www.shakespearetheatre.org

THE SHAKESPEARE THEATRE OF NEW JERSEY, Madison, NJ,
www.shakespearenj.org

SHATTERED GLOBE THEATRE, Chicago, IL, www.shatteredglobe.org

SHOTGUN PLAYERS, Berkeley, CA, www.shotgunplayers.org

SIERRA REPERTORY THEATRE, Sonora, CA, www.sierrarep.org

SIGNATURE THEATRE, Arlington, VA, www.signature-theatre.org

SIGNATURE THEATRE COMPANY, New York, NY, www.signaturetheatre.org

SITI COMPANY, New York, NY, www.siti.org

SOCIETY HILL PLAYHOUSE, Philadelphia, PA, www.societyhillplayhouse.com

SOLANO COLLEGE THEATRE, Fairfield, CA, www.solano.edu

SOUTH COAST REPERTORY, Costa Mesa, CA, www.scr.org

SOUTHERN REP, New Orleans, LA, www.southernrep.com

SOUTHWEST SHAKESPEARE COMPANY, Mesa, AZ, www.swshakespeare.org

SPEAKEASY STAGE COMPANY, Boston, MA, www.speakeasystage.com

ST. LOUIS BLACK REPERTORY COMPANY, St. Louis, MO, www.stlouisblackrep.org

STAGE ONE: THE LOUISVILLE CHILDREN'S THEATRE, INC., Louisville, KY,
www.stageone.org

STAGES REPERTORY THEATRE, Houston, TX, www.stagestheatre.com

STAGES THEATRE CENTER, Los Angeles, CA, www.stagestheatrecenter.com

STAGES THEATRE COMPANY, Hopkins, MN, www.stagestheatre.org

STAGEWORKS/HUDSON, Hudson, NY, www.stageworkshudson.org

STARK RAVING THEATRE, Portland, OR, www.starkravingtheatre.org

STATE THEATER COMPANY, Austin, TX, www.austintheatre.org

STEPPENWOLF THEATRE COMPANY, Chicago, IL, www.steppenwolf.org

STUDIO ARENA THEATRE, Buffalo, NY, www.studioarena.org

THE STUDIO THEATRE, Washington, DC, www.studiotheatre.org

THE SUGAN THEATRE COMPANY, Cambridge, MA, www.sugan.org

SUNDANCE INSTITUTE THEATRE, Beverly Hills, CA, www.sundance.org

SWINE PALACE PRODUCTIONS, Baton Rouge, LA, www.swinepalace.org

SYNCHRONICITY PERFORMANCE GROUP, Atlanta, GA,
www.synchrotheatre.com

SYRACUSE STAGE, Syracuse, NY, www.syracusestage.org

TADA!, New York, NY, www.tadatheater.com

TALKING BAND, New York, NY, www.talkingband.org

TAPROOT THEATRE COMPANY, Seattle, WA, www.taproottheatre.org

TARGET MARGIN THEATER, Brooklyn, NY, www.targetmargin.org

TEATRO DEL PUEBLO, St. Paul, MN, www.teatrodelpueblo.org

TEATRO VISION, San Jose, CA, www.teatrovision.org

TEATRO VISTA, Chicago, IL, www.teatrovista.org

TEN THOUSAND THINGS THEATER COMPANY, Minneapolis, MN,
    www.tenthousandthings.org

TENNESSEE REPERTORY THEATRE, Nashville, TN, www.tennesseerep.org

THALIA SPANISH THEATRE, Long Island City, NY, www.thaliatheatre.org

THEATER ALLIANCE, Washington, DC, www.theateralliance.com

THE THEATER AT MONMOUTH, Monmouth, ME, www.theateratmonmouth.org

THEATER BY THE BLIND, New York, NY, www.tbtb.org

THEATER FOR THE NEW CITY, New York, NY, www.theaterforthenewcity.net

THEATER GROTTESCO, Sante Fe, NM, www.theatergrottesco.org

THEATER J, Washington, DC, www.theaterj.org

THEATER OF THE FIRST AMENDMENT, Fairfax, VA, www.gmu.edu/cfa/tfa

THEATER PREVIEWS AT DUKE, Durham, NC, www.duke.edu/web/drama

THEATRE ASPEN, Aspen, CO, www.theatreaspen.org

THEATRE DE LA JEUNE LUNE, Minneapolis, MN, www.jeunelune.org

THEATRE FOR A NEW AUDIENCE, New York, NY, www.TFANA.org

THEATRE PROJECT, Baltimore, MD, www.theatreproject.org

THEATRE WEST, Los Angeles, CA, www.theatrewest.org

THEATREWORKS, Palo Alto, CA, www.theatreworks.org

THEATRICAL OUTFIT, Atlanta, GA, www.theatricaloutfit.org

TOUCHSTONE THEATRE, Bethlehem, PA, www.touchstone.org

TRAVELING JEWISH THEATRE, San Francisco, CA, www.atjt.com

TRIAD STAGE, Greensboro, NC, www.triadstage.org

TRICKLOCK COMPANY, Albuquerque, NM, www.tricklock.com

TRINITY REPERTORY COMPANY, Providence, RI, www.trinityrep.com

TRUE COLORS THEATRE COMPANY, Atlanta, GA,
    www.truecolorstheatrecompany.com

TRUSTUS, Columbia, SC, www.trustus.org

TWO RIVER THEATER CO., Red Bank, NJ, www.trtc.org

UNDERMAIN THEATRE, Dallas, TX, www.undermain.com

UNICORN THEATRE, Kansas City, MO, www.unicorntheatre.org

URBAN STAGES, New York, NY, www.urbanstages.org

UTAH SHAKESPEAREAN FESTIVAL, Cedar City, UT, www.bard.org

VALLEY YOUTH THEATRE, Phoenix, AZ, www.vyt.com

VERMONT STAGE COMPANY, Burlington, VT, www.vtstage.org

VICTORY GARDENS THEATER, Chicago, IL, www.VictoryGardens.org

THE VINEYARD PLAYHOUSE, Vineyard Haven, MA, www.vineyardplayhouse.org

THE VINEYARD THEATRE, New York, NY, www.vineyardtheatre.org

VIRGINIA STAGE COMPANY, Norfolk, VA, www.vastage.com

VITAL THEATRE COMPANY, INC., New York, NY, www.vitaltheatre.org

VOICES OF THE SOUTH, Memphis, TN, www.voicesofthesouth.org

WALDEN THEATRE, Louisville, KY, www.waldentheatre.org

THE WAREHOUSE THEATRE, Greenville, SC, www.warehousetheatre.com

WATERTOWER THEATRE, Addison, TX, www.watertowertheatre.org

WELLFLEET HARBOR ACTORS THEATER, INC., Wellfleet, MA, www.what.org

WEST COAST ENSEMBLE, Los Angeles, CA, www.wcensemble.org

THE WESTERN STAGE, Salinas, CA, www.westernstage.org

WESTON PLAYHOUSE THEATRE COMPANY, Weston, VT,
    www.westonplayhouse.org

WESTPORT COUNTRY PLAYHOUSE, Westport, CT, www.westportplayhouse.org

WHEELOCK FAMILY THEATRE, Boston, MA, www.wheelock.edu/wft

WILLIAM INGE CENTER FOR THE ARTS, Independence, KS, www.ingecenter.org

WILLIAMSTOWN THEATRE FESTIVAL, Williamstown, MA, www.wtfestival.org

THE WILMA THEATER, Philadelphia, PA, www.wilmatheater.org

WING-IT PRODUCTIONS, Seattle, WA, www.wingitproductions.org

WOMEN'S PROJECT & PRODUCTIONS, New York, NY, www.womensproject.org

WOOLLY MAMMOTH THEATRE COMPANY, Washington, DC,
    www.woollymammoth.net

THE WOOSTER GROUP, New York, NY, www.thewoostergroup.org

WORKING CLASSROOM, Albuquerque, NM, www.workingclassroom.org

THE WORKING THEATER, New York, NY, www.theworkingtheater.org

WRITERS' THEATRE, Glencoe, IL, www.writerstheatre.org

YALE REPERTORY THEATRE, New Haven, CT, www.yalerep.org

YOUNG PLAYWRIGHTS' THEATER, Washington, DC,
    www.youngplaywrightstheater.org

YOUTH ENSEMBLE OF ATLANTA, Atlanta, GA, www.fhyea.org

ZACHARY SCOTT THEATRE CENTER, Austin, TX, www.zachscott.com

THE Z SPACE STUDIO, San Francisco, CA, www.zspace.org

250+ SHAKESPEARE FESTIVALS

Will Power Rules as Shakespeare Thrives in America's Theaters

The bookstores are brimming with new editions. Video rental firms have dozens of copies of each title. Copycat directors and producers are turning the originals into cute romantic comedies filled with teenage angst. Attendance is up. People are traveling hundreds, even thousands of miles to see the latest, greatest production. John Grisham's latest epic? Neil Simon's newest play? Nope—the Bard is back!

Who would believe that as the 21st century began, John Updike's latest novel would feature *Hamlet*'s Gertrude and Claudius, and *Titus Andronicus* would be on the must-see new-movie list? Did *Shakespeare in Love* really win seven Academy Awards in 1999 and gross $100 million in North America or are pop culture fanatics simply caught up in the same dream that captured Michelle Pfeiffer and Calista Flockhart in *A Midsummer Night's Dream*?

Big Bucks for the Bard?

Even the world's Shakespeare Festival leaders are scratching their heads and chuckling over the resurgence of all things linked to the great William. So far in the 21st-century, England's Sir Peter Hall moved to America to join the boom in all Bard-related business, the Royal Shakespeare Company farmed out Shakespeare to the hinterlands of Great Britain, and the Stratford Festival of Canada sold over 600,000 tickets in one year with an estimated economic impact of over $170 million.

In a world where audiences for serious plays and nonmusical work are often waning, tickets to Shakespeare plays are hot, hot, hot. There are over

250 Shakespeare companies in North America, and over 150 international Shakespeare festivals and companies around the world, including companies in Japan, Spain, South Africa, New Zealand, China, France, and Germany.

Over a million people braved America's great outdoors for Shakespeare's sake at the beginning of the 21st century, while millions of others attended Shakespeare productions in indoor theaters throughout the world. England's Royal Shakespeare Company typically hosts over 1 million patrons and the Oregon Shakespeare Festival welcomed nearly 400,000 audience members in a recent season. Add 600,000 attending the Stratford Festival of Canada and that's 2 million tickets to three theaters alone!

Shakespeare up the Creek?

Certainly, producers have almost always enjoyed producing Shakespeare. Aside from the diversity of comedies, romances, histories, and tragedies, there's a great bonus to budgeting Shakespeare: no royalties. There is also good news for actors, directors, stage managers, and production personnel: you don't have to travel to Stratford-Upon-Avon or even Stratford, Canada, to belly up to the Bard! The United States leads the way in Shakespeare productions. It might be Shakespeare Up the Creek, Shakespeare-on-the-Rocks, Shakespeare Under the Stars, or Shakespeare by the Book (all in Texas), Shakespeare at the Ruins (in Barboursville, Virginia), The Shakespeare Free-For-All (in Washington, D.C.), or the Fairbanks Shakespeare Theater (in chilly Alaska), but the Bard is alive and well in the United States.

Without question, Shakespeare is the most-produced playwright in world theater. Fortunately, given the large size of his casts, the Shakespeare phenomenon translates into myriad annual opportunities for artists, craftspersons, and producers.

The Shakespeare Theatre Association of America (STAA) provides direct links to many of the major festivals. Four other related Web sites offer insights into Shakespeare Festival work and career opportunities. One Web site (http://ise.uvic.ca), hosted by Internet Shakespeare Editions (ISE) and the Shakespeare in American Communities program (www.shakespeareinamericancommunities.org), is sponsored by the National Endowment for the Arts (NEA). The 250+ Shakespeare festivals promised in the chapter title may be accessed through the Curtain Rising Web site (www.curtainrising.com) and the Institute of Outdoor Drama Web site (www.unc.edu/depts/outdoor/).

Shakespeare Theatre Association of America (STAA)

WEB SITE: www.staaonline.org

The Shakespeare Theatre Association of America was established to provide a forum for artistic and managerial leadership of theaters whose central activity is the production of Shakespeare's plays; to discuss issues and share methods of work, resources, and information; and to act as an advocate for Shakespearean productions and training in North America. Membership is open to any producing theater organization worldwide that is primarily involved with the production of Shakespeare's plays. Limited associate membership is also possible. STAA membership now includes approximately 75 theaters, representing diverse types (indoor, outdoor, year-round, seasonal, university-affiliated, free) with wide-ranging budgets ($25,000 to $27,250,000), and Equity as well as non-Equity companies.

HISTORY

The Shakespeare Theatre Association of America was founded in 1991 by Sidney L. Berger, producing director of the Houston Shakespeare Festival, and Douglas N. Cook, longtime producing artistic director of the Utah Shakespearean Festival. The first meeting was held on January 12, 1991, in the Library Board Room of the Folger Library in Washington, D.C. Over the years, STAA has met at the Royal Shakespeare Company in Stratford, England; Shakespeare's Globe in London; the Stratford Festival of Canada; and at festivals large and small throughout the United States. The STAA *quarto* is published twice a year and details plans, productions, statistics, and strategies related to Shakespeare in production. STAA also holds an annual conference hosted by a member theater and creates an online directory for access to member theaters.

The STAA Web site offers lists of officers, an institutional history, an updated directory, links to member theaters, and recent copies of *quarto*. The STAA secretary handles membership information. Check out the Web site at www.staaonline.org for ongoing information and direct links to many of America's producing festivals. *Quarto* is edited by Jim Volz. Editorial information or *quarto* questions may be sent to jvolz@fullerton.edu. Information about the association is available from STAA co-founder Sidney Berger at sberger@uh.edu.

A Few High-Profile Companies

While the diversity of Shakespeare production in America is vast, here is a sampling of some high-profile whose work focuses on the Bard:

STRATFORD FESTIVAL OF CANADA

P.O. Box 520, Stratford, Ontario, Canada N5A 4M9

ADMINISTRATION: (519) 271-4040; BOX OFFICE: (800) 567-1600; FAX: (519) 271-1126
WEB SITE: www.stratfordfestival.ca

With more than $35 million budgeted for production and salaries for actors, musicians, artisans, and craftspeople, the Stratford Festival of Canada employs over 830 people who generally work on 14 productions and more than 600 performances annually. Over 60,000 students from Canada and the United States attend student performances and related enrichment programs each year. Stratford's mission is "to produce the best works of theater in the classical and contemporary repertoire, with special emphasis on the works of William Shakespeare, to the highest standards possible." According to the casting office of the Festival, actor résumés are collected in July and August—check the Web site for details on casting and other positions. To submit a résumé, e-mail: resumes@stratfordfestival.ca

Starting with two Shakespeare productions in a tent in 1953, the festival prospered in the early years thanks to the founding vision of Sir Tyrone Guthrie and Tom Patterson. "I hope that the great and timeless stories we have to tell will astonish, awe, and delight you," says longtime artistic director Richard Monette, who has led the company with power, perseverance, and a quiet panache since 1994.

OREGON SHAKESPEARE FESTIVAL

15 South Pioneer Street, Ashland, OR 97520

ADMINISTRATION: (541) 482-2111; BOX OFFICE: (541) 482-4331; FAX: (541) 482-0446
E-MAIL: administration@osfashland.org
WEB SITE: www.osfashland.org

The Tony Award-winning Oregon Shakespeare Festival (OSF) is the USA's largest non-profit theater, with a full-time company of 325 employees and a part-time company of 125. OSF produces 11 plays in three theaters for over 360,000 people, with a budget exceeding $21 million. Artistic director Libby Appel and the Oregon Shakespeare Festival staff are looking for company members and actors willing to make a commitment to a classical repertory theater and longer-than-usual contracts for regional theater. Auditions are usually held in the Festival's home of Ashland, Oregon, as well as in Los Angeles and New York. Check the Web site for audition and casting information. Bill Rauch, a 20-year veteran of the Cornerstone Theater Company, will replace Ms. Appel when she retires at the end of the 2007 season.

"We celebrate our uniqueness as America's largest rotating repertory theater," explains the ever-daring, always charming Appel. "Our outstanding company of theater artists makes possible ambitious productions of works whose courage and daring boldly carry us into the twenty-first century." A recent season included Robert Schenkkan's new play *Arturo and Catherine*, Octavio Solis's *Gibraltar*, *Ma Rainey's Black Bottom*, *Richard III*, *The Philanderer*, *Twelfth Night*, *Love's Labor's Lost*, and several other plays.

According to David Dreyfoos, associate producer at OSF, actors should have "extensive Shakespeare experience and must submit a photograph and a résumé" for consideration. OSF operates under a modified LORT B+ contract and hires approximately 52 Equity actors and 20 non-Equity actors annually. A special audition hotline is available at (520) 482-2111, ext. 366.

The Oregon Shakespeare Festival's mission speaks to the creation of "fresh and bold interpretations of classic and contemporary plays in repertory, shaped by the diversity of our American culture, using Shakespeare as our standard and inspiration." Founded in 1935 by Angus L. Bowmer, OSF is among the oldest professional regional theater companies in America. New Zealander Paul Nicholson is the OSF executive director and one of the United States' savviest administrators.

THE PUBLIC THEATRE/NEW YORK SHAKESPEARE FESTIVAL

425 Lafayette Street, New York, NY 10003

ADMINISTRATION: (212) 539-8500; BOX OFFICE (TELE-CHARGE): (212) 239-6200;

FAX: (212) 784-3856

WEB SITE: www.publictheater.org

New York Shakespeare Festival productions have captured the imaginations of audiences worldwide. Joseph Papp founded The Public Theatre/NYSF in 1954 and the NYSF held its first free production of Shakespeare at the Emmanuel Presbyterian Church on East 6th Street. Three years later, Papp staged his first Shakespeare in Central Park. The Delacorte Theater was completed in 1962. Of course, the rest is history. Upon Papp's death, JoAnne Akalitis, his hand-picked successor, became artistic director for 20 months. George C. Wolfe took over in 1993; Oskar Eustis was appointed in 2005.

Now, the Public stages two classics as part of Shakespeare in the Park at the Delacorte every summer free of charge and 80,000 to 100,000 patrons flock to the productions. The Shakespeare Lab is a nine-week summer program providing intensive classical training to young and culturally diverse actors, and the company continues Joseph Papp's emphasis on innovative stagings of classic drama and the development of new American plays and musicals. Over the years, the Public's productions have won 30 Tony Awards, 111 Obie Awards, and 3 Pulitzer Prizes.

Auditions for the NYSF are held on a show-by-show basis. Equity principal auditions are held with other Off-Broadway theaters annually and the NYSF casting office keeps headshots and résumés on file for ongoing consideration. The company operates under a LORT B contract. Check the Web site for current casting director, audition, and job employment information. Internships are available in various areas, including Joe's Pub cabaret.

THE SHAKESPEARE THEATRE

450 7th Street NW, Washington, DC 20004-2207

ADMINISTRATIVE OFFICE: 516 8th Street SE, Washington, DC 20003-2834

ADMINISTRATION: (202) 547-3230; BOX OFFICE: (202) 547-1122 or
     Toll Free (877) 487-8849); FAX: (202) 547-0226

E-MAIL: info@shakespearedc.org

WEB SITE: www.shakespearetheatre.org

In this Washington, D.C. company's own words, "The mission of The Shakespeare Theatre is to become the nation's leading force in producing and preserving the highest quality of classic theater. The Theatre endeavors to strengthen the tradition of classic theater in America through productions that reflect its current world." Artistic director Michael Kahn leads the way as TST presents five plays by Shakespeare and other classical playwrights in its 451-seat theater.

Kahn was named artistic director in 1986 and has consistently thrust the theater into the national spotlight with exceptional casting, unique interpretations of the classics, and crowd-pleasing performances. His vision for the theater is that it would "be not simply a home for the classics, an environment where museum pieces were produced, but a company that presented a challenging classical repertory in a way that illuminated issues and themes relevant to contemporary life." In the summer of 1991, he reintroduced the tradition of free outdoor Shakespeare to Washington with *The Merry Wives of Windsor* starring Paul Winfield. What has come to be known as "The Shakespeare Theatre Free-For-All" ran for three weeks and played to more than 30,000 patrons.

TST maintains a small resident acting company and casts other roles (both Equity and non-Equity) on an ongoing basis throughout the year. Check the Web site for audition sites and casting agent information. Internships in many areas are also available.

ALABAMA SHAKESPEARE FESTIVAL

One Festival Drive, Montgomery, AL 36117
ADMINISTRATION: (334) 271-5300; BOX OFFICE: (334) 271-5353 or
    Toll Free: (800) 841-4273; FAX: (334) 271-5348
E-MAIL: asfmail@asf.net
WEB SITE: www.asf.net

Located in the heart of Dixie, the Alabama Shakespeare Festival is the sixth-largest Shakespeare festival in the world and attracts more than 300,000 annual visitors. ASF typically produces 14 plays year-round in the 750-seat Festival Stage and the 225-seat Octagon. The ASF contracts around 57 Equity actors and 16 non-Equity actors for the repertory season based in Montgomery, the state capital. Administrative and production positions also open on a regular basis. Artistic director Geoffrey Sherman joined the company in 2005.

The Southern Writers' Project festival of new plays was founded by former artistic director Kent Thompson in 1991 as an exploration of the South's rich cultural heritage. It is dedicated to creating a theatrical voice for Southern writers and topics. In cooperation with the University of Alabama, ASF is also home to Master of Fine Arts programs in acting, arts administration/theater management, stage management, and scenic and costume design. Martin L. Platt founded ASF in 1972. Check the Web site's Career Opportunities area for job opportunities, casting plans, MFA program information, and internship openings.

CHICAGO SHAKESPEARE THEATER

800 East Grand Avenue, Chicago, IL 60611
ADMINISTRATION: (312) 595-5656; BOX OFFICE: (312) 595-5600;
    AUDITION HOTLINE: (312) 595-5693; FAX: (312) 595-5607
Web site: www.chicagoshakes.com

The fastest growing "newborn" on the Bard-block is the Chicago Shakespeare Theater on Navy Pier. The gorgeous seven-story theater complex features a 500-seat courtyard-style theater and thrilling views of Chicago's sparkling skyline. It is dazzling critics and attracting visitors from all over the world. "There is no better view of Chicago than standing on Navy Pier. And there is no better view into the heart of mankind than through the eyes of William Shakespeare," proclaims the sassy and jubilant founder and artistic director, Barbara Gaines. A 200-seat flexible black box theater also helps with CST's mission: to bring innovative and high-quality theater to a broad and diverse audience. In this new location, CST's annual budget has grown from $2.9 million in 1999 to over $12 million and the subscription base has increased to more than 22,000 patrons.

The company, originally founded in 1986 as Shakespeare Repertory, first performed on the outdoor terrace of the Red Lion Pub in Lincoln Park and prospered during 12 seasons at the Ruth Page Theatre in Chicago. According to executive director Criss Henderson, the company now employs 200 artists and operates under a Chicago Area Theatre contract. Check the Web site for information on casting and career opportunities.

UTAH SHAKESPEAREAN FESTIVAL

351 W. Center Street, Cedar City, UT 84720

ADMINISTRATION: (435) 586-7884; BOX OFFICE: 800-PLAYTIX

E-MAIL: usfinfo@bard.org

WEB SITE: www.bard.org

The Regional Theatre Tony Award–winning Utah Shakespearean Festival, located in scenic southern Utah, hires over 250 actors, administrators, musicians, technicians, and educational tour positions for the summer and fall seasons, as well as technicians and managers for its touring production. Applications are accepted beginning October 1 for the following year. Seasonal hiring is completed by March of each year. For detailed information and application instructions for current positions, check out the company Web site.

Fred C. Adams founded the festival in 1961 and continues to serve as executive producer emeritus. "I believe in dreams, and in the need we all have to be children again," he says. Committed to entertaining, enriching, and educating audiences "through professional rotating repertory productions of Shakespeare and other master dramatists," the company is happily situated within a day's drive of seven national parks, in the tiny, Bard-booming town of Cedar City.

"We are seeking classically trained actors eager to work in a repertory environment in scenic southern Utah," explains Festival director R. Scott Phillips. A headshot and résumé are required for auditions, which are held in Los Angeles, San Francisco, New York, Chicago, and other spots around the nation.

The Festival's budget is over $5 million and nearly 150,000 audience members attend annually. Founder Adams notes, "We are looking forward to the future with nothing short of an adrenaline rush."

American Shakespeare Festivals: An Alphabetical Listing

A COMPANY OF FOOLS THEATRE, INC., Ottawa, ON, Canada, www.fools.ca

A NOISE WITHIN, Glendale, CA, www.anoisewithin.org

ABILENE SHAKESPEARE FESTIVAL, Abilene, TX,
www.acu.edu/academics/cas/theatre/asf.html

THE ACTING SHAKESPEARE COMPANY, New York, NY,
www.actingshakespeare.org

THE ACTORS SHAKESPEARE COMPANY, Hoboken, NJ,
www.ascnj.org/home.html

ACTORS' SHAKESPEARE PROJECT, Cambridge, MA,
www.actorsshakespeareproject.org

ACTORS' THEATRE COMPANY, Columbus, OH, www.theactorstheatre.org

AFRICAN-AMERICAN SHAKESPEARE COMPANY, San Francisco, CA,
www.african-americanshakes.org

ALABAMA SHAKESPEARE FESTIVAL, Montgomery, AL, www.asf.net

AMERICAN GLOBE THEATRE, LTD., New York, NY, www.americanglobe.org

AMERICAN PLAYERS THEATRE, Spring Green, WI, www.americanplayers.org

THE AMERICAN SHAKESPEARE PROJECT, Albuquerque, NM, www.amshakes.org

AMERICAN STAGE THEATRE COMPANY, St. Petersburg, FL,
www.americanstage.org

THE AQUILA THEATRE COMPANY, New York, NY, www.aquilatheatre.com

ARCADIA SHAKESPEARE FESTIVAL, Glenside, PA, www.arcadia.edu

ARIZONA CLASSICAL THEATRE, Prescott, AZ, www.azshakes.com

THE ATLANTA SHAKESPEARE COMPANY, Atlanta, GA,
www.shakespearetavern.com

AUSTIN SHAKESPEARE FESTIVAL, Austin, TX, www.austinshakespeare.org

BAJA SHAKESPEARE, Los Barriles, Mexico, c/o Marin Shakespeare Company,
www.marinshakespeare.org

BALTIMORE SHAKESPEARE FESTIVAL, Baltimore, MD,
www.baltimoreshakespeare.org

BAND OF BROTHERS SHAKESPEARE COMPANY, Johnstown, PA,
www.willshakespeare.org

BARD ON THE BEACH SHAKESPEARE FESTIVAL, Vancouver, BC, Canada,
www.bardonthebeach.com

BOSTON UNIVERSITY SHAKESPEARE SOCIETY, Boston, MA,
www.people.bu.edu/bard

THE BREVARD FRIENDS OF SHAKESPEARE, Melbourne, FL, www.henegar.org

BRIDGEPORT FREE SHAKESPEARE, Bridgeport, CT,
www.bridgeportfreeshakespeare.org

CALIFORNIA SHAKESPEARE FESTIVAL THEATER, Berkeley, CA,
www.calshakes.org

CAPE FEAR SHAKESPEARE, Wilmington, NC, PHONE: (910) 392-3335

CAPISTRANO SHAKESPEARE FESTIVAL, San Juan Capistrano, CA,
www.caminorealplayhouse.org

CARMEL SHAKESPEARE FESTIVAL, Carmel, CA, www.pacrep.org

CAROLINIAN SHAKESPEARE FESTIVAL, New Bern, NC, www.csfest.net

CENTRAL COAST SHAKESPEARE FESTIVAL, San Luis Obispo, CA,
www.ccshakes.org

CHESAPEAKE SHAKESPEARE COMPANY, Baltimore, MD,
www.chesapeakeshakespeare.com

CHICAGO SHAKESPEARE THEATER, Chicago, IL, www.chicagoshakes.com

CHICKSPEARE, Charlotte, NC, www.chickspeare.org

CINCINNATI SHAKESPEARE FESTIVAL, Cincinnati, OH, www.cincyshakes.com

CLEMSON SHAKESPEARE FESTIVAL, Clemson, SC,
www.virtual.clemson.edu/caah/shakespr

THE CLEVELAND SHAKESPEARE FESTIVAL, Cleveland, OH, www.cleveshakes.org

THE COLORADO SHAKESPEARE FESTIVAL, Boulder, CO,
www.coloradoshakes.org

COMMONWEALTH SHAKESPEARE COMPANY, Boston, MA,
www.freeshakespeare.org

CORONADO PLAYHOUSE, Coronado, CA, www.coronadoplayhouse.com

THE CROMULENT SHAKESPEARE COMPANY, Minneapolis, MN,
www.soulsofwit.com/cromulent

DELAWARE SHAKESPEARE FESTIVAL, Claymont, DE, www.delshakes.org

DOOR SHAKESPEARE, Baileys Harbor, WI, www.doorshakespeare.com

THE ELM SHAKESPEARE COMPANY, New Haven, CT, www.elmshakespeare.org

EXCELLENT MOTION SHAKESPEARE COMPANY, San Diego, CA,
www.excellentmotion.com

FAIRBANKS SHAKESPEARE THEATRE, Fairbanks, AK,
www.fairbanks-shakespeare.org

FESTIVAL THEATRE ENSEMBLE, Los Gatos, CA, www.festivaltheatreensemble.org

FIRST FOLIO SHAKESPEARE FESTIVAL, Clarendon Hills, IL, www.firstfolio.org

FLATWATER SHAKESPEARE COMPANY, Lincoln, NE,
www.flatwatershakespeare.org

FLORIDA SHAKESPEARE THEATRE, Coral Gables, FL, www.afn.org/~theatre

FOLGER THEATRE, Washington, DC, www.folger.edu

FOOL'S CATHEDRAL THEATRE COMPANY, Edmonds, WA,
www.drizzle.com/~fools

FREE WILL PLAYERS, Edmonton, AB, Canada, www.freewillplayers.ca/archives.html

GARDEN VARIETY SHAKESPEARE, Birmingham, AL, www.come.to/gvs

GEORGIA SHAKESPEARE, Atlanta, GA, www.gashakespeare.org

THE GLOBE OF THE GREAT SOUTHWEST, Odessa, TX, www.globesw.org

THE GLOBE PLAYHOUSE, West Hollywood, CA, PHONE: (323) 654-5623

GRAND MARAIS PLAYHOUSE, Grand Marais, MN,
   www.arrowheadcenterforthearts.org/playhouse

GRAND VALLEY SHAKESPEARE FESTIVAL, Allendale, MI, www.gvsu.edu/shakes

GREAT LAKES THEATER FESTIVAL, Cleveland, OH, www.greatlakestheater.org

GREAT RIVER SHAKESPEARE FESTIVAL, Winona, MN, www.grsf.org

GREENSTAGE: SEATTLE'S SHAKESPEARE IN THE PARK COMPANY, Seattle, WA,
   www.greenstage.org

HAMILTON URBAN THEATRE ASSOCIATION, Hamilton, ON, Canada,
   www.hwcn.org/link/huta/index.html

HAMPSHIRE SHAKESPEARE COMPANY, Amherst, MA,
   www.hampshireshakespeare.org

HAMPTON ROADS SHAKESPEARE FESTIVAL, Virginia Beach, VA,
   www.summershakes.com

HAMPTONS SHAKESPEARE FESTIVAL, Amagansett, NY,
   www.hamptons-shakespeare.org

HARRISBURG SHAKESPEARE FESTIVAL, Harrisburg, PA, www.gamutplays.org

HAWAII SHAKESPEARE FESTIVAL, Honolulu, HI, www.hawaiishakes.org

THE HEART OF AMERICA SHAKESPEARE FESTIVAL, Kansas City, MO,
   www.kcshakes.org

HOFSTRA SHAKESPEARE FESTIVAL, Hempstead, NY,
   www.hofstra.edu/ACADEMICS/HCLAS/dd/DD_SHAKESPEARE_06.CFM

THE HOLLYWOOD PLAYHOUSE, Hollywood, FL, www.hbtheatrefest.org

HOUSTON SHAKESPEARE FESTIVAL, Houston, TX,
   www.class.uh.edu/theatre/performances_houstonshakespearefestival.html

THE HUDSON SHAKESPEARE COMPANY, Weehawken, NJ,
   www.hudsonshakespeare.org

HUDSON VALLEY SHAKESPEARE FESTIVAL, Cold Spring, NY,
   www.hvshakespeare.org

THE IDAHO SHAKESPEARE FESTIVAL, Boise, ID, www.idahoshakespeare.org

ILLINOIS SHAKESPEARE FESTIVAL, Normal, IL, www.thefestival.org

INDEPENDENT SHAKESPEARE CO., Chatsworth, CA,
   www.independentshakespeare.com

INWOOD SHAKESPEARE FESTIVAL/MOOSE HALL THEATRE COMPANY,
   Bronx, NY, www.moosehallisf.org

THE ISLAND PLAYERS, Anna Maria, FL, www.home.earthlink.net/~islandplayers

JUDITH SHAKESPEARE COMPANY, New York, NY, www.judithshakespeare.org

KENTUCKY SHAKESPEARE FESTIVAL, Louisville, KY, www.kyshakes.org

KINGS COUNTY SHAKESPEARE COMPANY, Brooklyn, NY,
  www.kingscountyshakespeare.org

THE KINGSMEN SHAKESPEARE COMPANY, Thousand Oaks, CA,
  www.kingsmenshakespeare.org

LAKE TAHOE SHAKESPEARE FESTIVAL, Incline Village, NV,
  www.laketahoeshakespeare.com

THE LARK PLAY DEVELOPMENT CENTER, New York, NY, www.larktheatre.org

LEXINGTON SHAKESPEARE FESTIVAL, Lexington, KY,
  www.lexingtonshakespeare.org

THE LONG BEACH SHAKESPEARE COMPANY, Long Beach, CA,
  www.lbshakespeare.org

THE LOS ANGELES WOMEN'S SHAKESPEARE COMPANY, Santa Monica, CA,
  www.lawsc.net

MARIN SHAKESPEARE COMPANY, San Rafael, CA, www.marinshakespeare.org

MARYLAND SHAKESPEARE FESTIVAL, Frederick, MD, www.mdshakes.org

MERCED SHAKESPEAREFEST, Merced, CA, www.mercedshakespearefest.org

MICHIGAN SHAKESPEARE FESTIVAL, Jackson, MI, www.michshakefest.org

MILWAUKEE SHAKESPEARE, Milwaukee, WI, www.milwaukeeshakespeare.com

THE MIT SHAKESPEARE ENSEMBLE, Cambridge, MA, www.mit.edu/~ensemble

MIXED MAGIC THEATRE & CULTURAL EVENTS, Providence, RI,
  www.members.cox.net/mixedmagic

THE MONTANA SHAKESPEARE COMPANY, Helena, MT,
  www.montanashakespeare.org

MONTANA SHAKESPEARE IN THE PARKS, Bozeman, MT,
  www2.montana.edu/shakespeare

THE MONTFORD PARK PLAYERS, Asheville, NC, www.montfordparkplayers.org

MURPHYS CREEK THEATRE, Murphys, CA, www.murphyscreektheatre.org

MURRAY SHAKESPEARE FESTIVAL, Murray, KY,
  www.murraystate.edu/chfa/english/shakespeare.htm

NAPA VALLEY SHAKESPEARE FESTIVAL, Napa, CA, www.napashakespeare.org

NASHVILLE SHAKESPEARE FESTIVAL, Nashville, TN, www.nashvilleshakes.org

NEBRASKA SHAKESPEARE FESTIVAL, Omaha, NE,
  www.nebraskashakespeare.com

NEVADA SHAKESPEARE COMPANY, Reno, NV, www.nevada-shakespeare.org

NEVADA SHAKESPEARE IN THE PARK, Henderson, NV,
  www.artscouncilhenderson.org/pages/SpInthePark.html

NEW DOMINION SHAKESPEARE FESTIVAL, Manassas, VA, www.vpstartcrow.com

THE NEW ENGLAND SHAKESPEARE FESTIVAL, Deerfield, NH,
  www.newenglandshakespeare.org

NORTH CAROLINA SHAKESPEARE FESTIVAL, High Point, NC, www.ncshakes.org

NORTHEAST SHAKESPEARE ENSEMBLE, New London, NH, www.nesetheatre.org

OAK PARK FESTIVAL THEATRE, Oak Park, IL, www.oakparkfestival.com

OJAI SHAKESPEARE FESTIVAL, Ojai, CA, www.ojaishakespeare.org

THE OKLAHOMA SHAKESPEAREAN FESTIVAL, Durant, OK, www.osfonline.com

OKLAHOMA SHAKESPEARE IN THE PARK, Edmond, OK,
     www.theshop.net/okshkspr

THE OLD GLOBE, San Diego, CA, www.oldglobe.org

OLYMPIC SHAKESPEARE PRODUCTIONS, Port Townsend, WA,
     www.olympus.net/community/olyshakespeare

OREGON SHAKESPEARE FESTIVAL, Ashland, OR, www.orshakes.org

THE ORLANDO-UCF SHAKESPEARE FESTIVAL, Orlando, FL,
     www.shakespearefest.org

OXFORD SHAKE-SPEARE COMPANY, Long Island City, NY, www.osctheatre.org

OXFORD SHAKESPEARE FESTIVAL, University, MS, shakespeare.olemiss.edu

PARK PLAYERS, Warrior, AL, www.bhamparkplayers.com

THE PASADENA SHAKESPEARE COMPANY, Pasadena, CA,
     www.pasadenashakespeare.com

PAX AMICUS CASTLE THEATRE, Budd Lake, NJ, www.paxamicus.com

THE PELLA SHAKESPEARE FESTIVAL, Pella, IA, www.pmscasting.com/festival.html

PENNSYLVANIA RENAISSANCE FAIRE, Cornwall, PA, www.parenaissancefaire.com

THE PENNSYLVANIA SHAKESPEARE FESTIVAL, Center Valley, PA,
     www.pashakespeare.org

PENOBSCOT THEATRE COMPANY, Bangor, ME, www.penobscottheatre.org

THE PHILADELPHIA SHAKESPEARE FESTIVAL, Philadelphia, PA,
     www.phillyshakespeare.org

POOR PLAYERS THEATRE COMPANY, San Marcos, CA, www.poorplayers.com

PRINCETON REP SHAKESPEARE FESTIVAL, Princeton, NJ, www.princetonrep.org

THE PUBLIC THEATER/NEW YORK SHAKESPEARE FESTIVAL, New York, NY,
     www.publictheater.org

PUCK'S SHAKESPEARE COMPANY, New York, NY,
     www.puckshakespearecompany.com

QUINTESSENCE: LANGUAGE & IMAGINATION THEATRE, Portland, OR,
     www.eamesharlan.org/quintessence/shows.html

REDUCED SHAKESPEARE COMPANY, Lowell, MA, www.reducedshakespeare.com

RENAISSANCE THEATRE, Roanoke, VA, www.vw.vccs.edu/theatre

REVOLVING SHAKESPEARE COMPANY, New York, NY,
     www.milesphillips.com/page16.html

THE RICHMOND SHAKESPEARE FESTIVAL, Richmond, VA,
     www.richmondshakespeare.com

RIVERSIDE THEATRE, Iowa City, IA, www.riversidetheatre.org

ROCHESTER COMMUNITY PLAYERS/SHAKESPEARE PLAYERS, Rochester, NY, www.rochester.lib.ny.us/clubs/920jnw8q.htm

ROSEBRIAR SHAKESPEARE COMPANY, Groveport, OH, www.rosebriarshakespeare.com

SACRAMENTO SHAKESPEARE FESTIVAL, Sacramento, CA, www.SacramentoShakespeare.net

SALT LAKE SHAKESPEARE, Salt Lake City, UT, www.saltlakeshakes.org

SANDSTONE PRODUCTIONS, Farmington, NM, www.farmington.nm.us/sandstone

THE SAN FRANCISCO SHAKESPEARE FESTIVAL, San Francisco, CA, www.sfshakes.org

SAN JACINTO VALLEY SHAKESPEARE FESTIVAL, Hemet, CA, www.ramonabowl.com

SARATOGA SHAKESPEARE COMPANY, Saratoga Springs, NY, www.saratogashakespeare.com

SEATTLE SHAKESPEARE COMPANY, Seattle, WA, www.seattleshakespeare.org

SEBASTOPOL SHAKESPEARE FESTIVAL, Sebastopol, CA, www.the-rep.com/stage_ssf.aspx

SHADY SHAKESPEARE THEATRE COMPANY, San Jose, CA, www.shadyshakes.org

SHAKEFEST, Winnsboro, SC, www.pinetreeplayhouse.com

SHAKESPEARE '70, INC., Lawrenceville, NJ, www.shakespeare70.org

SHAKESPEARE & COMPANY, Lenox, MA, www.shakespeare.org

SHAKESPEARE & COMPANY, White Bear Lake, MN, www.pigseyetheatre.org/shakesco

SHAKESPEARE & MORE THEATRE COMPANY, Greenwood, IN, www.geocities.com/shakespeare_and_more/theatre_company.html

SHAKESPEARE & ORIGINALS, Carrboro, NC

SHAKESPEARE AT CHAFFIN'S BARN, Nashville, TN, www.dinnertheatre.com

SHAKESPEARE AT STINSON, Stinson Beach, CA, www.shakespeareatstinson.org

THE FOUR COUNTY PLAYERS, Barboursville, VA, www.fourcp.org

SHAKESPEARE AT WINEDALE, Austin, TX, www.shakespeare-winedale.org

SHAKESPEARE-BY-THE-BOOK FESTIVAL, Richmond, TX, PHONE: (281) 341-2611

SHAKESPEARE BY THE SEA, Halifax, NS, Canada, www.shakespearebythesea.ca/New/index.html

SHAKESPEARE BY THE SEA, Redondo Beach, CA, www.shakespearebythesea.org

THE SHAKESPEARE COMPANY OF GREATER ROCHESTER, Rochester, NY, www.ShakeCo.com

SHAKESPEARE DALLAS, Dallas, TX, www.shakespearedallas.org

THE SHAKESPEARE FESTIVAL AT TULANE, New Orleans, LA, PHONE: (504) 865-5105

SHAKESPEARE FESTIVAL/LA, Los Angeles, CA, www.shakespearefestivalla.org

SHAKESPEARE FESTIVAL OF ARKANSAS, Little Rock, AK, PHONE: (501) 376-7529

SHAKESPEARE FESTIVAL OF ST. LOUIS, St. Louis, MO,
www.shakespearefestivalstlouis.com

THE SHAKESPEARE GUILD, Washington, DC,
www.sparrowsp.addr.com/miscellaneous/shakespeare_guild.htm

SHAKESPEARE IN ACTION, Toronto, ON, Canada, www.modworld.com/sia

SHAKESPEARE IN DELAWARE PARK, Buffalo, NY,
www.shakespeareindelawarepark.org

SHAKESPEARE IN SANTA FE, Santa Fe, NM, PHONE: (505) 982-2910

SHAKESPEARE IN THE PARK, Minneapolis, MN, PHONE: (612) 341-0882

SHAKESPEARE IN THE PARK, Fort Worth, TX,
www.stagewest.org/FWShakespeareFestival.htm (on hiatus)

SHAKESPEARE IN THE PARK, Calgary, AB, Canada,
www.mtroyal.ab.ca/conservatory/sitp

SHAKESPEARE IN THE PARQUE, Arlington, VA, www.theparque.org

SHAKESPEARE IN THE ROUGH, Toronto, ON, Canada, www.sitr.ca

SHAKESPEARE IN THE RUINS, Winnipeg, MB, Canada,
www.shakespeareintheruins.com

SHAKESPEARE-IN-THE-SCHOOLS, Pittsburgh, PA, www.pitt.edu/~sits

SHAKESPEARE KELOWNA THEATRE SOCIETY, Kelowna, BC, Canada,
www.shakespearekelowna.org

SHAKESPEARE NOW! THEATRE COMPANY, Westwood, MA,
www.shakespearenow.org

SHAKESPEARE NYC, New York, NY, www.shakespearenyc.net

SHAKESPEARE ON THE GREEN, Wilmington, NC, www.shakespeareonthegreen.us

SHAKESPEARE ON THE HUDSON THEATRE COMPANY, Athens, NY,
www.shakespeareonthehudson.com

SHAKESPEARE ON THE SASKATCHEWAN FESTIVAL, Saskatoon, SK, Canada,
www.shakespeareonthesaskatchewan.com

SHAKESPEARE ON THE SOUND, Norwalk, CT, www.shakespeareonthesound.org

SHAKESPEARE ORANGE COUNTY, Orange, CA,
www1.chapman.edu/comm/td/soc

THE SHAKESPEARE PROJECT OF CHICAGO, Chicago, IL,
www.shakespeareprojectchicago.org

SHAKESPEARE SANTA CRUZ, Santa Cruz, CA, www.shakespearesantacruz.org

SHAKESPEARE SEDONA, Phoenix, AZ, www.shakespearesedona.com

THE SHAKESPEARE SOCIETY, New York, NY, www.shakespearesociety.org

SHAKESPEARE THEATRE COMPANY, Washington, DC,
www.shakespearedc.org

THE SHAKESPEARE THEATRE OF NEW JERSEY, Madison, NJ,
www.njshakespeare.org

SHAKESPEARE UNDER THE STARS, Wimberley, TX, www.emilyann.org

SHAKESPEARE VENTURES, Fairfield, CT, www.shakespeareventures.com

SHENANDOAH SHAKESPEARE'S AMERICAN SHAKESPEARE CENTER,
Staunton, VA, www.americanshakespearecenter.com

SIERRA SHAKESPEARE FESTIVAL, Nevada City, CA, www.foothilltheatre.org

THE SOUTH CAROLINA SHAKESPEARE COMPANY, Columbia, SC,
www.scshakespeare.org

THE SOUTH FLORIDA SHAKESPEARE FESTIVAL, Coral Gables, FL,
www.new-theatre.org

SOUTHWEST SHAKESPEARE COMPANY, Mesa, AZ, www.swshakespeare.org

STAGE WEST/ALLIED THEATRE GROUP, Fort Worth, TX, www.alliedtheatre.org

STERLING RENAISSANCE FESTIVAL, Sterling, NY, www.sterlingfestival.com

ST. LOUIS SHAKESPEARE, St. Louis, MO, www.stlshakespeare.com

THE STRATFORD FESTIVAL OF CANADA, Stratford, ON, Canada,
www.stratfordfestival.ca

SUMMER SHAKESPEARE, Notre Dame, IN, shakespeare.nd.edu

SUN VALLEY SHAKESPEARE FESTIVAL, Sun Valley, ID, www.nexstage.org

TAVERN SHAKESPEARE, Bloomington, IN, www.geocities.com/boarsheadtavern

TENNESSEE STAGE COMPANY, Knoxville, TN, www.tennesseestage.com

TEXAS SHAKESPEARE FESTIVAL, Kilgore, TX, www.texasshakespeare.com

THE THEATER AT MONMOUTH, Monmouth, ME, www.theateratmonmouth.org

THEATRE FOR A NEW AUDIENCE, New York, NY, www.tfana.org/index.html

THEATREWORKS, Colorado Springs, CO, www.uccstheatreworks.com

THEATRICUM BOTANICUM, Topanga, CA, www.theatricum.com

UNSEAM'D SHAKESPEARE COMPANY, Pittsburgh, PA, www.unseamd.org

UPSTATE SHAKESPEARE FESTIVAL, Greenville, SC,
www.upstateshakespearefestival.org

UTAH SHAKESPEAREAN FESTIVAL, Cedar City, UT, www.bard.org

VALLEY SHAKESPEARE FESTIVAL, Livermore, CA, www.valleyshakes.org

VERMONT SHAKESPEARE COMPANY, North Hero, VT,
www.vermontshakespeare.org

VIRGINIA SHAKESPEARE FESTIVAL, Williamsburg, VA, vsf.wm.edu

WASHINGTON SHAKESPEARE COMPANY, Arlington, VA,
www.washingtonshakespeare.org

THE WATER WORKS THEATRE COMPANY, Royal Oak, MI,
www.waterworkstheatre.com

WESTERLY SHAKESPEARE IN THE PARK/THE COLONIAL THEATRE, Westerly, RI,
www.thecolonialtheater.org

WOMAN'S WILL, Oakland, CA, www.womanswill.org

WOODEN O THEATRE PRODUCTIONS, Mercer Island, WA, www.woodeno.org

WOODWARD SHAKESPEARE FESTIVAL, Fresno, CA
www.woodwardshakespeare.org

YONKERS SHAKESPEARE PROJECT, Yonkers, NY, www.alltheworldsastage.org

THE YORK SHAKESPEARE COMPANY, New York, NY, www.yorkshakespeare.org

YORK SHAKESPEARE FESTIVAL, Newmarket, ON, Canada, www.resurgence.on.ca

YOUNG SHAKESPEARE PLAYERS, Madison, WI, www.ysp.org

130+ CHILDREN'S THEATER AND YOUTH THEATER PROGRAMS

Children's theater, educational theater, participatory youth theater, or theater for young audiences (known as "TYA" in contract terminology at Actors' Equity and throughout the business) is a growing enterprise in America.

"Leading artists in every discipline are finding that working in this field not only expands their aesthetic possibilities but connects them to an audience which challenges, inspires, and reconnects them to the profound power of theater," notes Peter Brosius, artistic director of The Children's Theatre Company in Minneapolis. "We need artists of skill, passion, and dedication," adds Mr. Brosius.

Many theaters and theater leaders are firmly committed to the goals of theater for young audiences, believing in the artistic, cultural, social, audience-building, family-values virtues of theater for children and teens. Some companies perform for children using adult actors, others perform with children in their casts, and many produce plays for family audiences including children and adults. Anyone who thinks that children's theater is for beginners obviously hasn't directed, acted, or produced children's theater or visited any of the major children's theaters in America. Long a staple in community theaters, schools, and parks and recreation programs, children's theater is now in remarkably creative hands. Check out the work of the Tony Award–winning Minneapolis wonder The Children's Theatre Company, and the Seattle Repertory Theatre's commissioning work from Pulitzer Prize–winning playwright Robert Schenkkan. St. Louis's Metro Theater Company; Tempe, Arizona's Childsplay; Dallas Children's Theater; Bethesda, Maryland's Imagination Stage, and many others have elevated the art form and continue to entertain children and their families.

However, it should be noted that many theater outreach and educational programs have surfaced to a prominent place in theater schedules for financial, fund-raising, marketing, and audience-development purposes. For example, at various times in our nation's recent history when art and theater were being threatened by censorship issues and minimized by business, corporate and government granting institutions, many theaters broadened their horizons to include significant educational programs as a way of attracting individual, business, corporate, foundation, and government support.

Some theater leaders have turned into "true believers" and others simply enjoy the subsidies. In either case, it's always good to research the theater's philosophy, mission, and real commitment to youth theater before plunging in.

Fortunately, there is the ASSITEJ/USA, the national service organization promoting the power of professional theater for young audiences through excellence, collaboration and innovation across cultural and international boundaries. The address of the United States Center for the International Association of Theater for Children and Young People (ASSITEJ/USA) is 724 Second Avenue South, Nashville, TN, 37210. The telephone number is (615) 254-5719, the fax is (615) 254-3255, or e-mail usassitej@aol.com. The Web site, www.assitej-usa.org, includes listings for over 130 producers with contact numbers. A few are listed below to give you an idea of the range of producers in this genre:

ADVENTURE THEATRE, Glen Echo, MD, www.adventuretheatre.org

ALLIANCE CHILDREN'S THEATRE, Atlanta, GA, www.alliancetheatre.org

ARKANSAS ARTS CENTER CHILDREN'S THEATRE, Little Rock, AK, www.arkarts.com

ATLANTA'S FIRSTSTAGE, Atlanta, GA, www.atlantasfirststage.org

THE BUSHNELL, Hartford, CT, www.bushnell.org

THE CHILDREN'S THEATRE COMPANY, Minneapolis, MN, www.childrenstheatre.org

CHILDSPLAY, INC., Tempe, AZ, www.childsplayaz.org

COLUMBUS CHILDREN'S THEATRE, Columbus, OH, www.colschildrenstheatre.org

COTERIE, INC., Kansas City, MO, www.thecoterie.com

CREATIVE ARTS TEAM, New York, NY, www.nyu.edu/gallatin/creativearts

DALLAS CHILDREN'S THEATRE, INC., Dallas, TX, www.dct.org

DENVER CENTER THEATRE ACADEMY, Denver, CO, www.denvercenter.org

FLINT YOUTH THEATRE, Flint, MI, www.flintyouththeatre.com

FORT LAUDERDALE CHILDREN'S THEATRE, Fort Lauderdale, FL, www.flct.org

GEORGE STREET PLAYHOUSE, New Brunswick, NJ, www.georgestplayhouse.org

THE GROWING STAGE THEATRE, Netcong, NJ, www.growingstage.com

HARWICH JUNIOR THEATRE, INC., West Harwich, MA, www.hjtcapecod.org

HONOLULU THEATRE FOR YOUTH, Honolulu, HI, www.htyweb.org

KENNEDY CENTER YOUTH & FAMILY PROGRAMS, THE JOHN F. KENNEDY
CENTER FOR THE PERFORMING ARTS, Washington, DC,
www.kennedy-center.org

KRANNERT CENTER FOR PERFORMING ARTS, Urbana, IL,
www.krannertcenter.com

LEXINGTON CHILDREN'S THEATRE, Lexington, KY, www.lctonstage.org

MAGIK THEATRE, San Antonio, TX, www.magiktheatre.org

METRO THEATER COMPANY, St. Louis, MO, www.metrotheatercompany.org

NASHVILLE CHILDREN'S THEATRE, Nashville, TN, www.nct-dragonsite.org

OKLAHOMA CHILDREN'S THEATRE, Oklahoma City, OK,
www.okchildrenstheatre.com

OMAHA THEATER COMPANY FOR YOUNG PEOPLE, Omaha, NE, www.otcyp.org

ORLANDO REPERTORY THEATRE, Orlando, FL, www.orlandorep.com

PAPER BAG PLAYERS, New York, NY, www.thepaperbagplayers.org

ROUND HOUSE THEATRE, Bethesda, MD, www.round-house.org

SEATTLE CHILDREN'S THEATRE, Seattle, WA, www.sct.org

SECOND YOUTH, Austin, TX, www.secondyouth.com

SEEM-TO-BE-PLAYERS, Lawrence, KS, www.lawrenceartscenter.com

SHENANARTS, Staunton, VA, www.shenanarts.org

SOUTH COAST REPERTORY, Costa Mesa, CA, www.scr.org

STAGE ONE: THE LOUISVILLE CHILDREN'S THEATRE, Louisville, KY,
www.stageone.org

STAGES REPERTORY THEATRE, Houston, TX, www.stagestheatre.com

STAGES THEATRE COMPANY, Hopkins, MN, www.stagestheatre.org

TEATRO HUMANIDAD, Austin, TX, www.teatrohumanidad.com

THEATRE IV, Richmond, VA, www.theatreIV.org

In addition to ASSITEJ/USA, there are many other TYA companies who use the Equity contract—some are LORT theaters, others are TCG theaters, and all of these are recent Equity Theatre Contract companies (contact the Actors' Equity Association for the full list and contact numbers):

ALABAMA SHAKESPEARE FESTIVAL, Montgomery, AL, www.asf.net

AMERICAN STAGE, St. Petersburg, FL, www.americanstage.org

BILINGUAL FOUNDATION OF THE ARTS, Los Angeles, CA, www.bfatheatre.org

CASA MANANA PLAYHOUSE, Fort Worth, TX, www.casamanana.org

CLASSICS ON STAGE, Chicago, IL, www.classicsonstage.com

CLEVELAND PLAYHOUSE, Cleveland, OH, www.clevelandplayhouse.com

DRURY LANE CHILDREN'S THEATRE, Oakbrook Terrace, IL, www.drurylaneoakbrook.com

FANFARE THEATRE ENSEMBLE, New York, NY, PHONE: (212) 674-8181

FIRST STAGE PRODUCTIONS, Milwaukee, WI, www.firststage.org

FLAT ROCK PLAYHOUSE, Flat Rock, NC, www.flatrockplayhouse.org

FREEDOM THEATRE, Philadelphia, PA, www.freedomtheatre.org

LARK THEATRE COMPANY, New York, NY, www.larktheatre.org

LINCOLN CENTER INSTITUTE, New York, NY, www.lcinstitute.org

NORTH SHORE MUSIC THEATRE, Beverly, MA, www.nsmt.org

OLD LOG CHILDREN'S THEATRE, Greenwood, MN, www.oldlog.com

PITTSBURGH CIVIC LIGHT OPERA, Pittsburgh, PA, www.pittsburghclo.org

PUSHCART PLAYERS, Verona, NJ, www.pushcartplayers.org

SEEM-TO-BE PLAYERS, Lawrence, KS, www.lawrenceartscenter.com/STB

SESAME STREET LIVE, Minneapolis, MN, www.sesamestreetlive.com

SHAKESPEARE & COMPANY, Lenox, MA, www.shakespeare.org

SHAKESPEARE LIVE!, Madison, NJ, www.njshakespeare.org/tour/live.html

STORYBOOK MUSICAL THEATRE, Philadelphia, PA, www.storybookmusical.org

THEATREWORKS/USA, New York, NY, www.theatreworksusa.org

WHEELOCK FAMILY THEATRE, Boston, MA, www.wheelock.edu/wft

140+ MUSICAL THEATERS
Including an Introduction to NAMT and ASCAP

NATIONAL ALLIANCE FOR MUSICAL THEATRE (NAMT)
520 Eighth Avenue, Suite 301, 3rd Floor, New York, NY 10018
PHONE: (212) 714-6668; FAX: (212) 714-0469
E-MAIL: info@namt.org
WEB SITE: www.namt.org

Musical theater is all the rage in theaters, arts centers, and civic light operas throughout America, and the National Alliance for Musical Theatre (NAMT) is the only national service organization dedicated to musical theater. Founded in 1985, the NAMT membership includes theater institutions, universities, and independent producers. In a recent year, NAMT reported that its members "cumulatively staged over 23,000 performances attended by over 17 million people and reached revenues of over $510 million."

In the organization's own words, the mission of NAMT is "to advance musical theater by nurturing the creation, development, production, presentation, and recognition of new musicals and classics, by providing a forum for the sharing of resources and information relating to professional musical theater through communications, networking, and programming; and by advocating for the imagination, diversity, and joy unique to musical theater."

PROGRAMS AND SERVICES
Member benefits include two annual conferences, a Festival of New Musicals, and various publications, and research services.

Members
A geographical index of NAMT members reveals theaters nationally and abroad. The main Web site provides direct links to each theater.

Alabama

SUMMERFEST MUSICAL THEATRE, Birmingham, AL, www.summerfest.org

California

42ND STREET MOON, San Francisco, CA, www.42ndstmoon.org

ACADEMY FOR NEW MUSICAL THEATRE, North Hollywood, CA,
    www.anmt.org

AMERICAN MUSICAL THEATRE OF SAN JOSE, San Jose, CA, www.amtsj.org

BROADWAY/L.A., Los Angeles, CA, www.broadwayla.org

CABRILLO MUSIC THEATRE, Thousand Oaks, CA, www.cabrillomusictheatre.com

CALIFORNIA CONSERVATORY OF THE ARTS, San Juan Capistrano, CA,
    www.ccarts.net

**CALIFORNIA MUSICAL THEATRE (MUSIC CIRCUS AND THE BROADWAY
    SERIES)**, Sacramento, CA, www.bushnell.org

CALIFORNIA STATE UNIVERSITY, FULLERTON, Fullerton, CA,
    www.fullerton.edu/arts/

CONTRA COSTA MUSICAL THEATRE, Walnut Creek, CA, www.ccmt.org

DEAF WEST THEATRE, North Hollywood, CA, www.deafwest.org

DEE GEE ENTERTAINMENT, Los Angeles, CA,
    www.coronet-theatrela.com/DEEGEE.htm

DIABLO LIGHT OPERA COMPANY, Los Angeles, CA, www.dloc.org

EAST OF DOHENY, Los Angeles, CA, www.eastofdoheny.com

FULLERTON CIVIC LIGHT OPERA, Fullerton, CA, www.fclo.com

LAS POSITAS COLLEGE, Livermore, CA, www.laspositascollege.edu

MCCOY RIGBY ENTERTAINMENT, Fullerton, CA, www.mccoyrigby.com

MUSICAL THEATRE WEST, Long Beach, CA, www.musical.org

THE OLD GLOBE, San Diego, CA, www.oldglobe.org

PERFORMANCE RIVERSIDE, Riverside, CA, www.performanceriverside.org

STARLIGHT MUSICAL THEATRE, San Diego, CA, www.starlighttheatre.org

THEATREWORKS, Palo Alto, CA, www.theatreworks.org

ULLMAN, STEVEN, Venice, CA

WESTERN STAGE, Salinas, CA, www.westernstage.org

WOODMINSTER SUMMER MUSICALS, Oakland, CA, www.woodminster.com

Connecticut

THE BUSHNELL, Hartford, CT, www.broadwayrose.com

GOODSPEED MUSICALS, East Haddam, CT, www.goodspeed.com

HARTT SCHOOL-THEATRE DIVISION, UNIVERSITY OF HARTFORD,
    West Hartford, CT, www.hartford.edu/hartt/

THE SPIRIT OF BROADWAY THEATER, Norwich, CT, www.spiritofbroadway.org

STAMFORD CENTER FOR THE ARTS, Stamford, CT, www.onlyatsca.com

District of Columbia

FORD'S THEATRE, Washington, DC, www.fordstheatre.org

Florida

FLORIDA STAGE, Manalapan, FL, www.floridastage.org

RIVERSIDE THEATRE INC., Vero Beach, FL, www.riversidetheatre.com

SEASIDE MUSIC THEATER, Daytona Beach, FL, www.seasidemusictheater.org

STAGE AURORA THEATRICAL COMPANY, INC., Jacksonville, FL,
www.stageaurora.org

UNIVERSITY OF CENTRAL FLORIDA, DEPARTMENT OF THEATRE, Orlando, FL,
pegasus.cc.ucf.edu/~theatre/

V.J. COLONNA PRODUCTIONS, INC., Miami Beach, FL

Georgia

ALLIANCE THEATRE COMPANY, Atlanta, GA, www.alliancetheatre.org

THEATER OF THE STARS, Atlanta, GA, www.theaterofthestars.com

Illinois

CHICAGO SHAKESPEARE THEATER, Chicago, IL, www.canstage.com

LIGHT OPERA WORKS, Evanston, IL, www.light-opera-works.org

THE LITTLE THEATRE ON THE SQUARE, Sullvian, IL, www.thelittletheare.org

MARRIOTT THEATRE IN LINCOLNSHIRE, IL, www.marriottheatre.com

MILLIKIN UNIVERSITY, DEPARTMENT OF THEATRE AND DANCE, Decatur, IL,
www.millikin.edu/theatre

**NORTHWESTERN UNIVERSITY, DEPARTMENT OF THEATRE, MUSIC THEATRE
PROGRAM**, Evanston, IL, www.newstage.northwestern.edu

PORCHLIGHT MUSIC THEATRE, Chicago, IL, www.porchlighttheatre.com

THEATRE BUILDING CHICAGO, Chicago, IL, www.theatrebuildingchicago.org

Indiana

DERBY DINNER PLAYHOUSE, Clarksville, IN, www.derbydinner.com

Kansas

MUSIC THEATRE OF WICHITA, Wichita, KS, www.musictheatreofwichita.org

Maine

MAINE STATE MUSIC THEATRE, Brunswick, ME, www.msmt.org

ROGOSIN, ROY, Kittery Point, ME

Maryland

NETWORKS PRESENTATIONS, Montgomery Village, MD, www.networkstours.com

PHOENIX ENTERTAINMENT, Frederick, MD,
www.phoenixontour.com/contact.htm

TROIKA ENTERTAINMENT, Gaithersburg, MD, www.troika.com

Massachusetts

THE BOSTON CONSERVATORY, Boston, MA, www.bostonconservatory.edu

BOSTON MUSIC THEATRE PROJECT AT SUFFOLK UNIVERSITY, Boston, MA,
www.cas.suffolk.edu/theatre

NORTH SHORE MUSIC THEATRE AT DUNHAM WOODS, Beverly, MA,
www.nsmt.org

REAGLE PLAYERS, Waltham, MA, www.reagleplayers.com

SPEAKEASY STAGE COMPANY, Boston, MA, www.speakeasystage.com

Minnesota

CHANHASSEN DINNER THEATRES, Chanhassen, MN,
www.chanhassentheatres.com

ORDWAY CENTER FOR THE PERFORMING ARTS, St. Paul, MN, www.ordway.org

SCALLEN, TOM, Minneapolis, MN

TROUPE AMERICA, INC., Minneapolis, MN, www.troupeamerica.com

Missouri

FOX THEATRE, St. Louis, MO, www.foxtheatre.org

MUNICIPAL THEATRE ASSOCIATION OF ST. LOUIS (THE MUNY), St. Louis, MO,
www.muny.org

STARLIGHT THEATRE ASSOCIATION OF KANSAS CITY, Kansas City, MO,
www.kcstarlight.com

THEATER LEAGUE, Kansas City, MO, www.theaterleaguue.com

Nevada

GILL THEATRICAL MANAGEMENT INC., Las Vegas, NV, www.gillmanagement.com

New Hampshire

SEACOAST REPERTORY THEATRE, Portsmouth, NH, www.seacoastrep.org

New Jersey

LENAPE REGIONAL PERFORMING ARTS CENTER, Marlton, NJ,
www.sjtheater.com

PAPER MILL PLAYHOUSE, Millburn, NJ, www.papermill.org

New York

AMAS MUSICAL THEATRE, INC., New York, NY, www.amasmusical.org

APT. 4A PRODUCTIONS, Brooklyn, NY

ARTPARK AND COMPANY, Lewiston, NY, www.artpark.net

ASCAP MUSICAL THEATRE WORKSHOP, New York, NY,
www.ascap.com/about/workshops.html

BMI LEHMAN ENGEL MUSICAL THEATRE WORKSHOP, New York, NY,
www.bmi.com/musicaltheatre/lengel.asp

BROOKS & DISTLER, ATTORNEYS AT LAW, New York, NY,
www.brookslawyers.com

COLUMBIA ARTISTS THEATRICALS, New York, NY,
www.columbiaartiststheatricals.com

DUKE MARKETING, INC., Haverstraw, NY

ERIC KREBS PRODUCTIONS, New York, NY

GORGEOUS ENTERTAINMENT, INC., New York, NY,
www.gorgeousentertainment.com

LARK PLAY DEVELOPMENT CENTER, New York, NY, www.larktheatre.org

LIGETI ARTISTS, New York, NY, www.theshowstore.com

MUSICAL MONDAYS THEATRE LAB, INC., New York, NY,
community.tisch.nyu.edu/object/OCC_int10.html

NYU, TISCH SCHOOL OF THE ARTS GRADUATE MUSICAL THEATRE WRITING PROGRAM, New York, NY, www.gmtw.tisch.nyu.edu/page/home.html

TOWN SQUARE PRODUCTIONS, New York, NY,
www.townsquareproductions.com

WAXMAN WILLIAMS ENTERTAINMENT, New York, NY

THE YORK THEATRE COMPANY, New York, NY, www.yorktheatre.org

North Carolina

NORTH CAROLINA BLUMENTHAL PERFORMING ARTS CENTER, Charlotte, NC,
www.performingartsctr.org

THE NORTH CAROLINA THEATRE, Raleigh, NC, www.nctheatre.com

Ohio

CAROUSEL DINNER THEATRE, Akron, OH, www.carouseldinnertheatre.com

THE HUMAN RACE THEATRE COMPANY, Dayton, OH,
www.humanracetheatre.org

UNIVERSITY OF CINCINNATI, DEPARTMENT OF MUSICAL THEATRE,
Cincinnati, OH, www.uc.edu/programs/viewprog.asp?progid=2088

VICTORIA THEATRE ASSOCIATION, Dayton, OH, www.victoriatheatre.com

Oklahoma

LYRIC THEATRE OF OKLAHOMA, Oklahoma City, OK, www.lyrictheatreokc.com

OKLAHOMA CITY UNIVERSITY COLLEGE OF MUSIC AND PERFORMING ARTS,
Oklahoma City, OK, www.okcu.edu

WEITZENHOFFER DEPARTMENT OF MUSICAL THEATRE, University of Oklahoma,
Norman, OK, www.ou.edu/bulletins/html/Fine_Arts_Musical_Theatre.htm

Oregon

ACTORS CABARET OF EUGENE, Eugene, OR, www.actorscabaret.org

THE BROADWAY ROSE THEATRE, Tigard, OR, www.bwayrose.com

Pennsylvania

ACT II PLAYHOUSE, Amber, PA, www.act2.org

ARDEN THEATRE COMPANY, Philadelphia, PA, www.ardentheatre.org

CARNEGIE MELLON UNIVERSITY, SCHOOL OF DRAMA, Pittsburgh, PA,
   www.cmu.edu/cfa/drama

THE MEDIA THEATRE FOR THE PERFORMING ARTS, Media, PA,
   www.mediatheatre.com

PENNSYLVANIA CENTRE STAGE, University Park, PA,
   www.pacentrestage.psu.edu

PITTSBURGH CLO, Pittsburgh, PA, www.pittsburghclo.org

PITTSBURGH MUSICAL THEATER, Pittsburgh, PA, www.pittsburghmusicals.com

Tennessee

CUMBERLAND COUNTY PLAYHOUSE, Crossville, TN, www.ccplayhouse.com

Texas

DALLAS SUMMER MUSICALS, Dallas, TX, www.dallassummermusicals.org

THEATRE UNDER THE STARS, Houston, TX, www.tuts.com

ZACHARY SCOTT THEATRE CENTER, Austin, TX, www.zachscott.com

Utah

UTAH MUSICAL THEATRE, Ogden, UT, www.community.weber.edu/umt

Vermont

WESTON PLAYHOUSE THEATRE COMPANY, Weston, VT,
   www.westonplayhouse.org

Virginia

BARTER THEATRE, Abingdon, VA, www.bartertheatre.com

MILL MOUNTAIN THEATRE, Roanoke, VA, www.millmountain.org

Washington

THE 5TH AVENUE THEATRE, Seattle, WA, www.5thavenuetheatre.org

TACOMA MUSICAL PLAYHOUSE, Tacoma, WA, www.tmp.org

VILLAGE THEATRE, Issaquah, WA, www.villagetheatre.org

Abroad

BRITISH BROADCASTING CORPORATION, Cardiff, Wales,
   www.bbc.co.uk/wales/music

CAMERON MACKINTOSH LIMITED, London, England,
   www.cameronmackintosh.com

GREENWICH THEATRE, London, England, www.greenwichtheatre.org.uk

THE INTERNATIONAL FESTIVAL OF MUSICAL THEATRE IN CARDIFF,
   London, England, www.cardiffmusicals.com

MERCURY MUSICAL DEVELOPMENTS, East Sussex, England,
www.mercurymusicals.com

THE TAMPERE THEATRE, Tampere, Finland, www.tampereenteatteri.fi

AMERICAN SOCIETY OF COMPOSERS, AUTHORS AND PUBLISHERS (ASCAP)

ASCAP/New York, One Lincoln Plaza, New York, NY 10023
PHONE: (212) 621-6000; FAX: (212) 724-9064
E-MAIL: info@ascap.com
WEB SITE: www.ascap.com

ASCAP/Los Angeles, 7920 West Sunset Blvd., Third Floor,
Los Angeles, CA 90046
PHONE: (323) 883-1000; FAX: (323) 883-1049

If you plan to focus on musical theater, you should also be aware of ASCAP, the association of over 200,000 US composers, songwriters, lyricists, and music publishers. In its own words, "through agreements with affiliated international societies, ASCAP also represents hundreds of thousands of music creators worldwide. ASCAP is the only US performing rights organization created and controlled by composers, songwriters, and music publishers, with a board of directors elected by and from the membership."

112+ OUTDOOR THEATERS

Theater and History Thrive in the Great Outdoors of America

So many theater, television, and film greats began and developed their careers in America's outdoor dramas. Sitting in the audience, there's a thrill unlike any other in the theater, when a group of whooping American Indians rides through the "theater" on a herd of horses, when Abe Lincoln reveals a personal discovery, or when Daniel Boone embarks on a new adventure. Dashing movie star Denzel Washington (Maryland's *Wings of the Morning*), television and movie icon Andy Griffith (North Carolina's *The Lost Colony*), voluptuous actress Raquel Welch (California's *The Ramona Pageant*), Tony Award–winning costume designer William Ivey Long, and many others worked (and many continue to work) on outdoor dramas throughout the United States.

INSTITUTE OF OUTDOOR DRAMA (IOD)

CB #3240, 1700 Martin Luther King Jr. Blvd., UNC–Chapel Hill,
   Chapel Hill, NC 27599-3240
PHONE: (919) 962-1328; FAX: (919) 962-4212
E-MAIL: outdoor@unc.edu
WEB SITE: www.unc.edu/depts/outdoor/

The Institute of Outdoor Drama (IOD) was founded in 1963 and at any given time represents approximately 37 historical dramas, 66 Shakespeare festivals, and 10 religious dramas throughout the United States. Collectively, these theaters employ over 5,000 people and, according to IOD figures, have an annual economic impact on the US travel and tourism industry of approximately $500 million. Perhaps most important to interested actors, directors, designers, production personnel, and administrators, the institute provides auditions, job placement, and career development potential for theater enthusiasts at virtually every level of their careers.

NATIONAL CONFERENCE

The institute organizes an annual conference, bringing together professional managers, directors, playwrights, promoters, designers, and composers, as well as representatives from communities planning new outdoor dramas, for workshops, tours, and open discussions on topics relating to the writing, producing, and management of outdoor drama in the United States.

AUDITIONS

The institute sponsors annual auditions in Chapel Hill, North Carolina, for performers and technicians seeking employment in outdoor drama. Typically, 150 to 200 auditionees from 50 or more colleges and universities in 20 states vie for jobs offered by 15 to 20 theaters in attendance from around the country.

OVERVIEW

The IOD is a public service agency based in the College of Arts and Sciences of The University of North Carolina in Chapel Hill. Under the astute, dedicated, and energetic leadership of executive director Scott J. Parker, the IOD fosters artistic and managerial excellence and assists in the expansion of the outdoor drama movement through training, research and advisory programs. The IOD serves as a national clearinghouse for more than 120 constituent theater companies across the nation.

According to Parker, "These dramas are delightful family entertainment and at the same time teach us about our heritage. We hear from public school teachers all the time, and from their students as well, about how much they've learned about North Carolina history through the dramas. They reinforce what students learn in class; they make history come alive. The outdoor dramas employ thousands of college and professional performers each season, and have been pioneers in nonprofit theatrical arts development. Most have been produced by cooperative organizational efforts of local citizens, foundations, and government on a noncommercial basis. These dramas have been produced out of community desire to commemorate the past and rededicate the future through theater."

The outdoor historical dramas are original plays, often with music and dance, based on significant events and include such past audience favorites as *Texas Legacies*, Ohio's *Tecumseh!*, North Carolina's *The Lost Colony*, Indiana's *Young Abe Lincoln*, and California's *Ramona Pageant*.

Religious dramas range from South Dakota's *Black Hills Passion Play*, Washington State's *Jesus of Nazareth*, and Arkansas' *The Great Passion Play*, to New York's *The Hill Cumorah Pageant*.

Among outdoor Shakespeare Festivals are Wisconsin's American Players Theatre, the Utah Shakespearean Festival, the Colorado Shakespeare Festival, the Oregon Shakespeare Festival, Kentucky Shakespeare Festival, Idaho Shakespeare Festival, and Shakespeare Santa Cruz.

PUBLICATIONS

The institute publishes more than 50 reference bulletins, periodicals, directories, and technical documents designed to keep professionals and the media informed, including *U.S. Outdoor Drama* (newsletter), the *Directory of Outdoor Drama in America*, and a *Bibliography on American Outdoor Drama*. The Web site is a great place to start and the profiles and links to America's outdoor theaters are a terrific way to begin your research.

Other Institute of Outdoor Drama services include consulting, assistance in the development of new dramas, personnel searches, a speakers bureau, and archival, library, and research support.

OUTDOOR DRAMA FACTS

According to the *Directory of Outdoor Drama in America*, the states with the most outdoor theaters include California (16), Texas (9), and North Carolina (11). North Carolina has the most history plays (12), and California has the most Shakespeare festivals (14).

Today, the Institute of Outdoor Drama consists of over 112 member organizations. Institute of Outdoor Drama member theatres are listed below, with the exception of member Shakespeare festivals, which can be found on page 302.

Historical Dramas

AMERICAN FOLKLORE THEATRE: MUSKIE LOVE

Dave Hudson, playwright; Paul Libman, composer
American Folklore Theatre, P.O. Box 273, Fish Creek, WI 54212-0273
Administration and Box Office: (920) 854-6117

AMISTAD SAGA "REFLECTIONS"

Ann Hunt-Smith, playwright; Reggie Jeffries, composer
A mutiny aboard a slave ship in 1839 that marked the beginning of the end of slavery in the United States is brought to life through powerful speeches, song, and dance. *Amistad* dramatizes the plight of the ship's captives, from their removal from their native land to a revolt at sea, and their battle for freedom. African American Cultural Complex, 119 Sunnybrook Road, Raleigh, NC 27610-1827. Administration and Box Office: (919) 205-9336

THE ARACOMA STORY

Thomas M. Patterson, playwright; Faser Hardin and Dana Dorsey, composers
This is the tale of the Indian princess Aracoma and her ill-fated love for the British soldier captured by her father in 1780 in the West Virginia hills near their home. The Aracoma Story, Inc., P.O. Box 2016, Logan, WV 25601. Administration and Box Office: (304) 752-0253

BLACKBEARD: KNIGHT OF THE BLACK FLAG

Stuart Aronson, playwright; Joseph Distefano, composer
This drama tells the tale of one of the most notable characters of colonial sailing days, Edward Teach, otherwise known as the notorious pirate Blackbeard. Shown through the eyes of his bride, Mary Ormond, his character unfolds to reveal a man of many facets: ferocious and tormented at some times, sensitive and compassionate at others. Ormond Amphitheatre, Whitepost, NC 92, Bath, NC 27808. Administration and Box Office: (252) 923-4171

BLUE JACKET

W.L. Mundell, playwright; Michael Rasbury, composer
Blue Jacket invites audiences to relive the adventure, as Shawnee Indians, frontier settlers, and fugitive slaves forge the definition of American freedom on the very land where these legends once walked. Thundering horses, roaring cannons, flaming arrows, and torches bring history to life on the three-acre outdoor stage. First Frontier, Inc., P.O. Box C, Xenia, OH 45385-0692. Phone: (937) 376-4358; Box Office: (937) 376-4318 or toll free (877) 465-BLUE

DOCK BROWN: LEGEND OF AN OUTLAW

Honus Shain, playwright
Dock Brown tells the story of the infamous Kentucky outlaw who lived in Pine Knob, Kentucky, in the mid-1800s as a charming and well-respected citizen, while turning his farm—the theater site—into a hideout for himself.

DOWN IN HOODOO HOLLER

Honus Shain, playwright
Down in Hoodoo Holler is the folklore story of Pine Knob. A city slicker from Louisville travels to Pine Knob, Hoodoo Holler, in search of Dock Brown's gold, and learns that there is more to life than work and money. Pine Knob Theatre, Inc., 2250 Pine Knob Road, Caneyville, KY 42721. Administration and Box Office: (270) 879-8190

FIRST FOR FREEDOM
Max B. Williams, playwright
This drama celebrates events that led up to the signing of the Halifax
Resolves on April 12, 1776, the first formal declaration of independence from
Great Britain by an American colony. Eastern Stage, Inc., 14511 Highway
903, Halifax, NC 27839. Administration and Box Office: (252) 583-2261

FROM THIS DAY FORWARD
Fred Cranford, playwright
Told through music, dance and drama, *From This Day Forward* is the story
of the Waldenses, a religious sect that arose in southeast France in the late
1100s, centering on their struggle to survive persecution in their homeland,
and their eventual arrival in North Carolina in 1893 to establish a colony at
Valdese. Old Colony Players, P.O. Box 112, Valdese, NC 28690.
Administration and Box Office: (828) 874-0176

HATFIELDS AND MCCOYS
Billy Edd Wheeler, playwright; Ewel Cornett, composer
This musical dramatizes the fierce mountain pride that fueled the world-
famous conflict between the Hatfields of West Virginia and the McCoys of
Kentucky.

HONEY IN THE ROCK
Kermit Hunter, playwright; Jack Kilpatrick and Ewel Cornett, composers
This musical drama is a historical epic telling how West Virginia was born
out of the anguish of the Civil War. In addition, through a combination
of dance and imagery, it dramatizes what Indians encountered when they
first settled the land and discovered its strange natural gas wells, which they
called "honey in the rock." Theatre West Virginia, Inc., P.O. Box 1205,
Beckley, WV 25802. Phone: (304) 256-6800; Box Office: (800) 666-9142

HOOFPRINTS ON THE STAIRS
Gary Vidito, playwright
This musical drama tells the story of the "wizard in the saddle," the
"Rebel Raider" General John Hunt Morgan, who led three raids on Union
soldiers camped in the city of Lebanon, Kentucky, during the Civil War.
Hoofprints on the Stairs, Inc., P.O. Box 47, Lebanon, KY 40033. Phone:
(270) 692-0021

HORN IN THE WEST

Kermit Hunter, playwright; Peter MacBeth, composer
Set in the southern Appalachian mountain region of North Carolina during the American Revolutionary War, the drama follows frontiersman Daniel Boone and his band of mountain settlers as they struggle against the British militia. Southern Appalachian Historical Association, Inc., P.O. Box 295, Boone, NC 28607. Phone: (828) 264-2120; Box Office: (888) 825-6747

JOHN MUIR'S MOUNTAIN DAYS

Mary Bracken Phillips, playwright; Craig Bohmler, composer; conceived by Richard Elliott
Mountain Days is the story of the life and legacy of John Muir (1838-1914), Contra Costa resident, world-famous author, and naturalist. The drama depicts John's immigration from Scotland, his first visit to Yosemite Falls, camping in the Mariposa Grove, and a partnership forged with Louis Strentzel that withstands distance, illness, and earthquake. Willows Theatre Company, 1425 Gasoline Alley, Concord, CA 94520. Phone: (925) 798-1824; Box Office: (925) 798-1300

JOHNNY APPLESEED

Billy Edd Wheeler, playwright; Denis Burnside, composer
Set in the early 1800s and leading up to the war of 1812, this inspiring story told with song and dance is based on true accounts of John "Appleseed" Chapman's thrilling adventures in north central Ohio. Johnny Appleseed Heritage Center, Inc., 2179 State Route 603, Ashland, OH 44805. Administration and Box Office: (800) 642-0388.

LAURA'S MEMORIES

Terri Spyre and Pat Allen, playwrights
This outdoor drama follows Laura Ingalls Wilder and her family, from the Big Woods of Wisconsin to Plum Creek in the Dakota territory, and finally to Mansfield in 1894. The production brings to life the writings of Wilder's *Little House* books. Ozark Mountain Players, P.O. Box 113, Mansfield, MO, 65704. Administration and Box Office: (800) 642-0388

LONE STAR RISING

Phil Price, playwright; Neil Hess, Rusty MaGee, Art Greenhaw, and Terry Winch, composers

A musical celebration of the Lone Star State and the cowboy way of life through music, dance, and drama, *Lone Star Rising* showcases the Spanish, Indian, and cowboy cultures that played a significant part in early Texas history. Center for Texas Culture, P.O. Box 1157, Borger, TX 79008-1157. Box Office: (806) 677-1706

THE LOST COLONY

Paul Green, playwright

Performed in the Waterside Theatre, this symphonic drama depicts the valiant struggle of 117 men, women, and children to settle in the New World in 1587. They disappeared without a trace, and after 400 years, this continues to be one of history's greatest mysteries. Roanoke Island Historical Association, 1409 National Park Drive, Manteo, NC 27954. Phone: (252) 473-2127; Box Office: (252) 473-3414 or toll free (800) 488-5012

THE MIRACLE WORKER

William Gibson, playwright

This drama centers on Helen Keller, who lost her sight and hearing as a child. Her life changed when she came under the tutelage of Annie Sullivan, but only after turbulent, violent, and emotion-packed events. Performed on the grounds of Helen's childhood home. Helen Keller Birthplace Foundation Board, 300 West North Commons, Tuscumbia, AL 35674. Administration and Box Office: (888) 329-2124 or (256) 383-4066

OKLAHOMA!

Oscar Hammerstein II, playwright; Richard Rodgers, composer

Designated the "national home" of the famed musical, the 2,000-seat Discoveryland Amphitheatre is the setting for this all-American love story set in the days of the Oklahoma land rush. Discoveryland! U.S.A., 5529 S. Lewis, Tulsa, OK 74105. Phone: (918) 742-5255; Box Office: (918) 245-OKLA

THE OLD HOMESTEAD

Denman Thompson, playwright

Drawn from memories of Thompson's youth in Swanzey, New Hampshire, in the mid-1800s, this play tells the story of Uncle Josh, an unsophisticated

Swanzey citizen who travels to New York City in search of his son. The Old Homestead Association, P.O. Box 10414, Swanzey, NH 03446. Administration and Box Office: (603) 352-3251

THE PAUL SAWYIER STORY

Elexene M. Cox, playwright

Based on the remarkable life of the famed Kentucky watercolor artist and American impressionist Paul Sawyier (1865-1917), who lived on a houseboat and painted scenes of the Kentucky River, this musical play features renditions of "Ballin' the Jack," "Alexander's Rag-Time Band," "Hello My Baby," and "Wait Till the Sun Shines, Nellie." Jessamine County Special Events Committee, 103 Robin Road, Nicholasville, KY 40356. Administration and Box Office: (859) 885-4225

RAMONA PAGEANT

Adapted by Garnet Holme from the novel by Helen Hunt Jackson

Set in southern California in the 1850s, this is the tragic love story of Ramona, the half-Scottish, half-Indian bride of Alessandro, a member of the local Cahuilla tribe. Based on the 1884 novel, that inspired the song and five motion pictures, this outdoor drama was first presented in 1923, and is the California State Outdoor Play. Ramona Pageant Association, Inc., 27400 Ramona Bowl Road, Hemet, CA 92544-8108. Phone: (951) 658-3111; Box Office: (800) 645-4465

RIDERS OF THE FLOOD

Robert E. Tuckwiller, playwright

Set in Greenbrier County, West Virginia, during the 1880s when men risked their lives driving logs down remote and dangerous rivers, *Riders of the Flood* tells the tale of one young man who leaves the big city to start a new life as a woodsman in a white pine logging camp. Along the way he finds adventure, romance, and success in the high mountain country. City of Ronceverte, 601 Clay Street, Ronceverte, WV 24970. Box Office: (304) 645-2070

SALADO LEGENDS

Jackie Mills, playwright; Michael Rasbury, composer-arranger

Salado Legends follows the history of the founding of Salado, Texas. One of the original songs, "Be Careful What You Wish For," weaves the legends of the Tonkawa Indians, the dreams of the Spanish explorers, and the hopes of the Scottish settlers, into a panoramic tale that encompasses the Civil War. Tablerock Festival of Salado, P.O. Box 312, Salado, TX 76571. Administration and Box Office: (254) 947-9205

THE SHEPHERD OF THE HILLS
Adapted by Keith Thurman from the novel by Harold Bell Wright
Based on Wright's 1907 best-selling novel, *The Shepherd of the Hills* dramatizes the story of a gentle stranger from a faraway city who comes to the Ozark mountains as a shepherd, but with a mysterious mission that gradually unfolds as he befriends the members of the community. The Shepherd of the Hills Historical Society, 5586 West Highway 76, Branson, MO 65616. Phone: (417) 334-4191; Box Office: (800) OLD-MATT

SING DOWN THE MOON
Mary Hall Surface, playwright; David Maddox, composer
A rollicking, high-energy musical presentation of six Appalachian folk tales based on the oral traditions of the peoples who settled in the rugged mountains, which reflect homeland cultures of the British Isles and Germany. Theater at Lime Kiln, 2 West Henry Street, Lexington, VA 24450. Phone: (540) 463-7088; Box Office: (540) 463-3074

STAR OF THE HILLS
Dorey Schmidt, playwright; Gordon Jones, composer
Based on the history of Wimberley, Texas, *Star of the Hills* is a musical drama focused on the intrinsic values of the peaceful landscapes and virtues of small town living. The story begins with Native American Tonkawa in the 1820s, carries through early Spanish visitors, to millers bent on capitalizing on nearby Cypress Creek, and concludes with present day residents bent on protecting their natural heritage of the land. The EmilyAnn Theatre, Inc., P.O. Box 801, Wimberley, TX 78676. Administration and Box Office: (512) 847-6969

STEPHEN FOSTER—THE MUSICAL
Jonathan Bolt, playwright; Stephen C. Foster, composer; based on an original dramatization by Paul Green
Nestled in My Old Kentucky Home State Park, where music fills the night air, this musical tribute to America's famous composer Stephen Foster, contains over fifty of his most appealing songs, including "My Old Kentucky

Home." Dazzling costumes and lively dancing take audiences back to the 1800s. The Stephen Foster Drama Association, Inc., P.O. Box 546, Bardstown, KY 40004. Phone: (502) 348-5971; Box Office: (800) 626-1563

THE SWORD OF PEACE

William Hardy, playwright

The Sword of Peace dramatizes the conflict faced by members of the North Carolina Society of Friends during the Revolutionary War, when, as peaceful Quakers, they are forced to defend their basic tenet of nonviolence.

PATHWAY TO FREEDOM

Mark R. Sumner, playwright; Ann Hunt-Smith, composer

Pathway to Freedom is the story of how anti-slavery North Carolinians and freed African Americans helped hundreds of escaped slaves flee to the North prior to the Civil War, via the Underground Railroad. Snow Camp Historical Drama Society, Inc., P.O. Box 535, Snow Camp, NC 27349. Phone: (336) 376-6948; Box Office: (800) 726-5115.

TECUMSEH!

Allan W. Eckert, playwright; Frankie Laine, composer

Tecumseh! tells the story of the great Shawnee Indian leader's lifelong effort to protect his homeland, the Scioto River Valley of southern Ohio, from white settlers, ending with his self-prophesied death at the Battle of the Thames in the War of 1812. The Scioto Society, Inc., P.O. Box 73, Chillicothe, OH 45601-0073. Phone: (740) 775-4100; Box Office: (866) 775-0700

TERROR OF THE TUG

Jean Battlo, playwright

Terror of the Tug recaptures the turbulent times during the organization of the United Mine Workers. This drama tells the story of two events of the mining war—the May 19, 1920 Massacre, and the August 1, 1921, murder at the Welch Courthouse—during which time Sid Hatfield, sheriff of Matewan, earned the nickname "Terror of the Tug." McArts, Box 415, Kimball, WV 24853. Phone: (304) 585-7107; Box Office: (304) 436-6645

TEXAS LEGACIES: THE ADVENTURE OF A LIFETIME

Lynn Hart, playwright; James Gardner, composer

This play dramatizes the gritty determination and pioneering spirit of life on the frontier plains of the Texas Panhandle in the 1880s with galloping horses, special effects (thunder and lightning, Civil War battle, fire-works), and portrayals of legends Quannah Parker, Colonel Ranald "Bad Hand" Mackenzie, and buffalo hunter Billy Dixon. Heritage Entertainment, 1514 Fifth Avenue, Canyon, TX 79015. Administration and Box Office: (806) 655-2181

TRAIL OF TEARS—REBUILDING A NATION
Layce Gardner, playwright
Beginning in 1839, with the tragic march of the Cherokee Indian nation along the infamous Trail of Tears and through the present day, the drama follows the fate of the Western Band of Cherokee as they build a new homeland. Cherokee National Historical Society, P.O. Box 515, Tahlequah, OK 74465. Administration and Box Office: (918) 456-6007

TRAIL OF THE LONESOME PINE
Earl Hobson Smith and Gerald S. Argetsinger, playwrights; based on the novel by John Fox Jr.
This musical drama, designated the official outdoor drama of the Commonwealth of Virginia, weaves a tale of love, feuding, and defiance resulting from the discovery of coal in the mountains of Virginia in the early 1890s. Lonesome Pine Arts and Crafts, Inc., P.O. Box 1976, Big Stone Gap, VA 24219. Administration and Box Office: (800) 362-0149

TRUMPET IN THE LAND
Paul Green, playwright; Frank Lewin, composer
Set in Ohio's historic Tuscarawas Valley during the Revolutionary War, this is the compelling story of David Zeisberger, a Moravian missionary who, with a small group of Delaware Indians, established Ohio's first settlement, Schoenbrunn.

THE WHITE SAVAGE
Joseph Bonamico and Mark H. Durbin, playwrights; Frank Lewin, composer
This drama is the legendary and heroic story of frontiersman Simon Girty, nicknamed "The White Savage" due to his alliance with Native Americans and the British during the American Revolution. Ohio Outdoor Historical Drama Association, Inc., P.O. Box 450, New Philadelphia, OH 44663. Phone: (330) 364-5111; Box Office: (330) 339-1132

UNTO THESE HILLS

Kermit Hunter, playwright; Jack F. Kilpatrick and McCrae Hardy, composers
From the arrival in the Appalachian Mountains of Spanish explorer
Hernando DeSoto in 1540, to the removal of the Cherokee Indians to
Oklahoma along the tragic Trail of Tears, this drama paints a vivid portrait
of the Eastern Band of Cherokee and their brave leaders, Junaluska, Tsali
and Sequoyah, who fought for survival. Cherokee Historical Association,
P.O. Box 398, Cherokee, NC 28719. Administration and Box Office (toll
free): (866) 554-4557

THE WATAUGANS

Ronnie Day, playwright; Jon Ruetz, composer
The Wataugans, which depicts the early settlement of northeast Tennessee,
is performed in the Fort Watauga Amphitheatre, within earshot of historic
Sycamore Shoals on the Watauga River. This 18th-century settlement
comes to life on the site of the Watauga Association, described by
Theodore Roosevelt as "where liberty began when free men established the
first democratic government." Watauga Historical Association–Sycamore
Shoals State Park, 1651 West Elk Avenue, Elizabethton, TN 37643.
Administration and Box Office: (423) 543-5808

YOUNG ABE LINCOLN

Billy Edd Wheeler, playwright-composer
Filled with music and song, *Young Abe Lincoln* portrays this country's six-
teenth president as a young man living with his family in the Indiana
territory during the years 1816 to 1830, and highlights his devotion to
learning, the loss of his mother, and his travels down the Mississippi River
to New Orleans. *Young Abe Lincoln*, c/o University of Southern Indiana,
8600 University Blvd., Evansville, IN 47712-3596. Phone: (812) 465-1668;
Box Office: (800) 264-4ABE

Religious Dramas

This category includes versions of the Passion Play, which dramatizes significant events in the life of Christ and is based on the text of the Bible; and the Mormon drama, which chronicles the founding and early history of the Mormon church based on events described in the Bible and in the Book of Mormon, a scriptural text of the Church of Jesus Christ of Latter-day Saints published in 1830.

BLACK HILLS PASSION PLAY
Josef Meier, translator
With a summer season which began in Spearfish, South Dakota, in 1939, the *Black Hills Passion Play* is one of this country's best-known dramatizations of the last seven days in the life of Christ. Amphitheatre Affiliates, Inc., P.O. Box 489, Spearfish, SD 57783. Phone: (605) 642-2648; Box Office: (605) 642-2646

THE GREAT PASSION PLAY
Tom Jones, playwright; revised by Don Berrigan; Phil Perkins, composer
Accurately based on the Old Testament prophecies and the New Testatment accounts of Christ's life, death, and resurrection, *The Great Passion Play* portrays the significant events in the last days of Jesus of Nazareth. The Elna M. Smith Foundation, P.O. Box 471, Eureka Springs, AR 72632. Phone: (479) 253-8559; Box Office: (479) 253-9200 or toll free (800) 882-7529

THE GREAT NORTHWEST PASSION PLAY
Steve K. Munsey, playwright
This religious drama portrays the ministry of Jesus Christ, His baptism, the miracles He performed, His betrayal and trial before Pilate, the Crucifixion and Resurrection. The Amphitheatre, 14422 Meridian Street E, Puyallup, WA 98375. Administration and Box Office: (253) 848-3411

THE HILL CUMORAH PAGEANT
Orson Scott Card, playwright; Crawford Gates, composer
Taking its name from the hill in New York state where, according to Mormon doctrine, the Angel Moroni delivered metal plates of the Book of

Mormon to Joseph Smith, the pageant dramatizes ten stories from the Bible and the Book of Mormon. Church of Jesus Christ of Latter-day Saints, 66 Old Country Lane, Fairport, NY 14450. Phone: (585) 388-3864; Box Office: (315) 597-6808

THE LIVING WORD

Frank Roughton Harvey, playwright; revised by Mark Pedro

Beginning with the Sermon on the Mount, *The Living Word* reflects on the last three years of the life of Christ, with dramatic depictions of Palm Sunday, the Last Supper, Gethsemane, Pilate's court, the Crucifixion and the Resurrection. The Living Word Board, P.O. Box 1481, Cambridge, OH 43725. Administration and Box Office: (740) 439-2761

MORMON MIRACLE PAGEANT

Grace Johnson, playwright

Staged on the Manti Temple Hill in Utah by a cast of five hundred, this pageant recounts the struggle faced by Mormons following publication of the Book of Mormon in 1830, and tells of their migration from Nauvoo, Illinois, to Utah's Sanpete County in 1849. Church of Jesus Christ of Latter-day Saints, P.O. Box 155, Manti, UT 84642. Phone: (888) 255-8860; Box Office: (435) 835-3000

NARROWAY PRODUCTIONS—FISHES AND LOAVES: THE STORIES JESUS TOLD

K. Rebecca Martin, playwright

A dramatization of the parables (miniature plays taken from everyday life) Jesus told people to help them understand God and what His kingdom or reign is like.

TWO THIEVES AND A SAVIOR

K. Rebecca Martin, playwright

Two Thieves and a Savior dramatizes how two thieves, searching for treasure, follow Christ and are crucified with Him. It is there that one of them finds what he is looking for.

THE DELIVERER

K. Rebecca Martin, playwright; Yvonne H. Clark, composer

Willing to lose his life for his religion, Barabbas finds himself fighting the God he defends. In his attempt to deliver his people from Rome, Barabbas discovers he is the one in need of a Deliverer.

ANNO DOMINI
K. Rebecca Martin, playwright; Yvonne H. Clark, composer
The story of Stephen, the first recorded Christian martyr.
LORD OF LIGHT
K. Rebecca Martin, playwright, Yvonne H. Clark, composer
NarroWay's portrayal of the Resurrection. NarroWay Productions, Inc.,
2175 Gethsemane Court, Fort Mill, SC 29715. Phone: (803) 802-2300;
Box Office: (888) 437-7473

THE NAUVOO PAGEANT
David Warner, playwright
This pageant commemorates the birth of John Smith, prophet and founder
of the Church of Jesus Christ of Latter-day Saints. Navoo Restoration Inc.,
Box 215, Nauvoo, IL 62354. Phone: (800) 453-0022, ext. 315; Box Office:
(800) 453-0022, ext. 324

THE PASSION PLAY IN THE SMOKIES
Mark R. Pedro, author
This dramatic musical presents the life, death, and Resurrection of Jesus
Christ, combining authentic sets and costumes, live animals, and Hebrew
dance. Crown of Thorns Ministry and Chilhowee Baptist Association, 1549
Deer Browse Way, Sevierville, TN 37876. Phone: (865) 908-8904; Box
Office: (865) 982-0499

THE PROMISE
Jan Dargatz, playwright; Gary Rhodes, composer
As a grandfather and his grandchildren begin to talk about life, biblical
characters appear. This religious musical drama dramatizes significant
events in the life of Christ, from His birth through His ascension. The
Promise in Glen Rose, Inc., P.O. Box 2460, Glen Rose, TX, 76043. Phone:
(254) 897-3926; Box Office: (800) 687-2661

300+ THEATER OPPORTUNITIES YOU SELDOM HEAR ABOUT IN MAJOR TRADE MAGAZINES

Murder mystery cafés, glitzy cruise ship theaters, and a wild assortment of related dinner theater, touring theater, and theme park entertainments offer employment opportunities in virtually every area of the theater, including producing, direction, design, production, construction, costuming, acting, dance, and musical performance. If your interests and tastes include popular entertainment, musical entertainment, and contracts that might include a food plan with your paycheck, the possibilities are extensive!

25+ Cruise Line Producers

Even the sublime Cirque du Soleil has joined the "at sea" business of sailing entertainment. Since cruise ships navigate the world 365 days a year featuring actors, singers, dancers, magicians, musicians, comedians, and story-tellers providing welcome breaks from the buffet lines, this might be your best chance for exotic travel. With the most popular cruises visiting Alaska's glaciers, Europe's historic capitals, Russia's palaces, Greece's magical islands, and the glorious waterfalls and fjords of Scandinavia, there are perks that might be even better than the salary and stateroom. Having sailed to all of these spots myself, I've enjoyed the combination of "Vegas-style Shows," "Broadway Musical Revues," and "MTV-wannabe" productions that dominate the entertainment and I am always surprised by the quirky specialty shows that spotlight unique individual performances and group exhibitions reminiscent of Vaudeville.

Although some cruise lines book their own entertainment for their travels, many use entertainment agencies, booking agencies, independent contractors, and casting agents to help in their search for talent and productions. If you are interested, it's best to keep an eye on *Back Stage East* and *West* and all of the "10 Pertinent Publications" mentioned earlier in this book. It may also be useful to check directly with the cruise lines.

Web sites devoted to cruise ship jobs offer a very positive view of working at sea. However, before signing a contract, most theater professionals would suggest talking to past cruise ship entertainers and employees to make sure that cruising is right for you.

Selected Major Cruise Lines

CARNIVAL CRUISE LINES, www.carnival.com

CELEBRITY CRUISES, www.celebrity.com

COSTA CRUISE LINES, www.costacruises.com

CRYSTAL CRUISES, www.crystalcruises.com

CUNARD LINE, www.cunard.com

DISNEY CRUISE LINES, www.disneycruise.com

HOLLAND AMERICA LINE, www.hollandamerica.com

NORWEGIAN CRUISE LINE, www.ncl.com

ORIENT LINES, www.orientlines.com

PRINCESS CRUISES, www.princess.com

REGENT SEVEN SEAS CRUISES, www.rssc.com

ROYAL CARIBBEAN CRUISE LINE, www.royalcaribbean.com

SEABOURN CRUISE LINE, www.seabourn.com

SILVERSEA CRUISES, www.silversea.com

Selected Cruise Line Agents and Producers

ANITA MANN PRODUCTIONS, www.anitamannproductions.com (Santa Monica, CA)

BIG BEAT PRODUCTIONS, INC., www.bigbeatproductions.com (Coral Springs, FL)

BLUE MOON TALENT, INC., www.bluemoontalent.com (Evergreen, CO)

BRAMSON ENTERTAINMENT BUREAU, www.bramson.com (New York, NY)

BROADWAY BOUND, www.broadwayboundinc.com (New York, NY)

CIRQUE DU SOLEIL, www.cirquedusoleil.com (Montreal, Canada)

FIRST CLASS ENTERTAINMENT, www.gotofirstclass.com (Maplewood, NJ)

GREG THOMPSON PRODUCTIONS, www.gregthompsonproductions.com (Seattle, WA)

JEAN ANN RYAN PRODUCTIONS, www.jeanannryanproductions.com (Fort Lauderdale, FL)

MIKE MALONEY ENTERTAINMENT, www.mmec.com (Las Vegas, NV)

PETER GREY TERHUNE PRESENTS, www.pgtpi.com (Cape Canaveral, FL)

SPOTLIGHT ENTERTAINMENT, www.barryball.com (Miami, FL)

STILETTO ENTERTAINMENT, www.stilettoentertainment.com (Inglewood, CA)

40+ Dinner Theaters

Historically, dinner theaters represent the only home-based professional theater operation in many American cities and have nurtured loyal and dedicated followings. Opportunities for directors, designers, dancers, singers, musicians, actors, and production personnel abound. The National Dinner Theatre Association (NDTA) lists many producers.

The NDTA can be written at NDTA Audition Office, 3925 Sherman Blvd., Des Moines, IA, 50310. The telephone number is (515) 252-1942, the fax is (515) 252-1942. You can e-mail them at goodone@mac.com. Their Web site is: www.ndta.com.

Founded in 1978, the NDTA holds auditions and conferences annually and, in its own words, "includes some of the top theatrical producers in the country (both union and non-union)." NDTA provides information and networking potential and holds conferences twice a year. The annual auditions are held at the spring conference for performers from across the United States.

NDTA members must be professional (i.e., hire performers) and be owners, operators, or producers of a dinner theater that is a full-time operation with at least eight months of productions annually. NDTA members, listed below, may be accessed through direct links on the Web site.

ALHAMBRA DINNER THEATRE

12000 Beach Blvd., Jacksonville, FL 32246
BOX OFFICE: (904) 641-1212 or toll free (800) 688-7469
WEB SITE: www.alhambradinnertheatre.com

ARIZONA BROADWAY THEATRE

7701 West Paradise Lane, Peoria, AZ 85382
PHONE: (623) 776-8400; FAX: (623) 776-9974
WEB SITE: www.azbroadwaytheatre.com

THE ARMORY INC.

10 South High Street, P.O. Box 8038, Janesville, WI 53548
BOX OFFICE: (608) 741-7400; FAX: (608) 531-0188
WEB SITE: www.janesvillearmory.com

THE BARN DINNER THEATRE

120 Stage Coach Trail, Greensboro, NC 27409
PHONE: (336) 292-2211 or toll free: (800) 668-1764; FAX: (336) 294-8663
WEB SITE: www.barndinner.com

THE BARTOLOTTA RESTAURANTS
6005 West Martin Drive, Wauwatosa, WI 53213
PHONE: (414) 258-7885; FAX: (414) 258-8313
WEB SITE: www.bartolottas.com

BLACK BEAR JAMBOREE DINNER & SHOW
119 Music Road, Pigeon Forge, TN 37863
BOX OFFICE: (865) 908-SHOW
WEB SITE: www.blackbearjamboree.com

BRAVO! DINNER PLAYHOUSE
1476 West Route 6, Ottawa, IL 61350
Box Office: (815) 433-4331

BROADWAY PALM DINNER THEATRE
1380 Colonial Blvd., Fort Myers, FL 33907
PHONE: (239) 278-4422; FAX: (239) 278-5664
WEB SITE: www.broadwaypalm.com

BROADWAY PALM WEST DINNER THEATRE
5247 East Brown Road, Mesa, AZ 85205
PHONE: (480) 325-6700; FAX: (480) 325-6746
WEB SITE: www.broadwaypalmwest.com

CANDLELIGHT PAVILION DINNER THEATER
455 Foothill Blvd., Claremont, CA 91711
PHONE: (909) 626-1254
WEB SITE: www.candlelightpavilion.com

CHAFFIN'S BARN DINNER THEATRE
8204 Highway 100, Nashville, TN 37221
PHONE: (615) 646-9977; FAX: (615) 662-5439
WEB SITE: www.dinnertheatre.com

CIRCA '21 DINNER PLAYHOUSE
1828 Third Avenue, Rock Island, IL 61201
PHONE: (309) 786-7733 ext. 2
WEB SITE: www.circa21.com

CLOCK TOWER DINNER THEATRE
82 River View Drive, Verona, VA 24482
PHONE: (540) 849-9097

CONKLIN'S BARN II DINNER THEATRE
P.O. Box 310, Goodfield, IL 61742
PHONE: (309) 965-2545
WEB SITE: www.barn2.com

CROWN UPTOWN PROFESSIONAL DINNER THEATRE
3207 East Douglas Avenue, Wichita, KS 67218
BOX OFFICE: (316) 681-1566; FAX: (316) 681-1925
WEB SITE: www.crownuptown.com

DERBY DINNER PLAYHOUSE
525 Marriott Drive, Clarksville, IN 47129
PHONE: (812) 288-2632; FAX: (812) 288-2636
WEB SITE: www.derbydinner.com

DUTCH APPLE DINNER THEATRE
510 Centerville Road, Lancaster, PA 17601
PHONE: (717) 898-1900
WEB SITE: www.dutchapple.com

EMPIRE THEATRE COMPANY
2825 North Avenue, Grand Junction, CO 81501
PHONE: (970) 248-9091

THE FIRESIDE, INC. DINNER THEATRE
1131 Janesville Avenue, P.O. Box 7, Fort Atkinson, WI 53538
BOX OFFICE: (800) 477-9505
WEB SITE: www.firesidetheatre.com

GADE 2000
534 East 400 South, Saint George, UT 84770
BOX OFFICE: (902) 836-4697

GARBEAU'S DINNER THEATRE
12401 Folsom Boulevard, Rancho Cordova, CA 95742
PHONE: (916) 985-6361
WEB SITE: www.garbeaus.com

THE GASLIGHT DINNER THEATRE
The Renaissance Center, 855 Highway 46 South, Dickson, TN 37055
PHONE: (615) 740-5600
WEB SITE: www.rcenter.org

HUNTERDON HILLS PLAYHOUSE
88 Route 173 West, Hampton, NJ 08827
PHONE: (800) 447-7313
WEB SITE: www.hhplayhouse.com

JACKSON HOLE PLAYHOUSE
135 Deloney Street, P.O. Box 2788, Jackson, WY 83001
BOX OFFICE: (307) 733-6994
WEB SITE: www.jhplayhouse.com

MARRIOTT THEATRE
Ten Marriott Drive, Lincolnshire, IL 60069
BOX OFFICE: (847) 634-0200; FAX: (847) 634-7022
WEB SITE: www.marriotttheatre.com

MURDER MYSTERY INC.
18 Hollywood Place, Huntington, NY 11743
BOX OFFICE: (631) 673-4979
WEB SITE: www.murdermysteryinc.com

MURRY'S DINNER PLAYHOUSE
6323 Colonel Glenn Road, Little Rock, AR 72204
BOX OFFICE: (501) 562-3131
WEB SITE: www.murrysdinnerplayhouse.com

MYSTERY DINNER PLAYHOUSE
2025 East Main Street, Suite 206, Richmond, VA 23223
BOX OFFICE: (888) 471-4802; FAX: (804) 649-7419
WEB SITE: www.mysterydinner.com

OOPS INTERACTIVE DINNER THEATRE, INC.

P.O. Box 270447, Vadnais Heights, MN 55127

PHONE: (651) 777-4150

WEB SITE: www.oopstheatre.com

PRATHER THEATRES

WEB SITE: www.prathertheatres.com (see Web site for individual theaters)

RAINBOW DINNER THEATRE

Route 30 East, Box 56, Paradise, PA 17562

BOX OFFICE: (717) 687-4301

WEB SITE: www.rainbowdinnertheatre.com

THE RIVERSIDE INN

One Fountain Avenue, Cambridge Springs, PA 16403

BOX OFFICE: (800) 964-5173; FAX: (814) 398-8161

WEB SITE: www.theriversideinn.com

SLEUTHS MYSTERY DINNER SHOWS

8267 International Drive, Orlando, FL 32819

PHONE: (407) 363-1985

WEB SITE: www.sleuths.com

THE STATION DINNER THEATRE

4940 Peach Street, Erie, PA 16509

PHONE AND BOX OFFICE: (814) 864-2022

WEB SITE: www.canterburyfeast.com

THREE LITTLE BAKERS DINNER THEATRE

3540 Three Little Bakers Blvd., Wilmington, DE 19808

BOX OFFICE: (800) 368-3303; FAX: (302) 452-2535

WEB SITE: www.tlbinc.com

TOMMY GUN'S GARAGE

2114 South Wabash, Chicago, IL 60616

BOX OFFICE: (773) RAT-A-TAT

WEB SITE: www.tommygunsgarage.com

WELK RESORT SAN DIEGO THEATRE

8860 Lawrence Welk Drive, Escondido, CA 92026

BOX OFFICE: (800) 932-9355; FAX: (760) 749-9537

WEB SITE: www.welkresort.com

WESTCHESTER BROADWAY THEATRE

75 Clearbrook Road, Elmsford, NY 10523

PHONE: (914) 592-2268; BOX OFFICE: (914) 592-2222; FAX: (914) 592-6047

WEB SITE: www.broadwaytheatre.com

WOHLFAHRT HAUS DINNER THEATRE

170 Malin Drive, Wytheville, VA 24382

PHONE AND BOX OFFICE: (888) 950-3382; FAX: (276) 223-0721

WEB SITE: www.wohlfahrthaus.com

60+ Touring Theater Companies

Whether it's Baltimore's Funkopolis Central (www.funkopolis.org), an experimental touring theater that creates original plays by melding urban and tribal experiences, or Blue Lake, California's Dell'Arte, Inc. (www.dellarte.com), a touring theater company committed to physical theater traditions, touring theater opportunities still exist for theater professionals who like to stay on the move.

Just a few of the other American theaters committed to touring include Aesop's Touring Theatre Company, The Act!vated Storytellers (www.activated-storytellers.com), Adventist Christian Theatre (http://members.aol.com/actbrett/home.html), American Magic-Lantern Theatre (www.magiclanternshows.com), Atlantic Coast Theatre (www.atlantic-coast-theatre.com), Elevator Repair Service (www.elevator.org), GMT Productions (www.gmtproductions.com), Guerrilla Girls On Tour (www.guerrillagirlsontour.com), Hampstead Players (www.hamplay.com), Mad River Theatre Works (www.madrivertheater.org), National Players (www.nationalplayers.org), Paper Bag Players (www.paperbagplayers.org), Traveling Jewish Theatre (www.atjt.com), and St. Louis Black Repertory (www.stlouisblackrep.com).

The National Endowment for the Arts' Shakespeare in American Communities project and funding has inspired a number of companies to temporarily hit the road, but others tour on an ongoing basis to tell their stories and find new audiences. Direct links to the theaters mentioned below may be found in the 400+ TCG Theaters chapter (p. 280), or on the National Endowment for the Arts Web site (www.shakespeareinamerican communities.org). Many are TCG or LORT members. The largest Shakespeare tour in American history comprised: Alaska Theatre of Youth, Eccentric Theatre Company, Edgware, American Players Theatre, Asolo Theatre Company, Cincinnati Playhouse in the Park, Hartford Stage Company, Idaho Shakespeare Festival, Indiana Repertory Theatre, Montana Shakespeare in the Parks, People's Light & Theatre Company, Perseverance Theatre, San Diego Repertory Theatre, Shakespeare & Company, The Shakespeare Festival at Tulane, Shakespeare Santa Cruz, The Shakespeare Theatre, The Shakespeare Theatre of New Jersey, The Theater at Monmouth, Utah Shakespearean Festival, Will Geer Theatricum Botanicum, Yale Repertory Theatre, A Noise Within, The Acting Company, Actors Theatre of Louisville, American Shakespeare Center, The Aquila Theatre Company, Arkansas Repertory Theatre, The Atlanta Shakespeare Company, Fairbanks Shakespeare Theatre, Georgia Shakespeare Festival, Idaho Shakespeare Festival, Long Wharf Theatre, Nevada Shakespeare Company, The Old Globe, Oregon Shakespeare Festival, The Pennsylvania Shakespeare Festival, San Francisco Shakespeare Festival, Seattle Shakespeare Company, Shakespeare Dallas, Shakespeare Festival of St. Louis, Shakespeare Festival/LA, Teatro Avante, Trinity Repertory Company, The Warehouse Theatre, Artists Repertory Theatre, Alabama Shakespeare Festival, and Chicago Shakespeare Theater.

100+ Murder Mystery Theaters and Innovative New Live Theater Opportunities

There's *Here's Killing You, Kid*; *Frankly Scarlett, You're Dead!*; and *Marriage Can Be Murder* at the Great Smoky Mountain Murder Mystery Theatre in Pigeon Forge, Tennessee—and that's just the beginning! Murder mystery theaters are among the hottest, fastest-growing theater industries in America and you might want to check out the 6,110,00 listings in the Google directory for "Murder Mystery Theater."

Comedy Theater Productions, Teambonding™; Experience the Power of Play!, Scaventures; Team Building Scavenger and Treasure Hunts; and Mystery Café are just three examples of the innovative industries (check out www.mysterycafe.com) that have been developed by one company (Comedy Theater Productions). A whole new world is out there for theater folks, and this book doesn't even touch on video game and other digital media employment opportunities! For example, Comedy Theater Productions, founded in 1986, "combines interactive events, athletic challenges, and theater-based games to increase social interactivity." From America's first murder mystery dinner theater, the Mystery Cafe in Cambridge, Massachusetts, to the licensing of the business-to-theater producers in 21 cities in the United States, the genre has taken off and opened doors to a whole new generation of actors, directors, designers, and craftspersons.

You can find state-by-state listings of over 100 murder mystery dinner theaters at www.partypop.com/Categories/Murder_Mystery_Dinner_Theatre.html. More than 60 mystery dinner theaters can be found in the Yahoo! Directory: http://search.yahoo.com/search/dir?p=Mystery+Dinner+Theaters&srch=. You'll also find over two dozen listings at www.mysteryplayers.com

110+ Theme and Amusement Parks

Over 75 million people attend America's top 10 theme parks on an annual basis, so if you dream of dressing up as a cuddly mammal, drool at the thought of singing and dancing in a Wild West saloon, or just enjoy surrounding yourself with sunshine, roller coasters and silly families, theme parks are for you. There are hundreds of theme parks and amusement parks in America. Florida and California have at least 20 playful parks each, including Orlando's The Holy Land Experience and Tampa's Weeki Wachee Springs (where you could be the live Mermaid), and SeaWorld San Diego (where you can hang out with the real animals).

Theme parks are generally looking to hire street entertainers, tour guides, jugglers, directors, designers, choreographers, stage managers, impersonators, choreographers, musicians, dancers, emcees, voice-over specialists, prop masters, costumers, carpenters, sound engineers, lighting technicians, and administrators to mention a few of the common positions.

America's largest parks, according to Arthur Levine's theme park research, include Florida's The Magic Kingdom at Walt Disney World, California's Disneyland, Florida's Epcot at Walt Disney World, Disney-MGM Studios at Walt Disney World, Disney's Animal Kingdom at Walt Disney World, Universal Studios at Universal Orlando, Islands of Adventure at Universal Orlando, Disney's California Adventures in California, SeaWorld Florida, and Universal Studios Hollywood. The 110+ theme and amusement parks are listed alphabetically and by state with direct links at http://themeparks.about.com.

50+ UNIVERSITIES AFFILIATED WITH PROFESSIONAL THEATERS

UNIVERSITY/RESIDENT THEATRE ASSOCIATION
1560 Broadway, Suite 712, New York, NY 10036
PHONE: (212) 221-1130; FAX: (212) 869-2752
E-MAIL: info@urta.com
WEB SITE: www.urta.com

A key resource for emerging theater professionals is also the country's oldest and largest consortium of professional theater-training graduate programs and associated professional theater companies. The professional companies these universities with graduate programs are "consorting with" may be LORT and/or TCG, and they offer the opportunity for graduate students to develop a network, meet directors, designers, Equity actors, Equity stage managers, and others in the field, and to take classes from some of the best theater-training faculty in the United States.

Here's a thought for you: If you are a 20-year-old woman just graduating from college and heading into professional theater, you are competing with the thousands of other recent college graduates, as well as with all the Equity professionals who can still play roles in the 18-to-25 age range. Your key "competitive edge and venue" at 20 is your audition (plus perhaps your enthusiastic recommendations and support from your college faculty members). Of course, you are generally competing for the *one* ingenue or *one* young character woman available in the typical classical play or new play—where there are, all too often, 15 male roles and three women's roles (two of which will most likely be cast from former employees).

On the other hand, if you are successful in your graduate school auditions and are offered a scholarship in a reputable graduate school, you have two to three years to make friends with other professionals and prove yourself on stage (competing against younger undergraduate students). At the same time, you are presumably receiving advanced training, maturing in the eyes of casting directors, and developing your résumé and skills. Finally, instead of being judged on a three-minute audition, you have been networking with actors, directors, and artistic directors who will hopefully remember you from your larger body of work. Graduate school is well worth considering. Make sure you read the debate on education and training in other sections of this book.

U/RTA helps make these connections and nurtures relationships between students, graduate schools, and professional theater.

History and Services

Founded in 1969, U/RTA provides a variety of service, management, and informational programs to its members, and to non-member students, theater professionals, and producing companies, while serving as the primary liaison between the professional and educational theaters. U/RTA encourages the professional training of artists, and of future teachers in the performing arts for all levels of education.

Services include the National Unified Auditions and Interviews held each winter in New York, Chicago, and San Francisco, with candidates coming from around the world. Students interested in acting, design (scenic, lighting, costume, sound), directing, theater technology, stage management, playwriting, and theater management, are provided the opportunity to vie for numerous positions with graduate schools, and for seasonal employment with summer theater companies, Shakespeare festivals, and other professional producing organizations. Membership in U/RTA is *not* required for students to participate.

U/RTA also has a Contract Management Program that offers a complete contracting and employment system to organizations that, for many different reasons, are unable to directly engage professional, union artists.

Finally, U/RTA negotiates and maintains important agreements with Actors' Equity Association (AEA), the Society of Stage Directors and Choreographers (SSDC), and United Scenic Artists (USA), which are geared toward the needs of resident and university theaters. These agreements make it possible to successfully integrate professional actors, stage managers, directors, choreographers, and designers with theater students both on stage and in the classroom.

U/RTA members and Web sites include (*in alphabetical order*):

UNIVERSITY OF ALABAMA, www.as.ua.edu/theatre

ALABAMA SHAKESPEARE FESTIVAL, www.asf.net/ASF.html

UNIVERSITY OF ARIZONA–ARIZONA REPERTORY THEATRE,
  http://arts.music.arizona.edu/theatre

UNIVERSITY OF CALIFORNIA, IRVINE, http://drama.arts.uci.edu

UNIVERSITY OF CALIFORNIA, LOS ANGELES, www.tft.ucla.edu

CALIFORNIA INSTITUTE OF THE ARTS, www.calarts.edu

UNIVERSITY OF CINCINNATI COLLEGE/CONSERVATORY OF MUSIC,
  www.ccm.uc.edu

UNIVERSITY OF CONNECTICUT/CONNECTICUT REPERTORY THEATRE,
  www.sfa.uconn.edu

FLORIDA STATE UNIVERSITY, www.theatre.fsu.edu

FLORIDA STATE UNIVERSITY/ASOLO CONSERVATORY FOR ACTOR TRAINING,
  www.asolo.org/fsuconsv/fsu-intro.htm

UNIVERSITY OF FLORIDA, www.arts.ufl.edu/theatreanddance

ILLINOIS STATE UNIVERSITY/ILLINOIS SHAKESPEARE FESTIVAL, www.ilstu.edu

UNIVERSITY OF ILLINOIS, URBANA/CHAMPAIGN, www.theatre.uiuc.edu

INDIANA UNIVERSITY, www.indiana.edu/~thtr

UNIVERSITY OF IOWA/IOWA SUMMER REPERTORY, www.uiowa.edu/~theatre

UNIVERSITY OF MARYLAND, www.inform.umd.edu/ARHU/Depts/Theatre

UNIVERSITY OF MINNESOTA, http://cla.umn.edu/theatre

UNIVERSITY OF MISSOURI, KANSAS CITY/MISSOURI REPERTORY THEATRE,
  http://iml.umkc.edu/theater

UNIVERSITY OF MONTANA/MONTANA REPERTORY THEATRE,
  www.sfa.umt.edu/drama

UNIVERSITY OF NEBRASKA, LINCOLN/NEBRASKA REPERTORY,
  www.unl.edu/TheatreArts

UNIVERSITY OF NEVADA, LAS VEGAS/NEVADA CONSERVATORY THEATRE,
  www.unlv.edu/Colleges/Fine_Arts/Theatre/

NORTHERN ILLINOIS UNIVERSITY/SUMMER NITE, www.vpa.niu.edu/theater

NORTHWESTERN UNIVERSITY, www.communication.northwestern.edu/theatre

THE OHIO STATE UNIVERSITY, www.the.ohio-state.edu

OHIO UNIVERSITY/CINCINNATI PLAYHOUSE IN THE PARK,
  www.ohio.edu/theater

PENNSYLVANIA STATE UNIVERSITY/PENNSYLVANIA CENTRE STAGE,
  www.theatre.psu.edu/

PURDUE UNIVERSITY, www.purdue.edu/theatre

UNIVERSITY OF SOUTH CAROLINA, www.cla.sc.edu/THSP/index.html

SOUTHERN METHODIST UNIVERSITY, www.smu.edu

TEMPLE UNIVERSITY, www.temple.edu/theater/mfa.html
UNIVERSITY OF TEXAS—AUSTIN, www.utexas.edu/cofa/theatre/
UNIVERSITY OF VIRGINIA, www.virginia.edu/drama/index.htm
UNIVERSITY OF WASHINGTON, http://depts.washington.edu/uwdrama
WEST VIRGINIA UNIVERSITY, www.wvu.edu/~theatre/index.htm
UNIVERSITY OF WISCONSIN—MADISON, www.wisc.edu

U/RTA associated theater companies include:

ILLINOIS SHAKESPEARE FESTIVAL, www.arts.ilstu.edu
IOWA SUMMER REP, www.uiowa.edu/~theatre
KANSAS CITY REPERTORY THEATRE, http://cei.haag.umkc.edu/theater/index.html
NEBRASKA REPERTORY THEATRE, www.unl.edu/rep
PENNSYLVANIA CENTRE STAGE, www.pacentrestage.psu.edu
SUMMERNITE FESTIVAL, www.niu.edu

PART VI

SURVIVAL STRATEGIES AND DIRECTORIES FOR LIFELONG PLANNING

12 TIPS FOR STRESS REDUCTION: STAYING FIT FOR LIFE

"Live as long as you can. Die when you can't help it."

James Brown

Every opening night is a serious, strenuous, soul-searching series of deadlines if you work in the arts. In regional theater, artistic directors strive to achieve their vision and satisfy, sway, or soothe guest directors, actors, designers, board members, and critics with each new production. Actors, designers, and craftspeople work mightily to make directors and audiences happy while remaining true to the playwright and committed to their own sense of artistic integrity. Marketing directors have sky-high sales goals, development directors are on the line to meet wildly optimistic fundraising goals, and production managers coordinate the complex creation of hopefully dazzling scenery, costumes, lights, and sound with a generally unrealistic budget that would make most Broadway or movie producers gasp (or laugh . . . or cry)! Add the realities and frailties of a personal life to a highly charged, competitive work place, throw in high rates of unemployment, overwork, and low pay, and the arts are oftentimes a prime breeding ground for stress.

Unfortunately, few nonprofit arts organizations employ a human resources staff or even a specific individual who handles personnel matters. Most professional theaters have a company manager who is burdened with housing, transportation, scheduling, and contract assistance, with little time to tend to the morale of the company. Artistic directors, managing directors, and business managers oftentimes "handle" or "deal" with tense contract concerns or unhappy employees. Stage managers usually do their best to keep actors on track, and individual supervisors tend to bear the brunt of the personnel load. Actors are usually left to handle their own personnel problems, and if you are the Equity deputy—*Look out*! This is not an ideal situation and there's a reason that most businesses and corporations have a personnel office or a human resources division. It's important that employees work within their realm of training and experience, and few arts employees are hired, first and foremost, for their personal counseling skills, medical diagnostic training, or first-aid expertise.

With this in mind, it's crucial for artists, production personnel, and arts managers to know and communicate their expectations and personal boundaries. It's also a good idea for everyone to be familiar with referral sources (local counselors, doctors, psychiatrists, psychologists, etc.) and options when it comes to "handling personnel matters" vs. "personal counseling" or "offering advice."

1   Understand Your Limitations

As an individual, work to clarify the source of your stress and determine if the problem is within your control. Agonizing over concerns that are impossible for you to influence is most likely an exercise in futility. Are the sources of your stress related to fear, anger, anxiety, depression, low self-esteem, passivity, conflicts with friends, or control issues at work? Or are they related to world events, ethical concerns, family frustrations, or current or recent crises?

It is certainly appropriate to be helpful, provide a listening ear, and assist your friends, colleagues, or employees within your level of experience, training, and comfort. However, whether you are a supervisor, employee, friend, or colleague, make sure you understand your limits as a counselor and as an individual. If you are an employer, devise a company referral list of professional services for your staff to use when an employee's stress levels stray "beyond the norm."

> "Anger is a momentary madness, so control your passion or it will control you."
>
> Horace

2   Pay Attention to Number One

If you are in poor mental or physical health, it's difficult for you to be of help to anyone else. See your doctor for a complete physical and make sure you are healthy, eating appropriately, and meeting your sleep needs.

> "Adversity is the first path to truth."
>
> Lord Byron

3 Work Out

Physical activity and exercise help break up the day and may help you sort out myriad problems, achieve perspective, and relieve a host of psychological and physical challenges. If you've dedicated your life to the arts, you've certainly been taught that the mind and body work together in wonderful and mysterious ways. A consistent workout regimen may also assist with weight control, lowering cholesterol, and sound eating and sleeping habits. A brisk walk, yoga class, 50-minute racquetball game, or biking to work could make all the difference in the world.

4 A Little Research Goes a Long Way

Every Borders, Barnes & Noble, and downtown bookstore has a plethora of self-help, stress-reducing techniques. Many of them may work for you. In addition, many community centers and nearby universities offer stress reduction seminars, and the more progressive healthcare providers are scheduling ongoing stress reduction programs as part of their proactive health-screening services.

5 Accept Reality … or Change Your Realities

Don't waste time fighting institutional policies, horrid employers, or events that you can't control. Sometimes it's best to simply cut your losses and move on. Working with unethical, rude, or wildly obnoxious colleagues or employers can impact your day-to-day attitude, self-image, and long-term health. If you can make a difference and create change and a positive work environment, more power to you! If your work environment is getting the best of you and influencing your health and psyche, it's time to step back and evaluate your values, goals, and strategic plans.

6 Hunt for a Mentor and Develop a Support Group

Sometimes, just having someone or a group of people you respect with whom you can discuss issues, try out ideas, explore the corporate culture, share concerns, or help with priorities will make all the difference. Ask for help.

> "Never go to a doctor whose office plants are dead."
>
> Erma Bombeck

7 Use Those Acting Exercises

Many arts professionals started as actors, dancers, or theater students. Remember those deep-breathing exercises, muscle tension release improvisations, and sensory awareness seminars that seemed so silly in Acting 101 or Beginning Dance? Now is the time to revisit these great stress-reducing techniques that can lighten up your day and add a sense of balance to a tense moment.

8 Look Out for Burnout! Consider a Time-Out

Often, just hiding away, finding quiet time, vacationing, and regaining perspective can work wonders for the battered soul. Monitor sudden weight loss, rise in blood pressure, emotional swings, withdrawal, self-destructive thoughts or actions, feelings of desperation, or physical symptoms (ulcers, teeth-grinding, nail-biting, back pain, colds, flu, rashes, neck pains, headaches, lowered sexual interest, fatigue, reliance on alcohol or drugs, shaking, unusual sweating, or facial tension).

> "Never trouble trouble till trouble troubles you."
>
> Anonymous

9 Choose Your Battles

I once had a colleague who would consistently pick fights with subordinates in the morning, drive to McDonald's at lunch, and argue with the serving staff about cold French fries and long lines, return to work to irritate his direct supervisor, and leave at five every evening to complain to his wife about her housework. His extreme competitiveness; charged, accusatory speech patterns; relentless impatience; and body tension reflected his hyper-stress-filled existence. When he finally mellowed and decided to more carefully select his battles, he was a much happier individual (and do I need to mention the relief of everyone around him)?

10 Know the Big Triggers

Stress lists typically include these "events": death or illness of a family member, marriage, separation, divorce, personal illness or injury, being fired at work, going back to school, pregnancy, supervisor troubles, quitting smoking, change in residence, sexual concerns, financial difficulties, arguments with spouse, work changes, burnout/overwork, sleeping-habit changes, eating habit changes, major holidays, large purchases, family concerns, and legal problems.

11 Don't Play Doctor

Avoid self medication and self-prescribed over-the-counter drugs to temporarily avoid the main problem (which is whatever is causing the stress in the first place). See a doctor. Don't procrastinate!

12 A Mini-list of Stress Relievers

Play soothing music, get a massage, learn to prioritize, limit the hours you work, take a walk in the woods, read adventurous fiction, take a coffee break, go to an upbeat movie, read a little Norman Vincent Peale, think optimistically, question negative thoughts that haunt you, write down everything that's going right in a journal (and review it often), and, finally, believe that your personal best is just around the corner.

> "If I knew I was going to live this long, I'd have taken better care of myself."
>
> Mickey Mantle

A BRIEF DIRECTORY OF THEATER-RELATED LABOR UNIONS, GUILDS, AND ASSOCIATIONS

ACTORS' EQUITY ASSOCIATION (AEA)
New York: (212) 869-8530
WEB SITE: www.actorsequity.org

AMERICAN ALLIANCE FOR THEATRE & EDUCATION
Arizona: (602) 965-6064
WEB SITE: www.aate.com

AMERICAN ARTS ALLIANCE (AAA)
Washington, DC: (202) 207-3850
WEB SITE: www.americanartsalliance.org

AMERICAN FEDERATION OF TELEVISION AND RADIO ARTISTS (AFTRA)
New York: (212) 532-0800
WEB SITE: www.aftra.org

AMERICANS FOR THE ARTS
Washington, DC: (202) 371-2830
WEB SITE: www.artsusa.org

AMERICAN GUILD OF MUSICAL ARTISTS (AGMA)
New York: (212) 265-3687
WEB SITE: www.musicalartists.org

AMERICAN GUILD OF VARIETY ARTISTS (AGVA)
New York: (212) 675-1003
WEB SITE: www.americanguildofvarietyartistsagva.visualnet.com

AMERICAN THEATRE CRITICS ASSOCIATION (ATCA)
Minnesota: (651) 261-7804
WEB SITE: www.americantheatrecritics.org

ASSOCIATION OF FUNDRAISING PROFESSIONALS (AFP)
(formerly the National Society of Fundraising Executives)
Virginia: (703) 684-0540
WEB SITE: www.afpnet.org

ASSOCIATION OF THEATRE IN HIGHER EDUCATION (ATHE)
Colorado: (888) 284-3737; (800) ATHE-737
WEB SITE: www.athe.org

ASSOCIATION OF PERFORMING ARTS PRESENTERS (APAP)
Washington, D.C.: (888) 820-2797
WEB SITE: www/artspresenters/org

ASSOCIATION OF THEATRICAL PRESS AGENTS AND MANAGERS (ATPAM)
New York: (212) 719-3666
WEB SITE: www.atpam.com

BUSINESS COMMITTEE FOR THE ARTS (BCA)
New York: (718) 482-9900
WEB SITE: www.bcainc.org

THE DRAMATISTS GUILD OF AMERICA (DGA)
New York: (212) 398-9366
WEB SITE: www.dramaguild.com

THE FOUNDATION CENTER

New York: (212) 620-4230

WEB SITE: www.fdncenter.org

INSTITUTE OF OUTDOOR DRAMA (IOD)

North Carolina: (919) 962-1328

WEB SITE: www.unc.edu.depts/outdoor/

INTERNATIONAL ALLIANCE OF THEATRICAL STAGE EMPLOYEES (IATSE)

New York: (212) 730-1770

WEB SITE: www.iatsw-intl.org

INTERNATIONAL THEATRE INSTITUTE OF THE UNITED STATES (ITI/US)

New York: (212) 697-5230

WEB SITE: www.tcg.org/frames/iti/fs_iti.htm

LEAGUE OF HISTORIC AMERICAN THEATRES (LHAT)

Baltimore: (410) 659-9533

WEB SITE: www.lhat.org

LEAGUE OF RESIDENT THEATRES (LORT)

New York: (212) 944-1501

WEB SITE: www.lort.org

NATIONAL ALLIANCE FOR MUSICAL THEATRE (NAMT)

New York: (212) 714-6668

WEB SITE: www.namt.net

NATIONAL ASSEMBLY OF STATE ARTS AGENCIES (NASAA)

Washington, D.C.: (202) 347-6352

WEB SITE: www.nasaa-arts.org

NATIONAL ASSOCIATION OF PERFORMING ARTS MANAGERS AND AGENTS (NAPAMA)

New York: (888) 745-8758

WEB SITE: www.napama.org

NATIONAL CENTER FOR NONPROFIT BOARDS

Washington, D.C.: (202) 452-6262

WEB SITE: www.ncnb.org

NATIONAL ENDOWMENT FOR THE ARTS (NEA)

Washington, D.C.: (202) 682-5400

WEB SITE: www.arts.endow.gov

NATIONAL ENDOWMENT FOR THE HUMANITIES (NEH)

Washington, D.C.: (800) 634-1121

WEB SITE: www.neh.fed.us

NATIONAL THEATRE CONFERENCE (NTC)

c/o The Players Club, New York

(212) 475-6116

NON-TRADITIONAL CASTING PROJECT (NTCP)

New York: (212) 730-4750

WEB SITE: www.ntcp.org

SCREEN ACTORS' GUILD (SAG)

Los Angeles: (213) 954-1600

WEB SITE: www.sag.org

SHAKESPEARE THEATRE ASSOCIATION OF AMERICA (STAA)

(713) 743-2930

WEB SITE: www.staaonline.org

SOCIETY OF STAGE DIRECTORS AND CHOREOGRAPHERS (SSDC)

New York: (212) 391-1070

WEB SITE: www.ssdc.org

THEATRE COMMUNICATIONS GROUP (TCG)

New York: (212) 609-2900

WEB SITE: www.tcg.org

THEATRE DEVELOPMENT FUND (TDF)

New York: (212) 221-0885

WEB SITE: www.tdf.org

UNITED STATES INSTITUTE FOR THEATRE TECHNOLOGY (USITT)

New York: (315) 463-6463

WEB SITE: www.usitt.org

UNIVERSITY/RESIDENT THEATRE ASSOCIATION (U/RTA)

New York: (212) 221-1130

WEB SITE: www.urta.com

UNITED SCENIC ARTISTS (USA)

New York: (212) 581-0300

WEB SITE: www.usa829.org

VOLUNTEER LAWYERS FOR THE ARTS (VLA)

New York: (212) 319-2787

WEB SITE: www.vlany.org

PART VII

—◆—

LEAVING A LEGACY

LIVELY STORIES OF MENTORING GLORIES

It's time to write your own book! So many pioneers in regional theater are still around to tell their stories. A few will sit down and commit their thoughts and histories to paper, but many more need the next generation of theater professionals and writers to be their spokesmen. As I've discovered over the past 30+ years that I've been attending and researching regional theaters, these stories are adventurous, poignant, humorous, and heart-breaking. In my truncated "Brief History of Regional Theater," I couldn't begin to mention all the self-made pioneers and dedicated teachers who influenced our generation of theater professionals. But many names sur-faced in my discussions and correspondence with so many of the nation's working theater professionals, and I wanted to share our inheritance from a few of the mentors, role models, and pioneering theater professionals in my interviewees' own words.

> THE QUESTION I POSED IS:
> "ARE THERE KEY FIGURES IN AMERICAN THEATER
> WHO HAVE BEEN CRUCIAL TO YOUR CAREER
> OR INFORMED YOUR WORK?"

"John Houseman sat behind his enormous desk at the Juilliard, looked me in the eye, and said, 'You're good enough. Take the job.' It was my first LORT artistic directorship and I didn't know if I could handle it. John put some small part of his power into me, for which I shall always be thankful. Alan Schneider sat across from me in a Chicago bar and said 'screw 'em, do the shows you want.' I was uncertain about putting Brecht and Beckett in my next season. Alan put some of his courage into me, for which I shall always be thankful. Jean-Louis Barrault told me, 'It's our responsibility to pass along what we've learned to the next generation.' I thanked him; I've tried. I sat in the Guthrie Theater for the first season of that legendary director's productions in Minneapolis and I said out loud to myself, 'I have to do this. At least I have to try.' The list of figures and events that have shaped all our lives and careers stretches out to the crack o' doom. To paraphrase Sartre, 'We are the sum total of our mentors.'"

Tom Markus, Author/Director/Longtime Artistic Director

"I, of course, worked in a number of theaters in the 1980s—God, that's a long time ago . . . I was blessed by being mentored by a number of people, of whom two rise to the top: the late Tom Haas, who was perhaps the most important figure for me, steering me towards graduate school, nurturing me as a director, teaching me how to read text in an uncluttered but heartfelt way; and the late Peter Zeisler, who during my NEA days taught me to see a field, not a string of separate theaters, while teaching me to value concepts of service and leadership."

Ben Cameron, former Executive Director, Theatre Communications Group

"Joe Papp. He dared to do what he thought important. His reward was an audience of interested, earnest, and informed people."

Gilbert Cates, Producing Director, Geffen Playhouse

"Richard Wilbur, Tennessee Williams, Charles Ludlam, Julie Taymor, and David Ives."

Dana Gioia, Chairman, National Endowment for the Arts

"A young and vital Zelda Fichandler with her dream of an Arena Stage, a school teacher named Angus Bowmer with his passion for Shakespeare, an immigrant Brit called Tyrone Guthrie who founded not one but two regional theaters, stand out amongst the hundreds that have played a major role in my love of theater and love for my region of this land. The list could go on and on with Margo Jones, Craig Noel, and Keith Engar adding confirmation to my every decision."

Fred C. Adams, Founder, Utah Shakespearean Festival

"Roger Stevens, Rockefeller Foundation, New York City."

Paul Baker, Co-founder, Dallas Theater Center

"Let's look at *The Kentucky Cycle*. One play (of the nine) was read at New Dramatists and then produced at EST, both in New York City. The rest of the plays were first produced at EST West (in LA) or at two separate workshops at the Mark Taper Forum (thanks to artistic director Gordon Davidson). The play also received readings in Colorado Springs and New Haven. I owe special thanks to Liz Huddle, then artistic director of Seattle's Intiman Theatre, who read *The Kentucky Cycle* on a Friday and called Saturday to say she was going to produce the play, 'even if I have to play the rest of my season on a unit stage.' Which, in fact, she did. The play was later produced at the Mark Taper and then the Kennedy Center before finally arriving on Broadway.

Other places/people in the regional theater who have been crucial to me include Lloyd Richards and The O'Neill Theatre Conference, David Kranes and the Sundance Theatre conference, Jon Jory and the Humana Festival, and Vinny Murphy at Theatre Emory. Most recently, Libby Appel, artistic director at Oregon Shakespeare Festival, has championed my work."

Robert Schenkkan, Playwright

"When we were starting Bay Street and we hit a bumpy period about five years into our development, the great Jack O'Brien said something I'll never forget, and which had been said to him when he started out at The Old Globe: 'For the first five years they'll love you, for the next five years they'll try to get rid of you, and if you can make it to fifteen you can do whatever you want.' So far, truer words were never spoken! He also wrote an extraordinary article once called *Here Be Dragons* about the nature of risk taking in theater that resonated for us way beyond its original intentions."

Emma Walton, Co-founder, Bay Street Theatre

"All of those pioneers who participated in the diaspora of proven theater people from New York in the 1960s, '70s, and '80s: Zelda Fichandler, Jules Irving, Herbert Blau, Gordon Davidson, Des McAnuff, et al. The successful creation of a regional network (crystallized by TCG and collective bargaining agreements such as LORT) has made it possible for generations of theater students to believe they can have careers without migrating to New York."

Andrew Barnicle, Laguna Playhouse

"Almost all of the founders of the regional theater movement have impacted on my thinking and expectations of theater and myself. Their vision and fortitude are amazing. I think of the courage of Gordon Davidson, the intellectual brilliance of Zelda Fichandler, the genius of Bill Ball, the dogged determination of Adrian Hall, the vision of Mac Lowry, the commitment of Peter Zeisler, the consummate skill of Arvin Brown, the abstract imagination of JoAnne Akalaitis, and the work of so many others. All have supplied inspiration and an experience that I often wish that I had the courage to emulate."

Arthur Bartow, Artistic Director, Department of Drama, Tisch School of the Arts,
New York University

"God, yes! I've been very lucky. Joseph Anthony, Harold Clurman, Lloyd Richards, and Lillian Hellman changed my life. We all need teachers, mentors, people to turn to for all our lives."

Craig Belknap, Director, Theater, Film and Television, Senior Faculty,
California Institute of the Arts

"Artistic leaders who have informed my work include Gerald Freedman (former artistic director of Great Lakes Theatre), Libby Appel, and Daniel Sullivan. Crucial to my work have been the pioneers of the American Shakespearean theaters, such as Fred Adams and Michael Addison."

Kathleen Conlin, Associate Artistic Director, Utah Shakespearean Festival

"Philip Meister, National Shakespeare Conservatory; Josephine Farsberg, Second City; Michael Langham; Des McAnuff; Jack O'Brien; Michael Kahn; and my therapists."

Ben Donenberg, Artistic Director, Shakespeare Festival/LA

"As a theater critic/journalist, it would be another theater critic/journalist. The one I most admire is Frank Rich of the *New York Times* . . . thanks to his searing insight, uncommon eloquence, and tremendous love for the art form of theater."

Iris Dorbian, Editor-in-Chief, *Stage Directions* Magazine

"The writers and composers of the American 'Broadway' Musical. The Cohans, Kerns, Berlins, Rodgers and Hammerstein, Lerner and Loewe, A. L. Webber, etc. They have defined this art form and made it dynamic. Also, the Shuberts, Nederlanders, etc., who have produced these shows and created facilities to do this work, and Agnes de Mille, Jerome Robbins, Harold Prince, etc., who have made this art form so distinct and exciting."

Jan and Griff Duncan, Artistic and Executive Director, Fullerton Civic Light Opera

"Of course we would have to consider Mr. William Ball a pivotal figure in terms of our approach to the work, and to our passion for live theater in general, and classical work in particular . . . his passion for dynamic productions of the great authors of world literature, and his unabashed love for actors are powerful elements of his legacy that we hope we carry on. Another person who looms large in our consciousness is Mr. Sydney Walker, a longtime member of ACT's acting company. He was such a generous, passionate teacher, whose extraordinary exuberance on stage taught everyone who watched that truth has no size."

Julia and Geoff Elliot, Artistic Directors, A Noise Within

"Yes, Milton Smith, Milton Goldman, Harold Clurman, Robert Anderson, Audrey Woodward, and Robert Edmond Jones."

Richard G. Fallon, Dean Emeritus, Florida State University, Co-founder,
Asolo Theatre Company

"Producers and directors I was influenced by include Robert Porterfield at the Barter Theatre, Douglas Seale at Center Stage, John Reich and Douglas Campbell at the Goodman Theatre. The biggest influences, however, were the actors I met in regional theater . . . I knew that was the kind of life-in-the-theater that I wanted."

Joel Fink, Associate Dean, Chicago College of the Performing Arts

"Peter Donnelly in Seattle and Peter Culman in Baltimore were great leaders in the regional theater movement."

Bernard Havard, Producing Artistic Director, Walnut Street Theater

"Later influences included Sir Tyrone Guthrie and his work as a director and administrator, and Douglas Campbell, an actor whose strong, fearless, invigorating risks on stage (and off) have always reminded me that life need never be dull."

Theodore Herstand, Professor Emeritus, University of Oklahoma

"Joseph Papp, Gregory Mosher, Bernard Gersten, Tim Sanford, Adam Guettel, Jon Robin Baitz, Dan Sullivan, Hugh Masekela, Josh Rosenbaum, John Guare, Jose Rivera, Chris Durang, Spalding Gray, Scott Elliot."

Lynn Landis, Managing Director, The Wilma Theatre

"I've been fortunate to have worked with leaders in a generation of theater that saw the birth of the regional theater movement and the Off-Broadway movement. I was close to Joe Papp from the mid-'80s until his death. I was very close to Jose Quintero for that same period. I was and still am associated with many leaders who crossed over from educational theater to professional theater, especially in the LORT system at the Asolo and other venues, and was president of ATHE at a very fruitful time of exchanges in both directions between academic and professional theater. People such as Lloyd Richards, Gerald Freedman, Zelda Fichandler, Edward Albee, Ming Cho Lee, John Ezell, and many others still work in both arenas."

Gil Lazier, Longtime Dean, Florida State University/Asolo Theatre Conservatory

"The key figures in my life in the American Theater, those whose philosophy I have followed or have guided me personally, are Zelda Fichandler, Don Schoenbaum, and Richard Fallon. Zelda because she believed in a company of actors, Don because he was the most innovative managing director in the early days, and Dick Fallon because he was my mentor for so many years."

Howard J. Millman, Producing Artistic Director, Asolo Theatre

"One individual in particular: Sally Stearns Brown was managing director of the Peterborough Players, a small New Hampshire summer theater, from 1963 to 1983. She was the managing director by title, producer in fact, and truly the heart and soul of the place . . . she ran a summer theater not out of any desire to make a career for herself, but to give others opportunity and because she simply couldn't imagine a summer without a house full of actors."

Charles Morey, Artistic Director, Pioneer Theatre Company

"Sharon Ott, Joseph Papp, Tina Landau, Ingmar Bergman, Robert LePage."

Jonathan Moscone, Artistic Director, California Shakespeare Theater

"Zelda Fichandler, Ellis Rabb, Garland Wright, Andre Bishop. Lots more . . ."

Robert Moss, Artistic Director, Syracuse Stage

"Absolutely! I would have no career at all were it not for the influence, kindness, and great generosity of many people—Eva Le Gallienne, William Ball, Ellis Rabb, and Adrian Hall, in particular. As a young man living in Los Angeles I saw Le Gallienne's touring National Repertory company play Ibsen and Moliere. I went backstage and timidly asked Ms. Le Gallienne for advice. She met with me daily for the two weeks her company was in Los Angeles and much of my thinking about the theater—particularly regarding the importance of the classics, resident companies, and rotating repertory—was forged by those conversations. It was the annual visits of APA, the Guthrie, and ACT to Los Angeles (as well as many subsequent trips to see them in New York, Minneapolis, San Francisco, and my travels to Providence to see Trinity Rep) that forged my taste and taught me by example most of what I know about acting and directing. I saw Ellis's *School for Scandal*, *The Wild Duck*, and *Right You Are if You Think You Are* 18 times each and Guthrie's *The House of Atreus* and *The Resistable Rise of Arturo Ui* (directed by Edward Payson Call) 20 times each. (I would hide in the men's room after the matinee on two-show days so I could sneak back into the theater for the evening performance.) And I saw every production at ACT for almost ten years, most of them multiple times. It was the work of Bill Ball, Ellis Rabb, Tyrone Guthrie, and Adrian Hall that inspired me to train for the theater (I went to Carnegie because that is where Bill and Ellis had studied) and to pursue a career working in, and preparing others to work in, the regional theater with an emphasis on classic plays . . ."

Sandy Robbins, Director, Professional Theatre Training Program, University of Delaware

"Many. Some positive. Some negative. I won't say which are which. For me, Adrian Hall (Trinity Rep), Hal Prince, Zefferelli, Jon Dillon (Milwaukee Rep), Michael Maso (Huntington), Martin Charnin, Victoria Crandell (Brunswick Music Theatre), Chuck Abbott (director), Arthur Laurents, Jo Loesser, Dan Schay, and a pile of others. I have been an avid collector of information from which to learn. I am in regional theater today because I consciously decided that I did not like the commercial world of theater despite a possible direct career path to Broadway. I just did not like the way that art was created on Broadway or the way decisions were made: not always for the benefit of the play, but frequently for politics. I learned a lot from all of those whom I was able to watch and with whom I was able to work."

Richard Rose, Producing Artistic Director, Barter Theatre

"Robert Whitehead, Julie Harris, and a great many American playwrights."

Alan Rust, Director, The Hartt School Theatre

"Joe Papp embodied that entrepreneurial spirit, melding a fierce advocacy that theater deserved government support like libraries and schools with an equally indefatigable commercial producer's instinct for working the marketplace. Under his leadership, The Public Theatre/New York Shakespeare Festival championed a highly eclectic program something we emulate at the Laguna Playhouse. He certainly fired my passion for this career when I met him and heard him speak while I was a graduate student."

Richard Stein, Executive Director, Laguna Playhouse

"Richmond Crinkley was an influence and mentor. He is not well remembered, in part because unlike many artistic directors, producers, or founding fathers, he kept moving on to the next organization, which was often the next company he started. Richmond came to Washington from a tiny Virginia town, and started the Folger Theatre Group, now the Shakespeare Theatre. He produced the bicentennial season at the then relatively new John F. Kennedy Center for the Performing Arts, and then moved to New York City and helped develop Off-Broadway by establishing a producing arm of a long dormant organization called ANTA (where he produced, among other works, the original *The Elephant Man* and *Tintypes*). Richmond then moved to the Beaumont Theater and built the organization, or board structure, for the Lincoln Center Theater Company, which eventually achieved lasting success under Greg Mosher and Bernie Gersten. Richmond possessed an extraordinary intellect . . . "

Scott L. Steele, Executive Director, University/Resident Theatre Association

"As a director, I learned enormously from assisting both Michael Langham (at the Stratford Festival in Canada) and Mark Lamos (at Hartford Stage) . . . Michael is the single best director with text, language, and verse that I have ever observed. Further, he's brilliant, charismatic, insightful, and articulate— sometimes to a fault, he can be lacerating as well as illuminating. But his ability to bring clarity to a Shakespeare text is astonishing. Mark had been a protégé of Michael's at the Guthrie, but turned into a wholly different kind of Shakespeare director—he is an imaginative, daring re-conceiver of classical plays for a contemporary audience. He always pushes the boundaries of design and story telling, with a restless, impulsive creative energy. Mark is a visionary. Two people gave me much-needed perspective in running a major institution: Peter Zeisler and then Ben Cameron, both executive directors of TCG. Peter was irascible, outspoken, and courageous— he always pushed me towards better work and into rethinking my ideas about how to build a theater company. And Ben is simply astonishing in his cogency of thought, his deep and heartfelt belief in the power of live theater, and his passionate, articulate, and inspiring preaching—both to the field and about the field."

Kent Thompson, Artistic Director, Denver Center Theatre Company

"Howard Millman, who saved and reestablished both the Geva Theatre in Rochester, New York, and the Asolo Theatre in Sarasota, Florida . . . from Howard, I truly learned what it takes to make a LORT theatre stay alive both artistically and financially. He is a master of understanding an audience while still pushing the artistic envelope. Ed Stern, who co-founded Indiana Rep and reestablished Cincinnati Playhouse in the Park, showed me a way of dealing with artists that was loose, exciting, and filled with care and devotion. Gordon Davidson of the Mark Taper Forum, who served as a living example . . . "

Stephen Rothman, Chair, Department of Theatre Arts and Dance,
California State University, Los Angeles

"Key figures: hard question. Gerald Freedman and John Houseman."

Steven Woolf, Artistic Director, Repertory Theatre of St. Louis

"Having gone to undergraduate school at the University of Virginia, I became aware in the '60s of the remarkable work Zelda Fichandler was doing at Arena Stage. I grew up in New York City but, ironically, did not see in New York the range of work that was being done in Washington by Zelda. These productions solidified in my mind how regional theater is the American national theater in this country. I would, in the same vein, include Bill Ball and the remarkable work he did at ACT San Francisco for being a pioneer demonstrating the remarkable vitality and strength that is the regional theater movement."

Ed Stern, Producing Artistic Director, Cincinnati Playhouse in the Park

A FINAL NOTE

Discover a Life Worth Living

Pursue a career you enjoy and treat those you love with warmth and sincerity, and chances are pretty good that you'll discover a life that's worth living. This book was written and assembled out of love for America's artists, respect for America's producers and craftspeople, and true admiration for the pioneers and ongoing leaders of America's professional theaters.

Thanks again to everyone who offered his or her advice, guidance, and encouragement for this book. There are a lot of "would-be/could-be" mentors out there—go out and find individuals who may be able to help you establish a network, discover the joys of the arts, and take advantage of the ever-changing career opportunities in today's American theater.

If you have suggestions or advice regarding additions or changes to this book, please don't hesitate to contact me at jvolz@fullerton.edu.

BIBLIOGRAPHY

Branson, Clark and Mary Mann. *The Los Angeles Theatre Book*. North Hollywood: LA Theatre Book Publishers, 1984.

Brown, Lenora Inez. "West is West." *American Theatre*. New York: Theatre Communications Group, 2001.

Brubaker, Edward and Mary. *Golden Fire, The Anniversary Book of the Oregon Shakespearean Festival*. Ashland: The Oregon Shakespearean Festival, 1985.

Case, Evelyn Carol and Jim Volz. *Words for Lovers: Snippets, Sonnets and Sensual Sayings from William Shakespeare*. Columbiana: WaterMark Inc., 1990.

Celentano, Suzanne Carmack and Kevin Marshall. *Theatre Management*. Studio City: Players Press, 1998.

Churnin, Nancy. *The Old Globe at 60*. San Diego: Performing Arts, 1995.

Cincinnati Playhouse 30th Anniversary. Cincinnati Playhouse Press, 1990.

Cory, Joyce Burke. *The Dallas Theater Center, An Idea that was Big Enough*. Dallas Theater Center Press, 1980.

Eustis, Morton. *B'way, Inc! The Theatre as a Business*. New York: Dodd, Mead, & Company, 1934.

Farren, Mick. *Words of Wisdom*. London: Chrysalis Book Group, 2004.

Flanagan, Hallie. *A Brief Delivered by Hallie Flanagan, Director, Federal Theatre Project, Works Progress Administration, before the Committee on Patents, House of Representatives*, Washington D.C., February 8, 1938.

Flanagan, Hallie. *Dynamo*. New York: Duell, Sloan and Pearce, 1943.

Hewitt, Barnard. *Theatre USA, 1665 to 1957.* New York: McGraw-Hill Book Company, 1959.

Holmes, Ann Hitchcock. *The Alley Theatre, Four Decades in Three Acts.* Alley Theatre Press, 1986.

Hoyt, Harlowe R. *Town Hall Tonight, Intimate Memories of the Grassroots Days of the American Theatre.* New York: Bramhall House, 1955.

Humana Festival of New American Plays. Louisville: Actors Theatre of Louisville Press, 1986.

Klotkin, Joel. *The City: A Global History.* New York: Modern Library, 2005.

Kragen, Ken and Jefferson Graham. *Life is a Contact Sport.* New York: William Morrow and Company, 1994.

Krows, Arthur Edwin. *Play Production in America.* New York: Henry Holt and Company, 1916.

Langley, Stephen. *Theatre Management and Production in America.* New York: Drama Book Publishers, 1990.

Langley, Stephen and James Abruzzo. *Jobs in Arts and Media Management: What They Are and How to Get One!* New York: American Council for the Arts, 1989.

Livingston, Sheila. *The Guthrie Theatre, 25th Year Anniversary.* Minneapolis: Guthrie Press, 1988.

London, Todd. *The Artistic Home, Discussions with America's Institutional Theatres.* New York: Theatre Communications Group, Inc., 1988.

Lynch, Margaret. *The Making of a Theater, The Story of the Great Lakes Theater Festival.* Cleveland: Great Lakes Lithograph Company, 1986.

Macgowan, Kenneth. *Footlights Across America, Towards a National Theatre.* New York: Harcourt, Brace and Company, 1929.

Malloy, Merritt, and Shauna Sorensen. *The Quotable Quote Book.* New York: Citadel Press, 1990.

McDaniel, Nello and George Thorn. *The Workpapers: A Special Report, The Quiet Crisis in the Arts.* New York: FEDAPT, 1991.

Meserve, Walter J. *An Outline History of American Drama.* New Jersey: Littlefield, Adams & Co., 1965.

Moe, Christian and Scott J. Parker, George McCalmon. *Creating Historical Drama, A Guide for Communities, Theatre Groups, and Playwrights.* Carbondale: Southern Illinois University Press, 2005.

Mordecai, Benjamin. *Indiana Repertory Theatre* . New York: FEDAPT, 1977.

Morison, Bradley G. and Julie Gordon Dalgleish. *Waiting in the Wings: A Larger Audience for the Arts and How to Develop It.* New York: American Council for the Arts, 1987.

Newman, Danny. *Subscribe Now! Building Arts Audiences Through Dynamic Subscription Promotion.* New York: Theatre Communications Group, 1977.

Peale, Norman Vincent and Kenneth Blanchard. *The Power of Ethical Management.* New York: Blanchard, Morrow, and Co., 1992.

Peter, Dr. Laurence. *Peter's Quotations.* New York: Bantam Books, 1987.

Poggi, Jack. *Theater in America, The Impact of Economic Forces, 1870-1967.* Ithaca: Cornell University Press, 1968.

Price, Steven D., Editor. *1001 Smartest Things Ever Said.* Connecticut: The Lyons Press, 2004.

Ratcliffe, Susan, Editor. *Little Oxford Dictionary of Quotations.* Oxford: Oxford University Press, 2005.

Samuels, Steven, Editor. *Theatre Profiles 12.* New York: Theatre Communications Group, 1996.

Shakespeare Theatre Association of America Member Directory. Cedar City: STAA Publishers, 2005.

Sheehy, Helen. *Margo, The Life and Theatre of Margo Jones.* Dallas: Southern Methodist University Press, 1989.

South Coast Repertory 40. South Coast Repertory Press, 2004.

Steinberg, Mollie B. *The History of the Fourteenth Street Theatre.* New York: The Dial Press, 1931.

Steppenwolf @ Twenty-Five. Chicago: Steppenwolf Press, 2001.

TCG Theatre Directory. New York: Theatre Communications Group, Inc., 2003.

Volz, Jim. *Shakespeare Never Slept Here: The Making of a Regional Theatre.* Atlanta: Cherokee Publishing Company, 1986.

White, Rolf B., Editor. *The Great Business Quotations.* New York: Dell Publishing, 1986.

Wilson, Garff B. *Three Hundred Years of American Drama and Theatre, From Ye Bare and Ye Cubb to Hair.* New Jersey: Prentice-Hall, Inc., 1973.

* Special Note: The basic facts for each theater and institution overview generally derive from each institution's Web site, from theater directories, brochures, programs, historical information, and/or from the author's own experience with the theater.

ABOUT THE AUTHOR

JIM VOLZ is a national arts consultant, author, producer, and professor at California State University, Fullerton. He is a longtime critic/columnist for New York's *Back Stage* and editor of the Shakespeare Theatre Association of America's *quarto*. He has produced over 100 professional productions and published more than 100 articles on management, arts criticism, Shakespeare, and theater in Oxford University Press's *Theatre Research International*, Hollywood's *Drama-Logue*, New York's *Back Stage*, and myriad national and international publications. *How to Run a Theater, A Witty, Practical and Fun Guide to Arts Management* was published by Back Stage Books in 2004. *Buffett and the Bard: The Wit, Wonder & Wisdom of Warren Buffett and William Shakespeare*, co-edited with Cindy Melby Phaneuf, is his next major project.

Jim is president of Consultants for the Arts, past president of the National Theatre Conference, and a voting member for the prestigious Tony Award's Regional Theatre Award. He serves on the National Advisory Council for the Institute of Outdoor Drama based in Chapel Hill, North Carolina; the National Artistic Board of Directors for Florida's Orlando Shakespeare Festival; the board of trustees for California State University; Fullerton's Philanthropic Foundation; and the editorial board of distinguished scholars for the ISE Shakespeare project, based at the University of Victoria in Canada. He has served as a Strategic Planning/Time Management Program presenter for the National Association of Schools of Music, the National Association of Schools of Dance, and the National Association of Schools of Theatre. His loyalties to the Rocky Mountain region include longtime service as associate editor for the University of Colorado's *On-Stage Studies* and continued work as the national adjudicator for the University of Wyoming's National Theatre Essay Grant.

The Alabama Shakespeare Festival's board of trustees recruited Jim to spearhead the ASF's historic expansion from a small summer operation to the world's fifth-largest Shakespeare festival. From 1982 to 1991, as managing director, Jim orchestrated the tremendous growth of the Alabama Shakespeare Festival. As a tribute to the board and volunteers of that institution, Volz authored *Shakespeare Never Slept Here*, published by Cherokee Press of Atlanta.

Devoted to arts education, Dr. Volz has taught at six universities; administered MFA programs in acting, stage management, and arts administration; and served as head of the BFA in Arts Administration program and acting chairman of the Department of Theatre and Dance at Wright State University. He is a Ph.D. graduate from the University of Colorado, Boulder, and has a master's degree from Ohio's Bowling Green State University. At California State University, Fullerton, Dr. Volz has received honors and recognition for Teaching, Mentoring in the Arts, Service to the Campus as a Community, Enhancing Learning in the Classroom, External Community Service, Contributions to Student Leadership, and Service to the University.

Over the years, he has served as a presenter at Stratford, England's Royal Shakespeare Company; a grant reviewer for the National Endowment for the Arts and National Endowment for the Humanities; a consultant to the Cities of San Jose, La Quinta, Cypress, and Irvine, California; and a consultant to theaters and arts centers in Pennsylvania, Virginia, Nebraska, Utah, Ohio, South Carolina, North Carolina, Florida, New York, Idaho, Illinois, Tennessee, Texas, Florida, Colorado, and Arizona. As a concerned community member, Jim has served on the board of directors of Humana Hospital, the World Affairs Council, the Southeastern Theatre Conference, and the National Theatre Conference. As a civic leader, he has worked on chamber of commerce and state tourism committees and volunteered services for struggling artists, theaters, arts centers, arts councils, and dance companies.

On a national level, Jim has served as a steering committee member for the American Council for the Arts, a planning advisor for ACTER, and a long-time member of the League of Resident Theatres, the University/Resident Theatre Association, the American Arts Alliance, the Theatre Communications Group, the Authors Guild, the Dramatists Guild, and the Association for Theatre in Higher Education. He is a current member of the American Theatre Critics Association.

In the past few years, he has devoted his spare time to travel, basketball, community service, and writing for publication. Jim is married to professional actress and educator Evelyn Carol Case. As a writing team, they edited *Words for Lovers: Snippets, Sonnets, and Sensual Sayings from William Shakespeare* and *Simply Shakespeare* both for WaterMark Publishers. They have two adventurous children: Nicholas and Caitlin.